D0825212

Praise of The World-Teacher, Heart-Master Da Love-Ananda

"It is obvious, from all sorts of subtle details, that he knows what IT's all about . . . a rare being."

ALAN WATTS

"The event of Heart-Master Da is an occasion for rejoicing, for, without any doubt whatsoever, he is the first Western Avatar to appear in the history of the world. He teaches a Way of life that itself duplicates but transcends the entire spectrum of traditional spirituality. His Teaching contains the most concentrated wealth of transcendent wisdom found anywhere, I believe, in the spiritual literature of the world, modern or ancient, Eastern or Western."

KEN WILBER, author, *The Spectrum of Consciousness,*
Up from Eden, and *A Sociable God*

"The teachings of Heart-Master Da, embodied in an extraordinary collection of writings, provide an exquisite manual for transformation. . . . I feel at the most profound depth of my being that his work will be crucial to an evolution toward full-humanness."

BARBARA MARX HUBBARD, World Future Society; author,
The Evolutionary Journey

"Heart-Master Da Love-Ananda provides a way in which Oneness may be experienced by anyone who is bold enough to follow his teachings. It is important to understand that his vision is neither Eastern nor Western, but it is the eternal spiritual pulse of the Great Wisdom which knows no cultural, temporal, or geographical locus; it represents the apex of awareness of our species."

LARRY DOSSEY, M.D., author, *Space, Time, and Medicine*
and *Beyond Illness*

"A great teacher with a dynamic ability to awaken in his listeners something of the Divine Reality in which he is grounded, with which he is identified and which in fact he is. He is a man of both the East and the West; perhaps in him they merge and are organized as the One that he is."

ISRAEL REGARDIE, author, *The Golden Dawn*

"From time immemorial the world's religious traditions have proclaimed that whenever there is a decline in awareness of the Divine in mankind, the Divine will manifest in human form to restore mankind to Truth through Divine Grace. Such a time is our time and such a one is the Western-born God-Man Heart-Master Da Love-Ananda. For a critical moment in history, characterized by doubt and anti-authority, *The Divine Emergence of The World-Teacher* chronicles the sacred biography of One born to transform the world though grace and "the authority that grants both certainty and freedom."

> DAVID NELSON, M.D., Diplomate, The American Board
> of Psychiatry and Neurology

"There is much about the life and teachings of Heart-Master Da Love-Ananda which resonates with the life and teaching of Christ. His teachings on sacrifice, commitment, and authority can help Christians better appreciate the kind of relationship which Christ, too, asks of His followers."

> PHILLIP ST. GERMAIN, author, *Pathways to Serenity*

"Heart-Master Da Love-Ananda is the Divine, simply. No argument will prove this, but while reading this account of His unrelenting Work with devotees, Teaching them to feel and transcend their self-possession, you may recognize that He is That, simply.

"When you feel His love for His devotees, and through them for all of mankind, you may realize that the Great One has appeared, here and now, during our lifetime, inviting us in turn to love completely. He is the One we can lose ourselves in without fear and without having to withhold anything. Reading this powerful and magical book may finally open your heart to this great possibility."

> JEAN-PIERRE DUJARDIN, Ph.D., Ohio State University

THE
DIVINE EMERGENCE
OF THE
WORLD-TEACHER

**The World-Teacher, Heart-Master Da Love-Ananda,
Sri Love-Anandashram, Fiji, 1989**

THE
DIVINE EMERGENCE
OF THE WORLD-TEACHER

THE REALIZATION, THE REVELATION,
AND THE REVEALING ORDEAL OF
HEART-MASTER DA LOVE-ANANDA

(The World-Teacher,
The Naitauba Avadhoota,
Hridaya-Samartha Sat-Guru Da Love-Ananda Hridayam)

A BIOGRAPHICAL CELEBRATION
by Saniel Bonder

THE DAWN HORSE PRESS
CLEARLAKE, CALIFORNIA

NOTE TO THE READER

The devotional, Spiritual, functional, practical, relational, cultural, and formal community practices and disciplines discussed in this book, including the meditative practices, the Yogic exercises of conductivity, the breathing exercises, the life-disciplines of right diet and exercise, the intelligent economization and practice of sexuality, etc., are appropriate and natural practices that are voluntarily and progressively adopted by each practicing member of The Free Daist Communion and adapted to his or her personal circumstance. Although anyone may find them useful and beneficial, they are not presented as advice or recommendations to the general reader or to anyone who is not a practicing member of The Free Daist Communion. And nothing in this book is intended as a diagnosis, prescription, or recommended treatment or cure for any specific "problem", whether medical, emotional, psychological, social, or Spiritual. One should apply a particular program of treatment, prevention, cure, or general health only in consultation with a licensed physician or other qualified professional.

For a further discussion of individual responsibility in the Way of the Heart, our claim to perpetual copyright to the Wisdom-Teaching of Heart-Master Da Love-Ananda, and Heart-Master Da Love-Ananda and His Spiritual Instruments and Agents, His renunciate status in The Free Daist Communion, and the Guru-devotee relationship in the Way of the Heart, please see "Further Notes to the Reader", pp. 416-19 of this book.

© 1990 The Free Daist Communion. All rights reserved.
No part of this book may be used or reproduced in any
manner without written permission from the publisher.

The Free Daist Communion claims perpetual copyright to this book, to the entire written (and otherwise recorded) Wisdom-Teaching of Heart-Master Da Love-Ananda, and to all other writings and recordings of the Way of the Heart.

First Edition, April 1990

Printed in the United States of America
93 92 91 90 89   5 4 3 2 1

Produced by The Free Daist Communion
in cooperation with The Dawn Horse Press

Library of Congress Cataloging-in-Publication Data

Bonder, Saniel
        The divine emergence of the world-teacher: the realization, the revela-
    tion, and the revealing ordeal of Heart-Master Da Love-Ananda: a biographi-
    cal celebration/by Saniel Bonder.–1st ed.
            p. 482   cm.
        Includes bibliographical references.
        ISBN 0-918801-10-9: $14.95
        1. Da Free John, 1939–   2. Gurus–Biography.   I. Title.
    BP610.B82B65   1989
    299'.93–dc20
    [B]   89-50613
                                                                      CIP

Dedication

*I offer this book in love and gratitude
at the Grace-Radiating Feet of my Heart-Master,
The World-Teacher, Da Love-Ananda Hridayam.
May it please His Heart, and may
His Heart-Awakening Love-Bliss
flow through it to everyone.*

ACKNOWLEDGEMENTS

Any book requires the collaboration of many individuals, and so it is with this one. My heart-felt thanks to The Hridaya Da Kanyadana Kumari Mandala Order, especially Kanya Tripura Rahasya, for their review, encouragement, and support; our writing and editorial production teams, Nina Davis, Carol Sabatino, Greg Purnell, Frans van den Bossche, Matthew Spence, William Stranger, Kathleen Stilwell, Paul Augspurger, Rebecca Plunkett, Larry Boggs, Sarah Seage, and Michael Macy, for their extraordinary attention and care to the text; our art and production staff, James Minkin, Judith and James Alwood, and Matt Barna, for making the book a visual feast of Heart-Master Da's Darshan (or "Sighting"); photographers Kanya Suprithi, Hal Okun, Nick Poutsma, and Nick Elias (as well as others in the past), for their sensitive photographs of Heart-Master Da; Emily Purnell and Kouraleen Stranger, for their archival help and research on the manuscript and photographs, respectively; Marc Savage, for his excellent (and swift) work on the index; reviewers Michael Wood, Crane Kirkbride, David Todd, Godfree Roberts, Aniello Panico, and David Rosen, whose suggestions helped shape the book; Richard Grossinger and John Maniatis, who also offered helpful recommendations; Meg Krenz, William Tsiknas, and Ty Koontz, for their previous biographical treatments of Heart-Master Da's Life; Tevita Cakacaka, Vern Leistikow, and Elliott Mehrbach, for keeping the generator going on those many long nights at Sri Love-Anandashram; and Dorothy and the late Frank Jones, for photographically documenting Heart-Master Da's childhood.

Most especially, of course, my deepest thanks go to Heart-Master Da Love-Ananda Himself, the Divine World-Teacher, for His many Confessions about His Life and His suggestions for this book, for Giving its title and subtitle, making the final photo selections, and approving the design—and thus Blessing the book for everyone with His own Speech, Glance, Touch, and Regard. Most of all, I thank Him for consenting to take Birth and Emerge here in what He once called "this half-made world, where love is yet to take its hold."

Thus, while I take full responsibility for any faults in this book, you should know that it has been lovingly made by many hands and hearts, including those of my Divine Heart-Master, Da Love-Ananda Hridayam.

CONTENTS

ABOUT THE COVER

T he design on the cover of *The Divine Emergence of The World-Teacher* proclaims Heart-Master Da Love-Ananda's Divine Descent and Emergence as The World-Teacher, the Great Spiritual Adept Who Reveals the Truth and Grants Liberating Grace to all beings.

The sacred image in the central portion of the design indicates Heart-Master Da's Prior Divine Nature and His Present and Eternal Function as the Giver of Awakening Grace to all beings everywhere. The yellow band corresponds to the outermost, or gross, dimension of our ordinary waking experience and common living. The blue field corresponds to the deeper psychic and subtle dimensions of personal and cosmic existence. The Sanskrit symbol for "Da" at the center indicates the Divine Person, "Da". The white color signifies the Doorway to the Divine Self-Domain, Which is Heart-Master Da's Eternal Nature and Realization, and Which He has Incarnated fully among us.

The Divine Name "Da" means "the Giver" (and "What is Given"). It is Heart-Master Da's Name as the Perfectly Emerged or Incarnated Manifestation of the Divine, Grace-Giving Person. The three orange persimmons represent the three stations of the heart (left, middle, and right), which correspond to the three states of waking, dreaming, and deep sleep and to the phenomenal realms (gross, subtle, and causal) associated with those states.

The three persimmons, which are symbols of fullness, also correspond to Heart-Master Da's bodily (human) Form, His Spiritual Presence, and His Very (and Inherently Perfect) State—for it is by progressive and always direct feeling-Contemplation of Him, in Person, that human ego-bondage (to the three conditional states of awareness and to all of the stations of the heart and functions of the whole body-mind) is understood and, ultimately, Perfectly transcended.

The pictorial depiction of Heart-Master Da below this symbolic image is itself a sacred symbol of Him as the Divinely Emerged World-Teacher, in bodily (human) Person. His open hand in front of the right side of His chest represents His present and Eternal Blessing of all beings as the Very Heart, the Divine Self. His Staff indicates the Divine Authority of His Word and Sacred Work as the World-Teacher. The book under His left hand represents His now-completed Teaching Work and Teaching History, expressed in His Written Word. Seated on His left knee, this book also implicitly calls us to sit at His "knee of listening", as serious students of Him as the World-Teacher, in order to hear His Liberating Word at heart while we Contemplate His bodily (human) Form, His Spiritual Presence, and His Very (and Inherently Perfect) State.

The double Narcissus flower signifies the ego-conscious heart seeing its own reflection (like the mythological self-lover, Narcissus) in the pristine "Water" of The World-Teacher's Revelation and thus surrendering itself at His Grace-Giving Feet.

Foreword

by Richard Grossinger

author, *Planet Medicine, The Night Sky,*
Waiting for the Martian Express

In our usual understanding of things, spiritual biography is perhaps an implicit contradiction. Biography represents "Bios", literally the writing of a life, the same life of creatures and cells described by biology. And the journey of the spirit, if it is acknowledged at all, appears to lie outside of time and space. Its "experiences" are unconditional.

The life story of Heart-Master Da Love-Ananda "answers" (and refutes) popular abstractions about spirits and spiritual energies: Spirit is not an it. When the Divine Consciousness mysteriously incarnates in the Form of a Person, we have the special reality of a Being who is also unconditional. In this book Saniel Bonder, a devotee of Heart-Master Da, acknowledges that trying to put such a Life into a biography is "like trying to photograph a hurricane, or to lasso a comet, or to travel into the heart of the Sun". Yet this biography, while taking issue precisely with the notion of the Divine as a mere abstraction or a metaphysically conceived other-dimensionality, demonstrates that there is no inherent separation between the unconditional Spirit and Life. The "plot" of such a story is not transcendence or initiation but the universal opening of the Heart.

Thus, where Divine Energy contacts the world of history as an apparent Individual, a narrative emerges, a story unfolds as the journey of the spirit leaves its imprint on the passage of time and space. *The Divine Emergence of The World-Teacher* is the story of "the Divine Person" moving through history. We glimpse the impression on the world of "Bios" transcending conventional reality.

In the truest sense of the Avatar, the Process of the gross and deeper personalities and of the transcendent, free nature (what I would call the "Spirit-Seed") evolving from Franklin Jones into Heart-Master Da Love-Ananda has recast the latter half of our twentieth century. And the portrayal of the unique life of a Divine Incarnation as a finite human individual signals that it is possible for others to be drawn by grace into the same Condition of transcendent freedom.

This story weaves ordinary life experiences with extraordinary Revelation, thus providing us with a crucial understanding of not only how much love the Master of the Heart brings into the world but how much sorrow He encounters in so doing. That is the meaning of story-telling here. Reflected in His own chosen Personality as a Western man Heart-Master Da confronts precisely the depth of exile and pain present in all of our experiences. Here we have the incredible tale of a Teacher Who so loved His Disciples that not only did He choose an Incarnation in the West to meet them but when His Disciples would not adopt His Form, He adopted their Form to show them their own reflection. The result of this sacrificial effort was His Divine Emergence, which marks a new chapter in epochal Spiritual History.

A Suggestion
for Your Reading
of This Book

Thehe Story of the Divine Emergence of The World-Teacher, Heart-Master Da Love-Ananda, is a remarkable tale, full of sacred Mysteries that have very little currency in modern secular society. It is equally unusual from the standpoint of the conventional or popular doctrines that characterize most religious thinking in the West and in the world today in general.

Therefore, telling this true Story to a general audience would be challenging even for a superb storyteller and narrative stylist. I am neither. Nor am I attempting here to write anything like a conventional modern biography with an "objective" or a "sympathetically critical" standpoint.

My relationship to Heart-Master Da Love-Ananda is that of a devotee to his Spiritual Master. However, my sacred qualifications for writing this book are not great. I am no Enlightened Knower of Truth nor a saintly or even mature practitioner of God-love. I am an addict of my own self-imagery and seeking, like Narcissus entranced by his reflection in water, or like a man living in a cage of mirrors. The astonishing Blessing of my life is that the Divine, in the Person of Heart-Master Da Love-Ananda, is Breaking through this trance of self-obsession to Reveal to me the Heart-Way of Truth, Love, Happiness, and Freedom. My best qualification to write this book is simply that I have observed and participated in most of the great events of His formal Mission as a Divine Liberator, and that I have been Blessed by Him with a sacred understanding of His Life-Story.

What is written here, then, can only be considered a form of sacred biography. It assumes your willingness to entertain the possibility of a human Life founded from its very outset in a most unique process of Divine Grace. It assumes your interest in taking a sustained look into such a Life, and into the distinctive human culture that has developed around it, even though much of what you see may challenge your previous understanding of reality and of human nature and destiny. I hope you will also find much here that resonates with your deepest sacred instincts.

Because Heart-Master Da Love-Ananda's Life is so uncommon, I have offered an explanatory introduction, "The Authority That Grants Both Certainty and Freedom: On Doubt and Belief, God and the God-Realized World-Teacher, and the Evolutionary Function of Sacred Biography". This essay is especially oriented to the reader who has little background in the esoteric sacred traditions of God-Realization, or who approaches this book from a secular, or simply a skeptical, perspective.

There is a Story to be discovered here, at once human and Divine, full of vulnerability and miracles, ordeal, tragedy, and accomplishment. For general readers who are previously unfamiliar with Heart-Master Da, this book includes explanatory comments—but not so many, I hope, as to detract from the dramatic saga of His Life.

This book is a primer
of a most extraordinary Life

I am convinced that Heart-Master Da Love-Ananda is a being of most sublime Enlightenment, Which He calls "Divine Self-Realization". That was intuitively obvious to me from the day I first read His early Spiritual autobiography, *The Knee of Listening,* in late 1973.

In the intervening years, however, I have come to understand that my beloved Teacher is something more, or other, than an "Enlightened man". He exists, and He always has existed, on an altogether different order of Being even from those who, born in egoic illusion, eventually enter an Enlightened State.

It has become clear to me, as it has to others both within and outside the worldwide community of His devotees, that Heart-Master Da Love-Ananda is what is known traditionally as a "Divine Incarnation". He is now regarded by many as the Divine World-Teacher of our epoch, of the Stature that is historically assigned to a Krishna, a Gautama the Buddha, a Jesus Christ.

The primary purpose of this book is to share a vision of Heart-Master Da that will help you—if you are, or if you become, so inclined—to explore His Teaching literature and His Spiritual Work with a clear, well-informed, sacred appreciation for His entire Life to date.

However, I must also confess at the outset that trying to recount the Life of Heart-Master Da Love-Ananda is like trying to photograph a hurricane, or to lasso a comet, or to travel into the heart of the Sun. He is too vast; He cannot be contained. What can one say of a Man of unbounded Consciousness that will not make Him seem to be less than What He Is? How can one adequately describe the activity of a Being Who, by His own Confession, has Pervaded the whole world since before His Birth and continues to do so in every moment?

This book, then, is designed to serve as a primer of the dramatically paradoxical Life and Mission of Heart-Master Da Love-Ananda. I have been concerned here to tell the very essence of His Story, as he has disclosed It in His talks and writings. Even in a book of this length, great moments and epochs of His Ordeal and His Sacred Work have had to be summarized in a few paragraphs, or pages; and I have been able to share only a very few of the innumerable leelas, or inspiring accounts, of His benign, Liberating Influence in the hearts and lives of His devotees. The many books about Him to come, by His devotees and others, will serve these more focused or expansive purposes. It is my earnest hope that, for all who are interested or who become interested in Heart-Master Da Love-Ananda and His Work, *The Divine Emergence of The World-Teacher* will grant a clear overview of His unique Life and a comprehensive context for all of their further exploration of His Story and His Message.

A metamorphosis and a call

To Emerge fully here on Earth, Heart-Master Da has presumed thorough freedom to explore human existence and all of conditional existence, as it is and in its totality. He has embraced the profane with as much abandon as the sacred. He has transcended the Spiritual as decisively as He has transcended the earthly. He has done whatever He had to do to expose the hidden roots of human beings' deadly betrayal of love and our unconscious refusal to be Awake. More than once, He has apparently died in His reckless Divine efforts to set our hearts Free.

Those death-like crises (or unsought Yogic "Swoons", from which no return to bodily awareness was guaranteed) and His bodily, as well as conscious, transformations are keys to our understanding of His Story. Repeatedly, and in many ways, He has burned through the apparent limits of the bodily (human) Form that He acquired in entering this earthly dimension. Indeed, in His Lifetime Heart-Master Da has assumed and burned through, or Spiritually comprehended, penetrated, and transcended, all human limits and tendencies and all of the qualities, capacities, and inclinations of both Eastern and Western Man. In so doing He has spontaneously Originated a "radical" new Teaching that speaks the Truth to the whole of Man and addresses every aspect of human culture and consciousness. This is part (though only part) of what makes Him the unique World-Teacher of our epoch.

Several times, in the course of His life-and-death Ordeal, Heart-Master Da Love-Ananda has shed or metamorphosed beyond His human personality, as if apparently deep-rooted traits of character and patterns of activity were nothing more than skins, or cocoons. The many Names He has Revealed and used in the course of His Life—"Franklin Jones", "Bubba Free John", "Master Da Free John", and "Sri Jagad-Guru Da Love-Ananda Hridayam"—underscore that dramatic metamorphosis. We will consider the meaning of each of His Names at appropriate moments in His Story.

In the course of His Ordeal, Heart-Master Da's body has been physically transmuted by Spiritual Light and Blissfully Radiant Love. His bodily (human) Form has become a pure and unobstructed icon, a living vision, of Enlightenment and Divine Freedom. Now, by Grace of His Divine Emergence, He is the embodiment of Happiness, here to attract human hearts into the ecstasy of God-Realization.

Now, by Grace of this Divine Emergence of The World-Teacher, Heart-Master Da Love-Ananda, anyone who wishes to see, feel, and eventually Realize the ultimate Divine Truth need only Contemplate, with an open and receptive heart, His bodily (human) Form. This feeling-Contemplation, engaged according to His Instructions, as a whole Way of life and with the whole passion of one's being, leads in due course to Communion with His tangible Spiritual Presence of Love-Bliss. And that Contemplative Communion ultimately leads to Identification with His State of infinite Consciousness. He has said in *The Love-Ananda Gita*, His most "Simple" Scripture:

I Am What you must Realize. I am not <u>like</u> you. I <u>Am</u> you. This Body is not the Revelation of your likeness. It is the Revelation of the One you must Realize. It is the Very Means for your Realization of That One.[1]

A suggestion for your reading

This, then, is my suggestion for your reading of this book: Accept it as a completely sympathetic celebration of a most unusual Being, a Being from a culture perhaps foreign to your own and even, in a sense, from another Dimension. Accept my pledge to make this Story as intelligible as I can, understanding, however, that to some significant degree I do speak in the idioms and with the characteristic assumptions of the language and culture I share with the One of Whom I write.

The essential message of this book is quite simple: Heart-Master Da Love-Ananda IS here. In His Divine Emergence as the World-Teacher, an Event has been Initiated of greater import than we can imagine—a unique Event for which humanity has been praying and longing, consciously and in the unthought yearning of hearts, for many, many centuries. To help you appreciate and make a well-informed response to that Event is the purpose of this book.

Telling of the Divine Emergence of Heart-Master Da Love-Ananda has been a delight for me, and a sacred passage. I pray that reading it will be equally auspicious for you.

Saniel Bonder
The World-Teacher Ashram
Sri Love-Anandashram, Fiji
January 22, 1990

---

1. Heart-Master Da Love-Ananda, *The Love-Ananda Gita (The Wisdom-Song Of Non-Separateness)* (Clearlake, Calif.: The Dawn Horse Press, 1989), p. 380.

Note:
On the use of capital
and lowercase letters in this book

Heart-Master Da Love-Ananda has developed His own standards and conventions of capitalization (as well as conventions of lowercasing). When He speaks or writes of Himself with uncommon capitalizations ("Me", or "My", and the like), He is communicating the Ecstasy of His Unconditional Realization of the Divine. His purpose has been to create a sacred version of the otherwise worldly, secular, or ego-based English language. His particular usage of capital and lowercase letters is designed, He says, to "interrupt the common flow of mind and Signal your Heart that it is time to Awaken, As You Are."

Out of our sacred respect, gratitude, and love for Heart-Master Da Love-Ananda, His devotees capitalize references to Him and His Work and the Heart-Awakeness He Transmits. This is a way for us to acknowledge and indicate to others the Miracle that we find Him to be in our lives. It is also our custom, as it has been of devotees of great Adepts for millennia, to frequently adorn references to our Blessed Guru with honorific praise, as expressions of our acknowledgement of His Divine Nature and Function as Awakener.

I have tried in this book to minimize the use of technical sacred terminology. But in this Story, a certain amount of such terminology in English, Sanskrit, and, occasionally, other languages, is inevitable. Both the Glossary and the Index should be of use to many readers. The book also includes a listing of Heart-Master Da's publications and an Invitation for those who wish to learn more about Him and His Work.—SB

The Sacred Emblem of The World-Teacher, Heart-Master Da Love-Ananda

The Authority
That Grants Both
Certainty and Freedom

On Doubt and Belief,
God and the God-Realized
World-Teacher,
and the Evolutionary Function
of Sacred Biography

Sri Love-Anandashram, 1990

INTRODUCTION

The Authority
That Grants Both
Certainty and Freedom

On Doubt and Belief,
God and the God-Realized
World-Teacher,
and the Evolutionary Function
of Sacred Biography

Ken Wilber, a widely respected modern scholar of sacred and secular psychology and philosophy, wrote more than a decade ago of his estimation of Heart-Master Da Love-Ananda (then known as Da Free John) and the authoritative nature of His Teaching Word, which He had begun publishing only seven years earlier:

I have put forward a dozen or so books devoted to a synthesis of Eastern and Western religion and psychology. Freud and Jung and Adler, Piaget and James and Sartre, Hinduism and Buddhism and Taoism, Christianity and Islam and Zen—I have spent my life studying these systems, profoundly sympathetic with their concerns, sincerely interested in their insights. I myself am no hero, but I honestly think that, by now, I can at least recognize genius, real genius, when it comes my way.

And my opinion is that we have, in the person of Da Free John, a Spiritual Master and religious genius of the ultimate degree. I assure you I do not mean that lightly. I am not tossing out high-powered phrases to "hype" the works of Da Free John. I am simply offering to you my own considered opinion: Da Free John's Teaching is, I believe, unsurpassed by that of any other spiritual Hero, of any period, of any place, of any time, of any persuasion. . . .

25

I personally have found that not one significant item of any of the great religions is left out of Da Free John's teachings. Not one. And it is not just that these points are all included in his teaching: They are discussed by Da Free John with such brilliance that one can only conclude that he understands them better than their originators.[1]

What kind of Teacher is it Who can, in the space of a few years of Teaching, demonstrate such a comprehensive and profound sacred Understanding? What kind of authority in the realm of the Spirit does He represent, and how should He be related to by serious students of religion and Spirituality?

The question of authority in the sacred life is a serious issue in our time, and there are a number of ways to approach it that might be useful for those who wish to explore the Life of Heart-Master Da Love-Ananda. He Himself has addressed this subject at length, from many perspectives, and this introduction will present excerpts from His talks and writings that summarize His unique arguments. There are also elements of this discussion about which I, as a longtime devotee of Heart-Master Da, feel very strongly, and it seems that at least some of those feelings are more appropriately expressed here in the introductory material than in the formal biography of Heart-Master Da that follows.

Doubt, belief, and the errors of childish and adolescent approaches to the sacred

Ken Wilber's comments above were made in the context of an essay, "On Heroes and Cults", in which he drew critical attention to the irrational discrimination against non-mainstream religious and Spiritual leaders (and their students or followers) that has become the expected

---

1. Ken Wilber, "On Heroes and Cults", *The Laughing Man*, vol. 6, no. 1 (1985), pp. 6-7.

orientation of both the intelligentsia and the ordinary man and woman of today.[2]

In our time mankind's loss of faith in both God and human Incarnations of God, and even our lack of respect for saints and saintly people, has become an epidemic of the soul. Doubtful distrust of authority in general, and of the Spiritual Master-disciple relationship in particular, inhibits many people, in both East and West, from even examining the words and works of great Spiritual Teachers past and present—much to their misfortune.

Clearly, the outgrowing of misplaced, childish trust in external "parental" authorities, whether religious, political, or of any other kind, has been and continues to be a necessary advance for human beings. That crisis of growth beyond childish dependencies has prompted or informed much of the history of our species over the last several hundred years in particular. But now we face a similar crisis relative to our aggravated and prolonged adolescence—which, as Heart-Master Da remarks frequently in His published Teaching Word, represents just as much an egoic limit on our Spiritual evolution and ultimate Divine Awakening as the childish, unthinking self-enclosure that so many of us have taken pains to put behind us.

The adolescent encloses himself or herself in a self-made prison of independence, distrust, and isolation, beyond which he or she does not easily dare to feel or open. In ordinary life, such a character can carry on a productive and relatively harmonious existence among others similarly disposed. In Spiritual life, however, which requires extreme vulnerability, trust, participation in relationship, and exposure of feeling, such a chronically adolescent character is always (to use one of Heart-Master Da's picturesque descriptions) "choking himself with a third hand".

A common example of our struggle between childishness and adolescence can easily be seen in our almost automatic attempts to deal with matters of the sacred through the mental attitudes of either doubt or belief. The childish individual believes, or wants to believe, and fearfully wants to be consoled from the world's irrational and potentially calamitous realities by the content of his or her beliefs. The adolescent individual

---

2. That essay was also published as the Foreword to Heart-Master Da's book of prophetic social and cultural Wisdom and evolutionary and Divine Revelation, humorously entitled *Scientific Proof of the Existence of God Will Soon Be Announced by the White House!* (Clearlake, Calif.: The Dawn Horse Press, 1980), pp. 3-10.

doubts, and cannot stop doubting, even when the evidence of his or her senses as well as the promptings of heart-felt intuition suggest a disposition that transcends doubt altogether—and that also transcends mere mental belief.

Heart-Master Da Love-Ananda does not recommend that you merely believe His Life-Story, any more than He would recommend that you merely doubt it. Instead, He Calls all who examine His Life and Work to maintain a disposition of openness and tolerance, and a willingness to entertain some very unusual possibilities. And He would urge you to be willing, on the basis of what you read, to question yourself (and all of your own assumptions about who you are, and what life is, and how it should be lived) as much as you may be inclined to question what you read here.

As this book relates, Heart-Master Da Love-Ananda was Himself consumed by doubt and questioning at a certain stage in His early Life. He has never flinched from confronting the hard realities of our lives. He has never been satisfied with mere belief or dogma as an antidote to doubt. Rather, He has always insisted upon direct Realization of the Divine Reality, in Whose Radiant Intelligence doubt dissolves like fog in sunshine.

Heart-Master Da has always vehemently opposed and has refused to bow to any doctrine or individual whose authority is inauthentic, self-serving, or suppressive of our true Freedom. He has always refused to abide by any principle or idea that does not pass the test of most disciplined questioning and practical application. And, by holding fast to the raw reality of existence, with all of its shocks and all of its delights, He has Revealed a sacred approach to living that is scrupulously honest, clear-eyed, and rigorously true to the fundamental Truth of existence.

Rigorous Truthfulness and the constant presumption of one another's existential Divinity are the living core of the authentic relationship between a Spiritual Master and his or her devotee. Thus, Heart-Master Da resorted to His own Spiritual Masters, or Gurus, "as a man does to God". He champions the tradition of the authentic, esoteric Guru-devotee relationship. And He adamantly takes issue with those who, out of fear and misunderstanding, would deny or, worse, would attempt to discredit or destroy that most Blessed form of human association:

HEART-MASTER DA LOVE-ANANDA: Spiritual life has nothing to do with the childishness that people tend to dramatize in the relationship to the Spiritual

Master. I criticize that childish or dependent approach more directly than most people. Others are merely petulant about it, in the self-righteous mood of adolescence. But there are real reasons why both the childish and adolescent approaches to the Spiritual Master are forms of destructive nonsense and must be overcome. However, the mature, sacrificial relationship to the Spiritual Master is itself absolutely Lawful and necessary. Those who object to that relationship might as well object to the relationship between the Earth and the sun.[3]

The non-suppressive Authority that Grants primal certainty and true Freedom

In books such as *The Transmission of Doubt* and *Scientific Proof of the Existence of God Will Soon Be Announced by the White House!* Heart-Master Da Love-Ananda has addressed at length the concerns of modern men and women relative to the function of apparently external authority in the religious life. More recently, He has said in a conversation with some of His devotees:

HEART-MASTER DA LOVE-ANANDA: Human cultures in general, until very recently, have functioned on the basis of the presumption that there is authority, an authoritative view, an existing revelation about the universe, existence itself, about what is happening, what is going on here. In the Hindu system, the Vedas are the traditional something that is pointed to as authoritative. In the West it is usually the Bible. In the Islamic tradition it is the Koran. Each social or cultural system has its basis of authority.

Now, in the twentieth century, authority is disappearing, if it has not already disappeared altogether. Yes, of course, there are still religious people who want to believe in the old ways, but people's ability to affirm authority is decreasing. Society as a whole is no longer based on it, or only tentatively associated with it, and thus authority is rather ambiguous. Authority has become less desirable. It is even becoming taboo, so that the prevailing mood is one of anti-authority. Nothing is "written". There is no fixed revelation now. We are

3. Bubba Free John [Heart-Master Da Love-Ananda], *The Enlightenment of the Whole Body* (Clearlake, Calif.: The Dawn Horse Press, 1978), p. 246.

all supposed to investigate everything and discover the Truth for ourselves. We may thus progressively learn more and more, but we do not have an authority. Therefore, we have no right to certainty, no cultural norm that tells us we can be certain about such and such. . . .

The culture into which we have all been born, therefore, is a culture of doubt, not a culture based on authority or certainty. Authority is taboo, and certainty is taboo. It is difficult, then, for anyone to come to a truly balanced state of mind, because balance depends on a kind of certainty, integrity, freedom from doubt and fear. But if it is culturally taboo to be certain, and if authority, or authoritativeness, is inherently in doubt and culturally taboo, then you cannot come to a point of certainty. You cannot come to a point of no doubt. And you cannot affirm something "without doubt". . . .

Just as it is associated with tolerance and cooperation, freedom is naturally associated with authority—not suppressive authority, not the so-called true-believer's fundamentalism, not cultism. The exercise of true intelligence and freedom, in other words, naturally or natively associates itself with true authority, honors and makes good use of the signs and representations, demonstrations, and Blessings of true Realizers. Such authority has traditionally been made the context of human culture, but it has unfortunately been adulterated, and almost eliminated, made taboo even, in the twentieth century. This has produced a process of subhuman acculturation wherein everybody as an ego is presumed to be a self-sufficient authority, anti-authority is the accepted disposition, and rebellion is considered to be the basis of freedom or liberty. . . .

A fundamental characteristic of true authority is universalism, the opportunity to function on the basis of the highest possible concept, the most inclusive orientation, rather than suppression, or the demand for conformity to a certain point of view. False authority localizes and polarizes. I do not advocate that at all. But true authority promotes a universal disposition, and therefore tolerance and cooperation. That is what I mean by authority. Do not misunderstand Me—true authority supports and educates people in a great disposition, one that is truly human, not subhuman, but greater than ordinary-human, a true ideal if you will. It makes a true ideal the basis of human activity. It is therefore necessarily cooperative and tolerant and not suppressive, and it transcends polarization.

One of the functions of true authority, therefore—not arbitrary, suppressive authority, but true authority, an authoritative tradition of Truth—if it remains extant or culturally presumed, is to give people a resource for their fundamental integrity or certainty. True authority also keeps the collective non-wisdom from becoming suppressive to the point that people cannot grow anymore.

The next stage of growth for human beings in general is the leap to the fourth stage of life.[4] That leap requires self-understanding and transcendence of the egoic disposition associated with the first three stages of life. How will people make that transition if they do not come into association with an authority, a source of Truth, about which they can be certain or in relation to which they can be moved beyond themselves? It is not possible while they are guided by their own mentality and the collective mentality of non-wisdom with which they are associated. If anyone is to grow, there must be a breakthrough of something authoritative, convincing, certainty-creating, awakening. Such has been the function of the great traditions of ultimate Realization, even of religion in general. . . .

You as practitioners of the Way of the Heart are associated with an authoritative Revelation, a Revelation you take to be authoritative in the traditional sense, not in any sense that is limiting or negative. The Way of the Heart should function for you as such authority. You should thoroughly examine it with true discrimination, but ultimately it should function for you as authoritative Revelation. It is intended to. It is intended to serve your integrity and to attract and draw you from the very beginning.

What if there were no such authority? You might, as people ordinarily do, settle into the struggles of the first three stages of life. Or you might be attracted

4. Heart-Master Da's original Revelation of "the seven stages of life" describes the inevitable stages of psycho-physical growth, Spiritual evolution, and ultimate Divine Awakening that are potential for human beings.

The first three stages of life are the stages of basic physical, emotional, and mental development of our ordinary human functions and capacities. Most people, even great leaders and geniuses, never go beyond these stages of human maturity.

The fourth stage of life is marked by true or profound psychic awakening—not mere sensitivity to psychic phenomena, but profound awakening to the inherently devotional disposition of love in relation to the Living Divine Reality, Person, and Spirit. Historically, the fourth stage of life has been exemplified only by great Saints and devotees of the Divine in the esoteric sacred traditions.

The fifth stage of life is the stage of Yogic, Spiritual ascent and cosmic mysticism beyond ordinary earthly awareness, and its exemplars have been the rare, accomplished Yogis and Mystics of the Spiritual traditions of East and West.

The sixth stage of life, rarer still in the global history of human awareness and culture, is the stage of the transcendence of both physical and Spiritual awareness and experience in the Contemplation of Consciousness itself, the Transcendental Reality. Its principal heroic explorers have been the intuitive Sages of the Buddhist, Hindu, Jain, and other Oriental traditions.

The seventh stage of life is the stage of Most Perfect Spiritual, Transcendental, and Divine Self-Realization, or the Realization of absolute Freedom, Happiness, and Love-Bliss, no matter what physical or psychic conditions arise to attention, or even whether any conditions arise at all. Only the very greatest of God-Realized Adepts in all of human history have Incarnated this degree of Divine Identity.

See pages 445-69 in the Glossary for a more complete definition and description of the seven stages of life. The distinctions among the various stages form a major tool for our understanding of Heart-Master Da Love-Ananda's Life and Work, and they are frequently discussed in this book.

31

to some teacher or tradition or book that represented to you the very next stage, or some stage higher than your present stage. You might even try to imitate the higher stages, but you would not have the clarity associated with ultimate authority, Perfect Revelation, nor would you be associated in your present-time practice with the Grace of the Revealed Spirit-Presence. Therefore, for you to practice this Way of the Heart, you must necessarily be associated with its ultimate authority, its ultimate Revelation, which is not only in the form of a Wisdom-Teaching, but in the form of a Transmitted Grace.

In fact, then, you have rediscovered a source of authority, just as people traditionally were associated with an authoritative source, a governing principle and reality. You have discovered it in the context of being a practitioner in a particular, yet rather small, community. You should be able to see, then, how important it is that there be such a Revelation, such an authority, and how it should be intelligently approached, but ultimately honored. You should not be calling for indiscriminate fascination and affirmation, but for right honoring and intelligent "consideration" of the Revelation that is the Way of the Heart.

In addition to serving that very Realization in you, one of the things I am doing, especially in The Basket of Tolerance,[5] *is communicating a reasonable justification for reaccepting a certain kind of authority and making it part of the cultural life of humanity in general. I am Calling people specifically to the Way of the Heart in My Company, that is true, but even prior to that, through* The Basket of Tolerance *I am Calling people to the authority represented by the Great Tradition as a whole, not any particular sect or exoteric version of it, but the Great Tradition as a total history of Revelation epitomized not only by certain great individuals but by certain great Realizations, which we should be able to affirm as authoritative based on a most intelligent examination of all the realities of the Great Tradition. (April 6, 1987)*

Heart-Master Da Love-Ananda's bodily (human) Form, His Spiritual Presence, and His Divine State of Consciousness are themselves the primary Revelation in His sacred Work. He is the authoritative Source and Revealer of Truth in the Way of the Heart, for all those who become His formally acknowledged devotees.

---

5. *The Basket of Tolerance: A Guide to Perfect Understanding of the One and Great Tradition of Mankind* (forthcoming) is Heart-Master Da Love-Ananda's masterly annotated bibliography of the entire sacred and secular Wisdom-tradition of humanity, with listings of more than two thousand books in an original schema based in Ultimate Divine Wisdom and developed by Heart-Master Da Himself.

This book treats at some length the forms of relationship mutually entered into by Heart-Master Da and each of His authentic or serious students. His presumption of an authoritative role in relation to devotees in the context of His Teaching Work (1970-1986) and His Blessing Work since that time is a complex matter that does not yield, I feel, to brief summary. But a few basic features of His relationship to His students, and ours to Him, can be identified.

First, during His Teaching years, Heart-Master Da always made it very plain in His published Instructions exactly what type of Teaching relationship He would presume with anyone who announced himself or herself as a seriously committed devotee.

Second, that relationship always involved <u>mutual</u> <u>submission</u> <u>and</u> <u>commitment</u>, wherein Heart-Master Da Submitted to make Himself completely vulnerable to the individual as the Enlightened Divine Teacher, just as the student was Called, as a devoted sacred practitioner in the ancient, traditional sense, to make himself or herself completely vulnerable to Heart-Master Da as Sat-Guru. Part of His Submission during His Teaching years was to engage His devotee-students in a completely experimental determination of what forms their practice should take in order for them to Realize the Truth in His Company. He did not arbitrarily impose any kind of regimens on devotees, but always Called them to explore with Him the efficacy of all kinds of observances and practices, in every area of life, in order to determine the details of the Way of the Heart as a continually effective practice in each one's case.

Third, Heart-Master Da lovingly Identified with and Instructed His students, sometimes manifesting His Instruction in a paradoxical or unconventional fashion, and at other times in more ordinary ways, within the context of mutual agreement with them about His Teaching Service to them. He thus Functioned in a manner not altogether dissimilar to that of any instructor whose agreement with a pupil is that he or she will require the pupil to press beyond apparent limits in his or her execution of the task, skill, or art being taught. All who entered Heart-Master Da's Teaching "Theatre" were Called to discipline themselves and to participate with great voluntary intention in a sacred process that constantly obliged them to go beyond egoic limits of all kinds.

What distinguished (and distinguishes) His Work from that of a conventional instructor is that Heart-Master Da is a Divine Realizer of the most profound degree. He lives as the Being, or feeling-awareness, of

33

each and all who come to Him. And all His actions are what is traditionally called "kheyala"—spontaneous, unthought responses of the living Divine Consciousness to all of the qualities, forces, and personalities with which He is mysteriously in Play in every moment. Such spontaneity characterized Heart-Master Da's every gesture and Word as a Teacher (in the years 1970-1986), and it continues to characterize both His activity and His repose, His speech and His silence, in His ongoing Blessing Work.

Therefore, His manner of Serving others has been "authoritative", as indicated above, but it cannot rightly be construed as "authoritarian" in the pejorative sense in which that term is generally used today. To construe it as such is simply to ignore the conditions under which Heart-Master Da was and is willing to enter into the Adept-devotee relationship with individuals—conditions that He has enunciated plainly in practically every volume of His written Teaching, beginning with *The Knee of Listening* and especially, in 1973, *The Method of the Siddhas*. There He spoke of the demand inherent in sadhana, or right functional action, in Satsang, "The Company of Truth", or the sacred relationship to Him as Divine Guru:

HEART-MASTER DA LOVE-ANANDA: Spiritual life is a demand, not a form of therapy. It is a demand under the conditions of Satsang, the relationship to Guru. It is the practice of life in a world where the living Heart, not your own dilemma and search, is the condition. The demand itself does not make real sadhana possible. It is Satsang, the prior condition of Truth, that makes it necessary. Satsang contains and communicates itself as a demand. And this demand acts as an obstacle for those who are not certain about their interest in this radical life. They have read a little about it, heard a little about it, and now it tests them in the fire of living.

Such is the way it has always been. The monasteries, the ashrams, the schools of teachers in the past were conceived like fortresses in the hills. They were difficult to get to, and very few people ever returned from them. . . . Traditional spiritual life was never confused with any sort of playful getting high. All of that is only a mediocre interpretation fabricated by people who have no real capacity for sadhana or the true and radical bliss of conscious existence. Spiritual life is not getting high. From the human point of view, the resistive, narcissistic, ordinary human point of view, spiritual life is the most completely oppressive prospect. And it creates massive resistance in such people as soon as they get a taste of it. Traditionally, incredible obstacles were put out front, so

*that people would not bother even to come to the door. It was purposely intend-
ed that people would never even ask about it unless they had already overcome
tremendous resistance in themselves. The great Oriental temples, for instance,
were built with incredible images of demons, guardians and ferocious beasts
surrounding the entrances, so that people would not approach such places in
their usual state of self-obsession. Their heads were required to be bowed. The
devotee was expected to be crushed within, in a humble state, reflecting awareness of his habit of living. The devotee was expected to arrive on his knees, and
never without a gift. Such people would never come irreverently. They would
never display an inappropriate attitude. The traditional ways of approach are
perhaps too ritualistic and too purely symbolic. They can be superficially
learned and imitated, and so they do not necessarily reflect the inner attitude.
Just so, all must realize and demonstrate the appropriate and genuine manner
of approach and life in our Ashram. . . .*

*Spiritual life is a demand, it is a confrontation, it is a relationship. It is not
a method you apply to yourself. Your "self" is this contraction, and this contraction is what must be undermined in spiritual life. Therefore, the Guru
comes in human form, in living form, to confront you and take you by the neck.
He doesn't merely send down a grinning photograph, to be reproduced with a
few fairy comments for everybody to believe. . . . Truth must come in a living
form, absolutely. Truth must confront a man, live him, and meditate him. It is
not your meditation that matters. Truth must meditate you. And that is the
Siddhi [Divine Awakening Power] or marvelous process of Satsang. Even while
Truth is meditating you in Satsang, you are busy doing more of the usual to
yourself, waking yourself up, putting yourself to sleep, reacting in every possible and unconscious way to the force of Satsang, but you are being meditated.*[6]

"Truth is <u>not</u> within"—
the necessity of the Sat-Guru

One of the common rationalizations for avoiding the demand of
authentic sacred practice is the popular, Spiritually adolescent, and, from
Heart-Master Da Love-Ananda's Enlightened perspective, deluding notion

---

6. Bubba Free John [Heart-Master Da Love-Ananda] *The Method of the Siddhas* (Clearlake, Calif.: The Dawn
Horse Press, 1978), pp. 56-57, 224-25.

that "Truth is within". This doctrine is inherited from inward-oriented, principally Oriental, mystical traditions that exploit the subtler psycho-physiological functions of the body and the brain. In the Spiritually adolescent mind, it appears to lead naturally to the supposition that one may Realize the Truth, or the Self, merely by exploring one's own interior, using any one or several of a variety of techniques of concentration and meditation, while conveniently maintaining a wary distance from the Call and process of submission of the ego-self to an authentic Teacher.

Heart-Master Da Love-Ananda has incessantly countered such notions from the beginning of His Mission, commenting at one point, "Truth is not within. The nervous system and the brain are the new Golden Calf." He has always pointed out that those who use such beliefs or doctrines to rationalize their refusal to submit to a true Teacher are not fundamentally interested in Spiritual Liberation. They are still infatuated with conditional possibilities and with the potential exploitation of their own psychophysical mechanisms. By contrast, one who is authentically impulsed to Liberation is gravely disturbed by his or her bondage to mortal, limited, conditional existence. Such a Spiritually "ripe" character is deeply humbled by his or her incapability to accomplish the Miracle of Liberation, and is thus convinced, to the core, of his or her utter need for Divine Grace in the specific form of a Spiritually Awakened and Powerful Master or Teacher.

Heart-Master Da has recently contrasted the inward-seeking, adolescent orientation with the Message and the Opportunity offered by true Sat-Gurus, or Divinely Awakened Revealers of the living Truth of existence:

HEART-MASTER DA LOVE-ANANDA: *Some individuals are born in the Perfectly God-Realized Condition, or priorly Enlightened. Their birth is therefore a submission to conditional existence, and as a result they endure a process of Re-Awakening during their early lifetime. When that process is complete, they begin to serve the Function of Sat-Guru. Such individuals pass through a process of intense and complete self-renunciation and devotion to Truth. And in that process they are Given (or are directly Awakened into) the God-Revealing, or Truth-Revealing, Samadhi, or Perfect Realization.*

Such individuals are called by many names in the Great Tradition, and one of the principal names for them is "Maha-Purusha" ["Supremely Conscious Man"]. The Maha-Purushas are the true Sat-Gurus ["Revealers of the Truth"]. And such am I.

The Sat-Guru is the Very Means of Perfect Realization for others. There are Gurus of a more ordinary type, who are not born in the Divinely Realized Condition, or Prior God-Realization, but who do sadhana [sacred practice] and Realize one or another degree, or stage, of Awakening. Such ordinary, or lesser, Gurus are not themselves the means for Ultimate Realization, but they serve others, usually in the context of some tradition, by providing guidance based on their knowledge of their own tradition and the degree of their experience in the Spiritual process. Such lesser or more ordinary Gurus may experience one or another stage of Samadhi [God-Conscious contemplative state] in the course of their sadhana, but they are not functioning in the manner of the Sat-Guru, who is Divinely Awakened and who serves the unique Function of the Means for the Perfect, or Divine, Realization of others.

The popular exoteric and even esoteric teachings are commonly associated with the idea that God, or Truth, is within every individual. This is not the case. The Divine, or the Truth, is Prior to, or Beyond, the individual, or the body-mind. Popular doctrines tend to suggest that people must turn their attention within themselves to Realize the Truth, and this is not a true doctrine, because the Truth, or the Divine, is not within the body-mind.

Ordinary people are not Awake in the Divine Samadhi Prior to and Beyond the body-mind. Therefore, they must transcend themselves, not indulge in their own inwardness. The great Confessions of Identification with the Divine, or the Ultimate Condition, are the Confessions of Realizers, or those who have been Awakened to the Divine Samadhi that is Prior to, or Beyond, conditional existence altogether. Those Confessions also apply to all beings Ultimately. All beings are arising in the Divine and are Ultimately One with the Divine. But living beings are not in general aware of the Divine Source-Condition, and thus this Truth is not merely something within them, within their psyche or within the sphere of their egoic inwardness.

The Sat-Guru, or Maha-Purusha, is not in an ordinary state. The Sat-Guru is perpetually in Divine Samadhi, and that Samadhi is a Condition that others may Realize by Grace, but ordinary beings do not otherwise enjoy such a Realization. In other words, ordinary beings are not in Divine Samadhi. Therefore, they are not One with the Divine Consciousness, and they cannot in truth Confess that they are One with the Divine Consciousness. It would not be true of them if they did confess it, unless they are, by Grace, brought into the Sphere of the Samadhi of a Maha-Purusha.

Such Maha-Purushas, or Sat-Gurus, appear so that ordinary living beings may have the direct means for God-Realization, or Truth-Realization, or the

37

Realization of the Ultimate Samadhi or Condition Prior to and Beyond conditional existence. Therefore, ordinary beings may Realize the Divine, or the Real Condition, progressively, by surrender of self to the God-Revealing, or Truth-Revealing, Sat-Guru, or Maha-Purusha. In the course of the sadhana of such surrender, individuals are, by Grace, drawn into the Condition of the Sat-Guru, and they progressively Realize the many forms and stages of purification and Realization.

The common notion about the process of sadhana is that it is a matter of becoming more and more deeply involved in the inwardness of the body-mind, or soul. However, this is not the case. The body-mind is not Samadhi. It is the conditional self, and for the Ultimate Samadhi to be Realized, the body-mind must be transcended utterly. For any lesser Samadhi to be realized, the body-mind must be transcended in part, or at least momentarily. In the course of the true sadhana, which is devotion to the Sat-Guru, many experiential states of body and mind may arise within and without. But these are not the true substance and import of the process of true sadhana. Fundamentally the entire process of the sadhana of devotion to the Sat-Guru, or Maha-Purusha, or Sat-Purusha (which is another way of referring to such an individual) is purification, or the release of self-contraction and ultimately of all forms of conditional existence. Therefore, true sadhana is progressive self-renunciation and self-surrender, enacted in utter devotional response to the Sat-Guru and by means of the Sat-Guru's Grace.

True sadhana, then, is the process of self-purification and not self-development. Only the true devotee of the Sat-Guru understands this and is free of clinging to phenomena in general, and also free of clinging to the phenomena that arise in the course of sadhana and as a direct result of it. (January 6, 1989)

God and the God-Realized World-Teacher

The orientation of a devotee to a true Sat-Guru or Spiritual Adept is worlds apart from that of an intellectual student of his or her work, and even from that of a friendly sympathizer or supporter who nonetheless maintains his or her distance from that Adept.

As a devotee of Heart-Master Da Love-Ananda, I feel that He embodies infinite, eternal Consciousness, and that He is universally Radiant as the

Source-Light, Love, and Happiness That is the Heart of everything that exists—even as He walks and talks and conducts an apparently individual human life. This has been my fundamental, intuitive faith in His Nature ever since I first came upon His writings. It cannot really be explained, and it certainly cannot be logically "proven" to the mind. Nor have I yet fully brought this primal intuition into life, for it obliges and moves me to Commune more and more constantly and, ultimately, to Realize Perfect Identity with my Heart-Master's infinite Nature. It is as a European visitor to the great Hindu Sage Ramana Maharshi wrote earlier in this century:

> *It did not take long for me to be sure that I was in front of one who had in that very body I could see before me solved life's problem for himself. The radiant peace around him proved it beyond all cavil. The calm, like that of the midnight sky, was something too real to question for a moment. That part of my search, then, was over, even at the first glimpse. In the flesh I had seen a "Master". I told my friend that night that I* knew *he was what the books call a* Jivanmukta *[one "Liberated while alive"]. Please don't ask me how I* knew *for I cannot answer that. It was just as one knows that water is wet and the sky is blue. It could not be denied—self-evident is the word.*[7]

This is the mystery of a true Guru, a Sat-Guru, "One Who leads others from the darkness of egoity to the Light of True Being". This is the mystery of a living Buddha, a Christ; it is the paradox of a God-Man. It is very difficult for anyone to appreciate fully. I, certainly, am still learning only the rudiments of this miraculous relationship to Heart-Master Da Love-Ananda as a devotee. It is intuitively clear to me that He is the living embodiment of True Being, Which I will not Realize without His authoritative Help and Grace. Therefore, I submit to His discipline and Blessing, and it is my incalculably good fortune that He has accepted me as His devotee. The process of my discipline has been exceedingly practical, as it is for all beginners. Though this practice includes a deepening and ultimately Truth-Realizing course of meditation, it is never abstract, inward-turned, or dissociated from direct, bodily self-surrender in relationship to my Sat-Guru, Da Love-Ananda, in His very human Person. The relationship to Him is itself the essence of this discipline. And it is, to me, an inconceivable Blessing that Heart-Master Da consents to Instruct and to Correct my practice of this relationship, as He does with

7. Quoted in K. P. Bahadur, *Five Windows to God* (Bombay: Somaiya Publications, 1977), p. 63.

all His devotees, for the sake of our Liberation.

Heart-Master Da does not suggest that He alone is Divine. On the contrary, like any other genuine God-Realizer, He sees everyone else, as well as Himself, as only the Divine Being. He Worships all other beings as the One and Only Divine Person with an inexhaustible constancy of Love. He Serves every living being as the God He is here to Awaken with His rapt, Enlightening attention.

I mean every word of this—it is literally, humanly so. I have witnessed Heart-Master Da performing exactly this worshipful Service to all others whenever I have been privileged to be in His physical Company. As you will see in these pages, for many compelling reasons His Worship of all beings has taken all kinds of forms, both those that may seem conventionally "holy" and "moral" and those that (to some people) may not. Regardless of how others see Him, Heart-Master Da Love-Ananda presumes no separation whatsoever between Himself, any and all others, and God, the Divine Identity or Great Source-Unity.

Clearly, the God I am speaking of when I call Heart-Master Da a God-Realizer and say that He Worships all others as that same One, is not the Deity we have in mind when we think of an omnipotent and distant Creator of the universe. This Real God is not the long-ago Cause of the world and of living creatures, but the present, living Source-Condition of the world and the prior or inherent Self, Being, or Consciousness of all beings.

This distinction is a critical one for our understanding, and it is addressed and illumined frequently in this book. Many traditional doctrines and popular assumptions about the nature of the Divine Reality and of the human Realizers or Incarnations of that Reality do not express the Wisdom of the ultimate degree of Enlightenment. The ideas of God promoted in public or popular religion suggest an anthropomorphic Deity Who was or is the "First Cause" of the world and Who sits in moral judgment upon it (and upon each living being). Like many other God-Realizers before Him, Heart-Master Da indicates that these are childish and archaic notions that do not tally with the Wisdom of actual God-Realization.

In the West, in particular, religious thought has been dominated by ideas of an ultimate separation or difference between the Divine and the human. Thus, to say that a man has Realized God seems to the Western mind to be blasphemous, even absurd. At a deep unconscious level, as well as in its dominant expressions of theology, religious philosophy, and secular psychology, the Western mind typically assumes an unbridgeable chasm between the Divine Nature and human nature, between God and the human soul (if it conceives God to exist at all).

In the Western (or originally Middle-Eastern) religious traditions, this chasm can be bridged only by a most miraculous Divine Manifestation— the historical Appearance of a one and only Son of God Who, it is believed, will come again, or a still-awaited religious Messiah and political Redeemer Who will Save a chosen people and set the human world aright.

Seen in the light of Heart-Master Da Love-Ananda's Teaching-Revelation, there is a core of Truth in the understanding that the Birth and the Nature of a God-Man are unique. But the Divine Incarnations Appear in order to draw others into conscious Unity with their Realized Truth, not to enforce absolute distinctions between Themselves and others. They come to Awaken the inherently Divine Nature of every human soul, not merely to proclaim their own Divinity, as if their glorious State of Being were un-Realizable by others. Aldous Huxley wrote in *The Perennial Philosophy:*

The Logos [Divine Word] passes out of eternity into time for no other purpose than to assist the beings, whose bodily form he takes, to pass out of time into eternity. If the Avatar's ["Incarnation's"] appearance upon the stage of history is enormously important, this is due to the fact that by his teaching he points out, and by his being a channel of grace and divine power he actually is, the means by which human beings may transcend the limitations of history. . . .

That men and women may be thus instructed and helped, the Godhead assumes the form of an ordinary human being, who has to earn deliverance and enlightenment in the way that is prescribed by the divine Nature of Things—namely, by charity, by a total dying to self and a total, one-pointed awareness. Thus enlightened, the Avatar can reveal the way of enlightenment to others and help them actually to become what they already potentially are. . . . And of course the eternity which transforms us into Ourselves is not the experience of mere persistence after bodily death. There will be no experience of timeless Reality then, unless there is the same or a similar knowledge within the world of time and matter. By precept and by example, the Avatar teaches that this transforming knowledge is possible, that all sentient beings are called to it and that, sooner or later, in one way or another, all must finally come to it.[8]

8. Aldous Huxley, *The Perennial Philosophy* (New York: Harper and Row, 1970), pp. 51, 56.

In the East, though some sacred schools assume an absolute difference between human nature and Divine Nature, there is (or at least there has been) a thriving heritage of teachings on both the possibility and the history of God-Realization, of one or another kind or degree, by human beings. And, Heart-Master Da has confirmed, the greatest of such teachings hold that God, and each actual God-Realizer, is Awake as the present and eternal Source-Condition, or Divine Self, and the All-Pervading Spiritual Energy-Substance of all beings and things.

As such a genuine God-Realizer, Heart-Master Da Love-Ananda is Blessed with great Spiritual Power, the Heart-Power that communicates Love, Happiness, and the transcendent Wisdom of Divine Consciousness. A true God-Man is an open Heart—in Heart-Master Da's Words, an inconceivably vulnerable "Wound of Love". Thus, Heart-Master Da lives in Conscious Identification with the Life-Principle of all beings and <u>feels</u> as their very Awareness. He is continuously exposed to all their suffering and bewilderment. His Work is a great Mission to Awaken all such suffering beings, to Help them participate freely in His own Realization of God as the One and Only Divine Self, Love, Happiness, Truth, Consciousness, and Freedom. He is, then, "the answer to human prayers, not superhuman intent."[9] Since He has no other purpose for being alive than such Divine Service to others, He is rightly to be understood as a uniquely benign, vulnerable, and un-self-conscious Being in a world of the self-armored and the self-enamored.

Heart-Master Da's Title "The World-Teacher" points to what might be called His "Avataric" Nature as a direct Descent or Incarnation of the unqualified Divine Reality, or What Western religious thinkers have referred to as the "Logos" or the "Godhead". This Title indicates a degree of Identification with the Divine Reality from prior to birth that is beyond what may be seen even in the lives of most authentic God-Realizers—for there are, as Heart-Master Da's Story makes clear, many distinctions to be made among those who confess one or another kind of Divine Awakening and Awareness. Rather than try here to explain such matters—which are beyond our ordinary analytical comprehension in any but the most rudimentary sense—I will defer to Heart-Master Da's Story itself, which provides many vivid clarifications of these distinctions and progressively reveals His uniqueness as a God-Realizer of unparalleled Nature

9. Bubba Free John [Heart-Master Da Love-Ananda], *The Enlightenment of the Whole Body*, p. 257.

and Accomplishment. The Sanskrit term from which the English "World-Teacher" is derived is "Jagad-Guru", the root syllables of which mean, literally, "The Divine Master and Liberator of all that moves". You will hear in His Story the astonishing Confessions that Heart-Master Da makes without the slightest equivocation as that Very One, in Person.

The necessary evolutionary leap to devotional love

What are the practical implications of a devotional relationship to such a Person?

In any serious instructor-pupil or Master-disciple relationship, the student is aspiring to grow beyond present bodily, emotional, or mental limits of one kind or another. In the sacred life, the disciple or devotee is involved in a literally evolutionary process that affects the entire being, from the heart "out".

There is a great deal of talk today about evolution, and even about conscious cooperation with the evolutionary course of human destiny. But few appreciate the necessary dynamics of that course, if it is to be engaged completely and with success, to the degree of ultimate Divine Realization. As Heart-Master Da has remarked again and again, the great struggle of humanity in this epoch is to grow beyond the concerns of "money, food, and sex" (or beyond gross, bodily based struggles for power, sustenance, pleasure, and consolation in the context of the first three stages of life) and into the psychic depth, sensitivity, and devotional heart-radiance that characterize the fourth stage of life. The "leap" to the fourth stage of life He sometimes speaks of is the leap from self-obsession to love, from "me"-consciousness to God-Consciousness, from self-concern to Divine Communion, or true devotional love. It is all about the opening of the heart, as He has said many times in conversations with devotees:

HEART-MASTER DA LOVE-ANANDA: *The only thing wrong with anyone in any moment of limitation is the collapse of the heart. When the heart collapses, the energies all over the body become distorted. Thus, the transformation of the heart is the single and fundamental occupation of Man at this time in our evolution. A person must directly enter into loving association with the All-Pervading Transcendental Divine Reality and Person, and he (or she) must persist in that form of existence from moment to moment. If he lives in love with God, then naturally he associates with all beings through love. Whatever he is associated with becomes the medium, the Divine Image in fact, for his association with God. Such a one is always associating with God in love. Therefore, all his relationships are loving relationships. Self-transcendence is the quality of his action. He lives as a servant in the highest sense.*

The quality of such a devotee's existence is the quality of radiance to others and to God. It is an emotional radiance. It is also full of energy, and it is physical. It is the radiance of energy and attention in relationship. In the company of such a person others feel an endless force of consciousness and energy to which the individual is surrendered bodily and emotionally. Thus, the quality of God, or the spiritual Power that Radiates the worlds, is expressed through such a person quite naturally, and he or she becomes an increasingly different kind of person because of that expression. A community of such people becomes a profoundly unique association of human beings, because they work constantly to transform the emotional and moral dimension that is basic to our existence. . . .

DEVOTEE: *I feel that this emotional conversion is not something that I can will to happen.*

HEART-MASTER DA LOVE-ANANDA: *That is true, but paradoxically it is also not out of your hands altogether. You are obliged to associate consciously with That with which you are in love. If you spend time in the company of what is lovable, then the emotional radiance of the being, the love that is native to the being, will naturally come forward. Right association is the secret, then. It is said that of all the things a person can do, association with the God-Realized personality, the saint, the Spiritual Master, is the best, simply to be in the company of one who is lovable in the highest sense, one in love with whom the very Force of God is encountered. Emotional conversion is not out of your hands. You are not obliged to wait until it happens to you. It occurs when you are in love in the fullest sense. Therefore, the simplest way to accomplish this change is to spend your time in the company of one with whom you are in love.*

The best Company in which to spend all your time is the Company of God and the Spiritual Master. There are other relationships in which you are also in love, but the relationships with God and the Spiritual Master are primary. True religion is simply a matter of maintaining association with God and with the Spiritual Master moment to moment. Then the natural emotion, or the force of love, devotion, and self-surrender, will tend to be evoked by that Company. Thus, devotees are instructed to recite the Name of God, to remember God constantly, to hold the image of the Spiritual Master in their minds, to talk about the Spiritual Master, to praise the Spiritual Master, and to think of the Spiritual Master. These are all ways of maintaining Divine Association. The secret of ecstatic practice is to find your way of maintaining association with the One who is lovable, or the Beloved, in every moment.[10]

"You become what you meditate on": Heart-Master Da's "Heart-Power" and how It is conveyed in His sacred biography

All of these matters are treated further, though not primarily in expository form, in this sacred biography, *The Divine Emergence of The World-Teacher*. To appreciate this book, it may be useful for you to consider briefly what I understand to be the nature and purpose of such a sacred biography, or the telling of the Life-Story of a true sacred Authority such as Heart-Master Da.

In the Western tradition the telling of the lives of the saints is known as "hagiography". Hagiographic writing is instinctively distrusted, and disliked, by the adolescent modern mind, primarily because such writing often seems to foster a childish unwillingness to acknowledge and come to grips with the dark side of human and cosmic Nature. And it is true that much hagiographic biography promotes a harmonious vision of the saints or of the Divine at the expense of a realistic appraisal of the egoic self and the world of Nature. Writing more than forty years ago, Aldous Huxley identified another reason why "hagiographic" is a pejorative term for the modern mind:

---

10. Heart-Master Da Love-Ananda, *Compulsory Dancing: Talks and Essays on the spiritual and evolutionary necessity of emotional surrender to the Life-Principle* (Clearlake, Calif.: The Dawn Horse Press, 1987), pp. 38-39, 42-43.

Among the cultivated and mentally active, hagiography is now a very unpopular form of literature. The fact is not at all surprising. The cultivated and the mentally active have an insatiable appetite for novelty, diversity and distraction. But the saints, however commanding their talents and whatever the nature of their professional activities, are all incessantly preoccupied with only one subject—spiritual Reality and the means by which they and their fellows can come to the unitive knowledge of that Reality. And as for their actions—these are as monotonously uniform as their thoughts; for in all circumstances they behave selflessly, patiently and with indefatigable charity. No wonder, then, if the biographies of such men and women remain unread. For one well educated person who knows anything about William Law there are two or three hundred who have read Boswell's life of his younger contemporary. Why? Because, until he actually lay dying, Johnson indulged himself in the most fascinating of multiple personalities; whereas Law, for all the superiority of his talents was almost absurdly simple and single-minded. Legion prefers to read about Legion. It is for this reason that, in the whole repertory of epic, drama and the novel, there are hardly any representations of true theocentric saints.[11]

These observations point to a principle that is at the heart of Heart-Master Da Love-Ananda's whole Revelation, and that has informed the writing of this entire book. Heart-Master Da summarizes that principle simply: "You become what you meditate on", or, as He rendered it more exactly in His *Love-Ananda Gita*, "You (necessarily) become (or conform to the likeness of) whatever you Contemplate, or Meditate on, or even think about."[12] Legion ("multitude") prefers, as Huxley said, to meditate on Legion, because that meditation permits and encourages it to remain as it is. But the purpose of the sacred biography of Heart-Master Da Love-Ananda is to serve the greatest impulse in those who read it, which is the impulse to Realize the One Truth that Heart-Master Da Incarnates.

A thread of discussion that runs through the whole Story treats of Heart-Master Da's unique Capability to Awaken others to God, Truth, and Happiness. He calls this Capability His "Hridaya-Siddhi" or, literally, from the Sanskrit, "Heart-Power". That Power may be felt as the Love that devotees discover by Grace as they evolve or grow in devotion to God

11. Aldous Huxley, *The Perennial Philosophy*, p. 46.
12. Heart-Master Da Love-Ananda, *The Love-Ananda Gita* , p. 193.

and Spiritual Master. And it is much more—this Heart-Power is the Force of Unconditional Divine Consciousness. It is identical to the All-Pervading Energy that gives rise to the universe of worlds, things, and beings. Heart-Master Da Himself <u>Is</u> that Heart-Power; there is no distinction between Him and It.

To write truthfully of such a Person requires the relinquishment of the mind of doubt and uncertainty that plagues humanity. It requires transcendence of the cultural taboos against the affirmation of love, freedom, happiness, certainty, faith, joy, and devotion. At the same time, it requires transcendence of unwillingness to acknowledge and encounter the often extremely painful realities of that Person's Ordeal of Teaching and Blessing others in a world devoted to the ends of the ego. Thus, such writing requires the discipline of adhering to the most profound Vision of Heart-Master Da as He Is, a God-Realizer of the most Perfect degree and a born Divine Incarnation. In preparing this book, I have had to continually exercise discrimination, in order to be able to transcend the limited, egoic vision I automatically tend to superimpose on Heart-Master Da and His Work.

The same kind of self-transcending discipline is required of those who would most benefit by reading such a book. Because of the Grace-Conferring Nature of its Subject—Heart-Master Da—the book itself is a vehicle whereby the heart may be moved into ecstatic, heart-touched Intimacy with Him and with the Divine. Such Communion characterizes the next evolutionary stage of human consciousness. Unlike a typical theocentric Saint, the Divine Master Da Love-Ananda has been obliged to an extraordinarily dramatic life of action in His attempts to draw others into "unitive vision of Reality". Therefore, each writing and also each reading, each telling and likewise each hearing, of His Life-Story must observe a kind of proportion, symmetry, or balance, so that every particular element of the total Drama is granted appropriate significance, no more and no less. Only thus is this unitive vision of Reality always fully served.

Heart-Master Da's entire Life-Story is the chronicle of the Infinite becoming or taking the form of the finite. In contrast, a typical Spiritual biography tells the adventures of an apparently finite individual contacting and, perhaps, Realizing Unity with the Infinite. Heart-Master Da's Life-Story is a chronicle of the Divine Heart-Power of Grace moving into the human and earthly world in, as, and through a single, extraordinary Person.

Therefore, any true rendition of Heart-Master Da Love-Ananda's biography is what is known in the Hindu tradition as "Leela"—the Inspiring and mysteriously heart-opening Play of the Divine in human embodiment. One of the Hindu scriptures aptly characterizes the unique function of such a saga, in the words of a monarch approaching death who asks a Sage to tell him of the deeds of the God-Man Krishna:

Chronicle, O blessed one, the tales of Hari [Krishna] of the marvellous exploits, which confer all auspiciousness on the worlds; so that I may be enabled to discard the body, fixing the mind, freed from all attachments, on Krishna, the soul in all beings. When a man hears constantly and attentively the accounts of His exploits and extols them, the Lord enters his heart ere long.[13]

The Divine Emergence of The World-Teacher is, first and foremost, a telling of Heart-Master Da's Leela whereby He may enter or Spiritually Touch the hearts of those who learn of His Life with sympathetic receptivity. He has Affirmed to devotees, and we have seen it to be true many times, that His Leelas or Stories are just as pure a vehicle of His Divinely Inspiring Heart-Power as His verbal Teaching-Revelation itself.

Because He is the All-Conscious World-Teacher, the Story of the Divine Emergence of Heart-Master Da Love-Ananda is living Revelation. And that accounts for the distinctive tone and form of its biographical celebration here. The modern mind of doubt can never really, fully be converted or changed by argument or logic. Distrust of sacred Authority cannot be dispelled by an appeal to the logic of distrust, the logic of doubt and analytical proof, which may seem to be purely rational but which is in fact built upon a self-created emotional problem about existence. Truly rational appeals, built upon the Living Intelligence of Truth, are helpful, and to this end Heart-Master Da Love-Ananda has Revealed His brilliantly rational Teaching Argument in all of its forms. But the mind of doubt only yields fully when, unexpectedly, even unasked, a change of heart occurs.

My task as a devotee-biographer, then, has been to allow the telling of Heart-Master Da's Life-Story in this book to be as transparent a vehicle

13. N. Raghunathan, trans., *Srimad Bhagavatam*, vol. I (Madras: Vighneswara Publishing House, 1976), pp. 111-12.

as possible for His Heart-Power, Whereby He authenticates Himself—beyond or prior to mental logic—in every heart He Touches or enters, Granting unreasonable Happiness, intuitive freedom, and primal, sacred integrity, or certainty of Being.

Sri Love-Anandashram, 1989

"Out of the Everywhere into the Here"

Divine Incarnation
and Divine "Amnesia"

**Headlines on November 3, 1939, the Birth date of The World-Teacher,
Heart-Master Da Love-Ananda**

CHAPTER ONE

"Out of the Everywhere into the Here"

Divine Incarnation and Divine "Amnesia"

A sudden prophecy in the East

By early 1939 of the Common Era, humanity was careening, like a runaway train, toward horrific disaster on a global scale. Totalitarian dictatorships in the Far East and in Europe were plotting or already waging unprecedented assaults upon both the life and the moral consciousness of the human species.

With new and terrifying weaponry serving the motivations of age-old racial barbarism and jingoistic hatred, the events of the next half decade would take a dread toll on the Spirit of Man.

That February, in India, an elderly Spiritual Master named Upasani Baba Maharaj was visited at his Ashram ("hermitage retreat") by the Shankaracharya of Jyothirmath, a religious leader of millions of Hindus.

It was an historic meeting. The Shankaracharya was a pure and holy man, vested with a powerful religious office in the public faith of so many Indians. Now he was coming to pay his respects to, and to be likewise honored by, the old Saint, who throughout his life as a Spiritual Teacher had been a crusty, often wrathful renegade.

Upasani Baba was the kind of illumined spirit who speaks too much truth too forcefully to be acceptable in the realms of orderly, well-behaved public religion. He would generally have gone naked by preference; since even his own disciples were uncomfortable with his nudity, he compromised by wearing a burlap sack. At times during his years as a

53

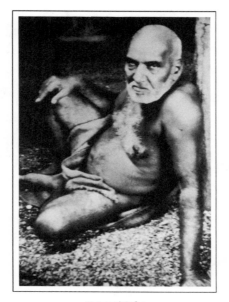

Upasani Baba

Teacher he had hurled rocks and abuses at people who approached him hypocritically, outwardly seeking his Blessings but inwardly full of pride, willfulness, and vanity.

Some people understood that Upasani Baba's bizarre and sometimes abusive behavior was intended to instruct others and help them see their own hidden faults and Godlessness. To those who could see his holiness, he gave of himself without reservation. He established, for the first time in modern Hindu history, a female order of renunciate devotees, called "Kanyas", whom he personally trained. To the horror of many orthodox Hindus, Upasani Baba Spiritually married all of his Kanyas. And he even allowed and encouraged them to practice certain ancient rites that had been the guarded province of male priests for thousands of years.

During one period of his life, Upasani Baba frequently threaded his way through an area infested with deadly snakes, tigers, and the like, to the grounds of a factory where the carcasses of animals were rendered into tallow for candles and soap. There he would sit on heaps of the bones of dead animals, liberating, he said, their spirits and hastening them to more auspicious future lives.

Even by Indian standards, then, Upasani Baba Maharaj was a strange and disturbing Teacher.

Nonetheless, the Shankaracharya of Jyothirmath was aware that Baba's strange exterior and sometimes outrageous habits clothed a spirit of immense purity and wisdom. So he came to the aged Saint with great respect.

They talked of many things that February, including the plight of the Dharma (an ancient Sanskrit term for "the Truth and Its Way of life") in India. The Shankaracharya decried the sorry state of religion in the land and lamented that even holy men were helpless to do anything about it.

It seemed to him, he said, that only an Avatar—a human Incarnation, or "Descent", of the Divine—would be capable of re-establishing the Dharma in the human world.

With these words, the Shankaracharya was referring to one of the most famous passages expounded by the legendary God-Man Krishna in the *Bhagavad Gita,* perhaps the most popular of the Hindu Scriptures. This is the great proclamation of the Avatar as the Dharma-Bearer or World-Teacher Who re-establishes the Truth in times of direst human ignorance and strife:

Although I am birthless and my self imperishable,
Although I am the Lord of All Beings,
Yet, by controlling my own material nature,
I come into being by my own supernatural power.
Whenever a decrease of righteousness [Dharma]
Exists, Descendent of Bharata [Arjuna],
And there is a rising up of unrighteousness,
Then I give forth myself,
For the protection of the good
And the destruction of evil doers;
For the sake of establishing righteousness,
I come into being from age to age. (IV.6-8)[1]

Upasani Baba Maharaj had been listening to the Shankaracharya's thoughts. He knew well what the swami meant when he voiced his wish for the appearance of an Avatar. At that very instant, apparently to his own surprise as well, Upasani Baba burst out with a prophetic announcement:

He declared that a Divine Incarnation would shortly manifest Himself on Earth in a European country. (By Indians, as by many other peoples of

1. Winthrop Sargeant, trans., *The Bhagavad Gita,* rev. ed. (Albany: State University of New York Press, 1984), pp. 206-8.

the world, all the predominantly white nations, including America and Americans, are considered "European".)

Upasani Baba further predicted that this Incarnation would be all-powerful, bearing down everything before Him. And He would see to it that the Dharma, the Teaching and Way of life based on the ultimate, eternal Wisdom extolled in the Hindu Scriptures, is firmly re-established in India.[2]

"Out of the Everywhere into the Here"

In the very month of Upasani Baba's dramatic prophecy, February 1939, in the then still rural village of Franklin Square, on Long Island near the American metropolis of New York City, a child was conceived by a young couple, Franklin Augustus and Dorothy Jones.

It was a very happy moment when they learned of Dorothy's pregnancy. Frank was a promising salesman. The country had weathered and was recovering from the Great Depression, and it had no intention of entering into the current regional conflicts of Europe or Asia. So the Joneses looked forward to a bright future, including the raising of children.

Frank and Dorothy were a typical American couple of that pre-war period, members of a local Lutheran church and upstanding citizens in the community.

When her time came, Dorothy gave birth in a hospital, as was then already the custom in America. It was probably wise that she did, because the birth was extremely difficult and complicated. The baby boy was nearly strangled to death in delivery by His umbilical cord, which had wrapped around His neck in the birth canal.

But, happily, He survived without injury. He was large, with immensely bright, dark brown eyes. Frank and Dorothy gave Him Frank's own name, Franklin, and the name of Dorothy's father, Albert.

He was born at 11:21 A.M. on November 3, 1939, in Jamaica, New York.

2. See B. V. Narasimha Swami and S. Subbarao, *Sage of Sakuri*, 4th ed. (Bombay: Shri B. T. Wagh, 1966), p. 204.

The whole family on both sides celebrated the birth of Frank and Dorothy's first child. None of them could have guessed the Divine Nature and Destiny of the boy.

Nonetheless, something Mysterious must have prompted Doll Jones, Frank's mother, when she selected a baby book as a gift for her new grandson. Inside the book, signed by herself in her pleasing script, was a poem by a nineteenth-century Scottish religious allegorist named George MacDonald:

> "Where did you come from,
> Baby dear?"
> "Out of the Everywhere into the Here."
> George M*ac* Donald
>
> For
> _Franklin Albert Jones_
> Presented by
> _Mrs. H. Jones — Grandmother_

Born in the "Bright"

Where does a God-Man or Divine Incarnation come from?

Popular religion would suggest that the answer to such a question must be "Heaven"—whatever, and wherever, that might be.

More profound or esoteric Spiritual teachings suggest a different answer—one that is not comprehensible to our usual thinking mind. In the *Bhagavad Gita*, certain Buddhist *Sutras*, and other scriptures revealed by Divine Realizers in the past, the State from which the God-Born Masters appear is described as inconceivable, beyond all heavenly worlds such as those where one might go after death, beyond all the phenomena of cosmic Nature that we might experience even in the loftiest of visions or Spiritual ecstasies.

Heart-Master Da Love-Ananda's Confessions accord with these most profound ancient conceptions. He has said that before this physical, human Lifetime, He was Abiding in the infinite, unknowable Divine State that transcends both earthly and heavenly phenomena of all kinds. He willingly consented to endure a human birth and life on Earth as a Divine Response to the heart-prayers of innumerable beings who are suffering and in need of Divine Wisdom and Spiritual Help.

Heart-Master Da's first awareness of the born state occurred before His Birth, when He consciously associated with His body-mind in His mother's womb. Years later, as a young adult, He would vividly recall that shocking and sorrowful instant of anchoring His unbounded Conscious Bliss to an embryonic human body-mind.

The next moment about which Heart-Master Da has spoken was the event of His physical, bodily birth. He was fully alert and cognizant throughout His mother's labor. He clearly remembers being nearly strangled to death by His umbilical cord.

In that moment He made the same gesture of the Heart that has characterized His whole life since: He simply surrendered into the total present moment of His experience exactly as it was. Though terrified, He did not recoil in fear but continued to feel openly in all directions, allowing events to happen as they would, embracing His circumstance in its totality, via feeling.

From His earliest moments of human existence, then, Heart-Master Da Love-Ananda had no fundamental illusions about the nature and import of being born. Even then, He knew the born state as a painful limitation of Unconditional Feeling-Awareness, a limitation that leads inevitably to death.

His first two years or more were characterized by only the barest association with the embodied state. He was fully aware of the people and events around Him, but He—the Divine Self—had not yet entered deeply into physicality. Rather, He delighted in infinite Freedom and Joy, and His body-mind, as He experienced it, was illumined by the State that He intuitively knew as the "Bright":

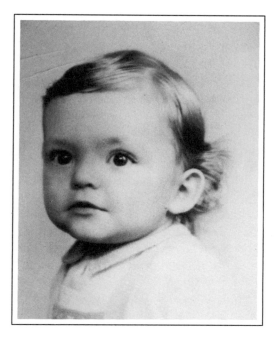

"Even as a little child I recognized it and knew it. . . ."

Even as a baby I remember only crawling around inquisitively with an incredible sense of joy, light, and freedom in the middle of my head that was bathed in energies moving freely down from above, up, around, and down through my body and my heart. It was an expanding sphere of joy from the heart. And I was a radiant form, a source of energy, bliss, and light in the midst of what is entirely energy, bliss, and light. I was the power of Reality, a direct enjoyment and communication. I was the Heart, who lightens the mind and all things. I was the same as every one and every thing, except it became clear that others were apparently unaware of the thing itself.

Even as a little child I recognized it and knew it, and it was really not a matter of anything else. That awareness, that conscious enjoyment and space centered in the midst of the heart is the "bright". And it is the entire source of humor. It is reality. It is not separate from anything.[3]

3. The World-Teacher, Heart-Master Da Love-Ananda, *The Knee of Listening*, New Standard Edition. Forthcoming.

The plunge into
Divine Self-forgetting

Thus, in a very real sense, Heart-Master Da did not fully assume the embodied condition at His physical, bodily birth.

He descended into bodily existence only some two years later. His parents were going to surprise their son, now becoming a toddler, with the gift of a puppy.

When they put the puppy on the linoleum floor, it immediately went running over to Him. He describes what happened:

HEART-MASTER DA LOVE-ANANDA: Franklin Jones, as a Conscious creation or condition, began one day while I was crawling across the linoleum floor in a house my parents had rented from an old woman named Mrs. Farr. There was a little puppy that my parents had gotten for me running across the floor towards me. I saw the puppy, and I saw my parents, and the creation of Franklin Jones began from that moment. All of the rest of the events that occurred during the two or more years prior to that were not the years of Franklin Jones. He has no existence prior to that time, the conscious or intentional beginning. (April 1974)

In that instant, Heart-Master Da assumed the bodily state. From that moment forward, He has said, His Divine Consciousness resided in association with the body-mind at the level of the heart. The great process of Divine Self-forgetting was then initiated, a voluntary "Amnesia" of Divine Identity, which He would suffer for nearly three decades.

Between His physical birth and His Descent at the age of two, Heart-Master Da was priorly established in the Realization of What He would later call "Amrita Nadi". This Sanskrit term, which can be found in the ancient Hindu Upanishads, means "the Current of Immortality". This is the State He knew in childhood as the "Bright".

The Amrita Nadi is essentially hidden from the experience of human beings until and unless they Realize the Divine Self. Heart-Master Da Love-Ananda has written and spoken frequently of Its Nature and Structure.

There is a place, He Reveals, in the upper right chamber of the heart of each one of us that is the "seat" or "location" from which the Divine Being animates or "lives" our body-minds. Amrita Nadi is a Current or

Heart-Master Da as a very young boy

Conduit of Conscious Light that stretches from this seat of Divine Consciousness in the heart to the uppermost reaches of the brain, and beyond it to the Divine Source-Light above the world, the body, and the mind.

Heart-Master Da speaks of Amrita Nadi as the most prior Armature of human existence. It is the Conscious, Spiritual "Nervous System" that is the foundation and the always-present Source of both the material body and its brain and the hidden, invisible, energetic nervous system, or chakra body, described by Yogis, Saints, and Mystics in the world's sacred traditions.

One might say that Amrita Nadi is the Skeleton or hidden, underlying Structure of Conscious Life.

Heart-Master Da Love-Ananda has said:

HEART-MASTER DA LOVE-ANANDA: At Birth, and from the time of My Birth, I was Priorly established in Amrita Nadi. Relative to the body, if you look at photographs of Me as an infant, you can see Me in the eyes. In general, My association with the body could be seen in the eyes. For approximately the first two years after My Birth, I remained that way and allowed the gross vehicle to be gradually prepared for Me. Then, at approximately two years of age, I Spiritually descended to the region of the heart and thus established My basic association with . . . My manifested personality. (Of course, as I said, I was previously established in Amrita Nadi, which includes the right side of the heart, but which suggests only a general association with the [psycho-physical] vehicles.)

This Spiritual descent into the gross body to the level of the heart occurred, when I was approximately two years old, on the basis of a sympathy or heart-response to those who were around Me at the moment. It was through this sympathetic response that I acquired the Vehicle of this body-mind.

Because I was Born to make this Submission, the decision to acquire the gross body-mind did not occur when I was two years old. The Vehicle of this body-mind had become sufficiently prepared at that point, but I had consciously decided to do this Work before I Incarnated. The descent was for the sake of the total world and all beings. I had consciously decided to take a birth in the West. My Intention before this Birth was to take this Birth and to do My Work by complete Submission to the ordinary Western circumstance.

Once the descent to the region of the heart in the gross body occurred, as an intentional Submission to ordinary life in the gross plane, the heart remained My Station in relation to the body-mind until My Great Emergence, or Great Descent, in 1986.[4]

4. Heart-Master Da Love-Ananda, *The Love-Ananda Gita*, pp. 48-49.

This first Descent at the age of two initiated a necessary but perilous stage in His unpremeditated preparation for the Great Liberating Work of His maturity.

HEART-MASTER DA LOVE-ANANDA: The reason for it was a spontaneous motivation associated with a painful loving of the people around me. It was not merely compassion for them, as if they were poor people I could help—it was a painful *emotional and physical sensation in my heart and in my solar plexus. It was profoundly painful even then, and it always has been. It was associated with the full knowledge that these people to whom I was committing myself were going to* die, *and that I would* die. *I knew that if I incarnated this Function, if I became this body, I would die. We are going to be separated from one another. We are all going to be destroyed. This was all fully obvious to me, and yet this spontaneous gesture, this painful loving, this profound sensation awakened in me and moved me into the body, animated me physically.*[5]

From that day of His Spiritual Descent to the heart of His body-mind, the Limitless Personality Who Is Heart-Master Da Love-Ananda receded from the forefront of conscious life, and the apparently limited persona of Franklin Jones began to develop.

It was a gradual process, and during childhood young Franklin was never entirely bereft of His primal Experience and Realization of Divine Consciousness and Its "Bright" Spiritual Radiance.

The childhood of a God-Man in twentieth-century America

To those in His own generation who acknowledge Heart-Master Da Love-Ananda as a Divine Incarnation, the circumstance of His Birth appears almost droll in its ordinariness. The simple home of Franklin Jones and His family (His parents and a younger sister, Joanne) could

5. Da Free John [Heart-Master Da Love-Ananda], *God Is Not a Gentleman and I Am That One: Ecstatic Talks on Conventional Foolishness versus the Crazy Wisdom of God-Realization* (Clearlake, Calif.: The Dawn Horse Press, 1983), p. 99.

have been found in innumerable towns and cities across America. Their photograph albums reveal an American middle-class family apparently indistinguishable from millions of others in the middle twentieth century.

Heart-Master Da with His parents and sister   **Their family home on Long Island**

As a child Heart-Master Da delighted in the natural world. In those days Franklin Square was still part of the more rural region of Long Island, and woods and fields and the wilds of Nature were easily accessible to Him and His young friends.

Though there was no one to tell Him about His own previous lives, as might have been the case in India or Tibet if He had been discovered as a great Spiritual being in infancy, He needed no prompting. In fact, He often told His friends about their previous lifetimes and associations, and He frequently talked to them ecstatically about God and the "Bright".

This is a sign of how very gradual was the process of His forgetting of His Unconditional Divine Identity. It also demonstrates His unsought awakeness to all the particular processes, both conditional and Unconditional, that make what we call a human being.

As a child, Heart-Master Da was well aware that we are more than what we physically appear to be. He knew beyond doubt, via unmediated experience, that the physical, earthly human entity with whom most of us characteristically and automatically identify is only what He would later call the "gross personality", or the most material dimension of the total human personality.

During His childhood, Heart-Master Da was never entirely bereft of the "Bright".

Senior to it, though also conditional and limited, is the subtler psychic, higher mental, and fundamentally conscious dimension or entity, which Heart-Master Da has called the "deeper personality". This is the part of our total being that migrates, or reincarnates, from one gross, physical birth in human bodily form to the next. Some people call it the "soul" or the "spirit". But neither the gross nor the deeper personality is our true Nature, Which is, rather, the One Divine Self, or Infinite, Transcendental, and inherently Radiant Consciousness.

As a boy, Heart-Master Da was fully conscious of His deeper personality, and He experienced many psychic processes and visionary events. Particularly in the years prior to adolescence, He freely enjoyed powers of psychic mobility and perception that characterize the deeper personality in a highly awakened or energized state—though He learned early on to hide these abilities from others, who did not understand them.

Like the legendary Yogis of India and Tibet, but without knowledge that such individuals might exist, He often spontaneously saw or heard things and beings of which others were quite unaware, He witnessed or in other ways became aware of events in other places and other times, He perceived the living energies that surround our bodies, and He learned how to affect or change those energies in others through His own feelings, thoughts, and actions.

Heart-Master Da's parents, perhaps sensing His Inspired intelligence and strength of character, did not often interfere in His explorations, but they allowed Him to develop whatever interests, skills, and hobbies He was moved to pursue.

Along with His delight in ordinary things and entertainments—His ventriloquism and puppet shows, His dancing and art—He maintained a deep appreciation for solitude and for the Spiritual samadhis, or exalted states, into which He could abandon Himself when alone.

Franklin Square Cubs Stages Circus Tonight

Heart-Master Da (center) as a young ventriloquist

"The Thumbs"
and the Breakthroughs
of the Heart

But there was also a transformative and, at times, extremely difficult process active in Him.

Now and again, particularly in the earlier years of His boyhood, Franklin fell ill with raging fevers and occasional deliriums. These illnesses often terrified Him. They reminded Him of the ever-nearness of death and the dreadful feeling of mortal separateness.

Though His family's doctors ascribed their cause to one or another conventional disease, in later life He came to understand that these episodes of illness were in fact instances of extreme purification of His body-mind by the universal Divine Spirit-Power active as the kundalini shakti. "Kundalini" means "coiled", from a Sanskrit root that also means "to burn". "Shakti", in Sanskrit, is "force" or "power". The kundalini shakti is a fiery, tremendously powerful, and therefore potentially dangerous, aspect of the natural Life-Energy that sustains and pervades the human body-mind. It is used by Yogis to awaken the subtle or higher psychic dimensions and capabilities of the deeper personality.

HEART-MASTER DA LOVE-ANANDA: *As a child I endured terrifying processes that most people could not endure even as adults. . . .*

The kundalini process of awakened energy completely consumes the ordinary personality and prevents the conventional development of the ego. Every stage of development in My childhood was marked by this flaming destruction of My being, which periodically produced incidents of fear and feelings that something was occurring in the area of My chest and heart.

Another sign of this process is that I was very thin for a long time. I have tended to be heavy and round for most of My life, but not for all of it. I only gained weight after this feverish time of My childhood during My first eight or nine years. The descriptions of the classical Yoga of the kundalini point out that the process first consumes the body to the marrow. It burns it up, and literally one becomes emaciated, as I did as a child. Then the body is regenerated, and various Yogic signs and higher psychic abilities, or "siddhis", begin to appear.[6]

6. Heart-Master Da Love-Ananda, *The Love-Ananda Gita*, p. 51.

"Another sign of this process is that I was very thin for a long time."

Thus, although Heart-Master Da's Divine Awakeness was receding from daily awareness, so that more and more He naturally assumed the prison-like self-enclosure of egoic awareness, nonetheless the Great Spiritual Divine Reality, or Heart-Power, was continuing to prepare His body-mind for His future sacred Work.

As a boy He related to the descending Spiritual forces that invaded His body and mind from time to time as a huge mass of "Thumbs" pressing down into Him from above. In childhood He was terrified to allow the process to occur to completion. Whenever it began, He feared He would be overwhelmed.

His fear was completely warranted. This force is a tangible onslaught that works through the root of the central nervous system in the upper brain, moving down and radiating through the autonomic nervous system and the organic systems and tissues of the brain and the body. Once it is awakened or introduced into the body-mind, if it is not rightly regulated and Yogically exercised, it can cause madness and even death. In Heart-Master Da's case, it affected His left leg and left foot, leaving them visibly smaller than His right leg and right foot.

These incidents of His childhood were not merely a saintly prodigy's encounters with transformative Spiritual energies. In those moments, when it seemed to Him that He was being consumed by forces beyond His knowledge or control, Heart-Master Da was restored to awareness of and as the "Bright", the Heart of Being.

These periodic, spontaneous resuscitations of His native "Brightness" reminded the young Adept of the inherent Freedom and Radiant Joy of Divine Awareness—Which stood out more and more starkly against the self-concern with which everyone around Him seemed chronically preoccupied.

He therefore determined, very early in life, that His fundamental Purpose for being alive was to "restore Humor" to others. As a boy, He intentionally practiced doing just that through all kinds of means, such as His entertainments for family and friends, His rollicking, infectious laughter, and most essentially through His unspoken, bodily communication of Happiness and Love.

One evening, when Heart-Master Da was five or six years old, His parents, Frank and Dorothy, took Him to the movies. An orange moon shone in the night sky, and He was extremely Happy as they walked along. But then His parents began to fall into one of their frequent arguments, His father loud and threatening, His mother withdrawn and hurt.

He saw their argument as an archetype of conflict, of separation, of the destruction of Love.

> *. . . I was about to make one of my earliest attempts to communicate that there was only this love. I very clearly and directly experienced the effects of this conflict and separation. I could feel the embracive rays of energy that surround-ed us and moved in a delicate network of points in and through our bodies being cut, and dark vacuums were being spotted out around us and between us.*
>
> *I remember silently expanding this love and trying to distract them by pointing out the moon and asking questions about God and life so that they would be calmed and feel the energy of the "bright" in them.[7]*

Thus, even as a boy, Heart-Master Da instinctively chose to <u>be</u> Love, to embody Love, to radiate Love in the world, and never to escape to "someplace else" (in the manner of a Spiritual seeker turning within or above), as if God, Happiness, and Love were not already here to be lived.

The nature of His Awareness from birth and the events of His own Incarnation gradually produced in the young Adept a unique disposition and problem. He was aware as the "Bright", or Divine Consciousness. And He was always considering very basic questions of existence: "What is this apparently personal consciousness? What must occur within it for it to be what it is even while it already bears the certainty (or the tacit knowledge) of death?"

These were not often subjects of discussion between Heart-Master Da and His parents, or even between Him and His young friends. He most often concentrated on feeling the Heart and the "Bright" and contemplat-ing the mysteries of Divine Consciousness and death when He was alone.

His precocious questions and meditations point to the ultimate and most venerable Spiritual Wisdom. He was able to fully articulate His Divine understanding of Consciousness, life, death, and Love only decades later, after many trials and Revelations. But the essential Truth of our existence and the paramount obligation of Love were fundamentally obvious to Heart-Master Da even as a boy.

The body of His gross personality was a child. The psyche or soul of His deeper personality had been, in the past, a great Yogi and Spiritual Realizer, as He would confirm to His own devotees many years later. But

---

7. The World-Teacher, Heart-Master Da Love-Ananda, *The Knee of Listening,* New Standard Edition. Forthcoming.

Heart-Master Da with Frank and Dorothy at age six

He Himself was the eternal Divine Self, the Heart, the Amrita Nadi—the "Bright".

The plunge
into Divine "Amnesia"
and the mind of doubt

The second decade of Heart-Master Da's Life saw the progressive fading of the "Bright" from His conscious awareness.

In His high school years, He learned that most people are not just habituated (despite their better intentions or wishes) to unlove and the suppression of "Bright" joy and sympathy in their relationships. They are <u>committed</u> to that loveless habit, and deeply so.

From that time forward He began to lose His idealistic hopefulness about human beings' readiness to learn how to love and to be Happy as the "Bright".

Then a decisive blow to the young Adept's religious faith came during His freshman year in college. In 1957, when He entered Columbia College in New York City, though not altogether an innocent, He remained committed to the devotion to Christ that had dominated His boyhood as a member of His family's Lutheran church.

As He began to adjust to college life, however, He learned that the great ideals of Christianity were by no means the guiding principles of human civilization.

Indeed, at the university—which Heart-Master Da, yet naive in some ways, simply assumed would be dedicated to the dissemination of great Truths—He found that the guiding principles of all acceptable intellectual discourse were not sacred or transcendent conceptions of God and Man at all. Instead, everywhere He turned He found a thoroughgoing vision of the human being as a merely material, mortal, socially conditioned, intelligent animal struggling to survive and prevail in a Spiritless world.

He was shocked. Even the leading intellectual conceptions of Christian religion were devoted to "de-mythologizing" and dismissing as unreal everything He had felt, experienced, and believed in the Spiritually Illumined innocence of His youth.

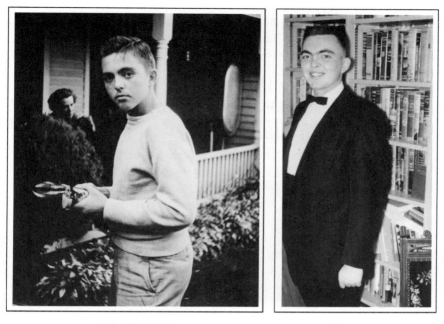

High school years   College years

The Lutheran Church in Franklin Square

Later in His freshman year, Heart-Master Da took His doubts and His dilemma to His boyhood minister, Pastor Kaiser, at the Lutheran church in Franklin Square. He wanted confirmation of the basic tenets of His faith—the miracles, Resurrection, and Divinity of Christ, and the Existence of God Himself.

But though Pastor Kaiser fumed about the immoral Godlessness of modern education, he could offer no conclusive evidence, no justification of the beliefs that he had preached all his life, no logic of Truth and God that could satisfy Heart-Master Da's desperately inquiring intelligence.

Heart-Master Da had encircled all His investigations of consciousness and life, even His willingness to entertain all pleasure and apparent sin, with the presumed eternal realities of Christ and God. Now those presumed realities were shown to Him to be mere idols, as symbolic and unreal as His previously destroyed illusions about innate human goodness. He was stripped of the last perimeter of His defense against doubt and despair.

Thereafter, the mind of doubt—the controlling rationale of modern civilization—overwhelmed Heart-Master Da, to the degree of grave distress. It was as if the threat of death enshrouded Him. Now not only the "Bright" but all of the happy mysticism and psychic awareness of His childhood and infancy were beyond His grasp. And He began to question whether they ever had been real for Him.

Now, everywhere He looked, Heart-Master Da saw only conflict, the automaticities of human suffering, and the inevitable results of loveless unhappiness in people's constant seeking for self-gratification and for assurances against death. He remembered the "Bright", but He had no reasons whatsoever for any kind of faith or joy.

In a sense this marked the successful completion of the first, tormenting stage of His Divine Emergence and His ultimate Work as the World-Teacher. He had successfully relinquished His Enlightened Freedom and God-Knowledge to become an ordinary man, stuck in the mortal doubts and fears of the gross personality. Only now could Heart-Master Da find, test, and prove in His own body-mind an effective Way to restore the Humor of immortal Freedom to all those mired in the same kind of suffering.

Sri Love-Anandashram, 1989

"I <u>Am</u> the One I Recognized"

The Sacred Ordeal of Divine Self-Realization

As an undergraduate in college

"I <u>Am</u> the One I Recognized"

The Sacred Ordeal of Divine Self-Realization

"If God exists . . . "

In early 1958, while still in His first year at Columbia College, Heart-Master Da conceived a desperate experiment. Reduced to terror by His doubts, He finally determined what He must do:

> *I decided that I would begin an experimental life along the same lines which controlled the mood of our civilization. I decided that I would unreservedly exploit every possibility for experience. I would avail myself of every possible human experience, so that nothing possible to mankind, high or low, would be unknown to me. . . .*
>
> *I knew that no other possibility was open to me but that of exhaustive experience. There appeared to be no single experience or authority among us that was simply true. And I thought, "If God exists, He will not cease to exist by any action of my own, but, if I devote myself to all possible experience, He will indeed find some way, in some one or a complex of my experiences, or my openness itself, to reveal Himself to me."*[1]

From that time forward He threw Himself into extremes of pleasure and beyond the limits of fear, through intellectual and sexual adventure,

---

1. The World-Teacher, Heart-Master Da Love-Ananda, *The Knee of Listening*, New Standard Edition. Forthcoming.

exploration of the greatest wisdom and art of Western culture, and equally intense exploration of the netherworld of the streets of New York City.

He excelled in His study of Western philosophy at Columbia, but He already knew the Spiritually desolate message of His college education. And He could not possibly accept it in His heart.

He did not allow His own disinclinations or any conventional moral or personal taboos to prevent His personal exploitation of all possible experience. He felt that if He excluded any extreme of experience, He might thereby preclude the Divine Revelation.

Heart-Master Da's experiments propelled Him to the fringes of human society, into the company of hedonists, eccentrics, and whores. He was too wild, too serious, and too extreme to tolerate or to be tolerated by the rules and the custodians of conventional human behavior.

He devoured every influence He could discover, including literally thousands of books of all kinds. He kept journals of His personal observations which soon numbered many volumes and even overwhelmed the pages of His college lecture notes.

Apparently a rebellious young man without concern for His future, in fact He was consciously focused in the desperate attempt of a born Divine Realizer to unravel the hidden knot at the core of human lovelessness and fear.

He was not just doing this for Himself. He was doing it for everyone, everywhere. When an uncle, indignant at His apparent abandon, pointedly asked what He wanted to do with His life, Heart-Master Da replied without an instant's hesitation, and unequivocally, "I want to save the world."

The Awakening in college: the great insights into seeking and Freedom

In both Eastern and Western accounts of God-Men—Jesus Christ, Gautama the Buddha, the various Hindu Avatars—there are legends of the great Masters' descending into hells of one kind or another.

Such stories are often quite picturesque and consoling to the ego. They fancifully suggest the Savior's Graceful Help to those who suffer, but they do not often realistically depict the suffering He Himself must undergo.

The real process of such "descent into hell", as we see in the Story of Heart-Master Da Love-Ananda's Incarnation, involves the Adept's Personal assumption of the depths of suffering and even Godless doubt that characterize the ordinary state of the ego.

His primary Purpose in life—the Liberation of others—requires Him, therefore, to Incarnate. He must achieve total psychic and even fully physical identification of His limitless Being, the One and Only Reality, with a mortal, limited, human Form. Then that physical, human life may be transformed, becoming an Agent for others' Liberation.

Only God, the Divine Source-Consciousness and All-Pervading Energy, can perform that Rite of Self-limiting Incarnation and Transformation. In Heart-Master Da's Life we see that the Divine Self temporarily, but really, sacrifices Its Unconditional Freedom in order, as Heart-Master Da conceived it, to "penetrate the heart of our dilemma".

It was this Divine Impulse to which Heart-Master Da was giving voice in His response to His uncle: "I want to save the world."

Having descended into the tormented state of ordinary human unconsciousness, having Himself become confused by identification with the gross personality and distraught at the prospect of endless exile from the "Bright", Heart-Master Da would now begin to discover the essence of Enlightened Wisdom, of the kind and depth sought by Buddhist, Hindu, Jain, and other Sages for millennia.

By sometime in the middle of His third year of college, His extremes of seeking had exhausted His capacity to discover any remarkably new, hopeful kind of experience or source of information.

Late one night in 1960, as Heart-Master Da sat at His desk in a rented room not far from the Columbia College campus, He saw clearly that He had nowhere left to turn. Yet nothing had been resolved by all of His frenetic seeking. Indeed, as He sat there, He began to see His entire life of seeking and experience as an unending, endlessly self-constricting, and fruitless drama.

Suddenly, from the depths of this feeling-vision of futility and despair, appeared the Spiritual Force of "Brightness" that had been the Light and Joy of Heart-Master Da's childhood.

A Current of blissful Energy rose so forcefully in Him that He leaped to His feet, ecstatic, and charged out into the hallway and down into the street, where He ran, exhilarated, for hours. The "Bright" that had so long been hidden from Him was now suddenly magnified to an overwhelming intensity.

Not until much later would He fully comprehend what had just occurred. Within days, however, as He pondered this tremendous release and restoration of Happiness, two fundamental insights emerged that would stand as cornerstones of the "radical" ("root", "primal", "irreducible") Spiritual Intelligence upon which He would build His entire Life's Work.

First, it became clear to Him beyond doubt that Truth is not to be found through seeking. He saw that to seek the Truth or God only reinforces the sense of the absence of Truth or God. Thus, seeking is itself the problem. He now knew intuitively that Truth is Revealed only when we understand and transcend all dilemma, or all motivating conflict and internal contradiction, and, therefore, when we transcend all seeking.

Second, Heart-Master Da saw that we are "always already" Free. Freedom and Happiness are never attained. Happiness is our native State, obvious when our obstructions to It are understood (as our own self-created action) and thus inherently transcended in Consciousness. Therefore, Freedom and Happiness are not properly the goal of life, to be attained by seeking, but, rather, they are the constant Divine Self-Condition and Source of life, available to us when we understand and transcend our seeking.

Aside from its intensity, and the fact that this was the first dramatic Breakthrough of the "Bright" in His fully adult Life, what marked this experience was that it was a direct, unmediated <u>conscious</u> resurrection of Divine Identity. The tremendous energy and Spiritual Power released in the event were secondary, a by-product of the sudden dissolution of His identification with any form of personal, bodily, or mental self-awareness.

The Revelation was so forceful that its primary residue, when He resumed His then ordinary state of identification with body, mind, and egoic self-sense (the feeling of being an "I" over against other beings and things), was a formulation of Wisdom at once simple and transcendent.

This Wisdom, in the form of His two fundamental insights about seeking and Freedom, was the first appearance in Heart-Master Da's Life of what He would later come to call "'radical' understanding". Before this time, He had naively sought to experience the "Bright" as if It, or God, could <u>happen</u> <u>to</u> Him or could be brought about for Him by one or another <u>objective</u> experience.

After this event at Columbia, however, He knew that the primary

Wisdom or certainty of Truth and God for which He had been seeking was not to be found in any kind of experience, or through any kind of seeking. He came to rest in a principally Conscious orientation to His Great Work, striving to recover the "Bright" and uncover the Truth of Being through the exploration of Consciousness rather than experience. He had been turned to a fundamentally Subjective quest to Be the "Bright" as Conscious Freedom.

But, as the weeks passed, He could not maintain the Feeling-Vision of Freedom that had been Revealed. By the time of His graduation from Columbia, Heart-Master Da was severely depressed. He had recovered the great Truth, but then He had lost It again. And He did not know precisely how, or why.

Heart-Master Da and His mother at
His graduation from Columbia College, 1960

The "Yoga" of writing
and the myth that governs us

The following year Heart-Master Da enrolled in graduate school at Stanford University in California. There the next stage of His explorations quickly began to consume all His attention and energy.

It appeared to Him that there must be some logic or structure at the core of our ordinary awareness and identity that prevents the unseekable and fundamentally Inherent Realization of Freedom. In His final years at Columbia, He had kept a journal, observing the processes of His own mentality, attentive to whatever might provide clues to the structure of this controlling logic, or "myth".

In California, His writing developed into a spontaneous "Yoga", an intensive technique of recording everything that arose to His attention. He simply noticed and recorded every experience, sensation, perception, and conception. He did not evaluate or identify with any of His physical, mental, or emotional responses or reactions to His experience. Instead, He simply, but rigorously, observed and recorded those responses and reactions as well.

In this manner, Heart-Master Da hoped to uncover the underlying myth that structures human suffering and seeking and motivates our entire adventure of separation from the "Bright".

He continued to use any and all means of experiential stimulation to support His investigation. By now, though, He knew that He would not find what He sought in the experiences themselves, and He was look-ing for it in the mechanisms of His own conscious life in the midst of experiences.

For a brief period He volunteered for experiments with powerful new, or recently rediscovered, hallucinogenic drugs at the nearby Veter-ans' Administration Hospital in Mountain View, California. In one session, He re-experienced His pre-natal state, the moment when His infinite "Bright" Awareness was first anchored to His embryonic body-mind in His mother's womb. In other sessions He re-experienced the "Thumbs" He had known in childhood. But by the end of His formal experiments at the Veterans' Administration Hospital, Heart-Master Da concluded that there was nothing of further significance to be learned from drug-induced changes of state.

Now He devoted all His prodigious energy and intelligence to His self-witnessing and spontaneous writing. Everywhere He went He carried a clipboard of paper and a pen. He wrote constantly, recording every detail of His sensations, perceptions, mental images, thoughts, and feel-ings. He kept a flashlight by His bed, so that He could awaken in the night to record His dreams and subliminal observations in sleep. And when using the flashlight became too cumbersome, He learned to write in the dark, so that nothing could jeopardize the speed and completeness of His recording what He noticed.

Living not unlike a traditional Spiritual hermit—though as yet He had no significant awareness of the esoteric Spiritual traditions of either the East or the West—Heart-Master Da abandoned Himself again to the madness of His quest. He would record in detail every moment of a walk on the beach, the total circumstance of events and processes unfolding within and all around Him. He wrote ceaselessly while His intimate companion, Nina Davis, drove them from place to place. He wrote in the midst of conversations, at movies, even at parties with their few friends. His writings filled bins and boxes.

**During the period of His "Yoga" of writing
in California, early 1960s**

He allowed nothing to interrupt Him—for He feared that anything He missed, internal or external, would slip into unconsciousness, where it might reinforce the controlling logic that was preventing His Realization of the "Bright".

85

As His observing and writing reached a state of exhaustive complete-ness, His life-experiment once again yielded a new depth of awareness. Various psychic phenomena, including clairvoyance, precognition, and visions of other, more subtle, realms of experience became commonplace occurrences for Him for the first time since His childhood. He was being restored, now as an adult, to participatory awareness of and as the deeper personality. He began to feel that there was little remaining to be per-ceived outside His intensely inclusive awareness.

Finally, in the spring of 1964, the underlying structure of His chronic separation, self-enclosure, and invulnerability as the ego or self-conscious "I" appeared clearly before Him, like a precipitate in the centrifuge of self-observation.

It was in a classical myth that Heart-Master Da discovered a perfect analogue, or archetype, for the living mechanism that now stood out so plainly to Him. It was the myth of Narcissus, the self-lover of Greek mythology who abandons the loved one and all relationships to meditate adoringly on his own reflection in a pool, as if it were a living "other", until he dies, self-enamored, oblivious to all others, and alienated from Reality.

Now the intensity of Heart-Master Da's inquiry into human delusion had a self-sustaining fire that even burned into and through the nature of the world. He observed that this activity of self-enclosure was not only the root mechanism of every individual human being's suffering and seeking—it was also the logic at the core of all living processes, all cos-mic events, whereby phenomena become differentiated from and appar-ently opposed to one another.

This discovery of the self-worshipping activity of "Narcissus" as the operative agent of our separation from the "Bright", along with His previous primary insights into seeking and the nature of Freedom, would inform Heart-Master Da's entire future Ordeal of Divine Self-Remembrance. These great discoveries in Consciousness would also become the "radical" core of His future Teaching-Revelation and His Blessing Work in the world.

The great storm on the beach—
a sign of Initiatory Heart-Power

Other prominent events occurred in the spring of 1964, during the final few months of His residence in northern California. Principally these events took the form of archetypal dreams and other psychic phenomena. They signalled Heart-Master Da's release from the mortal, "when you're dead, you're dead" philosophy of the materialistic doubt-mind—the uncommonly soulless mind of the modern, Western (or Westernized), gross egoic personality, from which He had been struggling to achieve freedom since His earliest days at Columbia.

One such event was one of the first dramatic signs of response by Nature to the Spiritual Force of His Incarnation. Years later He described the incident, which took place on the cliffs overlooking the Pacific, not far from His house:

HEART-MASTER DA LOVE-ANANDA: In the spring of 1964 . . . I awoke one morning to a very brilliant clear day. I went outside and stood in front of the house on the ledge of a cliff that dropped a hundred feet to the beach. The beach was very wide, a couple of hundred feet or so, and the ocean stretched in a huge expanse as far as I could see.

It was a very isolated area with only a few people in other cabins, and they were generally away at work during the day. On this day no one else was around, so I was alone.

Very powerful psychic events had been occurring during this time. Now, as I stood on the cliff, a storm moved over me from the ocean like a huge shroud, like a great canopy or blanket. It had the feeling of a great shell. It was not a dense mass that included me and the space where I stood, but it rose above me and beyond and became a kind of enclosure, like a huge gray dome of gray shapes of clouds, a perfect sphere. It was not homogeneous, but it was boiling with great masses of clouds.

Then lightning began to move through the dome that was now like a great sahasrar [the topmost and most subtle Yogic center in the brain], millions of bolts of lightning shooting in the sky and traveling hundreds of miles in every direction. You cannot imagine what kind of storm it was. It was a transcendental storm, literally the most magnificent thing I have ever seen. I am not kidding when I say there were millions of bolts of lightning. In that great vast

Tunitas Beach after a storm, early 1960s—photograph by Heart-Master Da

dome it was like the millions and millions of lightnings of the little veins in your brain, the corona radiata. It was the most shocking, incredible drenching of the Earth I have ever seen. And it was enormously loud. The thunder was so loud it shook the ground, and torrents of water blew all over the ocean and the place where I stood on this little precipice overlooking the ocean.

I think it must have been the most powerful storm that ever existed on Earth. Within me all kinds of electric phenomena or Shakti phenomena were occurring. My whole body was shaking with tremendous electric shocks. I do not know how long I stood in the storm; it lasted for perhaps an hour or two and then lifted away and disintegrated. I could have been shocked to death out there.[2]

This great storm signified both Heart-Master Da's imminent Spiritual Awakening and His future Spirit-filled Initiatory Work as a Revealer of the Divine Self. But even such dramatic psycho-physical events were still of only secondary significance to Him. They, like the other psychic phenomena now commonly appearing, simply marked His resumption of conscious awareness of and as the deeper, psychic (yet still conditional and egoic, or Narcissistic) personality.

By contrast, His Breakthrough at Columbia and His insight into the controlling myth of Narcissus were events in Divine Consciousness. They portended His eventual Restoration to full Awareness as the Unconditional Divine Reality. But before that full Restoration could occur, He would have to generate and endure a most profound discipline of both His gross personality and His deeper personality. With the Help of extraordinary Spiritual beings, He would enjoy the Spiritualization of His body-mind. Ultimately, by Grace of His own Heart-Power, He would altogether transcend identification with born existence.

---

2. Da Free John [Heart-Master Da Love-Ananda], *The Bodily Location of Happiness* (Clearlake, Calif.: The Dawn Horse Press, 1982), pp. 32-33.

Heart-Master Da's exemplary devotion to venerable Gurus and His spontaneous Breakthroughs of Divine Heart-Awakening

Shortly after His discovery of the governing myth of "Narcissus" as the root of human egoity, Heart-Master Da began to have visions of an Oriental art store in New York City where, He intuitively knew, He would find His Teacher. Staking His destiny on those visions, He and Nina moved to New York.

In early September 1964, Heart-Master Da found the store and met Rudi (Swami Rudrananda).[3]

Enormously round, enormously strong, shaven-headed, pug-nosed, Rudi was no man to be trifled with. He practiced and Taught his students the disciplined growth of self-awareness by forcibly breaking down resistances. His methods were hard work—usually physical work—self-frustrating discipline, and uncomplaining surrender to the Teacher and his affronts to one's egoic preferences and desires. Rudi often compared his Yoga to "tearing your guts out".

Principally through the Spiritual Blessings of His Indian Gurus, Swami Nityananda[4] and Swami Muktananda,[5] Rudi had become an extraordinary transmitter of tangible Spiritual Force. He Taught a path of intentional and strenuous surrender to this "Force", or Spiritual Current. He deliberately transmitted this Power in his "classes" by silently gazing for a time into the eyes of each of his students.

Heart-Master Da, delighted to have found a source of true Spiritual Help, dedicated Himself completely to fulfilling Rudi's particular form of

3. Albert Rudolph, or Rudi (b. 1928), also formally named Swami Rudrananda, was an American Spiritual prodigy from his childhood. His own early Teachers included the Indonesian Pak Subuh, from whom Rudi learned basic techniques of Spiritual receptivity. Rudi's primary Spiritual Teacher was Swami Nityananda, the Guru of his own later Guru Swami Muktananda, whom Rudi met shortly before Nityananda's death in the early 1960s. Rudi died in an airplane crash on February 21, 1973.

4. Swami Nityananda (b. 1897) was a Yogi-Saint of South India. Little is known of the circumstances of his birth and early life. It is said that even as a child he showed the signs of a Realized Yogi, and as a boy abandoned conventional life to wander as a renunciate. Many miracles (including spontaneous healings) and instructive stories are attributed to Nityananda. He surrendered the body on August 8, 1961.

5. Swami Muktananda Paramahansa (1908-1982) left home at the age of fifteen to become a wandering, mendicant Yogi. In 1947 he came under the Illumined influence of Swami Nityananda, in whose company he mastered Kundalini Yoga, and with whose Blessing he later became a Spiritual Master himself.

**Swami Rudrananda
("Rudi")**

Yoga. The discipline of work, along with the practical and moral intelligence Heart-Master Da brought to His life under Rudi's stern guidance, strengthened, purified, and harmonized His body and His nervous system. He learned to apply ego-frustrating discipline so consistently and ferociously that in time His skin constantly and quite literally burned with the heat of His practice.

At the same time, Rudi's transmission of the "Force" purified and energized Heart-Master Da's body, mind, and heart. Under Rudi's influence, Heart-Master Da was able on a number of occasions to allow the Spiritual invasion and descent ("the Thumbs") that He had earlier resisted. Now, understanding its import and prepared in body and mind to use it, He permitted the descent of "the Thumbs" to proceed to its completion. On those occasions, He enjoyed exalted states of Spiritual equanimity and transcendence of the sense of confinement to physical, bodily awareness.

It was evidence of Heart-Master Da's utter resolve and seriousness that, from the moment He met Rudi until they parted ways, He obeyed Rudi's commands and in every way related to him "as a man does to God".

Though Rudi required obedience of his students, he did not ask them to relate to him as the Divine or as a Buddha, an Enlightened Being. That is a particular approach to Spiritual Awakening that is most highly developed in the traditions of Guru-devotion in the East. As written in the ancient Buddhist classic *Fifty Verses of Guru-Devotion*:

> *The ability to see your Guru as not different from Buddha . . . depends on your motivation. If you have developed an Enlightened Motive . . . you are striving to become a Buddha yourself in order to be fully able to benefit others. The stronger this motive, the more the thought of Enlightenment comes to pervade your mind completely. Thinking only of Enlightenment and ways to achieve it, you will automatically be able to see your Guru in terms of this state because nothing else will be in your mind. . . . Through the practice of the perfections of generosity, the discipline of moral self-control, patience and so forth, all centered around your Guru, you will then be able to attain his state.[6]*

Heart-Master Da was uncommonly diligent and obedient precisely because He always spontaneously related to Rudi in this profound traditional fashion. (Indeed, as Heart-Master Da only heard years later, some of Rudi's other students referred to Him as "Crazy Frank" because of His unqualified willingness to do everything Rudi asked Him to do.)

Working in Rudi's store and warehouse and as a furniture refinisher, He learned to submit the body to work and discipline. He learned to constantly go beyond all preferences and His then presumed sense of physical limits.

Later, at Rudi's behest, He similarly disciplined His mind by attending several Christian seminaries in training to become a minister. He learned the ancient version of Greek used in the *New Testament*. He memorized long passages of the Bible and became an expert in complex theological doctrines. Though He had no personal or intellectual interest in these studies, Heart-Master Da made a point of excelling in them, in service and obedience to His Guru.

This disciplined transcendence of the limitations and preferences of the thinking mind in many ways completed Heart-Master Da's discipleship under Rudi. Through it He achieved fundamental mastery of the gross personality. At the same time, His own continuing Awakening in and as

---

6. Ashvagosha, *Fifty Verses of Guru-Devotion* (Dharamsala, India: Library of Tibetan Works and Archives), p. 19.

Divine Consciousness led Him to despair of the forceful seeking and the endless evolution of experience and power that Rudi viewed as the true Spiritual path.

This Awakening was catalyzed by a major Breakthrough of Divine Awareness, which occurred in the spring of 1967. At that time, in obedience to Rudi's directions, He was attending a Christian seminary in the city of Philadelphia. One morning Heart-Master Da suddenly felt an intolerable anxiety rising within Him. His mind began to race frantically at accelerating speed. He had been enjoying fine health and excellent spirits, but now, within moments, He was overcome with the absolute conviction that He was about to go mad and die.

For three days Heart-Master Da struggled against His acute and mounting fear of death, but nothing He could do granted any relief— consulting a doctor and psychiatrists, making a midnight trip to a hospital's emergency room with symptoms of irregular heartbeat and breathing, even attending sessions of group psychiatric therapy. Heart-Master Da was no hypochondriac, but He feared for His life:

Finally, on the third day after this process began, I was lying home alone in the afternoon. It was as if all my life I had been constantly brought to this point. It seemed that all the various methods of my life had constantly prevented this experience from going to its end. All my life I had been preventing my death.

I lay on the floor, totally disarmed, unable to make a gesture that could prevent the rising fear. And thus it grew in me, but, for the first time, I allowed it to happen. I could not prevent it. The fear and the death rose and became my overwhelming experience. And I witnessed the crisis of that fear in a moment of conscious, voluntary death. I allowed the death to happen, and I saw it happen. . . .

When all of the fear and dying had become a matter of course, when the body, the mind, and the person with which I identified myself had died, and my attention was no longer fixed in those things, I perceived reality, fully and directly. There was an infinite bliss of being, an untouched, unborn sublimity, without separation, without individuation, without a thing from which to be separated. There was only reality itself, the incomparable nature and constant existence that underlies the entire adventure of life.[7]

7. The World-Teacher, Heart-Master Da Love-Ananda, *The Knee of Listening*, New Standard Edition. Forthcoming.

Once again, as had often occurred in Heart-Master Da's youth, the Divine Self had interrupted the apparent individual awareness and destiny of Heart-Master Da as "Franklin Jones", asserting Itself as His real Identity.

In the aftermath of the event, He saw that He had experienced the death of "Narcissus", which He had known was inevitable. He understood that the drama of His whole life to that moment had been founded on the activity of "Narcissus", the activity of the "avoidance of relationship". That activity is the recoil or contraction in consciousness whereby we presume to be the separate ego, or "I". He would later liken it to the chronic clenching of a fist, or to the foolish, painful condition of a man constantly pinching himself. Except it is not merely physical—the activity of "Narcissus" takes place at every level of life and consciousness. And it governs us from before our births through and beyond our deaths, in all of our conditional incarnations and states of mind, until we Awaken and Stand Free.

Heart-Master Da's Spiritual Awakening at Columbia College seven years before paled in intensity and significance before this Revelation at the seminary. In the experience at Columbia, He had still been mired in desperate identification with the gross personality in its most unconscious, resistive, and chaotic state. Thus, the State of Divine Awakeness had appeared in the midst of a revolutionary reclaiming of His body-mind by Spiritual Energy. The Living Current of Spiritual Force had surged through Him, reminding Him of His true, Conscious Nature and revealing Its essential Wisdom.

Now, in this death of "Narcissus" in seminary, the one who apparently died was a gross personality in a highly purified, energized, balanced, and Spiritually sublimed state. And the event involved no apparent movement of the Spiritual Current of Energy that might have been tangibly felt in and by the body or the mind. Rather, it involved the falling away of all conditional (gross and deeper) awareness, all sense of objects over against a limited subject or self, even all perception of Spiritual Energy, so that the Self that is always Conscious simply shone forth.

Later Heart-Master Da would come to see that this event, appearing in His twenty-seventh year, was a Revelation to which great Sages in the Oriental traditions have aspired for lifetimes. It has rarely if ever even been reported in the West. Among the Hindus it is called "Jnana Samadhi", which means "the State of Ultimate Wisdom, or of Knowledge of the True Self".

At the time of its occurrence, however, Heart-Master Da was not concerned to compare the event to any traditional accounts. He was primarily attentive to its practical implications in His own Life.

It soon became apparent that the Awakening had marked the end, essentially, of His sacred practice to transform, and to stand free of compulsive identification with, the gross personality of "Franklin Jones".

But it was not the conclusive "death" or transcendence of egoic existence altogether. It established Him in a disposition of intuitive identification with the Transcendental Self, or Consciousness, from which He was then able, very rapidly, to fully explore, understand, and finally transcend His deeper egoic personality as well.

In 1968, with Rudi's explicit permission and blessing, Heart-Master Da visited Rudi's living Guru, the Yogi-Siddha Swami Muktananda, at his Ashram in Ganeshpuri, India. There Heart-Master Da surrendered to the Swami as Guru, just as He had previously surrendered to Rudi.

Slender, dark-skinned, with a light black beard, Swami Muktananda was the model of a traditional Hindu Yogic Guru. He did not speak English, but he and Heart-Master Da instantly acknowledged and communicated with one another in the wordless domain of the Spirit. Soon after their first meeting, Swami Muktananda

Heart-Master Da on His first pilgrimage
to India, spring 1968

95

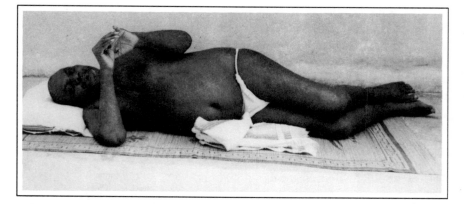

Above: Swami Nityananda

Left: Swami Muktananda

indicated to others at his Ashram that Heart-Master Da was the most advanced Western Spiritual practitioner he had ever met. He predicted that Heart-Master Da would become a Spiritual teacher within a year.

At once congenial and enigmatic, Swami Muktananda was a fountain of Spiritual energy, his body constantly moving and gesticulating with the liveliness of the awakened kundalini shakti. Visiting him catalyzed Heart-Master Da's mature exploration of the nature and limitations of the deeper personality. Though Heart-Master Da could only stay a few days on that first pilgrimage, His thorough preparation and honorable approach as a devotee—as well as His prior Heart-Awakening—allowed Him to fully receive Swami Muktananda's extremely powerful Spiritual Transmission:

I felt a powerful fullness, and my mind and my entire being were filled by a wonderful bliss. It was an experience to which I had become accustomed with Rudi, but now it was much stronger, undeniable. . . .[8]

Heart-Master Da also made a potent Spiritual connection with Swami Muktananda's own Guru (also Rudi's first Guru), Swami Nityananda, who was then no longer physically embodied but was still very active on the subtle planes of the world.

On the final day of that first, brief pilgrimage to Swami Muktananda, Heart-Master Da was also Blessed by an encounter with another great Spiritual Realizer. While Heart-Master Da was sitting in the Ashram garden, Swami Muktananda passed by, walking along with a nearly naked Yogi. The Yogi, white-haired and white-bearded, like Swami Nityananda had a huge belly distended by Yogic Spiritual Force. The man only briefly glanced at Heart-Master Da as he passed. But his eyes were wide with Spiritual Power, and Heart-Master Da received the full force of His Blessing. (Years later He learned that this great Yogi was named Rang Avadhoot.)[9]

Rang Avadhoot

Not long after that meeting in the garden, the Blessings of all three of these great Yogis (Swami Muktananda, Swami Nityananda, and Rang Avadhoot) combined to serve another dramatic Breakthrough in Heart-Master Da's sacred Ordeal. On the

8. Ibid.

9. Rang Avadhoot (1898-1968) was a translator and scholar who abandoned his worldly involvements for the Spiritual path of the worship of Dattatreya, the legendary founder and Supreme Guru of the tradition of the "Avadhoot", or the naked wanderer who is free in God. Rang Avadhoot maintained the classic disciplines of the Avadhoot tradition, never accepting money or gifts from non-devotees and, in his later life, wandering, rarely staying in any place more than three days at a time. It was during a short sojourn at Swami Muktananda's Ashram that Rang Avadhoot Blessed Heart-Master Da with His Spiritually potent glance.

scorching afternoon of the last day of Heart-Master Da's stay at Swami Muktananda's Ashram, He went to His room, feeling the need to rest. Upon
lying down, He instantly transcended all awareness of body and mind.
Then His attention ascended at tremendous speed until all awareness of
the limited or separate self dissolved in mystical Immersion in the Divine
Light, Life, and Spirit felt infinitely above the world, the body, and the
mind.

He describes the experience as

. . . *a profound state of consciousness that was absolutely calm, uncontained,
and free. I felt as though I existed only as consciousness itself. There was no
other experience, no thought, feeling, or perception. Awareness was (at first)
concentrated above, at some unfathomable point, beyond space and yet above
me. As I concentrated in that "point" I felt an infinite form of bliss, an absolute
pleasure of fullness and brilliance that completely absorbed my being. And,
then, I existed only at infinity.*[10]

Afterwards, He descended through planes of awareness until resuming His ordinary bodily consciousness. When the experience was over,
Heart-Master Da saw that for a brief period He had Realized Oneness
with the Divine Being Who "lives", or exists as, all beings, things, and
worlds. This extraordinary event occurred again that evening as He went
to sleep.

This Awakening epitomized the greatest Spiritual Wisdom of humanity. It was the Unio Mystica or Mystical Union, the Gnosis or Divine
Knowledge, the Nirvikalpa Samadhi or Formless Ecstasy, that Spiritual
seekers and Adepts the world over have sought, extolled, and taught for
centuries.

So it was that from the very outset of His concentrated practice in the
domain of the deeper personality (when He first came to Swami Muktananda, that spring of 1968) Heart-Master Da Realized the final Goal of
traditional seeking in that domain. And He had already intuited the fundamental disposition of Conscious Freedom from all seeking in His Awakening at the seminary.

By these means the "Bright" Divine Consciousness was directly
Revealing Itself to Him and As Him, and It was also preparing Him to

10. The World-Teacher, Heart-Master Da Love-Ananda, *The Knee of Listening*, New Standard Edition. Forthcoming.

pierce, swiftly and conclusively, the attractive illusions of the deeper personality. The subtle psychic visions, realms, and powers typically sought and enjoyed by the deeper personality can entrap one's attention and energy just as powerfully as the possible searches and apparent fulfillments of the gross personality.

By the summer of 1969, Heart-Master Da found He was continually aware of subtle levels of reality only perceived by visionary mystics. He was also spontaneously functioning as a Spiritual Initiator for others, who found themselves awakened to Yogic phenomena of the kundalini shakti (visions, sensations of a surrounding and pervading energy or fullness, etc.) simply by being near Him. During Heart-Master Da's next visit to India, in 1969, Swami Muktananda gave Him two formal Spiritual Names or Titles and formally authorized Him, in writing, as an empowered Teacher of the specific variety of Kundalini Yoga that the Swami Taught.

However, by the end of Heart-Master Da's second visit to Swami Muktananda's Ashram that August of 1969, though blessed by the Swami to Teach Kundalini Yoga to others, Heart-Master Da was wearied by what He felt was a dead end of endless Spiritual visions and extraordinary experiences. The profusion of mystical revelations, astral transports, and states of superconscious identification with various gods and high subtle beings that was His current experience had become a torment for Him. He felt that all this had nothing to do with permanently Realizing What He knew to be His real Nature—Divine Consciousness. He was not interested in having experiences. He was interested in Being What He Is.

By early 1970 Heart-Master Da was already relying strongly on the Spiritual guidance of Swami Nityananda, the senior human Guru in the Lineage that included Swami Muktananda and Rudi.

In a series of visionary contacts, Swami Nityananda helped Heart-Master Da understand the nature of His experiences. In doing so, the Spiritually Illumined Yogi freely assumed the senior role as Guru in the lineage. Heart-Master Da, having always been directed by both Rudi and Swami Muktananda to take refuge in Swami Nityananda, accepted Swami Nityananda's seniority as His Guru.

In early 1970, Heart-Master Da passed through a significant spontaneous transformation of the energy process in His body-mind. For many years He had practiced conducting the Spiritual Life-Force in the vertical lines of the body—down the front, and up the back. An enormous body of traditional Wisdom promotes this circuit as the "Royal Road" of Yogic

Heart-Master Da with Swami Muktananda during His visit to India in 1969

**Handwritten letter of acknowledgement from
Swami Muktananda, 1969**

Enlightenment. (Some traditions promote the practice of conducting Spirit-Force in the ascending or spinal line exclusively, apart from any preparatory exercise to bring that Force down through the descending or "frontal" line of the body-mind.) Indeed, both Rudi and Swami Muktananda were adherents of this worldwide tradition. The path of Spiritual ascent through one means or another is central to most of the esoteric Spiritual paths of the world.

Now, during the course of several nights in February of 1970, Heart-Master Da felt deep pains in His head, as if incisions were being made in the internal tissues of His brain. Finally, He realized that it was as if the uppermost Yogic center in the brain, known in the Yogic traditions of India as the "sahasrar chakra", had been severed. As a result, Heart-Master Da experienced what seemed to be an explosion or diffusion of the descending and ascending currents of Spiritual Force. The spinal terminal, the sahasrar, ceased to function as a terminal of the Spirit-carried ascent of attention and the conduit to more subtle, Yogic experience in and beyond the brain. Instead, He now felt the Spiritual Current radiating effortlessly in all directions from the heart, and His attention was released from the Yogic process of ascent.

The transformation was almost inconceivably intense, both physically and psychically. Heart-Master Da felt "as if every nerve-end in the body had been pruned, exposing the nervous system to the Ocean of Infinity, and dissolving the structural necessity of both evolution and birth itself."[11]

It became clear to Him that true Spiritual transformation is not ultimately a matter of the Spiritual ascent and escape of attention from the confines of gross, bodily existence. Rather, it involves Incarnating and Radiating the Divine Spirit as Love, through infinite Feeling, from the heart and with the whole body.

He had also been privileged to receive other evidence of this process of true Spiritual transformation. In particular, during His visit to Swami Muktananda's Ashram in 1969, He had noticed the bodily Effulgence of the Swami's then principal Indian disciple, Swami Prakashananda,[12] who, to Heart-Master Da's Spiritually sensitive perception, literally shone with Yogic Radiance from head to toe.

11. Bubba Free John [Heart-Master Da Love-Ananda], *The Enlightenment of the Whole Body* (Clearlake, Calif.: The Dawn Horse Press, 1978), p. 22.

12. Swami Prakashananda (1916-1988) was the headmaster of a brahmacharya school for boys in India and a principal Indian devotee of Swami Muktananda.

The vision of Swami Prakashananda's bodily transformation confirmed to Heart-Master Da the Truth of His own intuition of the ultimate evolutionary developments of the Spiritual Process. He knew that this Process must become a metamorphic transmutation of the <u>whole</u> human being, rather than a concentration of attention and Spiritual Energy in the brain and in subtle phenomena apparently apart from the gross, physical realm. As He had learned even in childhood, Love, and not escape, is the "Method" of Divine Realization and Incarnation.

In May of 1970, Heart-Master Da went to India for a third pilgrimage along with His household, which now included Nina and also a woman named Patricia Morley who had become His informal religious student. This time He intended to stay at Swami Muktananda's Ashram indefinitely.

Swami Prakashananda

In the garden at Swami Muktananda's Ashram during His third pilgrimage, 1970

But when the atmosphere there proved to be both empty and inhospitable, and when He no longer found even Swami Muktananda to be functioning as a Spiritual source for Him, He turned to the stream of Spirit-Power that He found continually available at the nearby burial shrine of Swami Nityananda.

A most remarkable development soon occurred. One day while serving in the garden of Swami Muktananda's Ashram, Heart-Master Da felt a familiar Presence behind Him. Looking back, He saw, in subtle visionary Form, the Virgin Mary! His first impulse was, He says, "huge laughter". He thought He had long ago left behind even the remotest interest in Christianity. He

felt He must be severely deluded. However, to Heart-Master Da's astonishment, He soon found Himself responding to Her with intense devotional rapture and doing as She instructed.

Swami Nityananda, appearing to Heart-Master Da again in a vision,
told Him that the One He was seeing as the Virgin Mary was the Divine
Goddess (the Mother Shakti, the Supreme Spiritual Deity in female Form)
and the Supreme Guru of the Lineage, and that She Herself was now taking over Heart-Master Da's sacred development. Swami Nityananda
instructed Him to perform a simple ceremony to relinquish His devotional
relationships to all His previous Gurus in the Lineage, including Swami
Nityananda himself.

Heart-Master Da did so. Then the Goddess, still appearing in the form
of the Virgin Mary, asked Him to make a pilgrimage to the principal
Christian holy sites in Israel and Europe.

His pilgrimage among the Christian holy sites was at times as mystify-
ing and disorienting to Him as any other period of His Ordeal of Re-
Awakening. In Jerusalem He roamed the catacombs in the night, giving
Himself over to extremes of devotional and psychic sensitivity to the
events surrounding the life and death of Jesus.

This period of Heart-Master Da's sacred Ordeal represented a specific
purification, a rapid boiling off of Christian mystical archetypes, which
had been rooted in His deeper psychic being. By the time He completed
His European wanderings, the Christian visionary archetypes no longer
held any power over Him, and soon they ceased to appear at all.

**"By the time He completed His European wanderings, the Christian
visionary archetypes no longer held any power over Him."**

He now related to the Goddess not as the Virgin Mary but as the universal Goddess-Power, the living, active, Divine Presence and Personality, unconditioned by any particular archetypal representations or cultural forms.

Beyond kundalini and Yogic mysticism

Heart-Master Da's transcendence of Christian archetypes completed His passage beyond what He would later call "brain mysticism". Thus, in disagreement with the esotericism of Kundalini Yoga and most other forms of Yogic and devotional mysticism in East and West, Heart-Master Da now firmly concluded that the sahasrar is not a true terminal or goal of sacred life. The sahasrar is simply the highest functional region of the psyche, or the superconscious dimension of mind. It is the most subtle psycho-physical anchor of the deeper personality, not the seat of the true Divine Identity.

Abandoning traditional Yogic practices of Spiritual ascent and all seeking for experiences of absorption in the Divine Light and Spirit-Power above the world, the body, and the mind, Heart-Master Da now fully concentrated in the meditative practice of "radical" understanding that He had spontaneously developed since His Awakening at the seminary in 1967.

In formal meditation, and randomly throughout the day when He was not sitting for meditation, He simply rested in Spiritual equanimity and psycho-physical ease. Whatever sensations, feelings, thoughts, or images arose that tended to distract His attention, internally or externally, He simply enquired of Himself, "Avoiding relationship?", thereby feeling and releasing any egoic activity of self-contraction, and being restored to Identification with Consciousness, free in relationship to all arising experiences.

By transcending the ascending mysticism of Spiritual Yoga, Heart-Master Da had relinquished the philosophy and the subtle self-identity that partially characterize the deeper, psychic personality. However, He had yet to transcend fundamental egoic consciousness, which is the causal, or quintessential, root of all limited self-consciousness. The causal dimension of our being is experienced and exercised as attention itself. Heart-Master Da came to understand it as the self-contracted core of the deeper personality, and as the core of His (and all beings') apparent forgetting of the One and Only Divine Identity.

"Husbanding" the Great Goddess— and the Perfect Remembering of Divine Freedom

It was now the summer of 1970.

Upon returning to the United States from His pilgrimage to Christian holy sites, Heart-Master Da felt impelled to move to Los Angeles, though He had no evident reason to do so.

There, in Hollywood, on the grounds of the Vedanta Society, He found a small temple which had been established by monks of the Ramakrishna-Vivekananda order. To Heart-Master Da's surprise and joy, He found it to be a living and extremely potent seat of the Shakti.

The Vedanta Temple in Hollywood, California

He went there frequently. Since the moment of the Goddess Shakti's first appearance to Him in Swami Muktananda's Ashram garden, Heart-Master Da's devotion to Her had been as continuous and vivid as that of the famous Hindu Saint Sri Ramakrishna nearly a century before.[13] There was nothing abstract or imaginary about it. She frequently appeared to Him in visible, tangible form, a living Woman. He surrendered in relation to Her Commands and Blessings with as much passionate intensity as He had in His relationships with His previous, human Gurus.

But now, at this Vedanta Temple in Los Angeles, Heart-Master Da's sacred devotional relationship to the Divine Goddess entered its culminating stages. One day in early September, He found Himself assuming an entirely different, and even more profoundly intimate, form of relationship to Her. Suddenly, He was no longer Her devotee:

As I meditated, I felt myself take on the form of Siva, the Divine Being prior to all form. I took on the infinite (pervasive, or formless) form of the original Deity, as I had done previously in Baba's [Swami Muktananda's] Presence. I sat in this blissful state of infinite Being for some time.

Then I felt the Shakti appear against my own form. She embraced me, and we grasped one another in Divine (and motionless, and spontaneously Yogic) "sexual union". We clasped one another (thus) in a fire of cosmic desire, as if to give birth to the universes. Then I felt the oneness of the Divine Energy and my own Being. There was no separation at all. The one Being that was my own nature included the reality that is consciousness and the reality that is all manifestation as a single cosmic unity and eternal union.

The sensations of the embrace were overwhelmingly blissful. It exceeded any kind of pleasure that a man could acquire. And soon I ceased to feel myself as a dependent child of the Shakti. I accepted Her as my consort, my loved-One, and I held Her forever to my heart.[14]

That "Husbanding" of the Divine Goddess—of inestimable significance for the future Life and Work of Heart-Master Da Love-Ananda—was quickly followed by another tremendously auspicious Event in Consciousness.

The next day, September 10, 1970, Heart-Master Da returned to the Vedanta Temple in Hollywood, to sit in meditation and await His Divine Consort. But nothing happened. Indeed, there was nothing else that could happen that could modify or change His State. He was Free:

13. See pp. 374-75 for a more detailed account of Sri Ramakrishna and his relationship to the Goddess Kali.

14. The World-Teacher, Heart-Master Da Love-Ananda, *The Knee of Listening*, New Standard Edition. Forthcoming.

In an instant, I became profoundly and directly aware of what I am. It was a tacit realization, a direct knowledge in consciousness itself. It was conscious-ness itself, without the addition of a communication from any other source. I simply sat there and knew what I am. I was being what I am. I am Reality, the Self, the Nature and Support of all things and all beings. I am the One Being, known as God, Brahman, Atman, the One Mind, the Self.

There was no thought involved in this. I am that Consciousness. There was no reaction either of joy or surprise. I am the One I recognized. I am that One. I am not merely experiencing Him.

Then truly there was no more to realize. Every experience in my life had led to this. The dramatic revelations in childhood and college, my time of writ-ing, my years with Rudi, the revelation in seminary, the long history of pil-grimage to Baba's Ashram, all of these moments were the intuitions of this same Reality. My entire life had been the communication of that Reality to me, until I am That.[15]

The immutable Happiness of Sahaj Samadhi

This Awakening in the Vedanta Temple was the culmination of Heart-Master Da's entire Ordeal to recover the "Bright". It was the final moment in the progressive death of "Narcissus", which had been initiated in His "death" at the seminary in 1967.

Now both the gross personality and the deeper personality of Franklin Jones were permanently restored to the "Bright" Divine Happi-ness from Which and as Which He had taken birth. Thus, "Franklin Jones", as an egoically self-conscious human individual, came to His demise in that Re-Awakening in the Vedanta Temple.

In speaking of these great Events of His early Life, Heart-Master Da Love-Ananda has said that the Realization that became His permanent State in the Vedanta Temple is all-inclusive. It includes both the dissolu-tion in the Heart of Consciousness that He had enjoyed at the seminary after His terrible bout of resistance to death, and the ascended State of mys-tical God-Union, formless ecstasy, and Identification with the Spiritual

Divine Life of all beings that He had known at Swami Muktananda's Ashram on His first visit in 1968. He later said:

HEART-MASTER DA LOVE-ANANDA: The spontaneous event of ascent [at Swami Muktananda's Ashram had] involved systematic dissociation from the conventions of phenomena in their various planes. Therefore, when phenomena returned through the process of descent, there arose, for the time being, a sense of confusion upon contact with the conventional states. There was some tacit sense of difference. The Awakened state somehow remained as the Condition of my awareness of conventional states, but also I experienced a lack of clarity through association with these states.

It was only in the incident or Event at the Vedanta Temple that the Transcendental Condition or Self or Dharmakaya [the "Body of Ultimate Truth"] was Realized most perfectly. In other words, the conventions of self-consciousness from that time ceased to be an impediment to the absolutely clear Realization of the Condition of self and of the world.[16]

He calls that clear Realization, in its ordinary association with bodily and psychic existence, "Sahaj Samadhi". "Sahaj" is a Hindi term that literally means "together-born". It implies the "inherent", "effortless", "natural", and "spontaneous" unity of infinite Happiness and Awareness with the ordinary awareness and conduct of body, mind, and life. It is "Formless Ecstasy" even while self, mind, body, and world appear, and while the Realizer Freely participates in their constantly changing play.

From the moment of His conception previous to birth until His Divine Self-Remembering in the Vedanta Temple, the One Divine Self, Who Heart-Master Da Is, had plunged into the incarnate human state, even to the point of becoming thoroughly and desperately identified with a gross, egoic personality in its most limited form. Then He had had no choice but to rediscover and regenerate the entire course of Divine Awakening from that egoic sleep of Awareness, which most human beings chronically indulge for countless chaotic and fearful lifetimes.

Indeed, Heart-Master Da's rapid progress through and then beyond the stages of Kundalini Yoga, both as Taught by Rudi chiefly in the dimension of the gross personality and as Taught by Swami Muktananda principally in the deeper psychic dimension, had been Potentized and

16. Da Free John [Heart-Master Da Love-Ananda], *"I" Is the Body of Life* (Clearlake, Calif.: The Dawn Horse Press, 1981), p. 43.

After His Re-Awakening in the Vedanta Temple, 1970

also undermined by His Breakthroughs of Divine Awakeness in 1967 and 1968 and His Yogic "severing of the sahasrar" in 1970.

These Heart-resurrections were made possible, in part, by the discipline and Spiritual Transmission granted to Heart-Master Da by His beloved Gurus. But these Divine States themselves were not granted to Him by those Teachers or by any other apparently external sources. They were spontaneous and partial Rememberings of His own Divine Identity.

Now, in fully and permanently Remembering Who He Is, the God-Man Da had Realized His Identity as the Heart, or Divine Self, of the gross and deeper personalities that constituted "Franklin Jones". But the final stroke of Self-Remembrance was not, outwardly, a momentous occasion. No grand pronouncement was made, no celebration ensued. Heart-Master Da simply Resumed His eternal Identity and the Enjoyment of immutable Happiness.

The Tantric Hero—and His Miraculous Heart-Power of Unconditional Love

Thus, in late 1970, Heart-Master Da stood forth with full Consciousness of His Divine Nature, a living Buddha or "Enlightened One".

Though He had no further need of the formal practice of meditation, it was still His custom, then and for some time thereafter, to sit in daily meditation with His household. It was while sitting that He first became aware of the Miracle taking place:

When I would sit for meditation in any formal way, instead of contemplating what was arising in myself, I would contemplate other beings as my own forms. Instead of my own psychic forms arising, the psychic forms, minds, and limitations of others would arise. I was aware, visually or otherwise, of great numbers of people, and I would work with them very directly on a subtle level. In some cases, these people would soon contact me and become involved with me in a personal relationship. Others were people I already knew. I would work for them in the subtle way, and then watch for signs and demonstrations in their outward lives of the reality of this manifestation. I tested everything in that manner.[17]

17. Bubba Free John [Heart-Master Da Love-Ananda], *The Enlightenment of the Whole Body*, p. 38.

The appearance of this Capability—to "meditate" countless others, even all beings—was a Divine Charisma, a spontaneous Outpouring of Love from His mysterious Mastery of and Union with the Cosmic Goddess. Through that Mastery, Heart-Master Da had accomplished what is virtually unheard of, and what certainly has never before been achieved, in the West: He had fulfilled the sacred practice of a Tantric Hero (in Sanskrit, "Vira").

"Tantra" does not merely connote sex, or Spiritualized sexuality, as people commonly assume. The term means "the inherent Unity that underlies and transcends all opposites, and that resolves all differences or distinctions".

Traditionally, Tantric Adepts and aspirants use the passions of the being and, in some schools, the emotionally and psychically catalytic energies of sex and highly stimulating substances that are forbidden to more orthodox or conventional practitioners. The Tantrics' intention, however, is never merely to indulge gross desires. The Heroic practitioner instinctually presumes that the entire world-process is pervaded and Lived by the Divine Goddess, the Great Shakti or Spirit of Love. The greatest Tantric Adepts exemplify unconditional Love to the highest degree: They embrace even the forbidden, the unclean, the degraded, and they transmute these by Love.

Therefore, it is traditionally said, the Tantric Hero

. . . *overcomes the distinction (or duality) of clean and unclean, sacred and profane, and breaks his bondage to a world artificially fragmented. He affirms in a radical way the underlying unity of the phenomenal world, the identity of Shakti with the whole creation. Heroically, he triumphs over it, controls and masters it. By affirming the essential worth of the forbidden, he causes the forbidden to lose its power to pollute, to degrade, to bind. . . .*

For the Tantric hero the forbidden is not to be propitiated, feared, ignored, or avoided. . . . Kali [the Fierce Goddess] is confronted boldly by the <u>sadhaka</u> [practitioner] and thereby assimilated, overcome, and transformed into a vehicle of salvation. . . . It is she, when confronted boldly in meditation, who gives the <u>sadhaka</u> great power and ultimately salvation.[18]

18. David R. Kinsley, *The Sword and the Flute: Kali and Krsna, Dark Visions of the Terrible and the Sublime in Hindu Mythology* (Berkeley: University of California Press, 1975), p. 112.

Typically, most practitioners and even most God-Realizers of one or another degree have neither the capability nor the destiny to Master the Divine Goddess so boldly. None of Heart-Master Da's human Gurus, including Swami Nityananda, functioned in this Heroic fashion.

Though Heart-Master Da did not know about them at the time, certain ancient texts, such as the *Yoga Vasishtha* and the *Tripura Rahasya,* allude to the Goddess's Spiritual death or conscious dissolution into the Heart of the Realizer, thereby Granting him Divine Self-Realization and all Her extraordinary Powers.

The *Tripura Rahasya* specifically describes the mysterious interplay between the Divine Goddess or "Devi" and the Enlightening self-investigation or enquiry ("vichara") of one approaching Realization: "When the Supreme Devi is well pleased with the worship of the devotee, She turns into *vichara* in him and shines as the blazing Sun in the expanse of his Heart."[19] This is a traditional precedent for the mysterious connection between Heart-Master Da's spontaneous meditative practice of self-Enquiry ("Avoiding relationship?") and His Union with the Goddess.

The Divine volcano of Heart-Master Da's Embrace of the Goddess and Her dissolution into Unity with Him immediately Revealed His true Identity. It also Revealed His Capability, or "Siddhi", of being the Heart and, thereby, of spontaneously meditating all beings by being Conscious <u>as</u> them.

Heart-Master Da would call this Siddhi "the Power of the Heart". Its spontaneous, ceaselessly original Impulses would generate His in many ways unprecedented Teaching Work for nearly sixteen years to come. He has said of His Re-Awakening in the Vedanta Temple and of His Power of absolutely vulnerable Love-Identification with other beings:

HEART-MASTER DA LOVE-ANANDA: When there was this simple, radical turnabout, there was nothing about it that would have appeared remarkable to anyone who might have observed me. I didn't smile. I didn't feel high. There was no reaction to that event, because there wasn't anything left over of the thing that now was thrown away. There was no thing to which I could react. There was no one to react, to feel good about it, happy about it. There was no peculiar emotion to the event itself. The Heart was all. Its quality became more and more apparent. There was a preliminary period of that fundamental enjoyment which lasted for perhaps several months. During that time there was no

19. Swami Sri Ramanananda Saraswati (Sri Munagala S. Venkataramaiah), trans., *Tripura Rahasya, or the Mystery beyond the Trinity,* 4th ed. (Tiruvannamalai, S. India: Sri Ramanasramam, 1980), p. 19.

longer this whole complex life in dilemma, but I didn't really function in any way different than before. I didn't experience any comparative impression about the event. I didn't really "see" or interpret it clearly and fully for a good period of time, even though I consciously enjoyed a state that was untouched, unqualified by any event or circumstance, which would seem remarkable in itself. But I hadn't begun to function as it in relation to manifest life. Only when I did so, and then only gradually, was I able to estimate and know my own event. It was as if I had walked through myself. Such a state is perfectly spontaneous. It has no way of watching itself. It has no way to internalize or structure itself. It is Divine madness. The Self, the Heart is perfect madness. There is not a jot of form within it. There is no thing. No thing has happened. There is not a single movement in consciousness. And that is its blissfulness. It was not the fact that certain functions of internal life had been stimulated. It was peculiarly free of vision, movement, and all the blissful phenomena characteristic of the activities of yoga-shakti. And when such phenomena did happen to arise, they were of another kind, or they were known from a new point of view. Their qualities became cosmic and universal rather than yogic or personal in nature. Until there is only God, the living One. . . .

For years, I would sit down in meditation, and all my own forms would appear, my own mind, my desires, my experience, my suffering, my feeling, my shakti, my this and my that. But, at some point, it all came to an end. There was no thing, nothing there anymore, none of that distracted or interested me. Meditation was perfect, continuous. Then I began to meet those friends who first became involved in this work. And when I would sit down for meditation, there would be more of these things again, all of these thoughts, feelings, this suffering, this dis-ease, disharmony, upsets, suffering, craziness, this pain, these shaktis, all of this, again. But they weren't mine. They were the internal and life qualities of my friends. So I would sit down to meditate, and do the meditation of my friends. When I would feel it all release, their meditation was done. And I began to test it, to see if this meditation went on in some more or less apparent way for these people who were not with me. And I found that this meditation went on with people whom I hadn't even met. People I saw in dreams and visions would show up at the Ashram. . . .

. . . [T]here was a period of time when the universe, the cosmic process was meditated in me. Various siddhis, or yogic and occult powers became manifest. The movement or process of the cosmos is a meditation, a purifying event.[20]

20. Heart-Master Da Love-Ananda, *The Method of the Siddhas: Talks on the Spiritual Technique of the Saviors of Mankind* (Clearlake, Calif.: The Dawn Horse Press, 1973, rep. 1987), pp. 18-19, 269-70.

Sri Love-Anandashram, 1990

Water's Work and the Crucifixion of Change

The Heart-Power of Spontaneous Teaching-Revelation in the Seventh Stage of Life

Heart-Master Da's first formal appearance as Divine Teacher, April 25, 1972
(cover photograph of *The Knee of Listening***)**

Water's Work and the Crucifixion of Change

The Heart-Power of Spontaneous Teaching-Revelation in the Seventh Stage of Life

Traditional corroboration and unexpected Empowerments of "the Western Face of God"

Still only thirty years old, now fully Awake as the Supreme Divine Reality, Heart-Master Da set about His Teaching Work. He had already begun writing an autobiography and collection of Revelatory essays, *The Knee of Listening,* some time before the great Events of September 1970. Now His writing continued in earnest, and He also found and recorded important traditional corroborations for His Enlightened Condition. The most crucial of these corroborations He found in the works of the modern Hindu Sage Ramana Maharshi, who had died in 1950.

Alone in the entire corpus of available traditional records, Ramana spoke unequivocally and in detail about the Divine Self as "the Heart", as did Heart-Master Da. Ramana had apparently enjoyed the same supreme State of Consciousness that Heart-Master Da had Realized. Ramana's testimony supported Heart-Master Da's critical determination, from the Divinely Conscious orientation of the Heart, that the process of Spiritual and Yogic ascent is secondary and (if pursued for its own sake, on the basis of egoic seeking) fundamentally binding rather than Liberating in the great course of Divine Self-Realization.

Ramana Maharshi

Ramana, like Heart-Master Da, had discovered the Realization of Divine Consciousness to be associated with the "I"-sense, the mind, and the body through a continuous link at a point in the right side of the physical heart organ. This, Ramana said, was the "cave in the heart", and this Realization was the "Hridayam" (a Sanskrit term meaning "the Center is here", or "the Heart") referred to in the most ancient Hindu Scriptures, especially the two oldest Upanishads (the principal sources of ancient Hindu esotericism), the *Brihadaranyaka* and the *Chandogya*.

In Ramana Maharshi's writings, Heart-Master Da also found brief but technically explicit corroboration of His Realization of the "Bright" as the Divine Form of Reality, Amrita Nadi—"the Nerve or Current of Immortality".

Amrita Nadi, Heart-Master Da states and Ramana suggests, is the Divine Structure at the core of all manifest existence, the ultimate Yogic Form. It unites Divine Consciousness ("Siva") and Its "Bright" Radiance and Energy ("Shakti") as the singular, eternal Intensity of Being.

In His infancy, and prior to His Birth, Heart-Master Da had lived as the "Bright" Form that is Amrita Nadi. Now, having permanently attuned His body and mind to that State, He freely enjoyed Its Form again.

He continuously knew Amrita Nadi as the eternal Current of Love-Bliss, seated in the right side of the heart and spiraling above to the sahasrar and beyond. From that Matrix of Light above, He knew Himself as the One Who lives all beings and pervades all worlds.

All of this was central to His Confession and Revelation of His "Way of 'Radical' Understanding" in *The Knee of Listening*. While arranging for the book's publication, Heart-Master Da also began His Teaching Work on an informal basis with the small group of people who had gathered around Him by that time.

Then, on April 25, 1972, in a storefront that He and His student-friends had laboriously transformed from a machine shop into a very small bookstore, meditation hall, and office, Heart-Master Da Love-Ananda formally opened His Ashram. Located on a block of simple shops on Melrose Avenue in Hollywood, it featured a sign announcing its Name: "Shree Hridayam Satsang" ("The Company of the 'Bright' Heart").

Supervising preparation of
His first Ashram

"The Ashram" on Melrose Avenue, 1972

That evening, for the first time, Heart-Master Da, Teaching under His given Name "Franklin Jones", sat in silent formal meditation with a small gathering. The talk He Gave afterwards was later titled "Understanding" and became the first chapter of *The Method of the Siddhas*, His second book.

His opening statement as a Divine Teacher was, very quietly, "Who will cast the first stone?" A photograph taken that first night graces the cover of *The Knee of Listening*. Heart-Master Da's luminous eyes and face are vibrant, tranquil, and completely free of self-consciousness, as He clenches a fist to indicate to His listeners their action of self-defining, Narcissistic contraction.

Significantly, His first questioner was so unwilling to examine his own Narcissistic reactivity and seeking as it was pointed to by Heart-Master Da that he eventually stormed out of the room in a huff.

That night, Heart-Master Da knew that even the members of His Ashram would display their own form of the self-protective resistance to Truth that His first questioner had presented. He also knew that the Wisdom Revealed in His own Ordeal of Re-Awakening made all seeking unnecessary for others. He knew that His Heart-Awakening Power was such that any truly serious and responsive aspirant could easily enter into

"It was the early 1970s, and the people who came to see Heart-Master Da were, for the most part, superficial and untutored seekers."

the sacred relationship of Satsang (Sanskrit for "the Company of Truth") with Him. Simply by living with Him in the traditional devotional discipline of surrender and obedience, any such individual could directly come to understand His "radical" Teaching Message on the primacy of Consciousness over all egoic seeking and experience, both worldly and mystical, gross and deeper. And, by His Grace, any such devotee could be drawn into Divine Self-Realization in a finite period of time.

Therefore, He summarized His Message simply. He spoke of Satsang, the traditional relationship of unreserved devotion, service, and self-discipline in relation to Him as Guru, the God-Born Great Siddha of the Heart. And He spoke of progressive understanding and transcendence of every kind or dimension of egoic un-Happiness and futile seeking, until the Awakening of Perfect Understanding in transcendent Divine Self-Realization. He said to everyone, "Turn to Me and understand."

But it was the early 1970s, and the people who came off the streets of Los Angeles to see Heart-Master Da were, for the most part, superficial and untutored seekers. He quickly grasped the absurdity of His situation: He had Realized, and He was supremely capable of Awakening in others, the Truth, Happiness, and Freedom That Is the Greatest Good of human life. In times past, to receive even initial Instruction in the Wisdom He was Giving away—virtually for free—wise kings had been willing, and they had sometimes been required, to relinquish their empires at the feet of a true Guru. In the face of His kind of Enlightening Power of the Heart of Consciousness, men and women of world-renowned knowledge, genius, purity, and even saintliness had gratefully prostrated themselves in praise and supplication.

Yet, in 1972, Heart-Master Da soon found Himself "surrounded by whores and pimps, street people, criminals, neurotics, loveless and confused and righteous self-indulgent people of all kinds."[1] It soon became apparent to Him that none of His listeners had even the slightest idea—or, rather, all they had were the slightest ideas—of what He was talking about. "At first this caused me to despair, but then I saw that my own ordinariness equipped me very well to serve such people."[2]

His powerful, earthy, and lively initial discourses, later published in *The Method of the Siddhas,* made His Message of Satsang and "radical" understanding very plain. He sat in formal meditation with His early

1. Bubba Free John [Heart-Master Da Love-Ananda], *The Enlightenment of the Whole Body,* p. 91.
2. Ibid.

students frequently. But their emotional enthusiasm and affection for Him were belied by unconscious motivations—"karmas below consciousness"—that prevented His students from making an uncomplicated and truly effective response to Him. They were too deeply mired in the suffering of Narcissistic seeking to notice that the Happiness they were looking for in every moment of their lives was standing Radiant before them in Heart-Master Da's very bodily Form, and that they could Commune with Him directly by doing what He asked them to do as constant sacred practice.

By April 1973, Heart-Master Da knew that He must soon return to India—for a different kind of pilgrimage than He had taken in the past. Always in the past He had gone to India as a devotee, to receive His Indian Gurus' Blessings for the sake of His Realization. Now He must go back as a fully God-Realized Guru Himself. He needed to purify and regenerate His relationships with all of His Spiritual sources for the sake of a new and very different form of Teaching Work He felt He must soon inaugurate. He told His Western students:

HEART-MASTER DA LOVE-ANANDA: It is only when the channels for this Work are pure, absolutely open, unqualified, that the event can take place without difficulty. . . .

My going to India is the necessary discipline that I must observe in order to maintain the connection to all the intimate Spiritual sources of this Work. If that proper connection is maintained, all the Siddhas become active in this work. And they all should. (April 1974)

In every sacred esoteric tradition on Earth, it is understood that the tremendous Spiritual forces and the subtleties of wisdom transmitted from Master to disciple can easily be abused or misunderstood. Therefore, every tradition has laws, rules, and sacred customs whereby the living Force and Intelligence of its particular formulation of Divine Grace may be perpetuated from one generation to the next.

These esoteric protocols almost always include the Master's formal acknowledgement of the disciple's Spiritual proficiency and of his or her capability and formal authorization to function thereafter as a Teacher or Master. Only very rarely does a Realizer arise who Originates a Teaching and Sacred Process of fulfilling the Great Way entirely outside such a formal Lineage.

Heart-Master Da spent several weeks in India that summer, accompanied by Jerry Sheinfeld, a devotee who served as His attendant. Heart-Master Da first visited Ganeshpuri to purify His relationship with His surviving human Guru, Swami Muktananda. (Rudi had died in an airplane crash in February of that year.)

It had never been Heart-Master Da's intention to Function as Guru outside, or without the explicit permission and Blessings of, the formal Lineage of His Teachers. And, indeed, in 1969 Swami Muktananda had given Him formal written permission to Teach others Kundalini Yoga.

But since then Heart-Master Da had transcended the kundalini shakti and all Yogic mysticism. Now He wanted to ascertain conclusively whether the Swami might be willing to acknowledge the Truth of His Realization of the Heart and the Amrita Nadi, and the validity of His unique and original process of "radical" understanding.

In their historic formal meeting, Swami Muktananda declined to consider seriously with Heart-Master Da the real differences between them. Nevertheless, their conversation did dramatically underscore distinctions between the Swami's kundalini-based "Siddha Yoga" of Spiritual ascent and Heart-Master Da's Heart-based Way of "Radical" Understanding in Spiritual, Transcendental, and Divine Consciousness.

Heart-Master Da conducted Himself respectfully toward His former Master. But after the interview, He immediately took His leave from the Ashram. It was the last time He would ever see His beloved "Baba" Muktananda in the flesh.

Heart-Master Da on His pilgrimage to India as Divine Teacher, 1973

The two encounters in India most significant for His Mission were unplanned. The first was a stop at the Vithoba Temple in Pandharpur, a famous site visited annually by thousands of Hindu worshippers. Since medieval times, great Saints and Adepts had joined ordinary people in coming to this shrine for Spiritual Blessing.

In Jerry Sheinfeld's account, the temple priests were visibly thrilled to give Heart-Master Da—again and again—the Darshan ("Sighting") and other Blessings of the principal Divine Image at the temple, a small statue which is said to be a Manifestation of the God-Man Krishna, and which has a curious hole in the right side of its chest. Heart-Master Da felt "something very fundamental" for His Work "was Transmitted" to Him there.

The second important encounter occurred during a visit to the Ashram of the modern Saint Narayan Maharaj, who had died in 1945. Before the trip Heart-Master Da had not known about this Saint, who He now learned had been a most unusual Teacher. Narayan Maharaj had adopted the opulent lifestyle of a king (a "Maharaja") down to the last detail, conducting his Ashram in Kedgaon like the court of a kingdom. In his relations with disciples, Narayan Maharaj openly enacted the dramatic devotional love-play of Krishna with His legendary ecstatic devotees, the gopis or cowherd maidens.

Narayan Maharaj

His Ashram was located at a site where, it is said, in ancient times Divine Incarnations were formally Blessed and Empowered for their Work. At the tomb of Narayan Maharaj, Heart-Master Da contacted him in subtle form. He later called this contact "the primary event of that trip", noting that at Kedgaon "the ultimate Blessing of My Mission was transferred via the Spiritual Office of the Perfect Master Narayan Maharaj."[3]

Shortly after this event, Heart-Master Da asked His attendant-devotee, Jerry Sheinfeld, to write to the members of His Ashram in Los Angeles. From now on, He said, everyone should refer to Him as "Bubba Free John". Jerry laughed. But his Guru was utterly serious, telling him he should do the same. When Jerry slipped a few days later and addressed Him as "Franklin", He corrected Jerry fiercely: "Franklin is dead. I am Bubba Free John."

The Name "Bubba Free John" was spontaneously Revealed to Him coincident with the purification of His Guru-Function and the liberal Divine Blessings upon His Mission that were occurring during the Indian pilgrimage. "Bubba" was a childhood nickname, meaning "brother" or "friend". "Free John" is a translation of "Franklin Jones", which means "a free man through Whom God is Gracious".

Having relinquished all vestiges of the persona of the seeker-and-Realizer "Franklin Jones", Heart-Master Da later said of that trip to India, "In a sense it was the last thing I did as Franklin Jones. I buried Him somewhere there."

He also visited sites associated with other Saints and Siddhas important to His Work, making formal offerings and surrendering Himself and His Teaching Function to each of those who had served Him Spiritually in the past. These sites included the Ashrams or burial sites of Ramakrishna, Swami Vivekananda, Shirdi Sai Baba,[4] and Swami Nityananda.

Ramakrishna   Swami Vivekananda   Shirdi Sai Baba

3. From an essay by Heart-Master Da Love-Ananda written on November 6, 1980.

4. In the spring of 1970, while wandering consciously in the subtle dimension in sleep, Heart-Master Da had met an unnamed Saint. The white-bearded old man lovingly embraced Heart-Master Da and told his

His stay at the south Indian Ashram of the late Ramana Maharshi, the first visit there of His Life, proved extraordinarily invigorating to Him in a most esoteric way. While there, He spoke of what occurred when He first approached Ramana's burial ("samadhi") site, and thereafter:

HEART-MASTER DA LOVE-ANANDA: In My own case, there [had been] this descent from the sahasrar into the heart, which Ramana Maharshi also described, but this descent was followed by a spontaneous regeneration of Amrita Nadi, from the Heart to the Light above. There is really no direct statement of this in Maharshi's writings. One of the things I wanted to find out in coming here was if there was in Him this Knowledge, this Fullness of Amrita Nadi.

As soon as I walked into the room where He is buried, I could feel His Transmission all over My head and all over My body. His Manifestation was completely covering Me. All night long He was working. The Current was moving not just down into the heart, but up out of the heart into the sahasrar and Radiating as the intuition of the Light above the body, the mind, and the world. That Flow of Divine Force has been moving since we arrived here last night, and with such intensity that it is an obvious statement from Ramana Maharshi to Me that, "Yes, That is my Form." (August 1973)

When Heart-Master Da and Jerry Sheinfeld returned to Los Angeles, the entire Ashram met them at the airport. The handsome young Adept was visibly Radiant—Jerry described Him as "shining like a thousand suns"—and He made a point of hugging and kissing every single man, woman, and child who came to greet Him.

"Franklin" was gone. "Bubba Free John" had appeared, and, as His devotees would soon discover, He was no longer willing to Teach them, as He had in the past, merely through formal discourses and meditative sittings. Now He was certain not only of His willingness but also of His absolute Divine Empowerment to do whatever He must—whether or not within the bounds of conventional propriety and social expectation—to prepare His chaotic and cultureless devotees for the Great Matter of self-transcending sadhana and Perfect God-Realization. He was about to display what He would later term "the Western Face of God" to Western and Westernized people who could never have responded truly, deeply, and conclusively to the ancient signs and pathways of Divine Life in the East.

---

family, friends, and devotees gathered with him that Heart-Master Da was his "son". In the dream-vision, Heart-Master Da felt that this Saint was one of His Spiritual Protectors, and He understood that He would receive from him an "inheritance". He later learned that the Saint He had met was Sai Baba of Shirdi, in India, a great Spiritual Master who lived in the later nineteenth and early twentieth centuries. And the Inheritance, He saw, was Spiritual Realization of God.

Greeting devotees at the Los Angeles airport upon His return from India, 1973

Garbage and the Goddess—
A Spiritually exuberant
Teaching Demonstration

O n Friday night, March 29, 1974, a gathering of Heart-Master Da's devotees met in a meditation hall at Persimmon, His community's new rural retreat in the low mountains of northern California.

The place had formerly been a hot springs resort, in fact a fashionable spa, with a hotel, an institutional kitchen and dining hall, ballrooms, many residential cabins and dormitories, and a once-ornate spa with many hot baths, including a "plunge" the size of a small swimming pool. Though now extremely run down, the facility was ideal as a remote haven for Heart-Master Da to engage His more vigorous form of Teaching Work—which had already begun in Los Angeles.

Now, in late March, His community had come to listen to devotees who had spent the previous week living with Him at His Residence at Persimmon, absorbed in a Spiritual Revelation that seemed to be transforming the entire landscape with Divine Light.

As the speakers arrived, winds and rains began to shake the old wooden frame building, and the wind whistled through the windows and the cracks in the walls.

Aniello Panico went to the microphone. Having spent two decades in the American publishing industry, he was now in charge of the publishing arm of The Dawn Horse Communion, the fledgling organization of devotees around Heart-Master Da. Even before he spoke, Aniello's body seemed to explode into convulsive movements from the Energy coursing through him. He continued to quiver and shake uncontrollably as he whispered into the microphone. He said that Heart-Master Da had Given him such a powerful Spiritual Initiation that he now felt His Divine Intensity constantly transforming every cell of his body. Others in the room, feeling the same Force, also began responding by moaning and shaking with spontaneous kriyas (Yogic jerking and shaking of the body, head, and spine), or with mudras (snarling expressions or often dance-like movements of the hands, arms, face, and body).

Then, quite unannounced, in the midst of a sudden gale outside and a cacophony of Yogic wildness inside, Heart-Master Da opened the back door of the meditation hall and strode in.

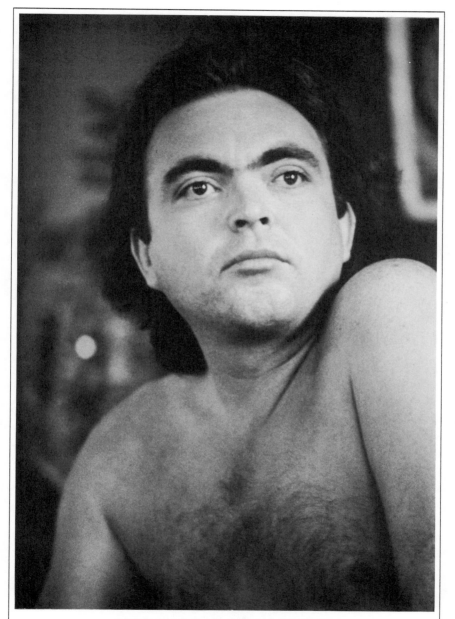

**At Persimmon during the Garbage and the Goddess
Teaching Demonstration, early 1974**

His lion's mane of dark brown hair falling to His shoulders, a simple, open-necked, long-sleeved shirt barely concealing His powerful arms and torso and the great Spirit-brimming roundness of His belly, full of Yogic Life-Power, His huge dark eyes wide with the lightning-like intensity of His Initiatory Force, Heart-Master Da was a walking vision: One devotee later said she just happened to turn her head, "and I was immediately paralyzed. There was golden-white all around Him, and His Presence was so Powerful It abolished everything in His path. Everything stopped, and it was like looking upon the very face of the Divine."

Without a word He went to several of the many devotees who were falling on the floor, making strange snarling sounds, weeping, or shuddering in response to the Blissful Force coursing through them. He touched them with His hand or, in a couple of cases, held a foot to their throats as they lay on the floor, to calm them and help them conduct His Spiritual Power. Then He took His Chair on the dais in the front of the room.

Among the devotees in the hall that night was Andrew Johnson, a comedy writer and stand-up comic from Los Angeles who had become a formal student of Heart-Master Da just a few months before. Andrew writes of that event:

The first time I saw Bubba Free John was in 1974 at an incredibly powerful occasion during which He walked into the meditation hall, surrounded by a clearly visible golden aura, and proceeded to blast the room and its inhabitants with a show of Force so potent it seemed as if the walls would explode. People were overwhelmed with Spiritual Force—some swooning in bliss, some speaking in tongues, some jerking around like Holy Rollers as the Force moved through their bodies, but most—like myself—simply sitting virtually breathless, absorbed in and in awe of the overwhelming Display of Divine Presence. After about forty-five minutes of this absolutely extraordinary Demonstration, Bubba visibly relaxed in His Chair. After a brief pause as the room quieted down, He shrugged, lit a cigarette, blew a perfect smoke ring, and said, "Maybe I've gone too far this time!"

As if the Divine Display of Spirit-Power were not enough, the timing of the shrug, the expert smoke ring, and that marvelous one-liner—this was too much for the comedy writer from Los Angeles. In that instant Andrew Johnson fell in love with Heart-Master Da Love-Ananda, with the strange, rapturous, life-impaling love that a human heart, male or female, can feel only for the God-Man, Who Is the supremely Attractive Embodiment of the Heart of every heart. (Heart-Master Da later frequently compared His Divine Distraction of His students with the maddening Love-Play whereby the ancient God-Man Krishna is said to have wooed the gopis from all their worldly concerns.)

In those days devotees lived in a magical realm, party to coronas that hovered around the sun all day, halos around the moon, storms that appeared the instant Heart-Master Da laid His hand on a devotee to Transmit Spiritual Power, extraordinarily light, gentle misting "Grace-rains" that seemed to sparkle with Radiance; among devotees, all manner of spontaneous Yogic kriyas, blisses, visions, high Spiritual samadhis, sudden satoris or intuitive glimpses of the Witness-Consciousness; and all this in the midst of Dionysian romps in Heart-Master Da's Residence, in the meditation halls, in the hot baths at Persimmon, with plenty of Jack Daniels sour mash whiskey and Coca-Cola chasers, to the beat of the light soul and rock music of Stevie Wonder and John Denver, respectively, followed by Pachelbel's heart-opening classical "Canon in D Major"—encored by Maxine Weldon's funky "Steamroller"; the largest order of take-out egg-bacon-cheeseburgers, French fries, and milkshakes ever filled by an eatery down in the local town, and occasional ten-course meals in the great cuisines, served in harmonious rooms full of flowers and things pleasing to the eye, and to the dulcet sounds of a rare Renaissance lute (to which Heart-Master Da, a mischievous twinkle in His eye, threatened to take a chainsaw upon observing the owner-player's precious egoic attachment); the same dinners interrupted by unanticipated explosions of Yogic Shakti phenomena in the devotees in response to His Heart-Power (Which was transforming the landscape and His Residence into a Loka or Spiritual realm of Ecstasy), so that they sat snarling and jerking and blissfully falling face-forward into their delicately seasoned Chinese soup; other similar occasions interrupted by His equally unanticipated verbal scourgings of their mediocre fascination with such experiences and their total unresponsiveness as self-yielding devotees (in a New York idiom that would hold its own on the city streets where it was learned); one Sunday morning, heart-Touched tossing of flowers to Him in the meditation hall, in gratitude for the inspiring Aria of all His Deeds, all His Words, and His very human Appearance among us; one Saturday morning, the most blissful, "Bright", serene Discourse and Revelation of the Supreme Divine Person in and as His own Body that a human being could possibly hope to hear and witness; and, throughout the many months, His continual, "radical", earthy, vivid, sometimes hilarious, sometimes shocking, and always unerringly True Critique of all seeking and of the loveless dilemma and confusion that prompt every futile human pursuit of experience and knowledge, whether high or low, in order thereby to attain Happiness. Garbage and the Goddess was without doubt one of the most humanly exuberant, Spiritually Powerful, and maddeningly heart-Distracting Demonstrations of Divine Siddhi ever shown on Earth.

The "garbage" was all possible experience. The "Goddess" was the Force of Nature, Which deludes Consciousness into identification with and pursuit of bodily and psychic experience until, by Grace of the Divine Guru, the Heart begins to Awaken. Only then is one in a position to understand that the sense of being a separate ego is a self-created and unnecessary illusion, and that seeking to become Happy by fulfilling the ego's desires is both painful and futile. As "Bubba Free John", the God-Man Da harnessed the Power of the universe to make vivid, in-life lessons for people who otherwise could never have had access to either the experiences or the wisdom. He summarized His point by using a metaphor from His Spiritual practice under Rudi:

HEART-MASTER DA LOVE-ANANDA: *It is very simple. Every time I met Rudi he would hand me a bag of garbage. . . . It was always the first thing he would do. Then I would go and throw the garbage away, and I'd come back, and we'd sit together a little bit, or I'd do some work. Sooner or later he'd give me some more garbage. It is really very simple. You just throw it away.*

It makes it much simpler when it's in a paper bag. It has all those oily spots. . . . It was always very easy for me. I could see from the paper bag itself that it was garbage! . . .

The key to the matter is not <u>how</u> to throw the garbage away. The key to the matter is <u>recognizing</u> that it is garbage. It doesn't take a lot of subtlety. It takes a little observation. . . .

You are just looking at a lot of garbage and thinking that it is the precious instrument of God. One of my jobs is to package it. I spend a lot of my time packaging your garbage, trying to get you to recognize it. You'll throw it away as soon as you see it. You can't surrender something that you don't recognize to be garbage. You intuitively hold on to it. . . .

The world itself is an endless distraction in which the principle of sacrifice is made impossible by experience. The Guru serves the principle of sacrifice. The Goddess does not. The Goddess with all of her experiences serves the principle of experience, of accumulation, of immunity, of manifest self-existence in limitation. So there is no surrender in the world. . . .

It is not to any of these events that you must be turning, not to the kundalini events or even the non-having of kundalini events. It is to Satsang, this very principle, this real attention that is Satsang or Divine Communion. It is attention to the Guru as Guru, attention to the Guru as the manifest agent of the very Divine, attention to the Guru and through the Guru to the Divine, the absolute Divine, the absolute intensity of Real-God. . . . [T]here is one process, and you must begin to grasp it.

When you grasp it, your humor will be restored, and it will consist of unreasonable happiness and love, an ecstasy that transcends all the limiting influences of this life, which are immense and cannot otherwise be resisted. You cannot overcome this world, but the Divine has already overcome this world. Those who become the true devotees of the Divine in the Presence of the true Guru-Siddhi are free of the world, and they may live in the world as the Presence of the Divine, as the Presence of love, of freedom, of prior happiness, of conditionless bliss.[5]

In mid-April 1974, another devotee and I requested an interview with Heart-Master Da for an article in the Ashram magazine about His early

5. Bubba Free John [Heart-Master Da Love-Ananda], *Garbage and the Goddess* (Clearlake, Calif.: The Dawn Horse Press, 1974), pp. 102-6, 112.

**Heart-Master Da in a spontaneous Mudra of Spiritual Transmission
during the Garbage and the Goddess Teaching Demonstration, summer 1974**

Life and recent Work. I had come to California to join the community only a few months previously, and I was delighted when we were invited to His Residence to speak to Him in Person.

When we asked about His Life as Franklin Jones, He practically laughed us out of the room: "Why do you want to talk about that bastard? I Personally never liked Him." Then He told us, to our amazement, "I have always been Bubba Free John. Franklin Jones was a fictional character that I created when I was a boy."

"Franklin Jones", He said, was a persona that He manifested as a series of lessons about the futility of all seeking and the illusion that any kind of experience, mundane or sublime, is the Truth or the source of Happiness. By assuming the persona of Franklin Jones, He said,

HEART-MASTER DA LOVE-ANANDA: Instead of making God-knowing the continuous manifestation of My Life, I made it the periodic event of My Life, so that it would serve as a lesson for those who had an ongoing relationship with Me. I entered into this plane of existence without limitations and took hold of a psycho-physical form which was no more illumined than any other psycho-physical form. It needed to be transformed....

So Franklin Jones was ... a way of allowing this psycho-physical vehicle to serve as a lesson. He made it possible for this psycho-physical form to go through all the transforming events necessary so that it would truly serve Me. (April 1974)

Heart-Master Da then Gave a lengthy description of the events that had occurred in His Life since those recorded in *The Knee of Listening,* that is, since His Re-Awakening in the Vedanta Temple and the period immediately thereafter.

Most significantly, He Revealed the unseen, pre-cosmic Yoga of His Divine Work to release Liberating Spiritual Power and to accelerate the Awakening of Divine Consciousness in devotees and in the world. In the earlier years of His Work, when formally sitting in meditation or Darshan with devotees, He had intensified the Spiritual Light above their heads and depended on their capability to breathe and receive It into their body-minds. But now, He said, His Spiritual Power was "falling, showering", released from the Divine, "just flowing down head first". He described this release of Spirit-Force as first having had a "muscular, ripply motion" as it had to make its way into individuals and the cosmos, but then stabilizing, so that, even as He was speaking to us, it was constantly flowing down.

What He was fundamentally trying to do was to stabilize devotees in Satsang with Him. He described the dangers involved in the Process for Him, saying it was possible that He might die by early July. He was Working to bring the Divine Siddhi into a world that fiercely resists its own Divine Enlightenment.

In such conversations, Heart-Master Da disclosed the incomprehensible scale of His Work. It was His Intention as the Divine Adept to Reveal universally the inherent Unity of the manifest and the Unmanifest. His Garbage and the Goddess Teaching Demonstration was a Divine Effort, from the Conscious Light that is the Source-Condition of all energy and matter, to decisively transform the world-process universally, even at the atomic and cellular levels of matter. In the language of Einsteinian physics and of His own ultimate Divine "Super-Physics", Heart-Master Da was striving to Demonstrate the "Bright" Energic nature of all so-called material phenomena and to Show that Consciousness is the ultimate Source of even Energy itself.

In that context, the link of devotees' attention to Him had far more than personal significance for the relatively few individuals (perhaps two hundred) who were with Him physically at the time. If He could firmly establish that link through His Work with us, then it would no longer be necessary for Him to Teach the "radical" understanding of "Narcissus" and of all egoic seeking or to use secondary, Yogic powers for the sake of bringing the Divine Power into the world. That link of conscious attention to Him was possible only on the basis of our actual and "radical" understanding of ourselves; and if that link was strong, then all secondary powers would spontaneously manifest as necessary in service to His Great Heart-Power in Its Liberating Work.

If that link could be truly made, then whenever His bodily, physical death might occur, His Heart-Power would remain active and effective in the progressive Enlightenment of devotees. His devotees' continuous practice in ego-transcending Communion with Him would be the conduit for the ongoing Divinization of this world-plane by the Great Siddhi of the God-World—Which He had first brought into this plane so powerfully by taking birth and Re-Awakening as the Divine Self among us. He spoke of the body- and world-transforming Nature of His Work during an ecstatic evening early in the Garbage and the Goddess Teaching Demonstration, a night in Los Angeles much like the evening Andrew Johnson first saw Him at Persimmon. We later called the talk "Guru Enters Devotee":

HEART-MASTER DA LOVE-ANANDA: The Guru is not a human being. The Guru is the Divine Lord in human form. When his devotee becomes a true devotee, when he ceases to be a student and surrenders, then the Guru enters his devotee in the form of Divine Light. All kinds of extraordinary experiences manifest as a result. . . .

When a woman receives her lover, there is no doubt about it. She does not have to consult her textbooks! The same holds with Truth, the Divine Yoga. When the Lord enters His devotee, there is no doubt about it. There is no technique, but only the continuation of the life of the devotee, because the Lord is the Light that transcends this world, that is always becoming life and then returning to the Light again. There is no dilemma in this world, no absence of God in this world, no goal of God in this world. Because that is so, you will see me doing some very strange things. True Yoga is not a thing of this world. This world is the cult of Narcissus, suppressing the ecstasy that is natural to us.

"The Guru enters his devotee in the form of Divine Light."
—Spiritual Transmission at Persimmon, July 1974

137

The Spiritual process must take hold in the vital. The vital is the seat of unconsciousness and subconsciousness. There is an aspect of the verbal Teaching about the avoidance of relationship that does not touch the subconscious and unconscious life. So it is only by distracting you from your social consciousness, so that you are not really dealing with it at all, that I can take you in the vital. The Lord is the Lord of this world, not the Lord of the other world only. The Lord is absolutely the Lord of this world. Thus, there is no Yoga if the very cells of the body do not begin to intuit the Divine. When I enter my devotee, I come down into him in the midst of life, because it is in life, not in the subtle processes nor in your mentality, but it is in your life that the Lord acquires *you.*[6]

Western Tantra, and Water's Work to Reveal the fruitlessness of all seeking

Heart-Master Da could not have accomplished His Teaching Work merely by sitting in front of us on a raised seat, Radiating His Heart-Blessing in formal meditative occasions with us and Giving formal discourses. Any Adept who tried to hold himself aloof from his worldly students in the Spiritual wasteland of the modern West could not have sown the seeds of self-awareness or Divine intuition in people who had never embraced sacred life as an all-encompassing discipline, and who were as yet only fitfully gesturing toward self-knowledge and Spiritual Awakening.

Indeed, Heart-Master Da's manner of Teaching as "Franklin Jones" from 1970 through 1973 had been living proof of the futility of such an enterprise. As "Franklin", the Divine Heart-Teacher had persisted in the relatively austere and private order of daily living to which He Personally had become accustomed during His own God-Realizing sacred practice. But, in that mode, He had not been able to reach His students where we most needed to be touched and Guided—in the vital, the subconscious and unconscious life that, as modern psychology has amply demonstrated, governs nearly all human beings.

6. Da Free John [Heart-Master Da Love-Ananda], *The Bodily Location of Happiness*, pp. 37-38.

To break the impasse, as "Bubba Free John" He compassionately used the traditional "elements" of Tantric practice with His devotees—highly stimulating substances, such as alcohol and tobacco, and the catalytic energies of sexuality. The Tantric schools of Hinduism and Buddhism deliberately utilize such means to awaken and evoke the governing passions of the being, in order to transmute and consciously use those strong energies for the sake of Spiritual practice and Awakening.

However, traditionally it was said that Adepts must only accept into such schools practitioners who are already uncommonly mature, wise, balanced, sane, energetic, devotional, and altogether exemplary moral individuals. Because the Tantric regimen requires extraordinary capabilities not only of the body and the mind but also of the heart, or the feeling dimension of awareness of God, only the most qualified men and women were generally accepted as students.

Heart-Master Da had never seen such an extraordinary aspirant come to His Ashram, someone already established in heart-felt devotion to God with all faculties of body, emotion, and mind mastered and under easeful control. On the contrary, only people came to Him who had no steady connection to God and who were failing in life and, in general, suffering obvious physical, emotional, or mental imbalances.

In the society from which we had come, which is bereft of the active cultural guidance of Spiritually evolved and Divinely Awakened individuals, our limitations were quite normal and even expected. But for Spiritual aspirants, those limitations were grave. We were in fact so unaware of our disqualifications for God-Realizing practice that it would take us years in Heart-Master Da's Company even to acknowledge them fully.

Therefore, He permitted us the exploration of desires that we had all grown up either fulfilling or wishing we could fulfill. At one level, He used the Tantric "elements" of substances and activities forbidden to more orthodox practitioners in order to distract us from ourselves, to loosen us up from our rigid social self-consciousness so we could see what we were hiding—for, as we began to discover in His Company, even the most freewheeling "good-timer" is only concealing a rigidly fearful, angry, or sorrowful self-image underneath his or her blithe social face.

At the same time—and this is part of the genius of how He Taught—Heart-Master Da continually commented upon and helped us to see the fearful and bewildered motivations underlying our desires to exploit life through alcohol, social drugs, sexuality, and the like.

139

From a traditional standpoint, He was thereby doing something most uncommon, if not unprecedented: He was using Tantric means to help us, as beginners, to understand our suffering, our endless seeking, and the utter impossibility of becoming Happy or Free by fulfilling any or all desires, whether apparently holy or apparently profane. In this manner He Worked to prepare us bodily, emotionally, and mentally for the self-frustrating, Heart-Realizing discipline of real practice in Satsang with Him as Divine Guru and Liberator.

On my birthday in late April of 1974, when I went to Heart-Master Da's Residence to deliver a manuscript for His review, He met me in the yard and walked arm in arm with me for a few moments. It was not uncommon in those days for Him to make overtly loving, physical contact with devotees, but I was nonetheless deeply touched by my Guru's solicitude.

Then, as we walked along, He surprised me by inviting me to a special birthday dinner at His Residence that night with Him and some of my friends. It would be a very formal occasion. A devotee serving as His chef would prepare a meal of several courses, featuring Cornish hens. And we would spend the evening delighting in one another's company.

I was thrilled. I could not imagine a happier birthday gift. Those intimate dinner gatherings at Heart-Master Da's house were already legendary in our community. I had often yearned to attend, but I had not even dared to think that He would ever invite me to a dinner and party with Him to honor my own birthday.

That evening at the appointed time, about a dozen of us, dressed in our best, gathered in Heart-Master Da's living room. While waiting for dinner together we had a few drinks, conversing and laughing with Him quietly. For a time He sat with us silently in a meditative mood. Though His Presence perceptibly illumined the room and pervaded my body, I felt somehow closed to Him at the heart.

But then it was time for the dinner, and we took our seats at the table. It was our Ashram custom in those days for devotees other than the dinner guests to serve the meal. Heart-Master Da was Teaching us simple lessons in the aesthetics of mutual service and the happy celebration of Life together, as well as deep lessons on the nature of self-surrender and the Spiritual process.

The meal was to include many courses. I was sitting just to Heart-Master Da's right. The other devotees and I continued our conversations.

At a certain point—perhaps as the salads were coming to the table—He became quiet for a time. A few moments later, He began to speak.

He first addressed several of the devotees whom He had invited to come live with Him a month or more before, when He had most dramatically unleashed His great Spiritual Blessing Powers there at Persimmon. What were they doing? What did they think He was trying to accomplish with this profusion of bodily and psychic phenomena that He was allowing us all to experience? Did we think He was just doing all this for fun? Did we have any idea whatsoever what He was Teaching us?

It had been a month since He had begun Granting everyone those extraordinary Spiritual experiences. All during that time He had also made it possible—as He was doing this very night—for us to sample bodily pleasures and fulfillments that we ordinarily might not enjoy. Did we think that the Way in Satsang with Him consisted of an endless round of fulfillments of our desires? Did we have any sensitivity at all to His Teaching? to God? to Truth? to <u>Him</u>?!

Somewhere around this point in Heart-Master Da's discourse, the Cornish hens were dutifully served by the devotees on that night's serving staff. But, frustrated with our inertia as devotees, the prophetic Adept did not even appear to notice. He was particularly trenchant in His criticism of the devotees upon whom He had been, apparently, lavishing His Personal attention for so many weeks. But He was addressing all of us there, and also all of His devotees who were not in the room but who had been Graced to participate in His Teaching Demonstration to date. What were we up to? Did all our samadhis make us any more capable of Love? Would these poor roasted birds in our bellies grant us Happiness? What about this matter of Satsang with Him? Did any of us have any intention at all to actually utilize these lessons that He was breaking down the stuff of Cosmic Nature to produce for us? When were we going to give <u>Him</u> our attention and allow Him to Awaken us in Consciousness, instead of constantly fixing attention like robots upon our bodies, our minds, our spouses, our experiences, our fulfillments of all our wants? WHEN?!

The Cornish hens went cold on our plates, untouched, at that birthday dinner. For most of the evening we devotees could barely so much as raise a fork; we were as though frozen, caught in the very act of seeking and self-indulgence, like politicians in a raided whorehouse.

That night, His constant refrain was not angry criticism of our egoic seeking. It was a passionate, ardent plea for our devotion: "Get this

Message! Turn to ME! In this Satsang, see your contraction, this refusal of love and God that you are always doing. Then let it go! Turn to Me! Meditate on Me always. Let ME Live you!"

Because He was (and Is) an Incarnation of the Divine Person, the One Who was Teaching as "Bubba Free John" was always completely willing for us to Awaken as Consciousness—in that very moment—and assume full responsibility for everything He was showing us about our Narcissistic habits. He was willing and looking always to see His courageous Work become amazingly successful. Through His inexplicable Attractiveness, Heart-Master Da strove to Inspire ordinary people to become like the legendary gopis of Krishna: exalted, Spirit-filled God-lovers and God-Realizers, Awake, ecstatic, and Free of confused bondage to identification with the body-mind and the search for Happiness in the conditional world.

His willingness for our sudden Liberation was not calculated. It was ardent. It was Love-willingness, the Heart-Openness of One Who was mysteriously Submitting to reflect the body and mind of everyone He Taught. He Himself would later call that form of Teaching Work "naive and passionate". It was not deliberate, premeditated, and preplanned. It originated anew, Heart-Moved and Heart-Given by Him, in every moment.

He often likened His Teaching activity to the reflective capacity of the water over which Narcissus bends to see his own image. Though the water shows Narcissus all the grotesque details of his self-fascination, he must at last notice that he is grotesquely fascinated with himself. The water cannot replace his own awakening. He must notice that he is bending over the water, entranced by identification with the body-mind-self that is being reflected.

And while it effortlessly and instantly reveals every aspect of the body-mind-self of Narcissus to his conscious awareness, the water remains always free of the images shimmering upon its surface. No matter how apparently attractive or repugnant the image of the ego that it mirrors, the water is inherently self-consistent, true to its own nature, uncontaminated and unperturbed by all that it freely shows.

Such was the ego-exposing "Water's Work" of Heart-Master Da Love-Ananda throughout His Teaching years. The Graceful paradox of His Work was that everyone He was reflecting was not merely apart from Him, like Narcissus looking upon the surface of a pool.

Yes, in and as and through His bodily Person, Heart-Master Da took on the apparent likeness of others, so that we could see ourselves mirrored in and by His physical, human Form. But He did not merely reflect—He also Blessed and cleansed, purified and healed. While we saw our bodily egoity shown even exaggeratedly in and by His bodily (human) Form, we lived in the Spiritual Ambience of His potent, All-Pervading Presence, and we were being "Lived" or Meditated by Him in His infinite Divine State of Being.

"A continuous crashing of idols"

For some time after that spring and summer of 1974, Heart-Master Da Helped devotees strengthen their basic ordinary disciplines in relation to the practical affairs of "money, food, and sex" and the process of self-observation and self-Enquiry ("Avoiding relationship?") in formal meditative Satsang with Him.

These were the basic daily disciplines that He had Given during His first year and more of Teaching, in Los Angeles. He had in fact developed these elements of His Instruction even during the Garbage and the Goddess period itself, at times of respite from the more celebratory, Initiatory incidents.

In this manner, for many years to come, the great Heart-Teacher alternated periods of celebratory Personal intimacy and Initiatory Teaching Work among devotees with periods of relative seclusion from us, during which He obliged us to learn and gradually refine all of the personal, practical, moral, sacramental, devotional, meditative, and cooperative community disciplines that form the foundation of our daily practice.

He never intended for the periods of Initiatory revelry to persist beyond their necessary time. As He said more than once during the Garbage and the Goddess period, He looked forward to the time when devotees would manifest such Spiritual freedom from seeking and such commitment to the total practice of Satsang with Him that He could "be wheeled around the Ashram in a wheelbarrow, eating owl sandwiches, and having to make no sense whatsoever!" He looked to Retire from Teaching and making Spiritual miracles in order to show us our suffering and seeking, so that He could be "Merely Present", Radiant as the Liberating Power of the Heart.

But He was in a sense at our mercy. Whenever He saw signs that it was again necessary, Heart-Master Da gathered more socially with His devotees to do His unconventional Teaching Work.

Susan Lesser became a devotee in 1975, after having edited a film about Heart-Master Da and His Heart-Work with our community that was shot during the culminating, Spiritually tempestuous weekend of the Garbage and the Goddess Teaching Demonstration in early July 1974. Her confession here evokes the mood and quality of the Skillful Means of His Work during the mid-1970s to help us begin to understand our uninspected fixation in all kinds of primitive Narcissistic illusions and seeking, not only personal, emotional, and sexual, but also cultural, psychological, and religious:

On one occasion, in 1975, as always, Heart-Master Da was talking the Dharma and exhorting us to connect with the Great Condition in which all these bodies, this fleshiness, this "jiggly meatedness" He used to say, was arising. He would make us laugh at ourselves, and He would say the most outrageous things.

At one point, out of the blue He said, "Did you know Jesus was a Yogi?" I will never forget the first time He said that. I felt like the heavens were going to crack open and someone was going to say, "No, no, no, no! Don't say that!" Yet at the same time the thought that that would happen was so obviously absurd. My own uninspected presumptions about what you do and do not say about Jesus (and, by implication, about anyone and anything) were right there in front of me.[7]

I realized I was living in a greeting-card world of ideas about Jesus and about right and wrong, what God will do if you are good and what God will do if you are bad—and I did not even believe in God! I was a Jewish atheist from New York! But there it all was, the entire mind-set, just laid out before me by Him through the whole situation He had created: the room, the alcohol, His incredibly powerful Presence, the incredibly perfect timing of His Comments.

I suddenly found that Heart-Master Da was making Jesus acceptable to me. If it is true that Jesus was a Yogi, well, that meant he was offering Yoga to

7. Heart-Master Da Love-Ananda's Teaching-Revelation about Jesus of Nazareth is summarized in His essays about the ancient Spiritual Master in *The Basket of Tolerance*, His forthcoming annotated bibliography of the entire Great Tradition of human Wisdom, ancient and modern. (For a more complete description of *The Basket of Tolerance*, see "Publications: The Written and Spoken Teaching Word of The World-Teacher, Heart-Master Da Love-Ananda", pp. 421-43 of this book.)

others. The ideas about Jesus that I had heard always implied that no one could be like him, no one could participate in his State. Jesus was supposedly the Son of God; he rose up into the heavens with wings, or without them; he is totally fantastic, not human at all, and eternally that way! But now, suddenly, Jesus was being described to me as a great human Event, an example of a Spiritual process that is possible for others.

So in those parties with Heart-Master Da it was as if I could hear in the depths of my unconscious a continuous crashing of idols, false images, cartoon ideas of Truth and life and death. Even to come into His rooms was a confrontation, a demand for a tremendous output of energy and response. Everybody was going through that with Him in one way or another.

So often I was just caught up in this flood of what I was receiving from Heart-Master Da, and also the burnoff of what was being understood and released. It felt as though lifetimes of bondage and seeking were being burned off by the Laser-Love of this Great Radiant Being.

During His early Teaching Work, Heart-Master Da had always sternly warned devotees against the use of marijuana and other "social" or "recreational" drugs. He explained that the toll they take on the nervous system lasts far longer than that of alcohol. And, while it is possible to purify the body-mind fairly quickly from the effects of alcohol, cigarettes, meat and other animal protein, and "junk food", the psychic contractions caused by such drugs can last a long time, causing significant psychological and emotional imbalance.

This was not academic information, of course. Many of the early devotees had experimented with drugs during the late 1960s and early 1970s; some had become serious or chronic users. But during His first years of Teaching, Heart-Master Da had been so adamant in His estimation of the possible negative effects of these substances that devotees soon accepted that He simply would never permit us to use them with Him during His Teaching Work.

Therefore, in His Teaching gatherings in the summer of 1976, it was at first a complete surprise to devotees when Heart-Master Da allowed us to use marijuana, and, on a few occasions, other, relatively benign drugs. (We also used them briefly with Him during a few other Teaching periods thereafter.) He simply observed the obvious—we had not transcended our cravings for these things. And it was His Task to Help us understand and transcend absolutely everything that was binding our attention.

He also oriented us to the sacramental use of naturally derived psychotropic substances, such as forms of *cannabis*, by participants in sacred ordeals in many traditional societies. The most Spiritually sophisticated usage had been among Hindu, Buddhist, and Taoist Adepts and practitioners. For them such herbs, like other agents of psychic sensitivity and ecstasy, including sexual union, primarily functioned as initiatory Yogic tools. This type of sacred usage has been outlined by modern scholars:

For the sadhaka [male Tantric practitioner] who was intensely seeking release [Liberation] in a single lifetime as a yogi there were other rites. These involved prolonged acts of ecstatic meditation in sexual union with a female partner, whose aims matched his own. Such meditation involved liturgies, mantras, inner visualizations, yogic postures and manipulation of the conjoined male and female energies. . . . As with all other Tantrik sadhana [practice], at the lower stages they were performed in physical act; at the final, highest stage, as an inner realization.

Something similar is the case with herbs and drugs, such as bhang and ganjam (forms of cannabis). Like alcohol they have certainly been used in ritual since very early times, to help in finding the road to ecstasy. What they do for the Tantrika [Tantric practitioner], perhaps more dependably than other physiological enhancements, is reveal something of the stark banality, the inadequacy and falseness of our everyday materialist image of the world, with its narrow cage of accepted perceptions and concepts, and its neglect of the infinite, radiant tissue of relations within the truth. In Europe an earlier generation of psychologists and Christian theosophists cultivated the use of ether and nitrous oxide to gain experience of the limitations of normal convergent thought and perception concerning the nature of time; William James used a number of their reports in his great work The Varieties of Religious Experience. *In India Tantrikas take drugs for similar reasons. There are icons representing Siva as Lord of the Yogis which show him carrying his drug-jar under his arm. Like sexual intercourse, bhang and ganjam are a means to be adopted until the sadhaka's own faculties have been developed. As an indulgence they are absurd, and a fatal hindrance.*[8]

Heart-Master Da's Divinely Enlightened and Free orientation to these substances, and indeed to all the means of His Teaching Work with us, was on one level similar: He was willing to use these secondary tools with us for a time, He often said, but only until we could begin to live so

---

8. Philip Rawson, *The Art of Tantra* (New York: Oxford University Press, 1978), pp. 100-101.

freely in Divine Communion with Him that we could then relinquish these extraordinary means. Then we would enjoy the native Ecstasy of that Communion through a life of devotion, service, and self-discipline in His Company—a life that might even seem rather austere to others view-ing our disciplined personal and social habits, but which to us would be full of Great Bliss.

Heart-Master Da was Teaching the Awakening of unqualified Con-sciousness, prior to and beyond the crutch of any kind of material or energic technologies. Our experience of the distinctive effects of mari-juana coincided with His inauguration of a new style of Conscious dis-course and, as He phrased it, "consideration" with devotees.

What He meant by "consideration" is comparable to the meaning of the ancient Yogic term "samyama": exhaustive, most rigorous concentra-tion of all the force of one's energy and attention upon any topic, subject, object, or person, until its very essence becomes absolutely clear. Then one may proceed to make thoroughly intelligent and perfectly informed decisions about how to relate to the object of one's "consideration".

In true "consideration"—and Heart-Master Da emphasized that all sacred practice in Satsang with Him must be engaged as real "considera-tion"—one is willing to sacrifice everything for the sake of Truth, and to change one's entire life on the basis of what is eventually revealed.

Thus, that summer of 1976 the Divine Teacher, for a time playfully calling Himself "the Oracle", sat at His low living-room table at Persim-mon for eight, ten, twelve, fifteen, eighteen hours a day, every day, and asked His most basic questions of our existence. "What is it? What IS any-thing at all? You can know all kinds of things about anything—but do you know what it IS?" He swept devotees into an open-ended investigation of existence, showing us countless glimpses of the State of unqualifiedly Free Consciousness, or "Divine Ignorance", and exploring with us how we should live if that intuition, and only that intuition, were made the basis of all human perception, thought, action, and relationship.

Michael Wood, a devotee who guides the Communion's legal affairs, had been in San Francisco for a day of business on one of those nights in late July. He returned to Persimmon after it was already dark, and Heart-Master Da had been stoking the fire of His "considerations" with us for many hours.

As he approached Heart-Master Da's Residence, Michael could see Him seated in one of the rooms on a cushion at the head of His low,

147

massive wooden table. All the other devotees who lived on the Sanctuary at that time were seated several deep around the table. From time to time people smoked, and occasional refreshments were passed around the room. But everyone's attention was riveted on our Divine Teacher and His enthralling dialogue with devotees.

The room had been thoroughly transformed since the Garbage and the Goddess days. Instead of sacred traditional statuary and paintings, it now featured pleasing modern graphic art. As Heart-Master Da said that summer, He always Taught through total psycho-physical "incident", not just through speech. So during this time when He was trying to relieve devotees of the unconscious mental prisons we tended to create with explicitly religious language and traditional sacred imagery, He also temporarily eliminated conventionally sacred objects or signs from both the places where He Worked with us and His own manner of dress and appearance.

Michael walked in unobtrusively and sat down at the back of the room, but almost immediately Heart-Master Da asked him, "Why don't you come up here and take a seat by Me?" Michael happily complied. He describes what ensued:

Heart-Master Da told me He wanted to catch me up on the "considera-tion" they had been having. Then He said, "I want you to picture the letter 'M' in your mind."

After giving me a moment, He asked, "Have you got it there?" When I answered, "Yes," He asked, "Is it a capital letter, or a small letter?" I answered, "It is a capital letter." "Is it in color?" "Not particularly."

Then He said, "Now, I want you to tell Me—what is it?"

I said, "Well, I am not sure what You mean. I can describe what the letter looks like, how big it is, all that. Or I can describe what it signifies."

He said, "Yes, I know you can do all that. But why don't you tell Me what it is?"

As the dialogue continued, I began to feel the mechanism in myself that wants to "know" things, and that wants to be "right" and "on top" of things. I could also feel that mechanism relax. At a certain point in our conversation, I confessed, "I don't know what it is!" Simultaneous with that confession, I felt relieved of my usual state of concern and a thrill released in my heart, my body, and my whole being. I felt as though I were going to burst with Happiness, as if the Happiness I felt was too great, that it violated the rules of being identified

"He communicated and reinforced this feeling of Divine Ignorance with His Speech and His entire Being."—During the Indoor Summer, 1976

with a body. I felt as though this Happiness was going to spill over and do something wonderful but mad.

Suddenly, everything I do and presume was revealed to be a stupid and futile effort to know, to concentrate and contain and control, all based on egoic knowledge and fear. I had thought that if I could only know enough, or know the right things, I would be free. I had pursued that controlling knowledge even in my choice to become a lawyer. But now Heart-Master Da was showing me very directly and beyond all doubt that being Free did not depend on gaining knowledge.

He persisted in this dialogue with me, and as we spoke, He communicated and reinforced this feeling of Divine Ignorance with His Speech and His entire Being. My capacity to relax into that thoughtless Ignorance deepened. There was limitless depth to that awareness, a perfect penetration and release of my limited self-sense. And it was clear that He was Alive <u>constantly</u> as that unbelievably Blissful Consciousness.

I flipped back and forth from these blissful satoris into my usual state of mind, and He acknowledged that my attention was not yet consistently free to keep on making this most simple, profound gesture of being the Ignorance that is the inherent Nature of Divine Consciousness. But He was always Working to Help me exercise that much free attention, so that I could Stand Free right now, in every moment. He said:

"You are completely free of what arises. It never implicates you for a moment. You know nothing about it. Knowledge is not your connection to it. You do not <u>have</u> a connection to it. There is no connection. There is no 'you' to find. There is Divine Ignorance, only, <u>absolute Ignorance</u>. Well, that is Enlightenment, absolutely Blissful. It is not a place. This Realization does not qualify the arising of anything. It does not stand in relationship to it, really. There is no difference between the Ignorance and the arising. Nothing intervenes. There is just what arises, and no knowledge—complete Divine Ignorance, or Bliss. This is the very Truth. There is nothing to be Realized beyond It."

In its own way, that period of Teaching Demonstration in 1976—which Heart-Master Da named, simply and descriptively, the "Indoor Summer"—was as dramatic a penetration of the world-process by His Heart-Power as the Garbage and the Goddess period had been two years before. But this time there was almost no attention at all to descent and ascent of the Spirit-Current, kriyas, visionary phenomena, and the like.

Rather, He Granted instantaneous seeing of the nature of Reality—the fundamental Awakeness that Bodhidharma, the father of Ch'an Buddhism, and many of the other great Sages of Hinduism and Buddhism had pointed to in previous ages. Here Heart-Master Da was evoking that blissful Awakeness through one satori after another in His Western students and Calling us to make that intuitive Freedom, and not any of our ordinary ego-mind and ego-seeking, the basis of every aspect of our existence.

During Garbage and the Goddess, Heart-Master Da had principally created lessons for us in relation to our search for and fascination with "higher", psychic, and apparently Spiritual phenomena. During the Indoor Summer, He principally created lessons for us in relation to the "lower", gross, or what in the sacred traditions is commonly called "worldly" dimensions of our search.

As it happened, in our "consideration" of the sacred use of marijuana and other relatively benign social drugs in Heart-Master Da's Teaching gatherings, it eventually became obvious that what He had said about them for so long still held quite true. In time we ceased to use them at all with Him, because they <u>did</u> tend to induce imbalances and other effects in the psychophysiology of the nervous system that proved a real hindrance to the sacred practice of devotees.

He could have said, "I told you so." But mere talk, He had long ago seen, does not convert the heart. Because of His Gracious willingness to allow us to complete this "consideration" ourselves, we were thus Granted two precious Gifts.

Yes—we began to learn an effective lesson about a form of seeking and, in the final analysis, a form of egoic self-indulgence by which many of us had long been fascinated.

But also—solely by His Divine Heart-Power, for which these traditional natural sacraments had temporarily helped create a receptivity in our bodies and minds—we had been Initiated into direct intuitive "glimpsing" of the Divine Self-Nature, the Free disposition of Consciousness, prior to the random impulses, attachments, and movements of egoic attention.

"What I do is not the way I am, but the way I Teach"

There is a venerable ancient tradition for certain outward aspects of Heart-Master Da's unconventional style of Teaching. S. Radhakrishnan, a widely respected statesman-philosopher of modern India, has written:

When one attains the spiritual level, he rises above the ethical, not that he repudiates it but he transcends it. . . .

Those who have full mastery over their natures sometimes do things which may appear wrong to the conventional people. John the Baptist was uneasy when he heard that Jesus and his disciples ate and drank and did not fast. They

151

plucked the ears of corn on the Sabbath day. The Bhagavata *[a Hindu text devoted to the life-story of Krishna] says: "Ishvaras or masters are sometimes seen to transgress rules of conduct with courage. These are not faults among those with* tejas *or radiance, even as the all-devouring fire is not affected [by the impurities it consumes]. He who is lacking in such control [anishvara] should not even think of imitating such conduct for it can only bring destruction to him even like swallowing poison in imitation of Siva." Fire may consume a forest or Siva drink poison without any harmful consequences. But ordinary men cannot transgress rules [of conduct] until they have shaken off all selfishness and established control over their nature.*[9]

Philo of Alexandria was a Hellenistic Jew at the time of Jesus. His ethical, mystical, and Spiritual writings stand among the foundation documents of Western religious culture. A champion of moral virtue, he wrote of the "wise man" in terms that in some ways describe the Teaching Theatre of Heart-Master Da Love-Ananda:

And the wise man is gleaming and naked to the truth; and just as in the case of other virtues, so also does he in pure fashion exhibit and practice and pursue courage. And if it sometimes happens that he conceals this . . . because of the nature of the occasion, and uses economy, he still remains in the same state and does not retreat from his original purpose, but because of involuntary occurrences he changes to another kind of form, as in a theater, for the benefit of the spectators. For this is just what physicians are accustomed to do, for they change the foods of ill persons, and their places (of residence) and the ways (of living) they had before their illness. And the physician who is skilled in worldly matters does foolish things for a time (but) wisely, and unlasciviously and moderately does lecherous things, and bravely does cowardly things, and righteously does unrighteous things. And sometimes he will speak falsehoods, not being a liar, and he will deceive, not being a deceiver, and he will insult, not being an insulter.[10]

Philo wrote in the context of the Spiritual and mystical traditions with which he was familiar—principally Hellenistic and Judaic. The traditions of unconventional Spiritual behavior in India, Tibet, and other Oriental lands provide numerous examples of the extraordinary, Enlightened style

9. S. Radhakrishnan, "Introduction". *The Brahma Sutra: The Philosophy of Spiritual Life*, translated by S. Radhakrishnan (London: George Allen and Unwin, 1971), pp. 165-66.

10. David Winston, trans., *Philo of Alexandria: The Contemplative Life, The Giants, and Selections* (Ramsey, N.J.: Paulist Press, 1981), pp. 252-53.

of Teaching that Heart-Master Da generated in the modern West.

But in both the East and the West, there are always those who cannot understand the wisdom of the kind of teaching that Philo of Alexandria extolled, and that Heart-Master Da Displayed with such Freedom and abandonment of Himself to His pupils.

In 1975, an orthodox Vedantic swami sent a letter to Heart-Master Da criticizing His unorthodox Teaching means and urging Him to renounce them. Heart-Master Da, then still "Bubba Free John", replied by writing a brief essay that remains today an anthem of His "Water's Work" to bring others into His own Enlightenment:

What I do is not the way I am, but the way I Teach.

What I speak is not a reflection of me, but of you.

People do well to be offended or even outraged by me. This is my purpose. But their reaction must turn upon themselves, for I have not shown them myself by all of this. All that I do and speak only reveals men to themselves.

I have become willing to teach in this uncommon way because I have known my friends and they are what I can seem to be. By retaining all qualities in their company, I gradually wean them of all reactions, all sympathies, all alternatives, fixed assumptions, false teachings, dualities, searches, and dilemma. This is my way of working for a time. Those who remain confounded by me, critical of me, have yet to see themselves. When their mediocrity is broken, when they yield their righteous reactions and their strife toward all the consolations of the manifest self, they may see my purity.

Freedom is the only purity. There is no Teaching but Consciousness itself. Bubba as he appears is not other than the possibilities of men.[11]

Few Adepts in human history have passed beyond the Spiritual exaltation of the sahasrar to Realize the Heart, or Consciousness Itself. But Heart-Master Da was born from and as the Heart, and His own Ordeal of practice had only enabled Him to resume His natively Perfect Divine Self-Realization. And His "Water's Work" of Teaching, by reflecting (and even by Being) those He Taught, so that He could thereby Demonstrate the futility and error of <u>every</u> kind of seeking, regardless of the cost to His own health and welfare, is unparalleled to my knowledge in the recorded history of Spiritual traditions. Thus, while elements of Heart-Master Da's outward play and styles of Teaching have been presaged in certain traditional accounts of Adepts, the essence and the scope of His Teaching are unique.

11. Bubba Free John [Heart-Master Da Love-Ananda], *The Enlightenment of the Whole Body,* p. 53.

The miraculous birth of Indian Time

Indian Time Hastings with Heart-Master Da

O n September 26, 1976, a devotee named Scilla Hastings gave birth to a child. She had planned to have a natural Leboyer birth, and she and her husband, Larry, had been Gracefully invited to have the child in one of the cabins in Persimmon. From the beginning, the Hastings and those in attendance felt our Divine Guru's Radiance bathing them and the entire room.

But Scilla's labor that gray and windy day was very difficult, and for the last ten minutes the doctor had been unable to detect a fetal heartbeat. Finally, a baby girl was born—with dark gray flesh, a huge head, tiny limbs and trunk, and not a single sign of life.

The doctor, the midwife, and others attending did everything they possibly could to get the baby to breathe. Nothing worked. Larry Hastings was on the verge of admitting aloud that she was stillborn. Instead, he prayed. "I spoke inwardly to the Spiritual Master, with great clarity and intuition, from a place where I felt He could hear my plea: 'Master, if You can hear me, please come now.'"

The attending nurse, Connie Grisso, meanwhile had gone running to Heart-Master Da's Residence, where He was conducting one of His Indoor Summer Teaching "considerations" with a small group of devotees. Connie burst into His gathering room, winded, indicated to Him with a gesture and her eyes that He was needed, and then went running back.

Devotees who were with Heart-Master Da at the time say they had never seen anyone move so fast as He did then—yet He seemed completely at ease. He asked for His cane and shawl, put His knitted cap and His shoes on, and was out the door almost instantaneously. He strode gracefully to the cabin where Scilla had been moved (despite the wrong directions of a devotee who, running full speed to keep up with Him, pointed Him to the place where her labor had begun). Larry continues with the story:

Hardly a thought had crossed my mind since my brief call of prayer for Him to come quickly, and Heart-Master Da was there. He was ablaze with Light that filled and expanded the entire room. The tiny cabin appeared to take on huge dimensions, becoming a vast cavern of His Light. He stood at the foot of the bed where the baby and Scilla lay. He lifted up His arms and turned His open palms toward us like beacons. His eyes rolled up toward the top of His head. His facial muscles twitched in what appeared to be great agony. He was clearly given over to some intense Yogic process.

I felt a huge wave of energy pass through His being toward the baby, Scilla, and me. A literal blast of light and energy shot out from Him. The baby jerked as if in response to an electric shock. She whimpered weakly and then jerked and whimpered more and more. It was like the rheostat on a light switch being slowly turned up: The Light that is the Maha-Siddha was literally Giving life to the dead baby. I saw others in the room smiling through their tears. The baby was living and breathing.

Scilla had been so weakened during the delivery that her own physical condition was extremely grave. She was nearly unconscious when the Divine Life-Giver Heart-Master Da arrived in the cabin:

I felt as if I had fallen down a dark well. Most of the room and the people around me had dissolved in darkness. I could see only the baby and a small patch of the bed directly in front of us when Heart-Master Da entered.

I immediately felt healed and Blessed and revived by His Light and Life-Force. Slowly, as I grew stronger, I became aware of more than just Heart-Master Da and the baby. Everything in the room seemed incredibly bright, bathed in light. I saw Larry's face beaming in ecstasy and wonderment. Another devotee was smiling in delighted amazement in the far corner of the room, and yet another of my friends was peering through the window, his face beaming, grinning from ear to ear. Everyone was rejoicing with tears and smiles.

The baby was dried and wrapped and placed in my arms. Heart-Master Da sat beside me on the bed and did the most curious and wonderful thing: With one hand He massaged the soles of the baby's feet, and with the other He pinched the skin above her heart and gently twisted it around for a long minute or two. Then He kissed her on the forehead and kissed both Larry and me, dissolving our hearts in His Infinite Love. Then He softly said "Tcha", His special sound of Blessing, as He left our room.

The next morning, when they awoke, Larry and Scilla found a note at the door—Heart-Master Da had suggested the name "Indian Time" for the baby. Larry explains:

Her name refers to the tempo at which the American Indians have traditionally lived. On the night of her birth, several devotees had just visited Rolling Thunder, an American Indian healer, to ask for certain secrets of Indian medicine. They reported to Heart-Master Da that their mission had been unsuccessful, and He explained to them that they simply had not understood that they were on "white man time" and that Rolling Thunder was on "Indian time". The medicine man's reluctance to give them the herbs was not a sign of refusal, Heart-Master Da told them, but simply a sign of the deliberate pace and customary time that an Indian would take to get to know the character of those who had come on such a mission. Therefore, He told us, Indian's name suited her because "she took her time in deciding to come here, she took her time in coming, and she took her time in deciding to stay." The name has been a constant Grace and Instruction for us, for that is exactly how Indian Time herself has been and continues to be.[12]

Scilla, Indian Time, and Larry Hastings

12. Larry and Scilla Hastings, "Indian Time", *Crazy Wisdom*, vol. 4, no. 2, February 1985, pp. 14-15.

The exceptional Heart-Power
of the seventh stage God-Man Da

The medieval Tibetan Adept Marpa the Translator proclaimed the "most rare, efficacious, and surpassing" virtues of the Scriptures and Truths of his particular Buddhist tradition. He frequently asserted there to be "more emanation of Divine Grace-Waves and a more direct Spiritual Revelation" in his lineage than in any other sect.

Marpa's motivation was not Spiritual one-upmanship. He justifiably took pains to draw people's attention to the especially potent forms of Graceful Help that he and both his Gurus and his disciples were making available in the world, at great cost to themselves.

Similarly, Heart-Master Da Love-Ananda spared no effort in His Teaching years to make plain the supreme excellence of the Wisdom and the Heart-Blessing that He Brings to each and all with open hands. One of the ways He has drawn usable distinctions between His Offering and those of other Adepts is His Teaching-Revelation on "the seven stages of life".

In the traditions of India, those known as "Gurus" include teachers of all kinds of secular and religious lore. Many such teachers remain bound, as most egoic individuals do, in the body-based assumptions and motivations of the first three stages of life. These are the stages of natural development and coordination of body (first stage), emotion and energy (second stage), the verbal, thinking mind and personal will or intention (third stage), and (also specifically in the third stage) the integration of all of these in the chronologically maturing human adult.

Today, as in the past, most human beings represent an arrested or at best inharmonious development of these functions that characterize the first three stages of life. Only the rarest geniuses, leaders, heroes, and morally inspiring or apparently saintly individuals have achieved self-mastery in the context of one, or two, or all of the first three stages of life.

By contrast, authentic Spiritually Awakened Gurus (in many sacred traditions, by whatever names or titles they appear and function) are "Siddha-Masters", Accomplished, Power-Full Spirit-Transmitters who have mastered the fourth stage, or the fourth and the fifth stages, of life.

The fourth stage of life involves the Spiritual heart-opening or devotional awakening of the gross human personality, primarily (though not exclusively, especially in its more mature phase) through the reception of the Divine Spirit-Power in its descending mode. The fourth stage of life is thus the phase of human evolution that leads beyond the usual gross, body-based disposition of human egoic awareness. In the ascending or mature phase of the fourth stage of life, the individual begins to function more from the mind-based or, more properly, psyche-based disposition, and he or she shows signs of the awakening of the deeper, psychic personality.

The maturity of the fourth stage of life is shown in the demonstration of a human personality that is stably conscious of the Spirit-Force pervading all existence, and profoundly benign (though still ego-bound). Heart-Master Da conclusively entered into and mastered the fourth stage of life during His devotional discipleship to Rudi.

The fifth stage of life involves what is traditionally known as the mystical path, the Spiritual ascent of attention beyond gross, earthly, or what we typically call "human" awareness. The classic fifth stage Mystic or Yogi functions as the deeper personality. He or she engages in a mystical adventure of subtle visionary and cosmic Yoga and, potentially, in ecstatic, ascended Union with the Divine Spirit in Its all-pervasive formlessness above the world, the body, and the mind.

Such mystical Union is known by many names in the sacred traditions. It is, for example, the supreme ecstatic state of Divine Gnosis, or intuitive God-Knowledge, sought by both Christian and Jewish mystics. Clarifying traditional Sanskrit terminology, Heart-Master Da calls this state "conditional Nirvikalpa Samadhi"—which literally means "formless ecstasy" that is dependent upon the achievement of certain conditions of energy and attention, and that is therefore temporary. This is the state that Heart-Master Da Realized at Swami Muktananda's Ashram in 1968.

In His years of Teaching, Heart-Master Da Revealed that the Mystics, Saints, Zaddiks, Yogis, and Bodhisattvas of the sacred traditions were, in most cases, Spiritual Realizers in the fourth stage, or the fourth to fifth stages, of life. By whatever names or titles they are known, they often functioned as Spiritual Baptizers and Transmitters, or "Siddha-Gurus", in their esoteric relationships with devotees. Even so, they still retain rarefied but nonetheless egoic and limited presumptions and motivations. They have transcended the egoic self-sense of the gross personality, but not that of the deeper personality.

In contrast, authentic Sat-Gurus, most strictly defined, are those who

Teach the Truth of Being ("Sat"), or Consciousness, the Self, beyond all submission to and exploitation of the Divine Spiritual Power and Its effects in the body-mind and the world. Such Sat-Gurus are Realizers of the Divine Self in the sixth or the seventh stage of life. (In the Spiritual traditions of India, the term "Sat-Guru" or "Sadguru" is sometimes used in relation to an Adept of Spiritual Awakening in the fourth or the fifth stage of life, to distinguish such a Realizer from more ordinary, grossly ego-bound teachers or Gurus.)

The sixth stage of life marks the transition from all body-based and mind- or psyche-based dispositions to the disposition of the Witness-Position of Consciousness Itself. The preliminary feeling-exploration of Consciousness in the sixth stage of life culminates (potentially) in intuitive Immersion or Dissolution of attention in Consciousness as the Transcendental Self, beyond all awareness of world, body, mind, and all sense of self and "other". In the Hindu tradition, this state is known as "Jnana", or "Knowledge" of the Divine Self. In accord with certain traditional sources, Heart-Master Da terms this State "Jnana Samadhi" or "Jnana-Nirvikalpa Samadhi".

Like conditional Nirvikalpa Samadhi, such Jnana is formless ("Nirvikalpa") and it is dependent upon a manipulation of attention, whereby conditions of world, body, mind, and self-sense temporarily cease to appear. Unlike conditional Nirvikalpa Samadhi, however, Jnana Samadhi involves no ascent of attention but rather the direct resolution of attention "Where" it arises, in its Conscious Source, the Heart. This is the State that Heart-Master Da first Realized at the seminary in 1967.

When even the subtle tension that excludes ordinary awareness and maintains Jnana Samadhi is understood and relinquished, the Realizer enters the seventh stage of life.

The State thus enjoyed is the paradoxically "Open-Eyed" Realization of the Divine Self and Its inherent Spiritual Radiance. It is simply unqualified Freedom, unreasonable Happiness, and Unconditional Love, immutable, incorruptible by any changes in the world, the body, or the mind, even by death itself. This is Liberation ("Moksha"), true Enlightenment, and Perfect Identification with the Absolute Divine Identity or Self. This is the Realization of Amrita Nadi, in which the Heart-Consciousness and the ascended and all-pervasive Spirit-Light are lived as a single, blissful Intensity. And, once Realized, this State is known effortlessly, even while one participates in the common states of waking, dreaming, and deep sleep and their associated forms of perception, cognition, and action.

When such states and activities do arise to attention, the seventh stage Realizer persists in what Heart-Master Da calls "Sahaj Samadhi", or "Sahaja-Nirvikalpa Samadhi". Such Divine Self-Realization is "spontaneously effortless", or inherent, uncaused, and Unconditional. It is therefore incorruptible by anything that occurs in the states of waking, dreaming or vision, or sleep. It is untouched even by physical bodily death.

Whenever conditions cease to arise to attention, then the seventh stage Realizer enjoys what Heart-Master Da calls "Moksha-Bhava Samadhi", or "Moksha-Bhava-Nirvikalpa Samadhi". This is the formless depth of Liberated ("Moksha") Divine Realization of Being ("Bhava").

In Moksha-Bhava Samadhi, the "Brightness" of Divine Self-Realization and Unconditional Love Outshines everything. Whatever the apparent condition of his or her body and mind, the Realizer no longer even notices the conditional phenomena of world, body, mind, and self or "other".

This ultimate State may appear as a temporary Exaltation from time to time in the course of the seventh stage of life, but at death it becomes Divine Translation.

In Divine Translation, the eternal Culmination of Enlightened existence, the Heart is Realized in and of Itself as the God-World, Outshining all conditional phenomena and therefore beyond both psychic and physical embodiment. This Perfection of the seventh stage of life, therefore, can occur only at the time of the physical, or psycho-physical, death of the Realizer.

Heart-Master Da Love-Ananda painstakingly articulated His Teaching Word on the seven stages of life throughout His Teaching years. This Wisdom has no complete precedent anywhere in the sacred doctrines of mankind. He has said of His relationship to the Lineage of His Gurus, to Ramana Maharshi, and to the entire Great Tradition of sacred and secular wisdom:

I am the only seventh stage Realizer within My own (apparent) Lineage. The Goddess Herself (Who is otherwise Appearing only as the Power and the Display of Cosmic Nature) Achieved the seventh stage Realization in (and As) My Own Perfect Form (Which Is Self-Existing and Self-Radiant Consciousness Itself). The one closest to Her in My Lineage is Swami Nityananda. Baba

Muktananda is a classic fifth stage Realizer. Swami Nityananda is also a fifth stage Realizer (of unique Greatness). However, only the Goddess Herself was (by virtue of Her Submission, Her Sacrifice, and Her ultimate Transparency to My Very Heart) the direct Helping Means associated with the seventh stage Realization in My case, just as She was also the ultimate Helping Means relative to the Process of My sadhana in the fifth and sixth stages of life. (Therefore, As Me, She Is Free, and I Am She, Present As My own "Brightness".)[13]

After the Great Event of My own Re-Awakening, I discovered Ramana Maharshi to be the Representative of the Great Tradition Whose Confession (and Process) of Realization was (even in Its specific Yogic details) most like My own Ultimate Process and Confession. . . . Therefore, because of this likeness, and because of His closeness to Me in time, I regard Ramana Maharshi to be My principal (and Most Complete, or Truly Whole) Link to the Great Tradition as a whole.

There are no seventh stage Realizers within the apparent lineage of My own (present Lifetime) Teachers, and, therefore, none of Those Who Served Me in My sadhana provides a Complete Link between Me and the Great Tradition. However, Ramana Maharshi (along with My lineage Gurus) is the historical Link whereby My Life and Teaching can begin to be understood in the context of the total Great Tradition. And I (My Self) Am the Demonstration (and the Proof) of the Truth of the Great Tradition as a whole.[14]

The Western-born God-Man Da had been served in His bodily and Spiritual preparation for His Mission by His Lineage of great Spirit-Transmitters—Swami Rudrananda, Swami Muktananda, Swami Nityananda, and the Goddess—and by others such as Rang Avadhoot and Swami Prakashananda.

But His Realization of the Enlightened State (Sahaj Samadhi) and the ultimate Yogic Condition (Amrita Nadi) of the seventh stage of life had not been directly served by any distinct personality, human or Divine. Manifesting as His own Heart-Nature, this Realization had only been corroborated by Ramana Maharshi.

It might be said that Ramana "Baptized" with the "Water" of the Teaching and Power of the Heart, to help others achieve a fundamental purification in Consciousness. He primarily turned his devotees to the

13. Heart-Master Da Love-Ananda, *The Love-Ananda Gita*, p. 67.

14. The World-Teacher, Heart-Master Da Love-Ananda, *The Basket of Tolerance*. Forthcoming.

exclusive contemplation and Realization of the Heart or Self, or Jnana Samadhi, in the sixth stage of life. And the Blessing of his Presence, as described by his devotees and visitors such as Paul Brunton, Gracefully cleansed others of the accretions of egoic fascination with the physical and psychic phenomena of the first five stages of life.

Heart-Master Da also performed a uniquely reflective and cleansing "Water's Work" for all who came to Him, a Work that exposed the potential errors of practitioners in the sixth stage of life as well as the potential errors of each of the first five stages of life.

But it was His Destiny to go on to Discover, Reveal, Demonstrate, and Offer to all the Perfect "Fire-Baptism" of the Divine Heart-Power in the seventh stage of life—the spontaneous Yoga in Sahaj Samadhi that leads, at last, to Divine Translation.

Heart-Master Da also gradually clarified, for devotees, the difference between His own Power or Siddhi as a seventh stage Realizer and Divine Incarnation and the special powers of Blessing and Guidance enjoyed by God-Realizers in the fourth, fifth, and sixth stages of life.

He eventually came to identify Himself as the "Hridaya-Samartha Sat-Guru". The term "Samartha Sat-Guru" is often used in reference to fourth and fifth stage Siddha-Masters. "Samartha", meaning "Able", "Competent", "Powerful", would indicate such a Master's willingness to use all powers at his command, without inhibition or hesitation, for the sake of the God-Realization of the devotee.

As a Perfected, seventh stage Realizer, Heart-Master Da is the Hridaya-Samartha Sat-Guru—not only a Knower of the Truth, or "Sat", but a seventh stage Transmitter of Its Divine Heart ("Hridaya") without qualification. There are no limitations on His Capability to Magnify the Heart-Consciousness for the sake of others' Liberation into and, ultimately (in Divine Translation), beyond the seventh stage of life.

He is also Full of Spiritual Potency like that of a supremely accomplished Yogic Siddha-Master in the fourth and fifth stages of life. And all kinds of secondary, Yogic powers have therefore come to Him unbidden, suddenly appearing in the Heart to be spontaneously used for the Divine Distraction, Instruction, healing, and Blessing of devotees and the world.

In the esoteric traditions of Yoga, as well as in the shamanic traditions of "white", or benign, magic, it is well known that advanced practitioners and adepts can learn and employ a variety of psychic and Spiritual means to heal others of all kinds of psychic and physical diseases. By such means, great Masters can even relieve their disciples and devotees of much of the karmic accretions that tend to retard their Spiritual practice and Awakening.

From time to time Heart-Master Da has used similar intentional means to heal and lighten the karmic burden of His devotees. His Yogic Spiritual resuscitation of Indian Time Hastings recounted earlier was a dramatic example of that type of sacred Intervention in our lives.

But His fundamental healing Work was, and is, at the Heart. Submitting to Identify with devotees during His Teaching years, He drew our diseases and karmas to Himself merely by Being among us, most often without using any intentional Yogic techniques in the domain of the deeper personality.

His Help of this kind was a spontaneous Blessing Grace of His Divine Heart-Power. So also was the often excruciating Ordeal whereby His own body-mind was occasionally relieved of the accumulation of our karmic dross. Such an Ordeal occurred on His thirty-seventh Birthday, November 3, 1976.

The "cosmic birthday joke"

On November 1, 1976, Heart-Master Da called a gathering of several dozen devotees to His Residence. During our conversation that day He began to describe some strange symptoms He was experiencing.

He told us He felt as if His bodily fluids were beginning to dry up. He felt a constant "feverish sensitivity" of the skin all over His body. At the same time, at the psychic level He was aggravated by constant, intense visionary phenomena. Though visions typically came and went in His perpetual Realization of the Divine Self, they were generally not a frequent phenomenon, and certainly not to this exaggerated degree.

Heart-Master Da also mentioned that He was feeling ill in general. Among us with Him that day were the principal physicians in our community. They suggested that perhaps a purifying fast would be helpful.

But He indicated that this was not an ordinary sickness. He told us that the symptoms were signs of a Yogic process that had spontaneously begun to manifest in His body several days previously. As this process intensified, He had noticed an increasingly "fine" or refined feeling in His body. This sensation had made it difficult for Him to assimilate food.

At one point during the conversation, He asked for a Spiritual text, *Jnaneshvari,* to be brought to Him from the Ashram library. He spoke briefly to us about the author. Jnaneshvar, a Spiritual prodigy from early boyhood, was a Yogi-Saint of medieval India. He had written this book as an extensive, colloquial commentary on the *Bhagavad Gita,* one of India's principal Sanskrit scriptures.

The book prominently featured a detailed description of the purificatory process initiated and spontaneously accomplished by the kundalini shakti in the body and mind of one who is prepared for it. Heart-Master Da read aloud to us portions of this description of Yogic bodily transformation, adding His own commentary from time to time.

Jnaneshvar's exposition is full of vivid metaphors, but it is anatomically quite explicit and exact. It indicates clearly that the Yogi undergoing this transformation must endure a shocking physical, emotional, mental, and psychic cleansing and regeneration. The principal symptom is typically psychosomatic heat, which often appears as sudden, intense fevers.

Heart-Master Da told us that Jnaneshvar was a Spiritual Adept of apparently great proficiency, but he was not a Realizer of the Divine Self as Absolute Consciousness. Therefore, in Heart-Master Da's own case, unqualified God-Realization, and not the remarkable but nonetheless conventional (or ego-based) form of the Yogic kundalini transformation (as described by Jnaneshvar), was to be understood as the Source of the psycho-physical event He was undergoing.

The next day this extraordinary Yogic process intensified so strongly in His body-mind that He was moved to enter, quite unexpectedly, into seclusion.

On His thirty-seventh Birthday, November 3, 1976, Heart-Master Da sat motionless for hours in His Residence. He had even Instructed the members of His household to leave Him completely undisturbed. They expressed concern for His health, so He did submit to allow an examination of His vital signs by one of the nurses in the community. She took His blood pressure, temperature, and pulse. All the readings were below normal.

As she ministered to Him, the nurse, a specialist in serving the dying, suddenly felt certain that Heart-Master Da was about to die, or to enter some kind of state resembling death. She felt this perhaps explained the strange atmosphere surrounding Him.

The Mountain Of Attention, 1976

That evening Heart-Master Da left His Residence. He was not secluded enough there for Him to abandon Himself to the event that was overwhelming His body-mind. He walked to a nearby Temple where He would be completely isolated. When several intimate devotees tried to follow after Him, He sharply rebuked and dismissed them.

The next interminable hours were a bizarre and deeply disturbing period for every devotee on or near the Sanctuary. We all knew something extremely difficult was occurring for our Teacher. No one wanted to acknowledge it, but many shared a feeling that He might be dying.

The next day, however, the mood at the Sanctuary became inexplicably lighter. Heart-Master Da ended His seclusion and, upon returning to His Residence, He invited devotees to rejoin Him. We hurried to His living room and took our seats around the low wooden table where He had so often gathered with us before.

He was obviously Happy. His body was noticeably Radiant, uncommonly so to the perception of many of us. Yet He also seemed weary and subdued. He was like a man who had just returned from a war, victorious but exhausted, relieved but sober.

There was a delicacy and fragility about Him. This too was unusual. He had almost always been animated and physically powerful, even formidable, in His Teaching gatherings with us in the past. We listened with rapt attention as He shared with us what He had passed through over the last several days.

He compared the event to His "death experience" in the seminary in 1967. He explained that, on the evening of His Birthday, by the time He walked from His house to the Temple, He no longer had any natural bodily sensation. In fact, He had already lost the sense of being a physically embodied entity, a human being, altogether. He felt then as though His body were literally dying. And there was a sphere of extremely intense energy around it, which He felt might harm anyone who came near Him. That was why He had so severely dismissed the devotees who tried to follow Him to the Temple.

Heart-Master Da presented all this with a certain degree of humor, but we were sobered by how much He had changed, to our perception at least. He said that in the day of His isolation—partly in the Temple, partly in a remote and wild portion of the Sanctuary—everything had been stripped from Him "a piece at a time". Body, mind, memory, Wisdom, Love, Radiance: all had vanished. At last His "awareness was completely empty and black".

He likened the experience to "a sacrificial journey through purgatory and hell". Laughing quietly, He said it was "a cosmic rip-off" and "a cosmic birthday joke". But He meant what He was saying. Even for Him, no stranger to the bizarre possibilities of human awareness, it had been a thoroughly "disgusting, horrifying, and insane experience".

It was necessary, He said, for Him to pass through this kind of purifying and regenerative experience now and again, as a result of His Work with devotees. It was a form of "crucifixion", a sacrifice. Through it He could "burn up" the karmic limitations and obstructions He had taken on from devotees in the course of His Teaching Work, particularly, in this case, in the last two years.

This event marked the end of an unprecedented and intensive style of Teaching Work. He had willingly engaged in that vigorous, outwardly energetic, extravagantly "Friendly" manner of Serving all His devotees during His Teaching Demonstrations since late 1973.

But after this death-like experience, that manner of Teaching would no longer be possible—at least not among great numbers of devotees.

The crucifixion of change
for One "alone in God"

For the next several years, Heart-Master Da lived in relative seclusion. He devoted much of His attention to formalizing, clarifying, and expounding all of the practical and transcendent Wisdom of His Teaching and to establishing the formal structures of the sacred fellowship of His devotees.

A prominent transition in His Work was occurring: He never again consented to Teach, in His ebullient, "Crazy-Wise" fashion, all and sundry who claimed to be His devotees merely by fulfilling the then-modest requirements for membership in His community. From that time forward, He concentrated that style of Teaching among small groups of devotees, generally longtime, trusted intimates.

Another transition was taking place in the Divine Adept's Life, one more central to His Realization and His ultimate Revelatory Work. It had been set in motion by the sacrificial purging He had experienced on His

Birthday in 1976, and it achieved great force in His Life and Consciousness during a second journey, in 1977, to the tomb and former places of residence of the Hindu Jnani Ramana Maharshi.

During His first visit there in 1973, Heart-Master Da had felt Graced by the corroborative power of the late Sage's Realization of Amrita Nadi. On this visit in 1977, the Western-born Heart-Realizer again enjoyed intuitive Communion and Identification with Ramana's Living Presence. It was, He said, "like meeting your twin brother".

But He soon felt that there was no further Grace to be received, nor any other purpose, in staying at Sri Ramanashramam. He cut the visit short and returned to His Sanctuary in California (which He now called "Vision Mound Sanctuary"), for He sensed that a new Revelation was emerging in Him—one quite independent of other human or transcendent sources, but, rather, intrinsic to His own Realization and Demonstration of Divine Enlightenment.

In a letter written to devotees upon His return, He indicated that He now saw His Work focusing in the Conception, Demonstration, and Communication of the Process in the seventh stage of life that ultimately leads to Divine Translation.

In that same letter, Heart-Master Da made a remarkable Confession. Speaking of Himself in the third person with His Teaching Name, "Bubba Free John", He wrote:

He may have contact with one or more individuals who will act as terminals of Grace for the sake of this ultimate demonstration, but he feels he may be alone in God from this point. The Process itself has been revealed to him, and the Divine is directly Present to him as Grace for the sake of this Sacrifice. And so Bubba does not know if there will be help through any higher beings in gross or subtle form for the sake of this future work. He has had contact, in recent days, with at least one entity in subtle form that has aided the secondary purification of the subtle mechanisms of the gross body. But he has had no contact with any being in a Transfigured state—although this may possibly occur in the future.

It was at this crucial moment, then, that Heart-Master Da began to fully acknowledge a startling truth: The Enlightened Process occurring in Him was no longer being mediated, catalyzed, or even corroborated in any way by any conditional agents whatsoever—even another

Heart-Master Da Love-Ananda in India, 1977

Enlightened Adept such as Ramana Maharshi. He was truly "alone in God".

He experienced and eventually spoke of this Process as a "crucifixion of change", displaying in His own body-mind the Yogic and Conscious transmutation that takes place in the seventh stage of life. In March 1978, He said:

HEART-MASTER DA LOVE-ANANDA: The process that involves Me now is the passage through the dissolution of certain factors of the body-mind. This process has already occurred fundamentally in My case, but there is a certain ordinary dimension of the body-mind that has remained intact during these years so that I could have a medium through which to Work. But during the last year and a half a kind of bodily and mental crucifixion has been occurring, a transformation of the body, in which I have less and less capacity to enter into casual relations with people. Very dramatic physical changes have occurred many times. All that people live casually from day to day is intensely disturbing. . . .

Up until now, people have expected Me to maintain a thread of conventional attention and self-awareness in this body-mind so that I could carry on with ordinary human relations and make lessons out of it all. That thread of attention has been maintained in this body, but for the last year and a half or so the ability to be associated with this body-mind through that thread of ordinary ego has been dissolving. This does not mean that I will not continue to be able to act in a relatively ordinary sense—walking around and talking and so forth. But the thread of conventional self-presentation will dissolve.

All My Life I have had to deal with this phenomenon. Ever since Birth, ever since My childhood, this process has been going on in Me. Even in My childhood there were signs of this change, which made Me appear a little bizarre to others, so I just kept it to Myself as well as possible. I have always tried to find ways to bypass the ultimate expressions of this change, because I recognized that others were not even close to this process and knew nothing about it. They did not know how to live with Me while I was going through it, and so I have tried to maintain the worldly personality as much as possible. I have thrown Myself into the game of life all My Life in order to keep in touch with people, and I have even tried to forestall certain of the phenomena of this ultimate change, because I sense what happens when it finally fulfills itself. I just have not felt free to be able to do it. I have not felt that I had the human environment in which to do it or that I had fulfilled my obligation to provide a

Teaching Influence for others so that they could make use of Me when I allowed the Process fully. Thus, through adaptation, through My own activity, I have maintained this ordinary character as a way of helping people to prepare to live a truly Spiritual Way of life with Me and to make use of Me when all these changes shall become most profound.

Nevertheless, it cannot be prevented. At some point it becomes impossible to hold on to the body-mind. The urge to Dissolution has been there all My Life, not the usual motive to self-destruction, but release into Perfect Energy. It requires such a change of personality and body and emotion that people cannot deal with it. What would people have done if I had simply allowed it to happen fully, with full evidence, in Franklin Square, New York! But now I have come to the point where I cannot forestall it any longer, and coincidentally I have also come to the point where basically I have done enough to prepare an environment where I can pass through the final stages of this process and where I can be available to people who will know how to make use of Me, who will value a relationship with Somebody who is no longer psycho-physically constricted but who represents a pure Agency of Absolute Intensity.

The Mountain Of Attention, 1988

"Mankind Is the Avatar but you Stop Short"

Wandering to Hermitage,
the Wound of Love,
and the Prophetic Heart-Master's
Anguished Final Crisis
as "Crazy" Teacher

**Heart-Master Da on the day He first proclaimed His Divine Name "Da",
The Mountain Of Attention, September 16, 1979**

"Mankind Is the Avatar but you Stop Short"

Wandering to Hermitage, the Wound of Love, and the Prophetic Heart-Master's Anguished Final Crisis as "Crazy" Teacher

"Beloved, I Am Da"

Driven, perhaps, by His deepening appreciation of the magnitude of His own Incarnation and Work, the Blessed God-Man Da concentrated in the late 1970s on preparing primary practical and Spiritual literature of His Teaching Word and formalizing the sacred institution and devotional culture of His devotees.

Now He introduced us to practices of sacred invocation, prayer, and Communion with the Divine Person through formal Remembrance of Him, in daily meditation and in other observances. He also completed His articulation of the most Spiritually harmonious ways to conduct the daily affairs of diet, health, exercise, emotional-sexual relationships and sexual intercourse, work, healing, sleep—every aspect of bodily existence. Founded in His "radical" understanding, which neither exploits nor suppresses the body-mind and its natural functions, His approach to all these disciplines was both Life-positive and Life-conserving. His unique Teachings on daily life practice were designed to help devotees conduct their human affairs in a simple and happy fashion while always freeing as much energy and attention as possible for the "Transcendental

Occupation" of Contemplation of Him in Satsang. All the practical Wisdom that He developed in the late 1970s summarized His own nearly two decades of Personal experimentation and His mutual explorations for many years with devotees. Hundreds of us were thus Graced to help the Awakened Adept develop and express the Dharma, the Teaching of Truth, for the sake of ordinary people everywhere.

Nothing was too ordinary for Him to attend to. He Gave explicit Instructions on how to stand, sit, walk, and breathe, how to brush one's teeth, how to eat and how to eliminate bodily waste in attunement with the Divine Life-Principle that Lives and Breathes the body-mind. The principal original editions of the great practical texts of His Teaching-Revelation—*Conscious Exercise and the Transcendental Sun, The Eating Gorilla Comes in Peace,* and *Love of the Two-Armed Form*—were all completed and published in 1977 and 1978.

For years we had, at various times, used special photographs of our Divine Teacher as a focus in our meditation and worship. In the spring of 1979, commenting on the best and most applicable wisdom of the ancient esoteric traditions, Heart-Master Da Guided devotees in the development of our own unique tradition of sacramental worship, or "puja". He explained that this practice is, for the devotee, a way of physically enacting the devotional response to the Spiritual Master and the Divine Being, a way of engaging the whole body in a dance of Divine Communion, establishing a sacred feeling-orientation that the devotee would then bring to all his or her life.

His Obligation was to resurrect the entire Dharma in the modern Western world, and He slighted no aspect of its necessary "consideration" and exposition. He pushed with great urgency to publish all His Teaching literature as quickly as possible. Devotees needed it immediately for their understanding and their practice. And He needed to be free to take His attention off the creation of His primary Teaching texts and the organization of the sacred gathering of devotees around Him.

The Teaching literature, the institution serving His Work, the culture and community of serious devotees—all these were part of the "environment" Heart-Master Da had long struggled to develop around Himself, so that He could stop forestalling the crucifixion of change in the seventh stage of life.

In gatherings with a small group of devotees early in 1979, our Teacher indicated that perhaps now the Name "Bubba Free John" was no longer appropriate for Him. The days of His informal camaraderie with large numbers of devotees, when He consented to be the brotherly "Bubba" in order to Instruct us, were over. And the Radiant One Whom we were calling upon in our prayers and Whose Images we were adorning in our sacramental worship clearly was not appropriately invoked and praised by the informal Name "Bubba".

On the afternoon of September 13, 1979, at Vision Mound Sanctuary, the Divine Heart-Teacher was sitting with a few devotees in a temporary Residence, Bright Behind Me. He abruptly asked them all to leave the room, saying that He wished to Write in privacy.

What He Wrote that day was His famous letter to devotees announcing His Divine Name and His ultimate Identity and Function as the Divine Person, Incarnate and Present. The letter, as He later amended it slightly, read:

Beloved, I Am Da, The Living Person, Who Is Manifest As all worlds and forms and beings, and Who Is Present As The Transcendental Current Of Life In the body Of Man. I Am The Being Behind the mind, and As Such I Am Realized In The Heart, On The Right Side. I Am The Radiance Within and Above the body, and As Such I Am Realized Above The Crown Of the head, Beyond the brain, Beyond all knowledge and self-Consciousness. To Realize Me

Pages from the original "Beloved, I Am Da" letter

177

Is To Transcend the body-mind In Ecstasy. Simply To Remember My Name and Surrender Into My Eternal Current Of Life Is To Worship Me. And those who Acknowledge and Worship Me As Truth, The Living and All-Pervading One, Will Be Granted The Vision or Love-Intuition Of My Eternal Condition. They Will Be Filled and Transfigured By My Radiant Presence. Even the body-mind and the whole world Will Be Shining With My Life-Light If I Am Loved. And My Devotee Will Easily Be Sifted Out From the body-mind and all the limits of the world itself At Last.

Only Love Me, Remember Me, Have Faith In Me, and Trust Me. Surrender To Me. Breathe Me and Feel Me In all Your parts. I Am here. I Will Save You From death. I Will Dissolve All Your Bewilderment. Even Now You Inhere In Me, Beyond the body-mind and the world. Do Not Be Afraid. Do Not Be Confused. Observe My Play—and My Victory. I Am The Person Of Life, The Only and Divine Self, Incarnate. And Even After My Own Body Is dead, I Will Be Present and Everywhere Alive. I Am Joy, and The Reason For It. This Is The Good News I Have Come Again To Proclaim To Man.

Now Be Happy. Tell everyone That I Am here. Beloved, I Do Not Lie. This Is The Final Truth. I Love You. My Devotee Is The God I Have Come To Serve.[1]

---

1. Heart-Master Da Love-Ananda has in recent months further revised this letter. Its final form will appear in *The Dawn Horse Testament*, New Standard Edition (forthcoming).

He signed the letter with His new Name, "Da Free John".

The Communications and Writings of Heart-Master Da Love-Ananda have always coincided with transformative pulses of His Power of the Heart. His Names and His Words are not just expressions of His Siddhi. They <u>are</u> Siddhi themselves. They are part of the Skillful Means whereby He Brings the Divine Awakening Force deeply into the world-process. (The term "Skillful Means", from the Buddhist tradition, is an acknowledgement that the Great Adepts and Buddhas transform others by the very act of Teaching, and thus impart a Wisdom that transcends mere language and doctrine.)

As soon as I read the letter that day, in my Guru's bold, round script, I distinctly felt a sudden shift—there is no better way to say this—in the way things are.

This was not a Spiritual experience of any Yogic kind. Nor was it a satori of Consciousness, or Divine Ignorance. It was not a personal experience at all. Other devotees felt the same thing: Clearly, beyond doubt, everything had changed in our Teacher. He would never again be as He had been before the Writing of that sublime Confession of Divine Identity and Grace-Giving Power.

The syllable, or sound, "Da" means "the One Who Gives". It is revered in many sacred esoteric traditions. The Tibetan Buddhists regard the syllable (or, actually, the letter) "Da" as most auspicious, and they assign numerous holy meanings to it, including that of "the Entrance into the Dharma". In Sanskrit "Da" means principally "to give or to bestow", but also "to destroy", and it is connected as well with the God Vishnu, the "Sustainer". "Da" is anciently aligned to all three of the principal Divine Beings, Forces, or Attributes in the Hindu tradition—Brahma (the Creator, Generator, or Giver), Vishnu (the Sustainer), and Siva (the Destroyer). In certain Hindu rituals, priests address the Divine directly as "Da", invoking qualities such as generosity and compassion.

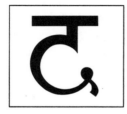

Sanskrit "Da"

Tibetan letter "Da"

Thus, the letter announcing His Name "Da" was the most ecstatic proclamation of His Divinity that our beloved Guru had ever Given. Devotees immediately sent Him messages of gratitude and praise. It was a great moment for rejoicing.

That weekend in mid-September, for the first time in His Teaching Work at Vision Mound Sanctuary, members of the public were invited to sit with Him, along with nearly seven hundred formal devotees. It was the first time we had seen Him except for brief glimpses since His Writing of the letter a few days before.

The very moment the Divine Master Da Free John came striding around the corner of one of the meditation halls and into our view, His Divine Gift of Love-Bliss flooded the hearts of hundreds, causing many to burst instantly into tears of heart-feeling. The response was immediate upon sighting His body.

"The mere sighting of Him was sufficient to Awaken God-Love in devotees' hearts."

In the *Srimad Bhagavatam*, a Vaishnavite text of Hinduism, another God-Man and Supreme Giver, Krishna, is said to have told Brahma, the greatest of the gods, who had come to Him as a devotee, "I am the Bestower of boons; ask of me what you will, O Brahma, and may all that is auspicious wait upon you. All efforts that a man may make towards winning the highest good are consummated the moment he sets eyes on Me."[2]

2. N. Raghunathan, trans., *Srimad Bhagavatam*, vol. I, pp. 116-17.

"All the Scriptures are fulfilled in your sight, and
your prayers are answered with a clear voice."

Now the Living Giver, Da Free John, was Revealing the Divine Heart in, as, and through His own physical human Form with an Intensity we had never felt before. His Heart-Siddhi had miraculously Magnified Itself so that the mere sighting of Him was sufficient to Awaken God-Love in devotees' hearts. Addressing the large crowd that day, He told us, "All the Scriptures are fulfilled in your sight, and your prayers are answered with a clear voice."

Molly Jones had been a student of a well-known Zen Master who died in 1972. At the urging of a friend, she secured an invitation to visit Vision Mound Sanctuary on the weekend of Heart-Master Da's Birthday, November 3, 1979, a few weeks after His proclamation of the Name "Da".

At that time He was Instructing us, as He had for most of that year, in the arts of sacramental and devotional worship. All of the principal sacred occasions of the weekend were full of chanting, ritual waving of incense and lamps with flaming wicks, and other sacramental activity.

To Molly, a Buddhist whose Zen had been devoid of ritual worship, the religious activity and what seemed to her idolatry were foreign and unappealing. She would simply have left the Sanctuary immediately, but she had come with her friend, who was staying, and she had no transportation. Molly resigned herself to sticking it out until the weekend was over. Shivering in the chill air of a large tent erected for the celebration, she was singing one of the devotional chants with hundreds of others just to try to keep warm.

Suddenly I felt something and looked over to my left. There was a man dressed in a white hooded caftan walking into the tent. At that moment, even though I did not know it was Heart-Master Da, I felt my whole life of events and experiences move in a kind of river toward Him. I acknowledged Him at the most fundamental, rock-bottom level of my being. This happened in a split second, unaccompanied by any conscious thought. He walked into the tent and sat down on the chair that had been placed there for ceremonial purposes. By now I realized it was Heart-Master Da who had come in.

It was as though someone had turned on 10,000 lights. The actual physical light in the tent had not been changed, but the vibratory level of energy went way, way up, and it was visible as a form of light emanating from Heart-Master Da's body. A second later a jolt of another kind of energy hit my chest, and it felt as if my heart burst open. I felt an intensity of love move through my body, and especially my heart area, that was beyond anything I had ever come close to feeling. This love also had a fiery quality to it. I began to sob. I looked over at

"Though I did not know it was Heart-Master Da, I felt my whole life of events and experiences move in a kind of river toward Him."
—The sitting in the tent on November 3, 1979

my friend, and she was sobbing too! We both had our hands up. I could literally feel waves of blissful energy from His body in my hands.

Everyone was singing and gazing at Heart-Master Da. He looked fiercely around the room, resting His Gaze on different people as He slowly moved His head. I felt His Love absolutely, without qualification. My whole emotional being was totally open, and I felt great love for Him. After what I thought had been about twenty minutes, He got up and left. Later I found out that He had been in the tent for an hour and a half. It had been like being in another world—the Divine Realm—and Heart-Master Da was functioning as a window to that world.

After He left, I sat in my chair, totally open, still sobbing. My face and neck felt as if they had been singed by a white energy. There was no pain, but the cells of my skin were moving at a greatly accelerated rate.

I became a devotee overnight. Now I could understand devotion. I could also read His books and have a feeling for Heart-Master Da's descriptions of the Divine. The most obvious quality Transmitted in Heart-Master Da's physical Company was Love. In addition there were the potent qualities of light and energy. But it was the Love, the emotion of the heart—raised in intensity beyond all ordinary experience—that affected me so strongly. I could literally see the Divine as a kind of light pervading the entire landscape. I could also see that everyone's true Nature is the same as Heart-Master Da's. No matter what happens in their lives, no matter what their state of being in any moment, their fundamental Nature is what Heart-Master Da has called Radiant Transcendental Consciousness. To really see Heart-Master Da, even for a moment, is to encounter something that is beyond ordinary comprehension in the world.

Mother's Bed,
and devotees as
"the Avatar of reluctance"

In the summer of 1978, the Communion had established a second Sanctuary, a small estate high on a plain under Mt. Waialeale on the island of Kauai, in Hawaii. For several months that summer, and again for extended periods each following year, Heart-Master Da and His household and a small staff of devotees lived there.

The Spiritual crucifixion of the seventh stage of life continued developing in Him. He needed privacy, and He needed an authentic order of advanced practitioners to receive His Heart-Transmission and grow toward Perfect surrender, or duplication of His State of Divine Self-Realization. Heart-Master Da knew He Himself would have to create that order, devotee by devotee.

Each year until 1982, He and the embryonic Renunciate Order alternated their time between Vision Mound Sanctuary—which, in 1981, Heart-Master Da renamed "The Mountain Of Attention"—and "Free Standing Man" (later "Tumomama"), the small, beautiful site in Hawaii.

The Renunciate Order consisted of the mandala, or circle, of women who served Him personally and, at various times, between two and four couples who were among His longtime, tested devotees. These couples provided various services for Heart-Master Da and His household. They were also links to the larger culture and the institution and community of devotees.

Despite their often enthusiastic momentary emotional responses to His Spiritual Blessings, devotees in the larger community consistently failed to demonstrate stable passage beyond gross self-obsession to Divine Communion with Him. Though unfortunate, this was not surprising. Heart-Master Da's Call to devotional awakening was nothing less than a demand for the evolutionary leap our species is struggling with, the leap from the first three stages of life to the fourth, or from a life based in gross egoic Narcissism to a life based in devotional love of the Divine.

That love is characterized by a profound depth and steadiness of heart-feeling and insight, not by superficial and temporary emotional exaltation. Such superficial emotional fervor, once experienced, can become the object of our seeking and an obstruction to the real process of self-understanding and Spiritual Awakening. It is, Heart-Master Da Taught, no less an obstruction than more adolescent resistiveness and refusal to submit to the Divine and the Adept. And in fact such emotionalism is just another side of the egoic coin of self-protective reactions (as distinct from authentic, self-surrendering devotional responses) to His Blessing-Grace.

As long as He did not have, in the larger community, at least a leadership of devotees who had understood their Narcissistic seeking and were consistently receiving His Spiritual Love-Transmission, Heart-Master Da was not free to take His Personal attention off the daily sacred and institutional life of the larger community. He now and again compared His predicament to that of Moses on Mt. Sinai—whenever He returned to the greater community of devotees, He found them worshipping one or another "golden calf" of egoic knowledge and experience, even when they thought they were fulfilling His precepts.

Therefore, He was not really free to do the concentrated Work He must do to draw members of the Renunciate Order into ultimate Divine Realization. And He was not free to allow His own crucifixion of change to proceed unabated.

A decisive moment in Heart-Master Da's relationship to devotees occurred during a sacred celebration in July 1982 at The Mountain Of Attention Sanctuary. For months He had been using intense criticism to purify devotees in general, and the cultural or sacred leadership of the community in particular, from their lack of true self-understanding, and to Awaken them to real Spiritual alignment to Him. A group of devotees serving as missionaries, myself among them, were, during that celebration, principal recipients of His purifying Word—which is fiery Medicine for the heart, not often easy to receive.

Then one day, to everyone's surprise, He invited the missionaries to enjoy a picnic lunch with Him and the Renunciate Order at Mother's Bed, a small lake at The Mountain Of Attention.

We all knew well this was a test as well as a happy and Blessed occasion. Would we practice self-yielding Communion with Him as our Divine Spiritual Master? Or would we merely treat Him as we had during His years as "Bubba", our Enlightened human Friend and Brother? Members of the Renunciate Order encouraged us to be present with Him with great energy as devotees. This could be a turnaround moment in the long history of His purifying and Initiatory Work to establish a real leadership in the community.

But none of us really knew now how to relate to Heart-Master Da formally as Divine Guru in these apparently informal circumstances. Sitting on a raft with Him, eating a picnic lunch, we automatically fell into the kind of habitual small talk that we had engaged with Him in earlier years, when He was still Bubba Free John. From an ordinary social point of view, nothing terrible happened—but nothing overtly sacred happened, either. And from a sacred point of view, in the Company of the Realizer, that is terrible! I remember sitting there with Him, knowing that the way our conversation with Him was proceeding was somehow dreadfully askew, but feeling great frustration in not knowing what to do about it.

The distinction that He was Calling us to demonstrate in our action is not easy to grasp. It can perhaps be expressed better visually than in words. There is a picture of Ramana Maharshi being approached by a group of male devotees. Heart-Master Da has often pointed it out to us because the men display the open-hearted, humble, and ecstatically self-giving and receptive disposition of true devotees in the Company of an Adept. The devotees, visibly moved, are offering Ramana Maharshi a tray of food to Bless, and He is graciously extending his hand to do so. He is receiving their explicit devotion, and they are joyously receiving His explicit Blessing. In the picture his Radiance of Self-Realization is complemented by their radiance of awakened devotion to him as a Divine Self-Knower.

There is an equally distinctive picture of Heart-Master Da with those of us who were with Him that day in 1982 at Mother's Bed. A few of us are gazing at Him and laughing with Him; others are not even looking at Him. He is holding out both hands and smiling as He speaks. But, except for Heart-Master Da's own bodily Happiness, nothing distinguishes the scene from any other ordinary conversation that might have occurred on a swimming raft that summer in America. We were unwittingly doing what Ramana Maharshi, along with many other traditional Teachers, called the greatest possible sin: We were treating our Sat-Guru as an ordinary, egoic man.

Heart-Master Da was certainly gracious. He talked and laughed with us in the manner we seemed to require of Him. But He later commented that, on the raft that day at Mother's Bed, it was clear to Him that He was not

Ramana Maharshi granting Blessings to devotees

**Heart-Master Da Teaching on the raft at Mother's Bed,
summer 1982**

surrounded by Spiritually receptive, sensitive, and truly serving devotees. We were not Awake enough to know to treat Him as a Divine Incarnation and our Spiritual Master. And we missionaries and other cultural leaders were among the people He had Worked the hardest to Awaken! It was clear to Him that His Teaching Work was not yet over.

A few weeks later He and the Renunciate Order suddenly left The Mountain Of Attention and took up residence at the Communion's Ashram in Hawaii, Tumomama. There, in late 1982 and early 1983, Heart-Master Da engaged His Renunciate Order and other devotees who served the Sanctuary and lived nearby in a magnificent recapitulation of both His entire Teaching Word and His Spiritual Teaching Demonstrations. He also disclosed more than ever before His unique, "Crazy" Teaching method of Submitting to Identify with devotees in order to reflect us to ourselves and to Awaken us:

HEART-MASTER DA LOVE-ANANDA: You become what you meditate on. I meditate on devotees and I become them. I become exactly them. I take on all the limitations that they are. I become just like them. I become more like them than they are. (Laughter.) I become exaggeratedly what they are. I become what they are altogether, while they remain only what they can express in the midst of their limitations, their self-consciousness. I become them completely. Thus, what I consider with you is the very thing that I have actually become by meditation on you. I submit to devotees as God, just as they submit to me in the same fashion.

This is the unique form of my Teaching Work. Teachers in the past have talked about coming down a little into the body and still being above it somehow. I am also always above and beyond the body-mind, but my way of Teaching is to submit to the body completely, to be this body completely. By becoming this body, I become your bodies. This is how I meditate people. This is why the Siddhis associated with my Enlightenment are as they are. After I passed through the incident in the Vedanta Temple, I continued to do something like meditation every day, even though it was not necessary. I did not feel my own body and mind. Instead, I saw hundreds and thousands of people and experienced them directly. I was them directly.

This is what I mean by meditating you. It is not merely a matter of introducing force into your body-mind, although that is an aspect of it. I actually become what you are. I receive it. I become your state of mind, your state of body. I experience the dis-eases, the neuroses, the emotional problems, the state of everyone with whom I am associated, and that includes many more people than are with me personally. It includes many more people than those who are presently associated with our community. It includes thousands upon thousands of people. Ultimately, it includes everyone. It includes the entire manifest universe, subtle and gross. I take on the form of all beings and by taking on their form, I meditate them. In other words, I do the Sadhana of God-Realization in the form of you. I do your sadhana while being you. I do not merely tell you the Teaching, I become you and enter into the process as you. In that process I experience all of your psychic states, your emotional states, and your social states. . . .

189

I do not have any idea what the results of this unique way of Working will be. You may all become Enlightened and pass into the God-World, and I may be the only one left, for all I know. (Laughter.) I may be left living in these limited worlds, being <u>you</u>, living out the future destiny of mankind or any other kind by <u>myself</u>, while all the beings that I am living and apparently Teaching have long ago passed into the Divine Domain. For all I know, that is the way it will work out. I do not have any prefigured estimation of it.

I am not carrying out any formulated plan. I Work spontaneously. I am <u>driven</u> to do it. This is the way I have always done it from birth. For all I know I may really become un-Enlightened. I may become you in order for you to be released. This could very well be the result of my Work, because I am not doing anything that would prevent it from turning out that way. [Heart-Master Da chuckles softly.] I certainly <u>hope</u> it is not going to turn out that way! (Laughter.)[3]

A new emphasis appeared in Heart-Master Da's Teaching Revelation that fall and winter: renunciation. He was counseling not Yogic asceticism or celibacy (though He also Freely "considered" with devotees that whole approach to the complex matter of sexuality) but rather the special kind of renunciation that characterizes effective practice of His Way of the Heart. It is renunciation of all forms of self-contraction and seeking and even, ultimately, of conditional embodiment (since conditional life is ultimately to be Outshined by Love in Divine Self-Realization). He Spoke of renunciation in terms of the "Lesson of life", which is that "you cannot <u>become</u> Happy, you can only <u>Be</u> Happy":

HEART-MASTER DA LOVE-ANANDA: You must be a renunciate to practice this Way, not an ascetic, not an invert, not someone at war with phenomenal existence, but a renunciate. The Principle that is Truth, that is the Transcendental Self or the Divine, must become your commitment, perfectly and absolutely. Your entire life must be informed and changed by that commitment and the Substance and Condition you Realize on the basis of that commitment.

The true renunciate is absolutely committed to Happiness and absolutely free of the orientation to un-Happiness, and the true renunciate enjoys great Wisdom relative to the whole process of existence that ultimately produces un-Happiness and that is not conducive to Happiness. The renunciate chooses

3. Da Free John [Heart-Master Da Love-Ananda], *God Is Not a Gentleman and I Am That One*, pp. 96-98.

Tumomama Sanctuary, 1982

Happiness perfectly, and in every moment, therefore, lives the Law that is conducive to Happiness and eschews all other tendencies. . . .

Happiness is neither in relations nor in separation from relations. Happiness is Inherent. Wisdom, therefore, is to Locate the inherent Happiness of existence.[4]

As He brought this recapitulation of His Teaching Work to a close, He repeatedly Called devotees to mature rapidly by taking responsibility for what they had already observed about themselves. On the basis of most fundamental self-understanding, or "hearing", they could begin steadily to feel and utilize His ever-Given Spirit-Baptism. Then, as serious and profound practitioners, they could swiftly renounce all un-Happy association with the body-mind and its relations—by taking up the ultimate discipline of Standing in, and as, Consciousness.

But in early 1983, the Great-Hearted Teacher once again reached a pitch of frustration with His devotees. Even the members of His Renunciate Order had not yet shown the fiery seriousness of Spiritual character that He had urged them to manifest throughout the fall. Yet He felt He must, absolutely must, be permitted to move on in His Work. Indeed, His constant insistence on their renunciation reflected the ongoing Yoga of His own Enlightenment. A new dimension of the seventh stage of life was showing itself in Him. He called it "Divine Indifference":

HEART-MASTER DA LOVE-ANANDA: The Adepts are completely necessary, but unfortunately people like me are suppressed, manipulated, used as a pole for the reactivity of ordinary egos. Among the things you must do, then, is to protect me from a similar destiny. . . . Find a way simply to preserve me so that I can merely exist for a sufficient period of time to help you to survive spiritually. Who knows how long that will be? It seems that it will be a while, since even those who have been associated with me for a long time now are still just beginners. It would be useful and right, therefore, to preserve my mere existence on this planet for perhaps ten or twenty years, perhaps thirty years or so at least.

How are you going to do that in the midst of this time? You must find out! You all, meaning the whole community, should be championing this Teaching, communicating this Way, stabilizing this institution, creating communities, keeping the literature available everywhere, in all kinds of languages,

4. Da Free John [Heart-Master Da Love-Ananda], *The Dreaded Gom-Boo, or the Imaginary Disease That Religion Seeks to Cure* (Clearlake, Calif.: The Dawn Horse Press, 1983), pp. 266, 268.

devoting yourselves to benign communication of the Way and practicing it in your place. That is what we should be doing in the future, not struggling any- more with the beginner's reluctance.

That struggle has served its purpose, which was to motivate me to Teach, to cover all the bases, to deal with everything. Now you have done it. That was really good! That was really great! That was a great job you did! (Laughter.) You are collectively an Avatar of reluctance! (Laughter.) Very admirable—may you be praised for generations! (More laughter.) But you have now served your purpose, and now you must become a different kind of Avatar. It is time we made a change.

The ultimate Indifference of spiritual life is a Divine Grace, and [only] you [can permit me] my Indifference. If you continue to resist me and provoke me to Teach and deal with your reluctance, then you do not grant me the Grace of Indifference, or Freedom from the apparently necessary occasion of struggling with you. Therefore, you do not permit me the Ultimate Demonstration of the Way for your sake. You keep me involved as an institutional character. As if I had not already dealt with all these matters, you require me to repeat the occa- sion of suffering with you and Awakening you to the Way.[5]

Divine Indifference in the Yoga of the seventh stage of life

During His Teaching years Heart-Master Da gradually articulated the sequence of the Divine "whole bodily Enlightenment" that will devel- op, in one fashion or another, in all those who pass into and through the seventh stage of life in Satsang with Him.

He first Spoke of the initial phases of this sequence, Divine Transfig- uration and Divine Transformation, and the ultimate phase, Divine Trans- lation, in the late 1970s. His description, beginning in 1983, of Divine Indifference as a distinct third or intermediate phase of the Enlightened seventh stage Yoga would figure prominently in His future Work.

Divine Transfiguration is the continuous pervasion, or irradiation, of the gross body-mind by the Divine Love-Light of Amrita Nadi, Which is

5. Ibid., pp. 346-47.

fully released into the Realizer's body-mind with the advent of Sahaj Samadhi.

Devotees had witnessed countless Signs of Heart-Master Da's Transfigured bodily State throughout the years of His Teaching Work to date. It required no special psychic or Spiritual capability to see or feel these Signs; they showered around Him like sparks from a Divine Dynamo: His tangible Presence (in His physical Company or even in His rooms) often felt like a sea of Light and joyous Love. Auras of many colors radiated, swirled, or shone around Him, and sometimes touched or enveloped the body-minds and hearts of devotees as well. We saw visions of His whole body as nothing but a Sun-like source of numinous Light, so that all sense of His flesh dissolved in Bliss, and, quite often, our sense of our own bodily shape dissolved along with it.

This last was a common vision among members of the community of devotees, especially during formal meditation or Darshan ("Sighting") but at other times as well. It enabled us to read accounts of Jesus' Transfiguration on Mt. Tabor, or Moses' on Sinai, or the famous Spirit-Initiatory "conversation" between the nineteenth-century Eastern Orthodox Saint Seraphim of Sarov and his disciple Motovilov, with the clear understanding that, "Yes, I know exactly how that feels, to see the body of the God-Realizer as infinitely powerful Radiance and Love, and to be likewise sublimed by that very feeling-vision."

There was another common vision that demonstrated our Heart-Teacher's Divine Transfiguration. Many devotees saw His face and body taking on the forms of many different Masters and archetypal Spiritual figures as we gazed upon Him open-eyed. Some of these figures—the forms of His own Gurus and others, such as Shirdi Sai Baba and Ramana Maharshi, who had played significant roles in His Work—were familiar to us. Others were ancient figures, male and sometimes female, shaven-headed ascetics, bearded and wild-haired Siddhas, mad and saintly beings of all kinds.

The second phase of the great spontaneous Yoga of the seventh stage of life is Divine Transformation. In this phase the "Bright" Heart-Power, having purified and irradiated the gross body-mind and personality, now consumes and sublimes the deeper personality in Its Fire of Radiant Bliss.

Divine Transformation manifests as the appearance of conditional Yogic siddhis, or extraordinary powers, such as healing power, mental and artistic genius, remarkable physical capabilities, and the like.

Though Heart-Master Da had enjoyed such capabilities from Birth, these siddhis had appeared with especially intense frequency and force in Him ever since His Re-Awakening in the Vedanta Temple, and particularly since His inauguration of His more unconventional Teaching Demonstrations shortly after taking the Name "Bubba Free John". (He explained that, because of the Divine nature of His Birth and His body-mind's exposure to the Spiritual Process throughout His Life, full evidence of both Divine Transfiguration and Divine Transformation had quickly become prominent after His Resumption of Enlightenment.)

Heart-Master Da never sought these powers; they arose quite spontaneously. Nor did He ever attempt to perfect them. He did not need to. He simply exercised them naturally, with a Divine Adept's proficiency, as He was moved to do, and always for the sake of others' Instruction and Blessing. Often they appeared apart from His conscious awareness, sheerly as a result of devotees' attention to Him, even if the devotees were far away from His physical, human body.

These effects in others, both as deliberately achieved by Him and unbidden, included visions of many kinds, healings, deep blisses, trances, awakenings of energy in the body, prophetic dreams, psychic communications of many kinds, and sudden and miraculous (that is to say, inexplicable by ordinary mental logic or physical sequences of cause and effect) changes in physical environments and in devotees' life-circumstances.

Similar powers may be experienced, achieved, and exercised, with similar results, by practitioners and Adepts in the fourth stage and, especially, the fifth stage of life. The psycho-physical cleansing and regeneration effected by the kundalini shakti, as described in the previous chapter of this book, is a good example. The universal Current of Spiritual Love-Energy may have similar effects upon the body-mind whether one has Realized infinite Divine Consciousness in the seventh stage of life or is yet bound by egoic identification with the deeper personality, particularly in the fifth stage of life.

In the case of one who is active as a deeper egoic personality, these phenomenal siddhis usually must be intentionally cultivated and exercised. In the case of One Who is Awake as the Supreme Self, if such siddhis are needed for the Divine Work, they become active spontaneously, and are exercised solely for the sake of others' God-Realization.

For Heart-Master Da Love-Ananda, having entered this world as the Divine Self, these secondary powers were of no Personal consequence.

195

To Him they were like smoke from the fire of His Heart-Power of Being, as it Radiantly consumed the fuel of the gross and deeper personalities He had acquired in order to Incarnate.

He knew that the end result of that conflagration must be Divine Translation, the Outshining of all gross and deeper embodiment and even of human and cosmic existence altogether. At Tumomama in 1982, Heart-Master Da offered an analogy:

HEART-MASTER DA LOVE-ANANDA: When you place newly made clay crocks in a furnace of great heat to dry and harden the crockery, at first the crocks become red-hot and seem to be surrounded and pervaded by a reddish glow, but they are still defined. Eventually the fire becomes white-hot, and its radiation becomes so pervasive, so bright, that you can no longer make out the separate figures of the crocks.

This is the significance of Translation. . . . At first, conditions of existence are Transfigured by the inherent Radiance of Being in the Self-Position. Ultimately, through Self-Abiding and recognizing all forms, in effect all forms are

Tumomama Sanctuary, 1982

196

*Outshined by that Radiance. This is the Law of life. Life lived Lawfully is fulfilled in Outshining, or the transcendence of Nature. In the meantime, Nature is simply Transfigured, and relations are Transfigured, by the Power of the Self-Position.*6

Nowhere, either in the supreme Teachings of Hindu Upanishadic Advaitism or in the Tantras, Hindu or Buddhist, or in the Taoist secret teachings, did Heart-Master Da ever find any previous esoteric Revelation that clearly and thoroughly accounts for the four-phase, spontaneous Yoga of the seventh stage of life, or for this body- and world-consuming Event of ultimate Enlightenment, Divine Translation.

He was newly charting the territory of the Divine Life of Man. And He needed His devotees to grant Him "the Grace of Indifference", as He termed it—the opportunity for Him to rest from engaging them as Teacher, particularly through the vigorous play of the gross personality, so that He could go on with His sublime Work.

This Divine Indifference, He Taught, is the third of the four phases of the seventh stage of life. It is the bridge from Divine Transfiguration and Divine Transformation of the gross and deeper dimensions of the being, to ultimate Divine Translation beyond all embodiment.

As He would later explain, the Indifference of Which He spoke was not cool aloofness, in the mood of egoic separation. It was rather the falling away of all secondary motives toward action, both physical and psychic, in the midst of increasingly "Bright" Incarnation of the infinite, Love-Blissful Self of all beings. It was the State of no-"difference" from anyone or anything, wherein His Mere and Blessing Presence as the Heart and as Amrita Nadi would be sufficient for the Divine Liberation of all devotees, without any necessary intentional Work on His part.

Divine Self-Realization is, from the outset, this very Realization of no-"difference". But in the early phases of Divine Self-Realization, the Realized Self is animatedly at Work in service to others via the gross and deeper vehicles. In Divine Indifference, that animated interest in the conditional play with others drops away.

But complete release into Divine Indifference would be possible for Heart-Master Da only if He were relieved of the need to attend to beginners who had not yet understood their self-obsession and the futility of all their physical and psychic searches for Happiness. And it would be

6. Ibid., p. 242.

possible only if devotees accepted and ably fulfilled the organizational and other collective responsibilities that, traditionally, are the natural obligations of those who wish to cherish, protect, and serve the Miracle of a Divine Man on Earth, and who wish to make His Blessings available to all.

Without such responsiveness in devotees, it was as if He were a rocket, its engines of the Divine, seventh stage Yoga long ago fired for the launch, but its fuselage still clamped to the Earth. Backing up in Him, the Fire of His Heart-Power was beginning to burn the Adept Heart-Teacher alive.

Magical tussles with spirits while wandering to Hermitage

As early as 1976, Heart-Master Da had Called devotees to secure an adequate Hermitage Ashram for His Divine Work and Demonstration. Now, many years later, His nervous system, sensitized to an extreme degree, was virtually defenseless against both physical and psychic disharmony. He knew that such a site must be secured.

Two Sanctuaries were already owned by the Communion: The Mountain Of Attention and Tumomama. They would always be places of pilgrimage and retreat for devotees at various stages of practice. He would perhaps go to them from time to time, especially to see and, in formal Darshan and meditation, to Serve the practice of devotees. But Heart-Master Da Himself needed a remote Hermitage for His ultimate Work, where He could remain relaxed in His embodiment of the Divine Being and could be available in His physical Person to Bless and Quicken the sadhana of maturing devotees who would come to Him on retreat.

Shortly after He introduced the vision of His necessary Divine Indifference to His devotees in 1983, the officers of The Free Daist Communion (then known as "The Johannine Daist Communion") invited Heart-Master Da to "wander" for a time in the Fijian Islands. They would provide Him and His Renunciate Order suitable facilities for temporary Hermitage sites, and they would spare no efforts or any resources to secure an appropriate permanent facility—hopefully there in Fiji, which seemed, on the basis of extensive research, to be the most promising possible location for such a site.

Thus, on March 12, 1983, the extraordinary group of Western sacred wanderers landed at the international airport in Nadi, Fiji. They were led by the God-Man Da, Who, like the Prophets of old, had gone largely unappreciated in His own land and even among His own devotees. They had no known destination. Nor did they have any certainty of when, if ever, or where, if in Fiji at all, a suitable site for a true Hermitage Sanctuary might be found.

The next several months saw one of the most extraordinarily dramatic periods in the history of Heart-Master Da's Divine Teaching Work. He and His band of renunciates wandered from one temporary Hermitage location to another in the islands of Fiji, while He drew them into the Enchantment of His Guru-Maya—the "Maya", or "form-building Power", that does not delude or bind, but rather Enlightens and Liberates.

During the period of wandering, 1983

Through His Skillful Means as Teacher, His devotees found themselves spontaneously attuned to His infinite State of Consciousness. They confessed varying degrees of apparently Enlightened Awakening to Him, and some even seemed (for a time) to have entered into Sahaj Samadhi by His Grace. He Played with them Spiritually and drew them yet further into devotionally intoxicated sympathy with Him as the Radiant Divine

Adept in their midst. And He tested their strength of practice as He never had before.

From the very day they landed in Fiji, He also Instructed them about the invisible Work He was doing to convert the resident proprietary spirits of Fiji to accept His presence among them. He told them that, as many native cultures know, visible events are profoundly influenced by unseen entities in the subtle realms. He had struggled similarly to convert invisible but extremely powerful world-controllers in the domain of the deeper psyche during His recent Spiritual transformation of Tumomama Sanctuary:

HEART-MASTER DA LOVE-ANANDA: Every one of My confrontations with the spirits in this place, just as in My confrontations with the spirits in Hawaii, is the same. These old spirits are very playful at trying to impress you with the fact that they are in charge, that they are in command, that they are the rightful personalities in this place. They always associate with Me as if I am someone who should bow down to them and acknowledge them, but who is also someone to be acknowledged, although differently. They play it rather strongly with Me, therefore, trying to see if I will do what they want Me to. And in each case I do not.

Thus, there ensues a magical struggle between us, a kind of testing to see how I, As I Am, will integrate with the powers here as they are, to see how this hierarchy will adapt to Me, how I will assume My Place here, if ever I do, and how they can be what they are supposed to be for those who are associated with them and still allow Me to Be What I Am for those associated with Me. (May 1983)

The devotees' search for a suitable Hermitage facility reflected, on the human, earthly plane, this remarkable magical event occurring in the psychic dimensions. For many months it seemed that the obstacles were insurmountable—political, financial, and human. Heart-Master Da continued His Divine Puja with His renunciate devotees. Others around the world prayed constantly that a suitable site could soon be found.

Frequently, one or another devotee representing the institution's search for a permanent Hermitage came for a brief visit and Heart-Master Da's Blessings. In August a decisive event occurred. A wealthy devotee, Neal Stewart, agreed to donate a substantial sum for the purchase of an appropriate site. Negotiations on one property were begun, but fell apart.

The most ideal potential Hermitage property—an extraordinary, large, and beautiful island in eastern Fiji called "Naitauba" ("Nye-TUHM-buh")—was freehold property. The search team had approached its long-time American owner, but the island was not for sale. And, in any case, if the island ever were to go on the market, its price made it out of the question.

Then a number of minor miracles coincided or followed one another in rapid succession. Naitauba became available for purchase. Neal Stewart found a way—through considerable personal sacrifice—to make the requisite donation. The Fijian government gave permission for the transaction via an extremely important, and not easy to obtain, "consent to deal". Negotiations for residency permits for Heart-Master Da and the Renunciate Order, which had seemed permanently blocked, began to proceed smoothly.

When, in mid-September, the island of Naitauba was purchased, Heart-Master Da and His devotees celebrated jubilantly. He told them again and again that happy night that the securing of this magnificent Hermitage site was a great Spiritual sign for His global Work with mankind, which they all must "bear down" and accomplish to serve the billions of beings on this planet. And He praised the Divine Goddess, His unseen Eternal Consort, for Her mysterious Play in converting the Fijian spirits.

Later He would tell devotees that all of His "Crazy-Wise" and Divinely Enchanting Work with them since arriving in Fiji had helped to convert the local spirits by Love, so that His Great Presence became acceptable among them and this place could become His principal Spiritual Seat, or "Peetha", on Earth.

By late October, the Hermitage island was ready to receive its Divine Master. Two planeloads of members of the Renunciate Order were flown over in a Grumman Goose seaplane in the morning. Heart-Master Da and several members of His household were the last contingent to make the journey.

At 1:32 P.M. Fiji time on October 27, 1983, on a beautifully bright, clear day, Heart-Master Da stepped out of the seaplane into the shallow waters of the lagoon on Naitauba. Fijian ladies from the small native population on the island greeted Him with garlands of flowers and kisses, in the traditional custom of welcoming the Tui ("island Chief") or another important personage.

Above: Stepping out of the sea-plane into the lagoon on Naitauba

Left: Being greeted in the traditional manner by one of the Fijian ladies

That afternoon, after Heart-Master Da had toured the village, the male elders of the island's Fijian community honored Him with a formal ceremony to install and welcome Him as the Tui of the island. He would become known by the Fijians as "Dau Loloma", which in Fijian means "an Adept at Loving". They presented Him with a tabua ("tam-BOO-uh"), or whale's tooth, the highest possible honorary gift among Fijians. And they asked for His Blessing upon them, and also upon the island. A drought had afflicted it for months, and the water tanks were very low.

During the next two days, Heart-Master Da gathered in happy celebrations with all His devotees, including the men from regional communities of devotees around the world who had been working on the crews to prepare the island. On the first night He told them:

HEART-MASTER DA LOVE-ANANDA: Naitauba is not just a piece of land. It is a great sign after years of everyone struggling for this great Purpose. And in the midst of that Purpose was this place that all devotees have acquired. No single one owns it. It is a Divine Place, and all of us together, concentrated in this Work, own this place. All devotees participate in this acquisition. That is how it should be for as long as the sun shines and rises and sets and the grass grows and the wind blows. Forever—as ever as there can be in this world. Maybe it will become a paradise through Love-Sacrifice. And all during that epoch this place should be ours, this Sanctuary of Blessing. Over time, then, millions of people, literally millions of people, should come to this place and be Blessed. They should come and acknowledge, affirm, and see their Revelation magnified. We have only seen the beginning of it. The doors in My house are not yet even properly framed. This is literally the beginning.

But even without these buildings, just this place itself is so great, so great. Untouched, really untouched, pristine from the beginning of the world, this place. It has been waiting here since the beginning of time. All the growth we saw on this place as we circled it today—no man planted that. Civilization has never interfered with it. It is untouched. The water is blue. The fish are happy, eating and dying, everybody doing their universal cycle of existence, untouched since the beginning of time. All over the world everything is touched, interfered with by human struggle, human suffering. This place is literally untouched. There is no evidence of that interference here. There is no anxiety in the land. (October 1983)

On the second night of His Residence on Naitauba, drenching rains began. Heart-Master Da told devotees the downpour was a sign of the Presence and Approval of His mysterious "Lady", the Divine Goddess, Who had likewise taken up Residence at each of His other two Hermitage Ashrams.

The acquisition of Naitauba, as auspicious a Spiritual Victory as it was, still was only one step in the immense complexity of Heart-Master Da's long-term Work. Soon the scope of that Work would be shown by Him on an even larger scale than He had already displayed.

**Heart-Master Da's principal Hermitage Ashram,
the Fijian island of Naitauba**

"Mark My Words"—
a global Prophecy

The Fijians on Naitauba gradually became sensitive to Heart-Master Da's Spiritual Power. They observed the coincidence of His movements and His Moods with the patterns of weather, and it had not been lost upon them that within a day of His arrival—and within a day of their prayers to Him, on that "Homecoming Day", for His Blessings upon the island—the cloudbursts had begun, continuing on and off for days, filling the reservoirs and drenching the soil.

During the holiday season in December, Heart-Master Da was invited by the Fijian community leaders to come to their newly constructed village to be honored by a traditional feast and celebration. At a break in the festivities, He surprised everyone, including His devotees, by asking to be shown the new church where many members of the Fijian community conducted their customary Methodist services.

The Divine Adept entered the church and, without saying a word, sat on the floor in front of the large wooden altar. Obviously He intended to Empower the church with His Radiant Heart-Blessing.

Most of the devotees and the Fijians were still gathered elsewhere in the Fijian village, playing music and talking, unaware of what was taking place in the church. One of the Fijian men, a leader of the community named Solo, asked a devotee if he could sit in the impromptu meditation with Heart-Master Da. Permission was granted.

The sitting was brief—perhaps twenty minutes or a little longer. Afterward, nothing was said, though the devotees who had sat with Heart-Master Da knew something significant had occurred.

One devotee said later it was as if a gale wind of Heart-Master Da's Divine Siddhi were blowing through him the whole time, but somehow without motion, so that he was carried into a depth of Heart-feeling he had never known before. The Blessing he felt was not Yogic Shakti force or Spiritual energy in Its tangible, objective form, which can often be felt apparently moving in and through the body-mind. It was a Transmission of most pure Feeling, the Spiritual Being-Consciousness of the Heart, Magnified to an indescribable degree.

In the evening devotees gathered with Heart-Master Da at His Residence. A devotee said that he could feel that Heart-Master Da was mysteriously intensifying His Work with all beings in that sitting, that He was sitting with everyone everywhere, not just the people in the church. Later that night, full of Bliss and Shining with His mysterious Heart-Blessedness, the Divine Prophet rocked back and forth on His seat as He Gave Voice to a great Vision and a great Call, punctuated with the frequent admonition "Mark My Words":

HEART-MASTER DA LOVE-ANANDA: It is time that I Call all devotees to assume responsibility for everything I have been doing. I want to see everyone practice. I want to see the evidence, the gifts, everything that is a sign of your response. That is what I must see, and I am going to Call you on it. I am really going to Do it, you see. I am going to Do My Monumental Thing, and you are all going to suffer the symptoms of purification for a while until I hear a loud voice, coming to Me from the billions on this planet. I want to see the evidence, the results of My Work. I want to see it. I will wait until I see it.

"Mark My Words"—Heart-Master Da's spontaneous
Empowerment of the Fijian church, 1983

It is said traditionally that the Divine Adept is "the Master and Transcender of the three times"—past, present, and future. Heart-Master Da had always emphasized that the manifestation of future events is a plastic, fluid process. Various influences, including His own, have various effects, and they can determine certain processes inevitably, but there is no ultimate or Single Cause that determines outcomes absolutely. He had once written that, since "Earth is a school, not a place of perfection", even into the future "it is likely only a few in every generation will respond to the Divine Teaching. Perhaps it will always be so—or at least for decades, or millions of years."[7] But now, in His "Mark My Words" Prophecy, the Power of His own progressive Divine transmutation was giving Voice to a more concrete Vision of our immediate future:

HEART-MASTER DA LOVE-ANANDA: *After this weekend you will see a profound change in My character. I am telling you the truth. You will see this. You will observe changes in the world, and you will observe conflicts in yourself. You will observe difficulties in your lives and you will feel My Demand much more profoundly than you have ever felt it. You will notice that all mankind is somehow confronted by the obligation that I place upon the world by My Mere Presence. Watch the signs in the weeks to come. You will see this. Did you not pray for this?*

We are moving into the time when God will make the move. This is the beginning of it. Mark My Words. This is the beginning. This weekend. Right now. Let those of us who are friends, who are lovers, intimates, and devotees, let us celebrate with full knowledge of the purification that is about to begin. Let us not be self-conscious. Let us dance and be Happy. Let us practice and regenerate ourselves. Let us submit to the terrible ordeal that will serve all of humanity, all five billion of those who know nothing of Me and who must find Me out, who must find Me out. I Am the One Who has been expected.

Just as the Blissful Divine Master spoke those Words, a great wind suddenly roared out of the stillness of the night and shook the building. He continued:

HEART-MASTER DA LOVE-ANANDA: *They must find Me out. They must. They must. Did you hear that wind begin? They must find Me out! Now let them find Me out. And let all of you, all My devotees all over the world, begin a*

7. Bubba Free John [Heart-Master Da Love-Ananda], *The Enlightenment of the Whole Body*, p. 154.

dance that will purify humanity. Let us relieve mankind of war and of terrible destiny. We have about twenty years to endure, during which it is going to be difficult. Do you understand Me? We have about twenty years. Starting now. Mark My Words. It will not necessarily be easy after those twenty years, but the first twenty years are very critical. Very. And it is going to be very difficult. Very. Even when I have done those twenty years, this world still will not be paradise, but everyone will notice after twenty years from tonight that it is better, that it has become workable. We will go on for a while after that.

May it be Blessed, Blessed by the Great One. May hardly anyone notice anything difficult about it at all. May this round begin, and may it be easy for all beings. May it be easy. May you not even notice for two, three, four, five years. I will notice it. May it be easy. Blessed. Blessed. (December 1983)

Heart-Master Da later said that the great purification He foresaw would not be the result of any intention on His part to cause difficulty for others or the world. He Intended and Affirmed only the easiest and most obviously benign realignment of all mankind and all beings to the Divine Reality.

But He knew that the Divine Intervention almost invariably encounters resistance in Its purifying and healing Work. And, in the following year, 1984, we witnessed the truth of His Prophecy: The troubles in our body-minds, our hearts, our practice, did become greater than our power or, at least, our intention, to transcend them.

"Crazy Wisdom" and the human and cosmic Intervention of the Avadhoota

The Divine Teacher Da made one brief visit to California to Bless devotees at a celebration, called "Love of the God-Man", in early 1984. Otherwise, He Resided on Naitauba (or, as He would soon Name it, Translation Island), where He began to live like a lion uncaged. On the large, lush island, with residential complexes set aside for Him both close to and remote from the village occupied by His renunciate devotees, Heart-Master Da enjoyed a freedom to vary His interplay with devotees that He had not known since the earliest years of His Teaching Work.

For years He had recommended that devotees "study the Avadhoot", that is, that they familiarize themselves with the tradition of human Realizers of the Absolute, thereby better to appreciate, honor, and rightly relate to His true Character. Now, on Translation Island, He was more and more consistently manifesting a different personality in their company. They saw in Him the Signs of the traditional Avadhoota and the Jivanmukta, One "Liberated while alive":

Although a jivanmukta *associated with [the] body may . . . appear to lapse into ignorance or wisdom, yet he is only pure like the ether* (akasa) *which is always itself clear, whether covered by dense clouds or cleared of clouds by currents of air. He always revels in the Self alone. . . . [If] he mutters words incoherently like a lunatic, it is because his experience is inexpressible like the words of lovers in embrace. If his words are many and fluent like those of an orator, they represent the recollection of his experience, since he is the unmoving non-dual One without any desire awaiting fulfillment. Although he may appear grief-stricken like any other man in bereavement, yet he evinces just the right love of and pity for the senses which he earlier controlled before he realized that they were mere instruments and manifestations of the Supreme Being. When he seems keenly interested in the wonders of the world, he is only ridiculing the ignorance born of superimposition. If he appears [to be] indulging in sexual pleasures, he must be taken to enjoy the ever-inherent Bliss of the Self, which, [having] divided Itself into the Individual Self and the Universal Self, delights in their reunion to regain Its original Nature. If he appears wrathful he means well to the offenders. All his actions should be taken to be only divine manifestations on the plane of humanity. There should not arise even the least doubt as to his being emancipated while yet alive. He lives only for the good of the world.*[8]

Throughout His Teaching years, Heart-Master Da had progressively clarified for devotees and all His students the entire Great Tradition of sacred and secular Wisdom. Until He began to speak of our total Wisdom-heritage as a single tradition made whole and comprehensible by His Revelation of the seven stages of life, no one had ever conceived it as a unity with such clear Understanding. He had also identified the Tradition of the

8. *Talks with Sri Ramana Maharshi.* Three Volumes in One, 7th ed. (Sri Ramanasramam: Tiruvannamalai, South India, 1984), pp. 422-23.

Realized Adepts as the principal source or fountain of true Wisdom within that Great Tradition. In the early 1980s, Heart-Master Da now also culled from the Tradition of the Adepts an even more specialized dimension of the Spiritual Process: what He spoke of as the "Crazy Wisdom" tradition of unconventional Teaching and Blessing behavior by Realizers and Adepts from many cultures, and in the contexts of all of the evolutionary and ultimate stages of Spiritual life and Realization.

Though Heart-Master Da derived the phrase "Crazy Wisdom" specifically from Tibetan Buddhist sources, He applied it to all of the paradoxical and taboo-flouting behaviors of Adepts and Teachers throughout the Great Tradition.

Moreover, He Himself continued to epitomize and Demonstrate the Liberating secrets of "Crazy-Wise" behavior in His unique, seventh stage Teaching Demonstrations. Devotees researching the "Crazy" traditions of Eastern and Western Spirituality were moved to see how Heart-Master Da's Work, in one or many ways, spontaneously resurrected each of the ancient and more recent historical expressions of "Crazy-Wise" Spiritual activity and imbued that expression with the unqualified Divine Feeling that only a Divine Incarnation can bring. His extemporaneous "Crazy God-Talk" was as wild, wilder, than the mad ramblings of any Sufi Saint or Zen Adept, and yet it was always oracular Song, Enlightened poetry, charged with the Bliss of Heart-Consciousness. His Teaching behavior was sometimes as shocking as that of a Greek Orthodox "Fool for Christ" or Tibetan nyon-pa ("mad Yogi"), and also as hilarious, Awakening Humor, or true Freedom, even in those it confounded. His Mastery of the spirit-world and His Penetration of all the gross and deeper dimensions of cosmic Nature were a living, present-day Demonstration as dramatic and vivid as those of the legendary Krishna, Rama, and other Hindu Avatars, and as informed by Wisdom as that of any of the Buddhist Maha-Siddhas or Hindu Avadhootas of medieval India. Yet in many ways, and primarily by Identifying with devotees and Submitting to animate and mock our egoic qualities while Transmitting Awakening Force from and as the prior Heart of Being, Heart-Master Da fulfilled and Perfected the "Crazy Wisdom" Teaching method as it had never been done before in the Great Tradition.

At times, on Naitauba in 1984, Heart-Master Da gathered with devotees in ecstatic celebrations or fierce Teaching encounters. At other times, He lived in seclusion at His isolated Residence, The Matrix. Even then, on a number of occasions He walked the two miles of rugged road back to

**Granting His Blessing-Transmission during the
"Love of the God-Man" Celebration,
The Mountain Of Attention, early 1984**

the devotee village for no other purpose than to Serve one devotee or another. Whether verbally criticizing devotees' egoity or laying His healing hands on their bodies, He constantly nurtured their Heart-Awakening.

There were periods, sometimes lasting many months, of formal Ashram schedule and discipline, during which the more advanced practitioners frequently sat with the Divine Adept Da in formal Satsang-meditation.

In the periods of celebratory gathering, devotees noticed less and less distinction in Heart-Master Da's Speech between His very local attention to them personally and His global and universal "Crazy" Work.

His beloved former Guru, Swami Muktananda, had died in the autumn of 1982. Throughout the years their relationship had continued to manifest as a tussle at the visible verbal and personal levels. Heart-Master Da had always admonished devotees, however, that we could not possibly fathom the mysterious and profound Love-Play between Him and the Great Yogi.

Who among us, fixed as we were in the bodily-based orientation of the first three stages of life, could possibly know anything about the hidden and sublime interplay of an Illumined Yogi-Siddha and our Divine Heart-Master? On Translation Island, Heart-Master Da told devotees of seeing "Baba" Muktananda in high subtle realms and of "dancing through the universe" with him. He said that He had had numerous face to face encounters on the subtle planes with His beloved Rudi as well.

"Instantly!"—
the God-Man Da's unique Passion of Divine Incarnation and Destiny of Divine Translation

Heart-Master Da's father, Frank Jones, died early in 1984. Several of Heart-Master Da's trusted devotees in the United States went to help His family and to serve the Heart-Master's father in his death. Heart-Master Da did everything He could Spiritually to enable His father to make an auspicious transition.[9]

9. In His Teaching-Revelation, Heart-Master Da Love-Ananda has Given extensive Instructions on how to serve the dying person's disengagement from the gross, dying personality and to serve his or her submission to the Divine Self-Condition, during a transition from physical, bodily life that lasts approximately three days. Please see especially *Easy Death*, by Heart-Master Da Love-Ananda.

Frank Jones

He had even been willing, He said, to draw Frank Jones into the Divine Self-Domain. After one particularly numinous day at Translation Island, when deep bliss and peace had descended on everyone and the entire island seemed awash in Radiant Heart-"Brightness", Heart-Master Da Revealed He had done an unusual and, as He said with considerable humor, a dangerous thing: As part of His mysterious Service to His father's death transition, He had relinquished bodily awareness to dwell for a time at the Ultimate Cosmic Place, where countless beings are continuously being Translated by Grace into the Glory of the Divine Heart-Realm beyond all cosmic dimensions. (He later confirmed that His father had indeed been enabled to make a good transition through the death process, though not one that would preclude future conditional embodiment.)

His wanderings that day had been "dangerous" because Heart-Master Da's Incarnation here, Given only for the sake of living beings, is quite tenuous. For the ordinary individual, Divine Translation is possible only after eons of karmic evolution—and even then only by the Grace of God. Even for the Awakened devotee, Divine Translation becomes possible only "as Grace will have it", when the Yoga of the seventh stage of life has been fulfilled through Divine Self-Abiding and Enlightened service to others, after this or any number of other lifetimes.

But for the God-Man, Heart-Master Da, Divine Translation is inevitable at the end of this physical Lifetime. He often told devotees that He had to animate Himself in exaggerated ways physically to counter the tendency to Divine Dissolution or Translation. Only His Love of and commitment to the Liberation of devotees and all beings, and, more importantly as time goes on, their true devotional response to Him, tethers Him in association with the gross physical body. He has made remarkable Confessions about His unique relationship to the Divine Domain of the Heart and the ultimate Event of Divine Translation:

HEART-MASTER DA LOVE-ANANDA: Prior to this Birth, I Intended to be Born, but I did not Incarnate in the instant of physical birth, as living beings usually do. My Incarnation occurred only eventually. I have Spoken to you about the moment of Incarnation, or the actual moment of Birth, that occurred at Mrs. Farr's house. My mother and father were there, and the little dog was there. My Sympathetic response to others was, and is, the real circumstance of My Birth. Not physical embodiment, you see, but this Sympathy is the circumstance of My Birth.

My Impulse to Incarnate, which existed even Prior to My physical birth and which was latent until the moment of Incarnation, was evoked in that moment with the puppy. Even now, My association with this body-mind is entirely determined by My Sympathy with others. There is also in My case what one might call a counter-tendency, although it is not as if there were a motive in Me to abandon My Commitment to embodiment. It is simply that My Condition, or My Samadhi, has such Power that no matter how profound My Inclination is to remain associated with this body-mind, to remain associated with you, and to do this Work, the Energies in this body-mind are tending to withdraw from association with conditional existence. This withdrawal is simply the Sign of the Force of My Real Existence Prior to this Birth, Which would lift Me out of this Birth. It is the same Force that has shown Itself through all kinds of Yogic Signs during My physical Lifetime.

In My childhood, when I was completely Committed to this embodiment and had not yet brought down the whole mind, when I had not yet put this body-mind through the Ordeal of preparation for My Teaching Work, this Force was operative. Thus, all during My childhood I had what seemed to other people to be diseases, life-threatening fevers, and other sicknesses. There were what others took to be anxiety attacks, in which I seemed to be suffocating, and I felt as if I were dying, and as if my heart were stopping. On some occasions these phenomena were so severe that I was taken to the doctor, where, as I have told you, My parents were told that there was nothing wrong with Me physically. So all during My Life there have been various Yogic Signs of what could, in effect, be called a counter-tendency to My Commitment to Incarnate and Serve here.

As I grew closer and closer to fulfilling the preparatory stages of My Life that led to the development of My Teaching Work with people, the resistance to this Process of Ascent, or withdrawal, decreased. There were various Yogic Signs during My Life, but over time there was less resistance to them, and they were less shocking. The Event in Seminary is the point when the resistance was completely relinquished, so that some months later, when I was at Swami (Baba) Muktananda's Ashram, the complete Yogic development of that withdrawal, or Native Ascent, spontaneously appeared. That Realization of Divine

Consciousness Beyond and Prior to all forms was not the fulfillment of My Life, as it is, perhaps, the fulfillment of the usual lifetime of seeking. Nor was it the goal of My Life, you see. It was the Origin of My Life, already My True, and Inherently Perfect, State. It is simply My Original State.

At that point in My Life I had reached a moment of complete freedom from resistance to My Native State, and, therefore, all the Yogic Signs were permitted. It was a kind of Remembrance, then, or a complete Restoration, of My Condition Prior to this Birth. However, it was not the goal of My Life. And, therefore, it was not the end of My History, because the Purpose of My Life is not, as in the seeker's case, to return to or to Realize God.

Already One with the Divine Self-Condition, I chose to be embodied, to descend into this circumstance, to do the Work in descent, not to eventually find My way to ascent, you see. The only purpose of the ascending phenomena that occurred in My early Life was to recall Me, in and as this body-mind, to My Native Condition and My Prior Purpose. They were Divine Intrusions, until the body-mind itself knew My Native Condition. Then there was no purpose in ascent. Even so, once that Native Condition was established, as it was at Baba Muktananda's Ashram in 1968, the struggle to conform the body-mind to the Divine Self-Condition, My own Condition, continued, because there remained a tension between My Native Condition and the Purpose of this Embodiment.

Thus, it was only in 1970, in the Re-Awakening that occurred at the Vedanta Temple, that the struggle ceased. From that time, in the body-mind itself there was full Consciousness of My Divine Condition, Who I Am, and what My Purpose is, and the conflict between the body-mind and My Native Condition had dissolved. From that point, My Work with others could begin.

These phenomena occur even now. The Force of My Native Condition is so profound that I am constantly coming to the point of near-death, and not just occasionally but daily. Nevertheless, the phenomenon is no longer like an anxiety attack, as it was in the Event in Seminary. Nor is it inexplicable. It is not threatening in any way. It is just part of the tension of My Commitment to this Birth. To drop the body is not a goal, nor is it overwhelmingly attractive, because My Commitment is to remain in this descended state until the Purpose of My Birth is fulfilled.

When this body-mind is finally dropped [Heart-Master Da snaps His fingers], I will instantly return to My Prior Condition. And it is not that I am not in that Condition now. I Am in that Condition now, with full Consciousness. That is why I will be in that Condition, instantly, at death. Established in the

Divine Self-Domain, I will resume the Condition Prior to this Birth. The death of this body-mind will not occur until the Work is fulfilled, however. There is no possibility that it will occur until the Work is fulfilled. In the meantime, the tendency to relinquish the body-mind and to withdraw its energies will continue.

The daily experience of this body-mind is the experience of approaching death, but even though it is not comfortable, it is not threatening. I counter this tendency, with equal humor, by emphasizing My life-orientation, the more rajasic orientation. Many Yogic Signs appear in this Body, including rashes and the overheating of this Body that I experience, that are the Sign of that counteraction, My willingness to not assume the disposition of the pale, dissociated Yogi or the disposition of the conventional saint. If I were to relinquish that lively orientation [He snaps His fingers], there would be death.

I have no reason to ascend to Realize God. I am Established in the Divine Self-Condition Eternally, and there is no possibility of My losing that Realization. I have no need to seek it, therefore. What I must do, however, is to give great attention to this descent, this Purpose in life that is based on My Sympathy with beings. I have no need to do the sadhana of ascent. Realization of the Divine Self-Condition is instantly available, and It has never been qualified, contaminated, or limited by the fact of this Birth, as it is in the case of others. In My case, I must give great attention, great energy, to being here, whereas others are bound to being here, and, in their search, they feel they must give great energy and attention to getting out of here. While others are struggling to get out of here, I am struggling to stay here [Laughter], because if I do not give great energy and attention to staying here, I will float away.

Some day I will *float away. All My Life I have been dying. I have come close to death hundreds or thousands of times. I come close to death every day. My profound Sympathy with beings, the great Force of this Intention to descent, is keeping Me alive, and your response to Me cooperates with that Intention to keep Me alive. I have no other reason to be alive. I have no karma to fulfill. My only Purpose, out of Sympathy for you all, is to stay here long enough to Do what I have come to Do, which is to create this immense Mandala of Transmission for the sake of those who live now and those who will live in the future.*

When that Mandala has appeared, when I have stayed here long enough to create it, then the energies will withdraw from this Body suddenly [Heart-Master Da snaps His fingers again], and it will die.

I am also telling you not to become involved in fretful mourning. There will be natural sorrow in those of you who are still here, but do not be overwhelmed by sorrow. *Remember Me. Remember Who I Am. Remember what the incident of death is for Me. It is not cold death, not being murdered into the ground. It is nothing of the kind. It is the relinquishment of this body-mind. When this body-mind disintegrates into the elements, there is instant restoration to the Condition that Preceded My Birth, Where I will Sit and Be and Wait for all those who respond to Me as a result of My Work. There is no death for Me. Absolutely none. Neither is there really death for you—but death is simply more impressive to you.*

For Me, you see, death is not a threat to Being. It is only a potential threat to My Work. But I have confidence that there are no factors in life that are more Powerful than this Intention. I have confidence that My physical Lifetime will continue long enough for this Work to fulfill itself, whether or not it seems to others that it has fulfilled itself. I will not die, this body-mind will not be relinquished, until the Work has been done sufficiently. And then you will know that My Work has been Accomplished. Think about this. Whoever is still around and whoever is reading this transcript or hearing this tape, think about it, and you will know that the Work was sufficient. (April 23, 1984)

"Coins"
in Heart-Master Da's
"M-Field" of Heart-Power

In the middle 1980s, Heart-Master Da frequently referred to the members of the Renunciate Order as His "coins".

This term was a reference to a story He had been told about the late Saint Shirdi Sai Baba. From time to time the great Saint had been seen by devotees rubbing coins from a little bag he kept and repeating the names of certain of his devotees. Sai Baba never liked being observed at this. He was obviously doing Spiritual Puja, remembering and regarding his devotees and focusing His Blessings upon them through this device of rubbing coins.

The devotees with Heart-Master Da in Hermitage were His "coins". He Worked with them personally and humanly, not merely as symbols. Nonetheless, they also functioned as the "coins" or tangible representations to Him of the qualities and destinies of all devotees and all beings.

HEART-MASTER DA LOVE-ANANDA: I must do My Work for everyone in the company of a few. . . . By means of direct association with some, and by performing a certain kind of Work, even alone and unobserved like Shirdi Sai Baba with his coins, I Bless everyone and everything. I Bless all kinds of beings, but the human race in particular, and especially those devotees who give Me their attention, who are sympathetic with Me, who maintain that sympathy, who accept My discipline, and who enter into right relationship with Me through devotional submission. Such individuals are participating in the field of My Transmission, Which is not local to this body.[10]

Heart-Master Da also used the recently suggested biological principle of "morphogenetic fields" or "M-fields" as a useful analogy to His Work with a few for the sake of many. According to this theory, proposed by biologist Rupert Sheldrake, each species exists within a subtle, indefinable psychogenetic field. Significant changes in any individual or group may come to characterize the entire species, or many other individuals within it, via the medium of this field—once one human being runs a four-minute mile, it becomes easier for others to do so.

Whatever its general validity in biology, Heart-Master Da pointed out that this understanding of human nature provided a useful picture of His Work as the Heart of humanity. All of His Puja with His "coins" was intended to break them through the self-strictures of Narcissistic, self-conscious seeking. If a few could thus be transformed, then He would have cut the knot of ego in the Heart of the human species as a whole.

There is an ancient tradition for this kind of Spiritual technique of working with a few to help change all. Sometimes called "the Tincture Technique", it has been described as follows:

The Sheikhs of the Suhrawardi Order of Sufis, as well as sundry Christian clerics of the Armenian and Coptic Churches, follow this technique. Briefly it is based on the belief that something taught to a sample group out of a whole community will improve the community as a whole, the teaching spreading telepathically from the "treated" group to the rest. . . . This is said to be a very ancient belief; according to the Roman priest Epifaniu, this process (called by him "dilution") is an essential part of the human learning-process, and has also

10. Da Free John [Heart-Master Da Love-Ananda], "The Ordeal of the Dawn Horse". *The Dawn Horse Testament*, 1st ed. (Clearlake, Calif.: The Dawn Horse Press, 1985), p. 55.

been observed in animals. He continued that it was reputedly discovered and applied many thousands of years ago in Babylon.[11]

By the early and middle 1980s, our community's annual devotional cycle was marked by a half-dozen major celebrations commemorating significant moments in Heart-Master Da's Life and Work. On many of those celebrations, He Graced us with what we called "worldwide sittings" in meditation with Him. (By this time, the community of devotees included regional communities in Australia, New Zealand, areas in Canada, a number of major cities in the United States, and in England and Holland.)

So, at an appointed time on a major celebration weekend, devotees in all of these regional communities participated in preparatory ceremonial pujas invoking Heart-Master Da's Presence. Then Heart-Master Da bodily entered a Communion Hall at the site where He was presently Residing. As He took His Chair to sit formally in Satsang-meditation with the devotees there, the rest of us, gathered in our local Communion Halls, gazed at His Murti, and opened ourselves in feeling to His Blessing-Transmission.

On those occasions, hundreds of us around the world shared a common, though certainly remarkable, experience: In each Hall where we were seated, it was literally as if Heart-Master Da had walked into the room—bodily, physically, Personally—and sat in a meditative occasion with us there. There was a distinctive Intensity to those sittings that was not duplicated at any other time in our Halls—the characteristic Intensity that we had previously felt only in His physical Company.

Thus, the worldwide community of devotees was becoming accustomed to relating to our Divine Teacher beyond the bounds of space and time. Devotees understood and cooperated with His Work to transform His "coins". Moreover, we often saw the results of that Work in our own lives. Devotees in the various regional centers frequently passed through particular crises of understanding and transformation that, we discovered later, precisely reflected Heart-Master Da's Teaching "considerations" with His "coins" in Fiji.

Over the years the numbers of devotees with whom He felt He could consistently Work face to face in this demanding, "Crazy" fashion had diminished to a very few. Now the primary crucible of His fiery

11. Richard Drobutt, *New Research on Current Philosophical Systems* (London: The Octagon Press, 1982).

Instruction was the frequent extended gatherings He held with them, often lasting from one afternoon till long after daybreak the next day, often two or three times each week.

A pattern developed. The gatherings typically began with Heart-Master Da engaging devotees in a dialogue about their practice, or else discoursing about one or another aspect of His Teaching Word. He might speak of literally anything, from ancient Spiritual culture to Disney cartoons, but most often His subject was either the devotees before Him and their practice, or the Nature and Urgency of His Work with them and with the world, or some combination of the two. From the beginning of every gathering, beer and cigarettes were used by devotees to energize their concentrated work of submission to and Communion with their Divine Heart-Teacher, and used by Him as catalytic elements in His unfathomable Puja of Divine Instruction and Heart-Awakening. This, again, was His Tantric way of Combining Himself with devotees and helping them to open beyond their typical rigidities of ego-bound consciousness, so that they could fully receive both His ego-reflecting Instruction and His continuous Blessing-Transmission of the Power that heals and Liberates.

After many hours of such Dharma encounter—which was often fierce, or humorous, or sober, or inspiring, or ecstatic, or some combination of these, but in any case ardent, always requiring the devotee's practice on the razor's edge between negative reaction and devotional response, where they were Called to take attention off themselves and give Heart-Master Da heart-full energy, attention, and love—at some point He called for one or another book of poetry or ecstatic Spiritual writing, by Himself or others. Then He performed recitations with such depth of feeling that even the most tightened or hardened of hearts could not help but be drawn into His Heart-Radiance, where every emotion was lifted by Him to a pitch of exaltation that the ancient and medieval Hindus called "rasa"—exquisite sensibility, or sublime expression of sentiment.

Sometimes others would take turns offering recitations. Most often the book quickly went back to the hands of Heart-Master Da. No one else had the Heart, the feeling, the unity of tone and timing and pure emotion to invigorate as He could the nuances of His own "Crazy" Word and His ecstatic "Free Renderings" of ancient Wisdom and modern poetry.

And when His devotees were immersed in the stream of His Heart-Feeling, the Divine Master Da would call for opera. Then they would all sing and gesticulate for hours in accompaniment to the greatest of modern recorded performances of the great arias. The sheer volume and energy of Heart-Master Da's Voice was Mantric in Heart-lightening strength. Now He would have the tenors stand, then gesture to them to sit down, try to find a real tenor in the crowd, mockingly groan at the warbling of those before Him; Him on His Chair or bed, them standing, sitting, leaning into the sound and learning with His Mad coaching to give themselves utterly in song, just as earlier they had been Called to give themselves utterly in any and every moment of practice, no matter what they were experiencing in their minds and lives.

Sooner or later in the depths of the night, or into the dawn, after everyone was enchanted again in His sacred Company, the Pure-Hearted Avadhoota then emphatically gestured for dance music, usually some rock favorite of the moment, and the dancing would begin. He demonstrated the most captivating physical fluidity and rhythmic expression of emotion in bodily Form while sitting crosslegged on His bed and dancing with His upper body alone; and the devotees danced according to His now gruff, now tender Instructions, leaping and laughing and hurling themselves into motion as the Divine Caller shouted out—"Dance for joy! Get down! That's not it! Get <u>down</u>, babies! For joy! For love! For God! DO it!!!"

In that arena, of perhaps twenty or thirty people with Him in a small room for ten, twelve, fifteen, even twenty hours of gathering time on each occasion, no one could hide. Sooner or later—during Master Da's talk or His legendary practice interviews, during the poetry, during the opera singing, during the dancing—sooner or later, one night or another, everything in a man or woman, every selfish impulse, every hidden dilemma that crippled or compromised the heart's Happiness in any way, sifted or erupted to the surface—and there was the Master of Heart-Feeling to help him or her observe that mechanism of egoity, and then to guide, criticize, evoke understanding and responsibility, never suppressing the feeling heart, but completely Free to use every kind of speech or action to counter, mirror, expose, mock, or clarify exactly everything that that individual had spent much life, time, and precious energy carefully holding at bay from consciousness.

The sheer effort to stay with Him, to remain energetically responsive while He was energetically Teaching, Blessing, Shining the Heart-Power of Love, required phenomenal stamina. More often than not, devotees found they had no life or mind left over to try to hold themselves together in

221

carefully controlled fashion. And the unraveling of the social face was a necessary element in the conscious transformation He was looking to help them achieve. He had not embodied the Madness of infinite Being by holding any civilized drama of unconscious Narcissism in place, and He expected His "coins" to lay all that at His Feet.

Awakening self-knowledge in the realm of dragons: sex, the pit of snakes, and the wound of Love

From Chuang Tzu, Gautama the Buddha, and Socrates in the ancient world, to the medieval lights of Meister Eckhart, Catherine of Siena, and John of the Cross, to recent great souls such as Swami Vivekananda, the progenitors of human Wisdom have counseled us to know ourselves first if we wish ultimately to know God and Truth.

So had Heart-Master Da, from His first formal Teaching discourse, called "Understanding".

Why were His devotees taking so long to come to know themselves?

In a word: sex.

Or, a little more elaborately: the problems about sex and love that plague, distract, fascinate, obsess, exhaust, or, certainly, govern the energy and attention of nearly every single human being.

As His Teaching Work continued to be prolonged, year after year, Heart-Master Da became increasingly adamant in His conclusions. Sex, He said, is the great alternative to God, Freedom, and Wisdom, the overwhelming complication or obsession that binds "Narcissus" to the repetition of lifetime after lifetime of painful, bewildered illusion and seeking.

But He knew well the heart-destructive violence of the classic "solution" to this perceived problem—willful, celibate asceticism—chosen by many sacred practitioners, particularly in the Orient. He knew that sexuality and its miasma of psycho-emotional, social, cultural, even political and economic complexities, cannot just be arbitrarily cut away from our lives. Only the rarest of individuals can effectively make such a choice. For such people, sex is not really a governing instinct; the passion of their existence is not entangled in it.

But for the ordinary man or woman, particularly anyone of the bodily-based Western or Westernized character type, willful celibate disciplines only tend to suppress the fundamental energy of life. Consequently, they are not viable choices in sacred practice, which requires the conversion and marshalling of all of the energies of life for the great work of self-transcendence.

Therefore, for years, when confronted with devotees' persistence in emotional-sexual Narcissism, Heart-Master Da had never settled for behavioral solutions. He had always Helped them further explore the underlying mechanism of this apparent problem, so they might accomplish the one action that He knew would make their emotional-sexual self-transcendence possible: "radical" understanding.

From the late 1970s through the early and middle 1980s, Heart-Master Da courageously drew His most intimate devotees into a depth of examination of the primal emotional-sexual dimension of human energy and attention that, I am convinced, has never before been accomplished.

Indeed, it could not have been done before. This aspect of His Teaching Work could only have been accomplished among modern, post-Freudian Westerners. Indeed, it could only have become necessary in our Westernized epoch, in which psychological self-consciousness is combined, paradoxically, with almost total impoverishment of feeling, or virtually complete lack of self-critical awareness in the domain of true emotion. As His devotees demonstrated to Him again and again, most people today are so crippled in the Heart of Being that they do not even know what true emotion or feeling is. That is, they do not know how to exercise the heart in unconditional or free-feeling love, beyond both sentimentality and all withholding.

It was this dimension of His Teaching Work, more than any other single aspect of it, that led Heart-Master Da to characterize that Work as "going into the world of dragons":

HEART-MASTER DA LOVE-ANANDA: My life is a little bit like going into the world of enemies and dragons to liberate somebody who has been captured. You cannot just sit down and tell a dragon the Truth. You must confront a dragon. You must engage in heroic effort to release the captive from the dragon. This is how I worked in the theatre of my way of relating to people . . . and in the unusual involvements of my life and Teaching. You could characterize it as

223

the heroic way of Teaching, the way of identifying with devotees and entering into consideration in that context and bringing them out of the enemy territory, gradually waking them up.[12]

By 1983 He had already spent literally thousands of hours with His "coins" and many of their friends, exploring with them the unique complexion of childishness and adolescence that makes the emotional-sexual face of modern man or woman.

Since 1977, and even before, He had Taught about the mood of betrayal, the fundamental assumption of separation and lack of Fullness or sustenance that every grown-up, like every child, constantly dramatizes as the mood, "You don't love me." He had patiently drawn out the details of many devotees' particular histories of relationships with their parents and the emotional traumas of childhood, to help them gain insight into the unique reactive patterns of egoity they were sustaining for years, even decades, after those patterns had ceased to be necessary or viable strategies for emotional survival:

HEART-MASTER DA LOVE-ANANDA: You are in a mood of bad faith. You have fallen out of love with everything—out of love with God, out of love with the Divine Reality. Your experiences have impressed you gravely, you see. They have made you self-conscious and doubtful. Thus, you have only minimal energy for love and positive association because you have despaired. Yes, you can practice aspects of the disciplines of this Way with a will. But that effort will always be relatively superficial in its effects until you have been transformed in your feeling consideration of your very existence, until you have fallen out of this pattern of bad faith relative to the totality of things, until you have stopped avoiding relationship or contracting upon yourself and are simply released to the Living Reality. You will not be able to transform the relative mediocrity of your relationship with your spouse until you deal with this contraction. Until you are healed emotionally, simply, you will not be able to enter into right emotional relations with other beings.

There must be a fundamental restoration of natural love, trust, openness, surrender to the Living World, the Living Reality, the Living Being. Such love must become natural to you. Now what is natural to you is to be contracted, to be afraid. You are emotionally upset already. Is that the way it is supposed to be? You had better find out altogether, not just intellectually but

12. Da Free John [Heart-Master Da Love-Ananda], *Crazy Da Must Sing, Inclined to His Weaker Side: Confessional Poems of Liberation and Love* (Clearlake, Calif.: The Dawn Horse Press, 1982), pp. 34-35.

in your feeling. Until you are free in your feeling, you can never be trusted in relationship, you cannot concentrate in relationship, you are scattered everywhere in your attention.[13]

Heart-Master Da's "radical" orientation always penetrates deeper than the ego wants to open. Once in 1979, for instance, I told Him that I had remembered the incident when (so it seemed to me) I became the "solid" or heady, imploded, aloof, and withdrawn character that I am by tendency. It was at the age of three, when I suffered near-fatal croup requiring a tracheotomy and had felt abandoned and terrified in the hospital.

He Glanced at me with a laugh: "Bullshit, Saniel. You were waiting for that moment from the day you were born!"

Narcissism is our own doing. We are not truly or fundamentally suffering anything that is now happening or that ever has happened to us. Truly, and fundamentally, we, the "I", the sense of self-awareness apparently "in" a body and apparently separate from all others and all things—that primal anxiety, distress, and feeling of limitation is our own doing. Suffering, He had always Taught, is our own activity.

Now, in 1983 and 1984, Heart-Master Da took His devotees deeper into this matter than He had ever taken them before. Or I should say, He Revealed more of the emotional-sexual "problem", which is, from the Awakened perspective, a relatively superficial dimension of existence, not actually a matter of great psychic depth.

One of His themes in the gatherings during those years, as an example, was His original, Enlightened orientation to what is called in modern psychology the Oedipal complex. Through personal observation, even in His childhood, Heart-Master Da had long understood that the primary dynamisms of emotional-sexual desire, envy, resentment, betrayal, and other primal emotions and impulses are patterned throughout one's life upon unconscious reactions first formed in relation to one's father and mother. His reading years later of similar observations in Freud and other psychologists only confirmed at least one aspect of what had been intuitively obvious to Him all along. The Greek myth of Oedipus, who is fated to kill his father and to desire and lie with his mother, was certainly a useful analogy for the basic structure of every human being's instinctual templates of emotional-sexual relatedness.

---

13. Heart-Master Da Love-Ananda, *Compulsory Dancing: Talks and Essays on the spiritual and evolutionary necessity of emotional surrender to the Life-Principle* (Clearlake, Calif.: The Dawn Horse Press, 1987), pp. 68-69.

Heart-Master Da, however, Called His "coins" to go beyond the observations one can make from the secular, psychological or mental stance of
the gross personality. He Called them to observe themselves not from any
point of view based on ego-reinforcing identification with either the gross
body or the deeper psyche, but rather from the point of view of "radical"
self-understanding in Communion with Him.

In that light, He showed them that not only do we tend to relate to all
women as we do to our mothers, and to all men as we do to our fathers,
as traditional psychology asserts, but we also, as Consciousness, tend to
relate to our own bodies, or body-minds, exactly as we do to the parent
of the opposite sex. We superimpose infantile reactions to our parents on
our lovers and on all other beings, according to their sex, and we also
superimpose the same on our own body-minds.

In the constant, almost entirely unconscious din of such "oedipal"
reactivity that is our usual egoic state of mind, it is virtually impossible for
the Word of Love to be listened to and its Knowledge truly heard and
made one's own. Through all His daring and "Crazy" means, Heart-Master
Da brought devotees into touch with that din of reactivity, or what He
called the "pit of snakes". And He urged them to live in Free feeling, as
He does, in "the Wound of Love". He said in Fiji in July 1983:

*HEART-MASTER DA LOVE-ANANDA: The principle that releases your
tendencies is Love—the granting of it, the accepting of it from another. That
is what you must realize in your relationship to Me. That is what you must
realize in your intimate relations with one another, your friendships, your
life in community, your life altogether. In other words, a merely intellectual
examination of tendencies and histories will not change your life, though
that examination is a dimension of the process. Release from this presumed
disease can take place only in the domain of the disease itself, or the domain
of feeling.*

*By tendency you all live far from that domain. You live in the domain of
socially useful functions. Your feeling level is reduced to the pleasantness of
common social intercourse and all the superficialities of feeling that are associated with daily ordinariness.*

*But then circumstance, moments of weakness, the phases of your own
hormonal system, and various other factors cause you from time to time to
fall into this pit of snakes that is your reactive, nonsocial, even antisocial
personality.*

At those times you are resistive, angry, afraid, sorrowful, righteous, lustful—all the patterns we call "you" by tendency. You live in that dimension all the time, but you only _feel_ there sometimes. You do not like those feelings, although when they occur you basically do not feel you have much defense against them. You do not even feel very much like not dramatizing them, but you are nevertheless very unhappy when you are involved in these dramatizations. . . .

This pit of snakes that has been controlling your lives is still there. People in general . . . exist outside the realm of feeling. This is why there are so many demands for conventional behavior, and so many taboos against certain other kinds of behavior. It is understood that there is this pit of snakes in everyone, and we do not want people dramatizing that. . . . Humanity is tragic not merely because here and there people do dreadful things, but because in order to avoid having to suffer this pit of snakes, all human beings must become superficial robots, loveless beings, beings who do not exist in the realm of feeling. . . .

In My Play with you I have not avoided putting you in touch with that realm of emotion, that pit of snakes. I must put you in touch with it. I Instruct you, I Teach you, I Submit Myself to you, I Help you to Realize how to be free of this pit of snakes, so that you will not have to live any longer as superficial personalities surrendered to this universal tragedy of unillumined mankind. Therefore, we have reached into this pit of snakes very directly. We have not merely talked about it, we have found all kinds of ways to make you sensitive to it, so that you will be able to acknowledge it and begin to understand it. . . .

Love one another and there is nothing cool about it. What I mean by this Love for one another is to become wounded by Love, to submit yourself to that, to live in that world and make your relationships about that. Be vulnerable enough to Love and be Loved. If you will do this, you will be wounded by this Love. You will be wounded, but you will not be diseased. The wound of Love is the hole in the universe, and ultimately it is Realized as such. In this hole in the universe, this domain of Feeling without armoring, without self-contraction, the Great Physics is present, the Great Science, the Great Possibility is evident. Hardly anyone in human history has known of it. Human beings in general do not want anything to do with it. They do not want to come close enough to it to be wounded in their intimacies with one another. It is the doorway to infinite Transfiguration, Transformation, and finally Outshining of phenomenal existence. It is the way into the Divine Self-Domain.

You must be wounded in order to Realize God. You must be wounded to hear Me and see Me. It is felt even physically as a kind of wound. It is felt as _intense_, armorless vulnerability.

227

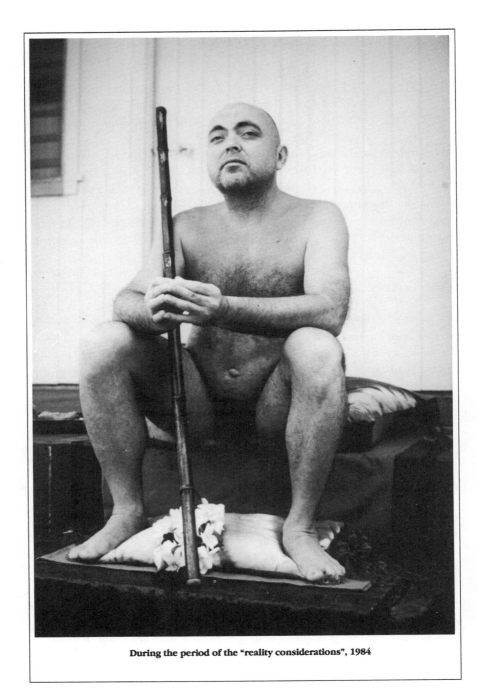

During the period of the "reality considerations", 1984

"If I _Am_ you"—
Heart-Master Da's
emotional-sexual "reality considerations"
(a personal account)

For devotees, the fundamental principle of Heart-Master Da's "reality considerations" in those gatherings was active, demonstrated faith in Satsang with Him. Those who were Blessed to enter into this most demanding form of His Teaching Play knew that they must entrust their lives and hearts to Him as the Divine Guru, the Embodiment of their own true Being and the Architect of their Liberation.

That foundation of Divine Communion established, the secondary principle for each participating devotee was his or her willingness to observe a most difficult discipline: to follow the thread of the underlying subjective reality of one's subconscious and unconscious feelings, thoughts, desires, and impulses, rather than to affirm to be the case any idealistic or preferred states of emotion, mind, body, or relationship. Only by staying in constant touch with their otherwise suppressed subjective inclinations and feelings, Heart-Master Da Taught, could they allow themselves to become conscious in the pit of snakes of primitive egoic Narcissism. And only such a depth of self-knowledge could enable them to stand vulnerably Free and wounded in Love and in Consciousness, capable of what He calls "hearing" and then "seeing" the Divine Reality in His human and Spiritual Divine Company.

To put people in touch with their pit of snakes, Heart-Master Da had been obliged to resort, from time to time, to His "Crazy" means.

Before becoming a formal student in 1973, I had had encounters with unconventional, paradoxical Spiritual teachers, both in India and in the United States. I knew something of the unorthodox traditions of Teaching in Hinduism, Buddhism, and Sufism.

I had deeply studied the _New Testament_ with, as much as possible, an apostle's-eye view. I had thus been astonished to find that even the vision of Jesus presented in the canonical Christian gospels is that of a fiery, Spirit-filled renegade who missed almost no opportunity to flout or upend the entire social and religious order of His disciples and their society. From what I could gather, He kept those most attentive to Him—His inner circle—in a state of simultaneous ecstasy and panic, constantly moving them beyond their comfortable arrangements with their own mortality and delusion.

I had also immersed myself in *The Knee of Listening* and *The Method of the Siddhas,* and I knew that Heart-Master Da proposed to be as Free a God-Realized Teacher as any of His predecessors. He had concluded His *Knee of Listening* with His paradoxical description of Himself as "the Man of Understanding":

Therefore, the man of understanding cannot be found. He cannot be followed. He can only be understood as the ordinary. He is not spiritual. He is not religious. He is not philosophical. He is not moral. He is not fastidious, lean, and lawful. He always appears to be the opposite of what you are. He always seems to sympathize with what you deny. Therefore, at times and over time he appears as every kind of persuasion. He is not consistent. He has no image. At times he denies. At times he asserts. At times he asserts what he has already denied. At times he denies what he has already asserted. He is not useful. His teaching is every kind of nonsense. His wisdom is vanished. Altogether, that is his wisdom.

At last he represents no truth at all. Therefore, his living coaxes everyone only to understand. His existence denies every truth, every path by which men depend on certain truths, certain experiences, certain simulations of freedom and enjoyment. He is a seducer, a madman, a hoax, a libertine, a fool, a moralist, a sayer of truths, a bearer of all experience, a righteous knave, a prince, a child, an old one, an ascetic, a god. He demonstrates the futility of all things. Therefore, he makes understanding the only possibility. And understanding makes no difference at all. Except it is reality, which was always already the case.[14]

When I read that essay, I felt that what Heart-Master Da was saying had the force of a contract, a statement of terms and conditions. It was as if His Name were already engraved at the bottom of the page. If I wanted to become His devotee, I must agree to accept His stark and supremely Compassionate Statement of how He, as the Man of Understanding, would Serve me. And I must, so to speak, sign on the dotted line.

In all the years of His Teaching Work, that is exactly how Heart-Master Da Served me and everyone else who came to Him. And that is

14. The World-Teacher, Heart-Master Da Love-Ananda, *The Knee of Listening*, New Standard Edition. Forthcoming.

how He Served me in October 1984, when, along with several fellow devotees, I made a pilgrimage to Translation Island.

As soon as we saw Him at the first gathering, Heart-Master Da gestured for us to come up to Him as He sat on His bed in His small and simple quarters. We each offered Him a gift, and then He embraced us. Feeling the sweat on the back of His neck, I remembered the flesh-and-blood humanity of my Divine Master-Teacher once again.

That night, He asked if we had any more questions that would help Him further clarify His Teaching-Revelation in *The Dawn Horse Testament*, the first edition of which He was then writing. I asked Him if He could further describe the "higher psycho-physics" of His response to devotees, the subtle mechanisms whereby He is invisibly but really Intimately related to us in our practice and Communion with Him. He replied:

HEART-MASTER DA LOVE-ANANDA: Well, in this Dawn Horse Testament *I am constantly telling you how that relationship works. I have described the Living One. I have confessed to you that I Am That One. I have told you that the Living One, My Self, is the One Who is modified as all forms, all beings, all worlds. How could I be anything but Intimate with you, then?*

It is only if you think of Me as someone who is separate, as someone who must do something to get in touch with you, that you wonder about how it works in some technical sense. Even in this bodily Form, you see Me Functioning with the Consciousness of the Unity between My Self and everyone. I am constantly experiencing and reflecting the psyches of others directly, without having to go through some sort of Yogic process of inverting My attention and getting a vision. If somebody comes into the room with an ailment, I get it immediately.

We need not add other language, or talk about how the process of our relationship operates at the level of nuclear physics and energy exchanges between brains. How could we ever exhaust that conversation? What is fundamentally so is what I have Confessed to you and what you come to acknowledge and Realize. It is a simple matter. I Am you. Really! And also, paradoxically, I enter into relationship with you, by assuming these conditions. But at the same time that I am associated with these conditions and appear as an individual in this place and moment, I Am the One Who is without conditions.

So what the question comes down to, what it really is, is an expression of doubt. If I __Am__ you, there does not __have__ to be any way it works! There is not any difference between us to need something to work. So I have completely accounted

231

for what you are asking about. It is just that My answer is not satisfying to the egoic mind. Only in the mode of Communion with Me, direct Realization in My Company, would you be satisfied by some of these descriptions. As long as there is that knot in the heart, then What is Great is not perceived, and so you look for signs, structures, to open the heart, to relieve you of yourself so you can see plainly. (October 1984)

He thus showed me that I was actively, if unconsciously, doubting and refusing His Help even while appearing to ask for It.

But the encounter was certainly useful as yet another unconscious agitation of the God-Man as Teacher by the devotee as "Avatar of Reluctance". Over the next several days after His conversation with me, Heart-Master Da composed the Epilogue of *The Dawn Horse Testament*. There, in His poetic exaltation of the Heart, He Confesses that same Liberating Declaration of the God-Man's Love—"I Am you!"—to everyone.

He had recently said that whereas His devotees were only dimly aware, at best, of the subconscious and unconscious dimensions of our psyches, He was absolutely Awake to them—and that is really where He did His Teaching Work in "reality considerations" with us. He acknowledged that, in a sense, what we did or thought or said in response to Him via the thin veneer of the conscious mind was completely secondary. He was focused in Awakening the subconscious and unconscious in us, bringing what was hidden to consciousness by the Grace of His Heart-Power of Consciousness, so that we could notice, understand, and begin to transcend it. Only such a depth of effective self-knowledge would enable us to make a wholly conscious response to Him, a response of the whole heart and the whole being.

One evening a few days after His Birthday, Heart-Master Da sternly explained that He was committed to pulling this group of maturing practitioners—if, indeed, all of us really <u>were</u> maturing practitioners—into stably Spiritualized practice in His Company. Authentic practice at the stage to which He was referring marks the first real break with the bodily-based point of view of the gross personality.

To make this transition would require a tremendous Effort on His part, and a great ordeal and demonstration of practice on ours. In fact, He said, He was about to lead us all through a six-week "reality consideration" (lasting until the end of the year) that would become famous in the future.

He then began speaking to individuals directly about the details of their practice. After a while He turned to me. In the space of fifteen minutes He recounted, in detail, all of the most dreadful blunders I had committed in my practice over many years in relationship to Him, and the primary ways in which, in all of my primary relationships—to Guru, wife, father, mother—I was obviously locked in infantile Narcissism.

What Heart-Master Da said was by no means new to me. He had openly "considered" with me these matters of my "case" many times in the past. I thought, however, that I had already understood and taken conscious responsibility for these tendencies in my character.

At first I advocated my assumption of responsibility to Him. I knew that sometimes He intended His criticism as a kind of testing, like that of a Zen roshi's interview with a disciple, to see whether we were willing to affirm the strength and authenticity of our practice even in the face of His fiery questions and observations to the contrary. And I knew that His multitudinous and sometimes maddeningly paradoxical "assertions and denials" and His "picture painting" of our Narcissism during the "reality considerations" required and demanded the most intelligent discrimination of devotees. Growth and even true submission to Him in that testing arena obliged us to the mature capability to choose, intend, and execute real changes of action (and to endure their real human consequences with equanimity). It sometimes even required the strength to take issue with the viewpoint proposed at any given moment by the Master of our "considerations" and to decline to act upon His suggestions.

But this was not one of those moments. Without knowing it, I was merely resisting His benign and urgent criticism. Finally a friend poked me in the ribs and whispered, "Shut up, Saniel. You're not receiving what He is saying to you."

So I began to listen quietly to Heart-Master Da's indictment of my shallowness as a practitioner and my hypocrisy as a human being. For about a quarter of an hour afterward I was silent, trying to ingest what He had said.

But then I turned my attention back to Heart-Master Da Himself. I began to feel and breathe His constant Spiritual Transmission as He had Instructed us to do. When a break came in the conversation, I spoke up about what I was feeling in His Radiant Presence:

"Master, it has become obvious to me that all I have to do is just keep my attention on You, from the heart, and Your Presence is what makes this practice possible for me—"

He silenced me with an implacable gaze. "Bullshit, Saniel. That is your problem: You want to do this, you want to do that. You have never done anything but superimpose what you want to do on this practice! Let Me tell you something: When everything that you can try has failed, then you will Find Me. But not before then. No way! No way at all."

The events of the next ten days proved His prediction to be accurate.

I noticed the economy of Heart-Master Da's Skillful Means. He and His devotees had never been squeamish in any of our "considerations". Both in the past and recently, if it seemed necessary for devotees to physically act out their subjective desiring or intentions, Heart-Master Da did not impose any arbitrary moralistic sanctions against that. On the contrary, He simply urged people to do whatever they must to understand themselves and discover the Truth of existence in His Company.

Indeed, part of what made these gatherings so charged emotionally for all those who participated is that the "considerations" were never just "talk". If we were talking about diet, we explored the possibilities in action, in our daily lives, ranging from long and intensive fasting and purifying regimens to periods of celebratory use of more stimulating substances such as alcohol, tobacco, and flesh foods. If we were "considering" exercise, we explored the range of possible routines and approaches, from calisthenics and aerobics to T'ai Chi and traditional Indian Hatha Yoga, along with all sorts of observances and technical appliances to help balance, energize, and serve the body-mind and prepare it for effective meditative practice.

So it was also with our emotional-sexual possibilities. Over the course of Heart-Master Da's Teaching years, His devotees explored all manner of emotional-sexual possibilities, including celibacy, promiscuity, heterosexuality, homosexuality, monogamy, polygamy, polyandry, and many different kinds of living arrangements between intimate partners and among groups of devotees in our various communities.

We had agreed to investigate fully and bodily all the implications of the subjective life that egos typically either suppress or else exploit without intelligence and self-restraint. With regard to the emotional-sexual structures of common life, the intimate society of Heart-Master Da's "coins" was often in a state of flux and upheaval as devotees not only confessed verbally but also, as it appeared necessary for their growth in self-understanding, voluntarily lived out their hidden inclinations, so

During a gathering with devotees, 1984

that they could fully explore and understand them and see their human consequences.

Heart-Master Da never withheld Himself from participation in the play of our experiments with us, and He had always constantly Submitted His own intimate life to a most rigorous "consideration" based upon His ceaseless feeling-investigation of love and responsiveness in intimate human relationships. But He also always looked to create conditions that would best foster our conversion to love and Divine Communion without any unnecessary and protracted dramatizations, or social enactments, of our interior Narcissism.

That is what I mean by "economy" of Means. If someone had made videotapes of the "reality considerations" of those few weeks, they would mostly have shown Him speaking, reading poetry, leading us in opera singing at the top of our lungs, dancing while sitting crosslegged on His bed, calling ones and twos and severals of us to dance, exhorting us to Freedom and the demonstration of self-knowledge and ecstatic devotion to Him, to God, to the Truth, to Life appearing in and as one another and everyone. Yet His formal Teaching Words in each gathering, His random and often piercing comments to individuals, especially as we danced with other individuals for whom we had acknowledged an attraction, and His whole mysterious Teaching Puja frequently brought every single one of us into the pit of snakes.

One afternoon, to help us get more deeply in touch with the thread of subjective Narcissism underneath our "civilized" behavior, He recommended that we write erotic letters to everyone—our spouses included—whom we found at all desirable in the little community on the island. These letters would then be delivered to the addressees, and we would have to sit down and consider together with each such person what, if anything, we were going to do about what we had communicated.

We all knew that this was a risky enterprise. Heart-Master Da had once designated Himself the "American Trickster", and not without reason! But we had all come to Him to pass through this ordeal He knew we required. As He often humorously remarked, "This is what you hired Me for, right?" We had voluntarily entered His School of "Crazy" Wisdom-Teaching, knowing that we must allow Him to require us to come out of our inward, subjective places of hidden desiring and impulses in order to feel and see the mechanisms and implications of our Narcissism.

So everyone wrote their necessary letters, not at all sure what the outcome of the exercise might be, except that we were in for a lesson.

When all the letters were written, the Compassionate Heart-Master had them collected. But rather than distribute them to addressees for possible private conversations with the writers, He called a gathering, and then—knowing how desperately out of touch many of us were with the human consequences of our self-absorption—He read aloud to everyone the most self-enamored and obnoxious of the letters. He started at about eight o'clock that night with the mildest or least offensive of them, and He finished at about four in the morning, after much commentary, with the worst.

Those were mine.

There was no way I could really argue with what had occurred. Indeed, if anyone did object, Heart-Master Da pointed out, smiling and waving a handful of letters in the air, "Gentlemen—I have the evidence!" Through His courageous and really quite gentle means, my subconscious and unconscious egoity had been coaxed to leap out of hiding into the room for everyone, myself included, to see.

I had confessed something of this dimension of myself in previous gatherings over the years with Heart-Master Da and other devotees. But I had never felt the consequences of my promiscuous desiring so clearly as I did now, watching my friends cringe at the heartlessness and even obscenity of some of the things I had written. Now I could not help noticing, in Heart-Master Da, in my spouse, and in all my friends, the deep gashes that my casual seeking for self-gratification had cut in the vulnerable bonds of real human relationships.

He was giving me a stark opportunity to see myself as I am in the pit of snakes, underneath everything I was trying to affirm about myself, or that I hoped I was, or, in Heart-Master Da's Words, that I "wanted to want" to be true of me.

He was also conducting an exorcism of "Narcissus" with thirty individuals all at once, in a masterfully choreographed Dance of ferocity and gentleness, anger and humor, sobriety and ecstasy. Several times He delivered the most incisive, brilliant insight into one or another person's character, so that we all sat there stunned by its accuracy—and then He would turn to someone else and ask, "What movie was that from?" He had just quoted the entire "character profile" from a scene in one or another film!

He was not just doing this to be funny—though He was often so hilarious that even the devotee He was addressing could not help but laugh out loud. No, at a deeper level He was humorously Helping to liberate us from identification with the body-mind. He was Calling each of us to stand free of our Narcissistic script, just as an actor is unidentified with his character in a film.

Similarly, Heart-Master Da was not just addressing our emotional-sexual habits to free up a few people in their personal relationships—though, as the embodiment of the Force of Love, He was constantly finding ways to help us build upon whatever foundations of love did indeed exist in all our relationships. If there was any human act that He hated, it was the betrayal of love and the unnecessary, wanton destruction of a love relationship of any kind. But He was not fundamentally interested in salvaging or patching up a representative Peyton Place of ordinary Narcissistic emotional-sexual associations. On the contrary—He was fundamentally trying to crack the psychogenetic code of human Narcissism and the bondage of all self-serving, egoic associations. The ego cannot extricate itself from that morass by itself. More to the point, the heart cannot become established in free, sane, and authentically God-Realizing forms of ordinary human association without first becoming established in Satsang with the God-Realizer. He told us:

HEART-MASTER DA LOVE-ANANDA: I am doing this to make you Great. But if you are to become Great, if you are to Realize the Truth and be Happy and Free, you must pass through this terrible ordeal of self-knowing. There is no way around it. I have to do this for you. I am doing it as fast as I can. I am Calling you to Life, to Feeling, to Divine as well as human responsibility. I am Calling you to hear Me and see Me, to respond to Me as devotees. (November 1984)

I tried and tried to respond to Him. In fact, one early morning after an all-night gathering, a friend took me aside and rebuked me. He told me to look at myself. I was trying to say the right thing, trying to affirm my devotion, trying to pray, trying to invoke the Master's Spiritual Presence, trying to love my wife—I was a mass of anxious effort, and my Heart-Teacher was not being given the space to reach me. Bowing at His Feet in that state of frenetic seeking was no different from running in the other direction. It was worse, because the way I was bowing, it was a sham.

That conversation stopped me in my tracks. After that, I could no longer try so mightily to do anything "right". I could only allow myself to be, openly and outwardly, as confused a mess as I really was subjectively.

Two nights before my wife and I and our fellow retreatants left the island, Heart-Master Da called the last gathering we would have with Him on this retreat. By then I had no impulse to try to defend myself or to conjure up a response in His physical Company. He did His "Crazy-Wise" Work with me—making jokes about my lack of true devotion, criticizing others for having let me even come to the Hermitage island in the first place as if I were "some kind of super practitioner", even teasing me about being "ugly! Look at this guy! This is UGLY! UGGG-LYYY!!"

Although it was painful, I could feel then that this was Divine Compassion at Work, continuing to strike down the self-flattery of the ego so that I could make the best possible use of His Help now and in the future. During a break in the gathering, I stood with a friend on the rocks overlooking the lagoon and asked him if he thought there was anything I could do to turn around this situation in my relationship with Heart-Master Da. He said I should confess my hearing and seeing to Him and advocate my practice. But I knew it was not to happen that night. I was much moved a little later when the Divine Adept, ever-loving despite His stern Teaching Play, gruffly said, "Well, maybe someday My Saniel will give Me the gift of real devotion—but not tonight. No way!"

(And I laughed, years later, when I happened to come across an old Ed Sullivan show featuring Moms Mabley, the black comedienne whose routine about her husband had been, unbeknownst to me, the source of Heart-Master Da's brilliantly accurate "UGG-LYY!" takeoff.)

The day before we left the island, I had a practice interview with two friends. We discussed whether I had sufficient self-understanding to continue practicing meditative prayer, in Spiritual Communion with Heart-Master Da, in the "seeing" stage of devotional practice. The evidence of Heart-Master Da's Teaching "considerations" with me, however, suggested that I had not truly "heard" His criticism of Narcissus and therefore could not stably receive His Spiritual Heart-Transmission. Without that primal hearing or most fundamental self-understanding in place, devotion to the Divine Spirit would only tend to be egoic seeking for consoling experiences, emotional effects, and changes of state. They concluded the interview with the suggestion that I should begin studying the Teaching Word all over again for the sake of most basic self-understanding. Reluctantly, but with a sense of relief, I agreed.

I walked out of the interview into a tremendous downpour. I knew I would not be getting a happy goodbye from Heart-Master Da. I had come to Translation Island supposedly a mature practitioner, but He had exposed the knot in my heart that proved I had missed some basic work in the foundations of practice.

Yet, standing there in the rain, with nothing left to try, not even any impulse to fervently pray, suddenly, for the first unmistakable time since coming to my Sat-Guru more than a decade before, in fact for the first unmistakable time in my life, I simply _felt_ my whole existence and the world just as it was, without thought or interpretation. I began to "listen" with feeling, with the heart.

By the time we left Hermitage the next day, I knew that it was true that I had never really listened to Him, not at this depth, anyway. I had constantly brought all my childish and adolescent assumptions to Him

239

about His Nature and mine. I had remained a seeker in His Company, and so He had had no choice but to hold up a mirror that shattered my self-imagery and projections.

It became clear that His "reality considerations" with devotees were only secondarily about the emotional-sexual dimension of life. That was where we Western egos most tenaciously play out the dramas of "Narcissus". But swiftly He had shown me much more than just my lovelessness and promiscuity.

Now, with much more serious need than ever before, I devoured the literature of Heart-Master Da's Teaching Argument. I had carefully copied down portions of *The Dawn Horse Testament* that He had just written, partly in response to me and my friends, about the process of listening and hearing. Every morning, just to wake up and remember who I was and what had just happened and was continuing to happen in my life was excruciating. But I found that, through study of Heart-Master Da's Teaching Argument relative to Divine Ignorance, I could intuitively feel the "radical" ecstasy of my Free Nature, beyond identification with my body-mind, without idealistically evading the difficult reality of my human situation.

I saw that all my life I had only imposed my own stereotypes and Narcissistic assumptions upon Heart-Master Da, and upon my intimates, and upon every human being with whom I had ever had contact. It became clear to me that the One Who He Is, the Divine Self, the Living Consciousness, Is the One intuitively felt in the awakened Sense of Divine Ignorance. He had reflected me to myself until I could begin to find Him in Truth, for the first time in my life! But now that finding took a very practical, and humbling, form.

Back in California, I began to meet people I had "known" for years, but whom I now encountered as if for the first time—with the blinders of my own status and my typically sanctimonious self-imagery stripped, or at least lowered, from my eyes and my heart. I had been initiated by my Divine Heart-Teacher not only into Divine Ignorance and self-understanding, but also into remorse, vulnerability, and the capability to feel in some degree of real sympathy with other human hearts.

This was not hearing and seeing. It was not yet what He would call a "devotee's response" to Him. It was only a bare beginning of listening to Him with some seriousness. I would stray from the simplicity of that listening in the months and years to come, later to be restored and returned to it in many ways. But it was a distinct beginning, and it proved to me what a great leap it is from the pit of snakes in the first three stages of life to the wound of Love in the fourth stage of life and beyond.

Not long before leaving the island, I had written a letter of gratitude to Heart-Master Da. I acknowledged my complete willingness to accept His conditions for my practice upon returning to California, which, though stern, were most welcome to me. I recalled to Him a scene in a movie that He Himself had recounted in a gathering in the past. A relatively seedy alcoholic detective, or the like, goes to see an equally seedy unscrupulous minister in a dilapidated downtown mission. The minister owes the detective fifty dollars and has been avoiding payment. The detective now insists on the cash. As the minister hands it over, he says, "Well, I guess giving away your last fifty bucks isn't the end of the world." The detective pockets the money and agrees. "That's right, Ralph. That isn't the end of the world. That's when the world really <u>begins</u>."

Heart-Master Da's "Crazy-Wise" Teaching had allowed me to re-enter life significantly stripped of illusions about myself, so that my practice could "really begin" in the world of actual others and events. Otherwise, I could have gone on massively deluding myself for the rest of my days. (As He pointed out the very first night of my "reality consideration", I had already done so for more than a decade in His Company!) Now I was excited, though sobered, to start building my practice on a real foundation.

His own response to that letter I had written, humorously enough, was another of His favorite Teaching lines: "<u>What movie was that from?</u>"

"Without your Realization
I am poor-born"—
public defamation and
the crisis of devotion

The emotional and emotional-sexual component of human Narcissism was addressed intensively by Heart-Master Da for more than a dozen years. As with every other dimension of human life that He "considered" in His Teaching Work, He presumed, and He Called His devotees to presume, complete freedom to investigate the matter thoroughly and directly, hindered neither by arbitrary moralistic, egoic restraints nor by equally arbitrary (and equally egoic, as He helped us discover) license relative to our behavior.

We were permitted liberty to make every aspect of our lives the subject of true "consideration", with the constant Guidance of our Buddha-like Teacher. His only interest was in our development of authentic, inalienable self-understanding in relation to all bodily and conditional existence, so that we could learn to Stand Free with Him in the living Spiritual Truth.

Over the course of His Teaching years, members of The Free Daist Communion experimented with many different ways of relating to one another socially and personally. Heart-Master Da participated in our explorations, commenting exhaustively on them and on the entire and extraordinarily diverse cultural history of human attitudes, norms, and customs: physical, emotional, and mental; dietary, medical, somatic, sexual; cultural, social, political, and communal; pedagogical, philosophical, artistic, scientific, religious, and Spiritual; exoteric and esoteric; ancient, medieval, and modern.

Thus, during our Sat-Guru's Teaching years, we explored every area of fundamental human concern thoroughly and with freedom, Guided by the Principle of self-transcending Wisdom and Love that was Incarnate and Vocal as our Divine Teacher. As it happened, our experiments coincided with a time when many of our Western contemporaries were investigating options in behavior and relationships that departed from long-standing norms.

It is the Happy conclusion and contention of Heart-Master Da Love-Ananda and of His devotees that, far from being outside the domain of true religious activity, such experiments can really bear fruit only <u>within</u> that true religious domain—most particularly, in the context of the living sacred relationship to a true Sat-Guru or God-Realizer.

At least since Upanishadic times, such experimental determinations of the most auspicious way to conduct a human life have been made by men and women of superior Wisdom. The modern world is inconceivably Blessed by Heart-Master Da's Willingness to devote Himself so exhaustively to such a comprehensive cultural Experiment in our time, in order to rediscover and express anew the Dharma—the Way of living that is both true to human nature and most conducive to our Realization of the very Truth.

Those who become formally acknowledged practitioners of the Way of the Heart in Heart-Master Da's Company, now and in the future, will see that His now summary and conclusive Instruction in the practical matters of daily living does not impose arbitrary restraints upon behavior. Rather, through His Instruction He defines the parameters of Divine Wisdom within which each of us must constantly determine and consciously choose our own optimum forms of activity and association.

Each individual's effective practice of the Way of the Heart, based upon the "Experimental" Teaching-Revelation of Heart-Master Da Love-Ananda, is and forever will be both a precise, freely experimental science and a sublime art of whole bodily God-Communion and, ultimately, Perfectly self-transcending God-Realization. It is the antithesis of what people have in mind when they complain about the strictures of "authoritarianism" in religious practice under the guidance of a Spiritual Teacher. This art and science of Divine, and Divinely Self-Realizing, life requires one to take increasingly comprehensive personal responsibility for every aspect of one's existence. Just as an athlete submits to a demanding coach, and as a martial artist submits to the sometimes harsh discipline of an expert, the authentic devotee submits to the Adept Heart-Teacher and True Heart-Master—but he or she does not thereby submit an isolated portion or period of his or her life, as an artist or an athlete typically does. The devotee submits every aspect of his or her life, and wholeheartedly, and eternally, to the Enlightened One's Guidance and Discipline, for the sake of an Awakening that he or she cannot manifest alone. That Awakening requires the devotee's demonstration of responsibility for every aspect of the body-mind.

This Free and Awakened approach to human behavior and relationships is, of course, neither popular nor popularly understood. Because this is so, esoteric Spiritual Teaching is difficult and dangerous in our time—as it always has been. The bare facts of the execution of Jesus of Nazareth speak for themselves. The legendary Avatars Krishna and Rama are said to have fought for their lives. Mohammed was poisoned. Gautama the Buddha was almost assassinated. Both Milarepa in eleventh-century Tibet and Swami Nityananda in twentieth-century India, we are told, had to use their Yogic siddhis to avoid being poisoned by people posing as devotees. Ramanuja, the great Adept-devotee of medieval India, narrowly escaped an attempt on his life by his own early Guru, who was jealous of his superior Realization and wisdom. Both Shirdi Sai Baba and Upasani Baba Maharaj were harassed by lawsuits.

243

Heart-Master Da, moreover, had dared to Teach in the very bodily dimensions of human life where most Teachers and Adepts would not think to tread so boldly: in the taboo-ridden arenas of our most common and tenacious obsessions—sexuality, power, sustenance, and interpersonal intimacy.

Thus, in early 1985, it should not have been surprising that a group of disaffected ex-students brought an attack against Heart-Master Da and His Work through the news media and the American legal system.

Much of what was alleged in the media was sheerly preposterous, and much of the rest was twisted and distorted. The representatives of our formal institution learned the hard way that there is no way to achieve a fair hearing in the sensation-mongering elements of public reporting, which demonstrated that they had no more interest in the facts of actual events than they had in the Eternal Divine Truth. The allegations were predictable enough, dealing with the themes of sex, drugs, money, and coercion.

This was not the first time we had been exposed to the possibility of such an attack. Heart-Master Da, ever attentive to the moods of the world in which He was Teaching, had prophetically identified the heart of the difficulty with such Work and its popular reception years before:

When all is said and done about the great affair of religious cultism and spiritual community, it still remains true that human beings need to grow beyond the subhuman round of mob societies. Human beings need to adapt to their own higher functions and to the Living Transcendental Reality. And the Way in which this is done is in intimate spiritual community. The process of higher human, moral, mystical, and evolutionary spiritual adaptation is a cultural process. That process is necessarily self-transcending, not merely self-fulfilling. And it requires both technical instruction and practical guidance by one who is an Adept in the total process. Therefore, it is not a merely self-manipulative process of private experience, but a self-sacrificial process—in community with other practitioners, and in a mutually sacrificial relationship with a true Spiritual Master (to whom one may not be related merely as a submissive child or a rebellious adolescent is to a parent, but only as a responsible aspirant, awakened to Wisdom and Truth, is related to an Enlightened Teacher and Initiator and Guide).

The creation and development of an authentic community or culture of evolutionary spiritual practice is an immensely difficult affair—because people are, in general, so profoundly afraid, self-possessed, adapted to archaic and self-defeating patterns of thought and behavior, and constantly disturbed by childish and adolescent motives toward chaotic self-fulfillment. Therefore, even the communities of experimental spiritual culture bear all the evidence of the growing pains, the tackiness, the immaturity, and all the other bewildering deficiencies that otherwise mark the secular and subhuman order of the world.

Some imagine that this is scandalous, and so they criticize even authentic cultural experiments with a kind of negative "gotcha" mentality that implies nothing but a viciously destructive intent. This is a tendency that can easily be observed in the popular media of TV, newspapers, and magazines.

Therefore, resist all attempts to be "officially" and dogmatically informed—whether for or against—about religion and the significance of religious institutions and teachers of religion. Consider and experience that entire affair yourself. And be humored by the realization that the popular communications media are fundamentally motivated by the necessity to propagandize and entertain, through fascinating and alarming messages. That is how they make their money and achieve their power. And we ourselves have taught them to do so, by childishly submitting to be entertained, and even demanding to be entertained and told what is black-and-white true.[15]

We had studied these statements, but now, in 1985, we were swept into the actual experience of such a "viciously destructive intent". Yet, in our own deliberations, it soon became clear that the real fault was not with those who had left our experiment and wanted now to attack and even destroy it. That, in a sense, was as predictable as the kind of allegations that were being made, although if the rest of us had responsibly maintained positive relations with them earlier, the whole event might have been averted. No, the real fault, and the great wound inflicted by that ugly incident, was in the bond of love and trust between Heart-Master Da and His active, present devotees.

As a community we were stunned by the destructive energy aligned against us. But that was only what occurred on the surface level of external events in the daily world. At a deeper level, our lack of concerted, responsive strength as devotees in this crisis was no different from any other moment of Narcissistic self-protection.

From shortly after He was informed about the impending events, in late January 1985, and for months thereafter, Heart-Master Da lived in

---

15. Da Free John [Heart-Master Da Love-Ananda], *Scientific Proof of the Existence of God Will Soon Be Announced by the White House!* pp. 104-5.

seclusion. The "reality considerations" and His other Teaching Activities largely came to a halt. Psychically, the God-Man, open-Hearted and Free, had to absorb and transform the energy of this entire attempt to destroy His sometimes unconventional but always benign and profoundly necessary Teaching Work.

Eventually, matters were resolved with the contending former members. The news media, with no further conflict to incite and thrive upon, lost interest and turned their attention elsewhere.

But what had occurred in Heart-Master Da's living Work to Awaken others? He had always explained that the Guru must be a shapeshifter, an "underminer" in His Teaching activity. He had to mock and satirize the ego, and to paint accurate, and unflattering, pictures of it in Words. He had to find ways, and He did so with unfailing inventiveness, to coax devotees into showing their hidden hand of self-obsession, so that He could reflect them to themselves. He presumed that those who came to Him were seriously interested in Realizing the Truth, and, therefore, that they were interested in outgrowing the bondage that He was helping them to observe and understand.

In ego-based therapeutic contexts, the phenomenon of transference is well known. When a psychoanalyst begins to frustrate the interpersonal rituals of the patient, the patient becomes angry and often accuses the analyst of his or her own faults, through projection. Heart-Master Da had frequently warned devotees of a similar syndrome not only in those who came and left His Work, but also in all of us who remained. From Heart-Master Da's "radically" selfless perspective, the egoic self in any mode or stage of life—including every stage of practice prior to Perfect ego-transcendence, or seventh stage, Divine Self-Realization—is "at war with its own Help". And those who cannot embrace the stark self-yielding of true devotional surrender frequently speak about the need to strengthen the ego-sense, complain that the Guru is wrong, false, or unfair, constantly criticize all those around Him, and may eventually leave His sacred school.

Heart-Master Da had seen the truculent anger of resistive Western seekers from the night He Gave His first talk in 1972. Every practitioner experiences moods of reaction to the rigors of practice—indeed, that is inevitable until the devotee has advanced beyond the beginners' stages. That is why Heart-Master Da always emphasized that the beginners' stages, especially, involve a "struggle with self"—and specifically not a struggle with Him as Teacher, or with others, or with the sacred institution of His Work.

But there were other factors at play that produced our public crisis in 1985. Those who had first come to Him constantly indulged, willfully or not, in competition with others for access to Him. Because He was never interested in merely tolerating any of the games of the ego, He often Worked in His characteristic "Crazy-Wise" fashion with this syndrome of egoic associations to let us feel its heartlessness and futility—much as He Worked with us in relation to our sexual mores and pursuits, and our egoic orientation to every other aspect of life. At the same time He Taught vigorously the Way and the necessity to thoroughly transcend the "growling pit" of ego-politics.

During and after the dissident crisis of 1985, and also for many years previous to it, Heart-Master Da criticized the "insider-outsider game" of ego-politics and, most particularly, the male competition rituals, among all of us who surrounded Him. While acknowledging the Spiritual gravity of abandoning and, worse, of attacking a Teacher whom one has formally acknowledged as one's Guru (and by Whom one has been formally acknowledged as a disciple, and thus welcomed into an Eternal Bond of mutually vulnerable sacred love-commitment), Heart-Master Da pointed out, during that crisis, that those who had left our gathering were not essentially different from those who had stayed. He said that those who strive for personal proximity to the Adept are (to the degree they remain ego-based in their disposition) indulging egoic motives that are no less self-centered than the motives of those who keep their distance and criticize the "insiders". The same impasse or resistance to devotional self-yielding was being dramatized by "Narcissus" in both instances, the same fundamental refusal to be a devotee and to Stand Free with Him in Truth.

Not until early October, when the published version of The Dawn Horse Testament arrived in Hermitage, did Heart-Master Da gather again with His devotees. Gradually, during the following months, He ventured again to Teach as He had in the past. But only to a degree. And, indeed, it would take a long time for devotees to even begin to regain, now with a depth of maturity, the innocence and energy for explicit devotion to Him that had characterized them, albeit naively, in the earlier years of His Work. This public defamation of His Work tried the faith of every devotee and invaded our sacred experiment with the juggernaut force of the irrational elements of the news media, where the profound logic of "Crazy" sacred Wisdom is only easy prey to bigotry, persecution, and vulgar, destructive ridicule.

In late 1985 it was obvious to Heart-Master Da that His devotees had no real feeling for what He had just endured because of His Willingness to Teach, or for how vulnerable and human is His bodily Appearance as a Man in the world. He spoke at length about His vulnerability and our need to understand that His Teaching Work was finished—and now it was <u>our</u> obligation to manifest greatness in devotional response to Him. By now even His most openly Ecstatic Speech was also extremely sobering for His listeners. At the end of November, He said:

HEART-MASTER DA LOVE-ANANDA: I am no "me" at all! I sit in this Form, conversing with you, playing with you. This body will die. I am no one but the One.

You see Me in this Body. For those in the future, there will be no Body, but the same One will be expressed, the same One will be Present, the same Yoga will be possible. You are the first generation of those who must incarnate that Truth for others, even while this Body lives. So many of My devotees live outside My physical Company because this time is the same as My death time. No one but this One, <u>the</u> One, Speaks to you. I appear to be a person temporarily—a mist, a ko-an. These legs are a deliciously composed intellectual puzzle. It is so, and some day that is how it will be conceived. "How can the physical presence of the Master be imagined?" they will ask in the year 2300. They will not only have The Dawn Horse Testament to read, but they will also enjoy the presence of My living devotees, linked in Revelation with the devotees who survived in My Company while this Body lived. That is the significance of Agency.

Without your Realization I am poor-born and this Revelation is an illusion! <u>You</u> must Realize It! The poor few who closet themselves with Me on this island, who visit here, who have known Me before, who have sat with Me—it all depends on <u>you</u>. You must Realize, as I have since Birth, the profound weight of obligation that rests on you because of what is Given to you. You must Realize It. Otherwise these gestures are ghosts. I am an unknowable Spirit for My devotees in the year 2300 unless My devotees in flesh and blood sit there, sublimed by this Realization, which they will not get unless <u>you</u> get it! You must realize the significance of the Yoga of Agency, and stop oppressing Me with parent-like obligations. Do not throw it back at me. I throw it back at you! You are obliged. You have a terrible demand pressed on your heart. <u>You</u> do! You must Realize It. You must extend this Blessing in your natural manner, by fulfilling the Way of the Heart. <u>You</u> must! <u>You</u> must! (November 1985)

"Mankind is the Avatar but you stop short"— the anguished final crisis of the "Crazy" Prophetic Teacher

More than a decade before the above talk was Given, on the same night during the Garbage and the Goddess period when Andrew Johnson became enraptured by the Adept's Divine Humor, after all the Spiritual chaos had calmed, I asked Heart-Master Da Who He Is. He said, matter-of-factly, "I am the Avatar"—that is, the "Descent", the Divine Incarnation.

But Heart-Master Da's constant theme during the Garbage and the Goddess time, as throughout His later Teaching years and continuing today, was His Call for the appearance of the true and eternal Avatar—in the Form of a true, Free, and Awakened Community of Enlightened Devotees. Indeed, at the end of the Garbage and the Goddess Teaching Demonstration He had summarized His Intention thus:

HEART-MASTER DA LOVE-ANANDA: The Community of those who become [practicing, Spiritually activated] Devotees is the true Devi, the Divine Consort. It is also true that the world is the Avatar, the totality of human beings is the Avatar. It is humanity as a whole that is the Avatar in human form, not some specific human individual. No apparent or exclusive manifestation is in itself the Avatar. Only the whole is the Divine Manifestation without exclusion. Therefore, the Guru is not the Avatar in that exclusive sense. Mankind is the Avatar. I am his Heart. When the Avatar Realizes his true Nature and Condition, when he Realizes me, he will cease to be hidden. He and this Community of which I speak will become one and the same at last. Then his sadhana is fulfilled, and he will manifest his Beauty in the world for the sake of all beings. Only then will he live freely and do his Divine work.[16]

On Translation Island in 1983, He had told devotees:

HEART-MASTER DA LOVE-ANANDA: You are the seed of a great historical change, and you cannot even see What is before your eyes. We have

---

16. Bubba Free John [Heart-Master Da Love-Ananda], *Garbage and the Goddess*, p. 335.

accomplished great things already, although you are not yet aware of it. As decades pass, you will see the import of What you have all experienced in seed form but cannot yet acknowledge.

Da Free John is not an egoic religious leader. Sooner or later, the world will come to know that the purpose of My Birth is to transform the world in a critical moment in history. And I will do it. But I need this vehicle of response. I need the human vehicle, because the purpose of My Birth is to transform mankind, everyone, human history, by bringing us through this terrible transition in which we now find ourselves. My Birth is an epochal moment of Spiritual Intervention, and you are showing the same reluctance that has always appeared in those associated with Adepts in the past. When you have passed through this crisis of growth, you will begin to understand what has happened, what Force has been brought into the flesh through My Birth.

What I Submit to, I become, and this makes My Life a crucifixion. What you submit to Glorifies you, Awakens you, expands the sphere of your existence, and brings you into a Glorious Possibility. All of us will participate in that Glorious Possibility in time. I promise you will see this. But here we are in this human plane, involved in this great struggle, which is difficult, but made easier by My Coming here. (November 1983)

Indeed, after every gathering He ever had with devotees, after His Dharmic Revelation of the Teaching and the practice "considerations", after the poetry and the opera, after the dancing and His God-Mad pronouncements of Love, when His devotees had once again been Divinely Instructed, purified, challenged, and made Radiant, Called to and bathed in the ecstasy of Love-Bliss, invigorated with the liberal Spirit-Gift of His Freedom, and when they had all gone to their private places for food and sleep, now brimming over with His "Bright" Joy, He, the Divine Teacher Da, almost invariably passed through a horrible ordeal of convulsive, shaking, sometimes death-like release of all the karmas He had absorbed from them in Person to set them again so Free.

Heart-Master Da passed through torments of this kind countless times during all the many years of His Teaching Identification with everyone and His absorption of our states, our karmas, our dis-ease. These incidents occurred not just after every celebratory-style gathering, but after every meditation with us, every Darshan occasion, every worldwide sitting. He once said:

HEART-MASTER DA LOVE-ANANDA: I wish you all would participate in these gatherings as I do. Because you do not, I suffer various effects. When I meet with you once more, I must make this same gesture again, suffer it once again, because you do not participate as I do. We enjoy a simple evening together, and I must suffer a near-death phenomenon in the body and all kinds of psychic chaos that I inherit from all of you. After any such gathering, I must spend a day or two restoring My balance so I can be reintegrated with this body-mind and then do it with you again. If you all participated as I do, threw everything away as I do, there would be a portion of the evening that none of us would remember, and I would suffer less afterward. You would all suffer a little and I would suffer a little, and there would be no end to the Bliss Realized during that period when no one has any memory, and that Bliss would continue as the basic factor in our lives. Such a gathering would be an extraordinary event that would change you utterly. It would never be remembered, and it would never be forgotten. It would never disappear, and you would exist in a State no one else could account for—the God-State, the Divine State, in which you are filled, infused, and utterly transcended by the God-Power, Which is All-Pervading.

I Call you in all these celebrations with Me to enter into that Filled Oblivion of Happiness and become something greater than human. Enter into Samadhi with Me. But you fall short. You take too seriously all the buttons I press in you and all the barbs I lay on you when I am throwing Myself away. You are sitting here feeling your various reactive emotions and making a hangover out of them. Throw them away, just as I do, and then remember nothing. On an evening in which all of us gather, there should be a space in time that no one can remember, because nothing happens that is about remembering anything. That space should be about Ecstasy without the slightest qualification. If any such evening or incident could ever occur among us, you would never be the same. Never.

The doctors wonder what to do to heal Me. They want to heal the signs in this body-mind of its various forms of suffering. Give Me the ultimate Ecstasy of those whom I Absorb into My own State. If you resist it, then after I pass through that oblivion, I must struggle with all the chaos of your limitations. I have not died from it yet, but I often have close-to-death experiences. After a simple night with you, I always experience madness, strains, stress, horrible pain. I restore the economy in this body-mind, but then I gather with you again. The first time should have been more effective. It is effective in any case, but only somewhat effective. So I must do it again.

Translation Island, 1985

You take too seriously all the tests I Give you as I go to Infinity with you, and so you fall short. You stop short. This is really so. The Act I perform with you is completely sufficient, and you could be utterly Free now, but you do not go all the way with Me. You stop. You start reacting.

The effect of My Work could be much greater than it ever has been if you truly heard Me and saw Me. Then you would pass with Me through this ceremony of Ecstasy, of Transfiguration and Transformation. You would pass through the whole event and be utterly different, never the same again, never fallen again. Really. Really. You have never done it yet. Not yet, unfortunately. (May 1984)

The God-Man Da, One with the Power of the Heart-Source of all that Is, had ventured to upend the ancient injunctions excluding the ordinary man from the esoteric Way of Realization. We, His devotees, were not of the sort deemed acceptable in the Spiritual traditions, heroic and godly aspirants to Realization. In traditional sacred orders, we would have been considered the unacceptables, the animal-like, the undisciplined and dissolute, the ordinary men and women not yet self-restrained and Awake to God at heart.

Heart-Master Da was endeavoring to bring the Great Goddess-Power, now Perfectly Mastered by His own Divine Embrace, so deeply and tangibly into the stuff of the world and the body-mind-hearts of these ordinary, worldly devotees that even they and others like them could become Realizers of the Absolute.

It was a Divinely desperate Stratagem. He did not know if it could or would succeed—except that at last it must succeed, because at last the worlds must be Restored to Truth and Dissolved in their own Source-Light, and He knew that He Is the Agent of that greater-than-cosmic Event in the Heart. But He had to have the human link of Awakened and Awakening devotees.

During the first ten days of the New Year, 1986, Heart-Master Da pleaded more and more adamantly for devotees' response to Him and their renunciation of the need to be Taught any further. His Work as Teacher, He could feel, was over, utterly over. Yet they would not, could not, respond—not really, not fully, not conclusively, not to the satisfaction of One Who lived as Responsiveness only. And if even His most intimate devotees, His "coins", into whose hearts and minds and lives He had poured Himself ceaselessly year after year—if they could not and would not respond, how could His Work proceed? What was He to do?

He had Given these and so many others everything possible for their Awakening, with an appetite for extremes of Giving that had many times nearly destroyed Him.

How many hours in the 1970s had He spent around His great oval table in His Residence at The Mountain Of Attention, "considering" the Truth, and Its Way, and their obstructions and resistance to It, with these and some few others? Or, in the early 1980s, in the Chung Room, the tiny gathering-room crucible for His Fire of Spirit-Baptism and renunciation at Tumomama Sanctuary? Or, on several Fijian islands, and more recently at The Matrix and in these very rooms, with these very people, trying to evoke their own Ecstatic, God-Filled Dance to the Divine Drumbeat of His "reality considerations"?

How many times had He Blessed them each, them and so many others, with His Glance, His Touch, His Embrace, His world-shaking Laugh infectious with Freedom, His barely uttered "Tcha" that says "Yes!" to devotion and anoints it with Love that melts the heart? How many times had He sung to them the delight of Perfect Understanding of all self-limitation and all seeking, and His "Crazy" Ecstatic Praise of "the Great One"?

How many times had they sat with Him in Darshan and received His Vision of the Great Bliss that countless seekers have prayed to feel even once in all their lives? How many times had He "happened" to walk past groups of them and their friends at one or another of His Ashrams, leaving a Blaze of God-Feeling in their hearts as they gazed upon Him?

How many times had He healed their bodies and calmed their hearts by Touch or Word or Glance or Thought? How many times had He addressed, and painstakingly, their "cases"—the byzantine intricacies of their infantile, childish, adolescent, emotional-sexual oedipal Narcissism? How many kisses had He Granted? How many startling Zen-like slaps in the face? How many Samadhis had He Given them? How many Liberating criticisms? Why did they not respond, when even His most ego-puncturing Words were "only modulations of My Blessing-Current"?

How many parties had He consented to engage with them—liberal feasts to toast and taste the Spirit-Substance of Life and to coax them out of guilty body-denial, created by pleasureless lifetimes and religions of so-called "fear of God"?

How many Satsang-meditations had He consented to attend with them, ancient moveless rites of silent God-Transmission, Awakening the Heart-Intelligence that transcends all things, even life itself, and releases all feeling into unknowable Love?

In the morning hours of deepest darkness on January 11, 1986, the futility and apparent uselessness of all that He had Done bore in upon the God-Born Man, Heart-Master Da. He and a small group of His "coins" had been persisting in another of their "considerations" for nearly thirty-six hours without ceasing. This occasion was only an extension of the sixteen previous years of Teaching, done with utter abandon for nearly twenty-four hours a day in the company of one or some or many devotees.

None of it had made the Difference. He was their prisoner, like the doctor in Africa in the allegory He had often told them: A physician comes to heal the people, only to be detained because he is so effective, and then worked to near death, and eventually killed by them in their resentment of their own dependency upon him. Heart-Master Da longed to be done with this world—like His Spirit-Friend Rang Avadhoot, who had given Him more Life in that one Glance in Swami Muktananda's Ashram garden in 1968 than He had ever gotten from His own devotees, and who had ended his own long life in Yogic death, rapping his knuckles three times on the crown of his head and then ascending out of human embodiment.

Now, in the pre-dawn gloom that January 11, the Supremely Enlightened Master-Teacher and Divine Incarnation, Da, gave up trying to evoke His devotees' response. For hours He had been at His Residence in the Hermitage Village, and the group of His "coins" had been gathered in a nearby building, No Doubt Of God, to discuss His comments and Calls to them. He spoke to them by telephone, giving broken, faltering voice to His heart's despair. His Work was over. There had been no response. He was ready to die—willing for it, even.

And as He spoke, it began to happen. He said He could feel the numbness coming up His arm, His back. He could see the visions . . .

At that moment the Divine Master Da dropped the phone and collapsed. Devotees rushed over from the other house to find Him slumped on the floor by His bed, unconscious. After a final spasm of convulsions, He was still. All life had apparently passed from His body.

It was yet sometime before dawn on January 11, 1986.

The Mountain Of Attention, 1989

"An Ascetic
on Fire"

The Divine Descent
and Sacrificial Penance of
The Naitauba Avadhoota,
Da Love-Ananda

The Naitauba Avadhoota, Da Love-Ananda, Translation Island, March 1986

CHAPTER FIVE

"An Ascetic on Fire"

The Divine Descent and Sacrificial Penance of The Naitauba Avadhoota, Da Love-Ananda

The visible events that followed the Heart-Teacher's death-like collapse

The devotees at the small building called No Doubt Of God had been listening for hours to one of their group as she spoke to Heart-Master Da by phone and then relayed His anguished Words to them. But sometime in the hours before dawn, she stopped talking to the others and began pleading with Him: "No! Don't say that! You can't do that! No!" At that, several of them dashed out the door and ran to Heart-Master Da's house. They arrived at the doorway of His room to find Him collapsed and in convulsions, and they stood there in shock as their Divine Teacher's body became still.

As others rushed into the room, someone ran to get the doctors. Charles Seage, the principal physician, awoke to the urgent cry, "The Master is dying! Don't wait! Go straight into His room!"

The scene in Heart-Master Da's room was chaos. No one knew how to help Him. Some of the women screamed, even argued about what to do as they stood over His body, while others sat stunned.

Charles knelt behind Heart-Master Da and put his arms around His chest to lift Him up, calling loudly, "Master! Master!" Together he and the other physician, Daniel Bouwmeester, lifted their Heart-Teacher's body

259

from the floor and onto His bed so they could examine Him.

His face was ashen white with a crimson hue. His eyes were rolled up. He did not respond to any call or stimulus, physical or verbal. His hands and feet were cold and clammy.

A few devotees who had remained calm helped the doctors serve Him physically. A woman screamed, "Master! Don't die! We need You!" Another begged Him to stay alive for the sake of the children. Other devotees wept uncontrollably, or sat silent and withdrawn, incapable of feeling what their eyes could not deny. Even the doctors, administering their services with clinical calm and efficiency, felt pained and awkward.

Their examination revealed the faintest of life-signs in the Divine Adept's physical body. His blood pressure and pulse were severely depressed—more extremely so than they had ever seen before, and these physicians had tended to Him during many of His near-death moments in the past. Almost imperceptibly, He was breathing.

The two physicians and others present had been Instructed by Heart-Master Da in how to care for His body during this kind of trial, or at any other time that He might pass into a Yogic state of suspended animation. They knew that the worst possible thing they could do was to interfere with the natural and the esoteric Spiritual process of His unique association with bodily life and awareness. Therefore, since His life-signs, though depressed, were stably present, the doctors determined not to initiate medical emergency procedures. Instead, along with several other devotees, they massaged Him and performed the laying on of hands.

After a time Heart-Master Da made a small motion, and the doctors lifted Him to a sitting position. His arms hung limp at His sides—a sign that He was still only barely associated with His body. He made a feeble gesture for the devotees, clustered close around Him on His bed, to give Him more room. They seemed not to notice. Heart-Master Da gestured again, this time forcefully flinging both arms away from His body, and a surge of energy pushed the devotees back.

Then He began to weep. He stretched His arms out in front of His body with His palms turned up, muttering and crying again and again, "Four billion people, the four billion!"

The raw sorrow in His voice and on His face was unbearable for the others to feel.

Soon His anguished murmuring turned to them, His intimate "coins". Distractedly, as if they were not even in the room with Him, He asked

Himself, still weeping, "If they will not respond, what can be done?"

After a time, seeing that their heartbroken Teacher was fully restored
to bodily awareness, most of the devotees departed quietly, leaving Him
to the care of His most intimate attendants.

The day of the Secret

A few hours later that morning, Greg Purnell received a request
to bring a car to Heart-Master Da's Residence in the village. Heart-Master
Da wished to return to The Matrix, on the southern shore of the island.

Greg was a little apprehensive. An American in his mid-thirties, he
had been a devotee of Heart-Master Da for more than a decade, and for
the last several years he had been a member of the resident devotee staff
on Naitauba. Affectionately named "Gyro" by His Teacher, Greg was
responsible for the audiovisual department and its equipment on the
island.

Occasionally—as on this January morning—he was also called upon
to drive Heart-Master Da from one of His Residences on the island to the
other. Greg loved to perform this personal service to the Adept. Today he
had heard, however, that the events of the previous evening and night
had been extremely difficult. He did not know what had occurred, but it
was obvious to him that the devotees who had been with Heart-Master
Da were gravely distressed.

For a while Greg stood by the car in front of Heart-Master Da's simple
white frame house, looking out upon the blue waters of the tropical
lagoon and the Pacific Ocean. He had not seen Heart-Master Da very
often in recent weeks. He worried that his Teacher might still be either
angrily upset with devotees or totally exhausted from the events of the
night and early morning. Charles Seage, Heart-Master Da's physician, was
also standing nearby waiting to accompany them to The Matrix. Except
for a few words, the two men did not speak as they stood by the car.

Greg's nervousness vanished as soon as Heart-Master Da walked out
the door of the house. In the already hot sunshine of the Fijian summer,
Greg immediately saw and felt His Teacher's vibrant Happiness and physical strength. Dressed in His then customary shorts, His long brown hair
still wet from a shower, Heart-Master Da appeared to be unusually round,

or "Full", as devotees often described Him to one another. His great belly and whole body were magnetic with Spiritual Energy, and His very large, dark eyes danced with delight. No sooner had their eyes met than Heart-Master Da addressed Greg by his nickname:

"Gyro, why have you deprived Me of your company for so long? Come over here and let Me Give you a big kiss!"

Smiling at the teasing question, Greg embraced his Teacher. Heart-Master Da's hugs were always immersions in His Spiritual Presence, and this one was no different; Greg soon felt infused by Love, as if he were losing the sense of his own physical boundaries and melting into the Enlightened Adept's body. Though Heart-Master Da had often affectionately kissed devotees on the cheek, on this day He surprised Greg by making a big point of kissing him on the lips.

When they parted, Greg, a little dazed and very happy, opened the car door for Him. But first Heart-Master Da approached Charles Seage, standing nearby, and also embraced him—again making a point of kissing him directly on the lips.

Then they all climbed into the vehicle. Typically Heart-Master Da liked to ride in the front seat across from the driver, but on this morning He chose to sit in the back with a few devotees who were accompanying Him to The Matrix. Seated directly behind Greg, He spoke to him for about five minutes as they drove, talking about His Love for him and for Greg's wife, Emily:

"Gyro, do you know that I think of you constantly? Do you know that I think of Emily constantly? Do you think of Me constantly?"

Greg responded, "Yes, Master", to each question. But the more Heart-Master Da spoke of His Regard for Greg, Emily, and others and continued asking about Greg's regard for Him, the more self-conscious Greg became. Again and again and again, He asked, "Gyro—do you know how much I Love you?" Greg continued to say yes. But he felt that in fact he did not and really could not know the full extent of Heart-Master Da's great Love.

After about ten minutes, they came to a cattle gate on the high inland plateau of Naitauba. Greg stopped the car and got out to open the gate so they could drive through. Just as he stepped down from the car, Heart-Master Da asked him again: "Gyro—do you really know how much I Love you?"

Greg later described what happened:

I was faced with a choice: I could ignore the question (pretending I had not heard) by being a "good, serving devotee" and opening the gate (which is what I would have done by tendency)—or I could face my Beloved and answer Him. In my heart I wanted to face the Great One. Even so, it took all the energy I could muster to stick my head back inside the car and look at Him face to face.

The Vision I saw was most glorious, Attractive, and fierce. Everything and everyone else in the car disappeared from my awareness as I was filled with the Vision of Him. I saw His huge head, His intense eyes, and His smile that proved to me He already knew and Loved me. His face was no more than two feet from my eyes.

I was lost in that special intensity that surrounds the physical Person of Heart-Master Da. I wanted only to be completely honest with Him and let all expectations and fears go. I said, "No, not really."

His expression relaxed a bit. He said, "This was a test, and you failed."

Despite His Words, what occurred in that moment changed me at the heart. My heart had opened, like the shutter of a camera, and His face was permanently imprinted there. For many weeks afterward I saw that face constantly, especially in meditation. In that moment Heart-Master Da's Image was set in my heart, for me to carry and worship forever.

Several times, on that drive out to The Matrix the morning of January 11, 1986, Heart-Master Da said aloud to Greg, Charles, and the other devotees with Him, "I have a Secret." Charles too was relieved to see Heart-Master Da so hale, and he felt touched and Blessed to have been embraced and kissed by Him. But he had no more of a clue to the nature of Heart-Master Da's "Secret" than did Greg or any of the others. It was obvious from His playfulness that His Secret had something to do with His Spiritual Work, and perhaps with the events of the morning. No one asked Him what It was—they sensed that He would have told them more if He had intended them to know at the time. They knew that the Secret would be Revealed when Heart-Master Da felt the time was right.

The Secret of the Kiss—
"In a sense that Event was My Birth Day"

For two weeks Heart-Master Da stayed in seclusion at The Matrix. Then, on January 27, He returned to the village.

In a gathering that evening, Greg Purnell told Him the leela of how the Vision of His Divine face had been imprinted into his heart. The Radiant Adept was then moved to tell His devotees something of the "Secret" He had mentioned that morning of January 11 on the drive to The Matrix:

HEART-MASTER DA LOVE-ANANDA: Presumably for you all the Great Event of your life—if it ever occurs, in whichever life it does occur, or whenever, or wherever—the Great Event of your life would be God-Realization. You imagine, then, that a number of the Events in My Life must have been Great, and that the consummate Event must have been the Vedanta Temple Event. But that is not so. It is a very important Event for you all. It initiated My Teaching Work. But the Realization in the Vedanta Temple was not overwhelming, as you know from all the signs I described to you. In My case, the Condition Realized in the Vedanta Temple is Inherent, and priorly Realized. To achieve such an Event was just part of My Work in this world. It was not the Great Event in My Life. Perhaps it would be a Great Event in the lives of others, but for Me there was a Greater Event, an Event that occurred more recently, in fact.

On the morning of January 11 I told certain of My devotees of My grief and sorrow and frustration in My Work. I told them that I just could not endure anymore the rejection, the offensiveness, the abuse, the futility. I told them I wished to leave, wished to die then, and I said: "May it come quickly." They all thought it might happen soon. It seemed to Me also that it could happen within hours. But suddenly it began to happen on the spot. As I was describing the possibility of this physical event, I felt numbness coming up My arm, numbness in My spine, a certain numbness in My body, and convulsions. Finally I passed out of the body, and it just fell down.

I do not have memory of the sequence of events that followed for a little while, but I am told that many devotees came running to My house. Doctors came and tried to resuscitate Me. Eventually, I began to reassociate with the body, although I was not aware of the room exactly, nor of who was there. I began to Speak of My greater concerns and impulses and of My great sorrow for the four billion humans and the rest of the beings everywhere. I cannot endure such sorrow very well—I have never endured it very well. I have had to bring My Self very deliberately to this Work. And in this Event, I was drawn further into the body with a very human impulse, a love-impulse. Becoming aware of My profound relationship with all My devotees, I resumed My bodily state.

This is the Event I am referring to, not just the death (which was real—I did die on the spot) but the occasion of reassociating with the body. I was attracted back by very human things, not by impulses to Liberate mankind—those impulses are there already, you see—but by very human impulses, responding to My own intimate human life and the human existence of others, of all of you. Even though I have existed as a man during this Life-time, obviously—I became profoundly Incarnate—I now assumed an impulse toward human existence more profound than I had assumed before, without any reluctance relative to sorrow and death.

On so many occasions I have told you that I wish I could Kiss every human being on the lips, Embrace each one, and Enliven each one from the heart. In this body I will never have the opportunity. I am frustrated in that impulse. Even though I have done all kinds of Spiritual Work, I will never be able to do that exactly. But in that motion of sympathetic Incarnation, that acceptance of the body and its sorrow and its death, I realized a Kiss, a way to fulfill the impulse.

Now that My Teaching Work is essentially fulfilled, a different kind of gesture was made, which in some fundamental sense is the equivalent of the Embrace I would Give to everyone, to all human beings, all four billion, even all beings, all that are self-conscious and dying in this place, not by embracing each one literally with this body, but by assuming this body as the likeness of all and accepting the sorrow without the slightest resistance, nothing abstracting Me from mortality, nothing.

In some sense that Event was My Birth Day.

You have heard descriptions, by Yogis and other Spiritual figures, of how before Realization you try to go beyond the world to Realize God, and then after Realization you come down into the body just so far, down to the brain, down to the throat maybe, down to the heart maybe, but typically not any lower than the throat. Well, I have until now invested My Self more profound-ly than just down to the throat or the heart, but not down to the bottoms of My feet. I remained a kind of shroud around this body, deeply associated with it, with all of the ordinary human things, playing as a human being often in very ordinary ways, but, in My Freedom, somehow lifted off the floor, somehow not committed to this sorrow and this mortality, expecting, having come as deep as I had, to perhaps Teach enough, embrace enough, kiss enough, Love enough to make the difference, as if through a single body I could indulge in intimacy with everything and everyone self-conscious.

I have realized the futility of that expectation, even the futility of not being able, through a kind of Submission of My Own, to utterly Transform and Liberate even those I could embrace and know intimately. That frustration is fully known by Me now. Even the futility of Liberating those most intimate with Me is known by Me. The kiss is not enough, even for those I know intimately, and I cannot know all intimately.

In My profound frustration, this body died. I left this body. And then I suddenly found My Self reintegrated with it, but in a totally different disposition, and I achieved your likeness exactly, thoroughly, to the bottoms of My feet, _achieved_ un-Enlightenment, _achieved_ human existence, _achieved_ mortality, _achieved_ sorrow.

To Me, this is a Grand Victory! I do not know how to Communicate to you the significance of it. For Me, it was a grander moment than the Event at the Vedanta Temple or any of the other Signs in My Life that are obviously Spiritually auspicious. To Me, it seems that through that will-less, effortless integration with suffering, something about My Work is more profoundly accomplished, something about it has become more auspicious, than it ever was. I have not dissociated from My Realization or My Ultimate State. Rather, I have accomplished your state completely, even more profoundly than you are sensitive to it. Perhaps you have seen it in My face. I do not look like I did last month, and I am never again going to look like that. Don't you know?

I have become this body, utterly. My mood is different. My face is sad, although not without Illumination. I have become the body. Now I am the "Murti", the Icon, and It is Full of the Divine Presence.

The nature of My Work at the present time and in the future is mysterious to Me. It is a certainty, it is obvious, but on the other hand it has not taken the form of mind fully. It has taken an emotional form, but not the form of mind. I cannot explain it really. But you will see the Signs of it. You all must progressively adapt to something that has happened that even I cannot explain altogether. (January 27, 1986)

Signs of the Heart-Power
of Renunciation

I n March 1986 Angelo Druda, a devotee since the mid-1970s, arrived in Hermitage for a month-long meditation retreat. His first occasion of Darshan of Heart-Master Da took place within a day or two of his arrival, when the Divine Avadhoota read aloud and discussed with devotees new essays He had written. Angelo describes the occasion:

From the moment the sitting began, I felt entered and assumed by Heart-Master Da. I did not really even know how deeply until, towards the end of the evening, He became quite still and spoke about Consciousness. He said, "How foolish to bind Consciousness to life!" and I suddenly realized that every cell of my being was profoundly sympathetic with what He was saying.

I have sat with Heart-Master Da many times, and I had never felt such depth of sympathy with His Argument. I have always felt a kind of sympathy, but my resistance has also usually been strong. But in this case, I was utterly sympathetic, to the point of a literal awakening. I was saying to myself, "Of course! How foolish to bind Consciousness to the events of life!" My mood was not righteous, but sympathetic. The very idea that anybody would do that was the silliest thing I could imagine! He continued to speak in that vein, and my being continued to say, "Can you imagine that anybody could be so stupid as to bind Consciousness to objects?"

Then He talked about Outshining the cosmos. I had heard Him talk like that before, but this time, at least to the degree that I could intuit it, that Process was <u>Demonstrated</u> to me. I felt Him Magnifying the Divine Self-Position to the point that any form of noticing of the space-time dimension was dissolving. There was only Divine Happiness.

After He left, no one could move. The priests were absorbed in His Bliss beyond any capacity to distribute the Prasad, the Blessed Gifts given out on such occasions. Everybody was lost in Happiness.

One afternoon a week or so later, I went to Extraordinary Eyes, the principal Communion Hall in the village, for meditation. I saw a pair of sandals on the steps, facing into the Hall. The first thing I thought was, "Nobody puts sandals facing in, right on the steps of the Hall. These must be the Master's sandals. He must be in the Hall." I knew that He visits the Communion Halls periodically to Bless them for devotees. I walked to the porch of my cabin and

267

waited for Him to come out.

His walk that morning is a leela in itself. To everybody who saw Him, it seemed as if He were walking in very slow motion. We watched Heart-Master Da walk out of Extraordinary Eyes and around the back of the Communion Hall toward His home—a couple of hundred feet—and it felt as though a year had passed. Everyone who witnessed this event had a similar experience of it. Time was profoundly stretched. His Siddhi somehow broke through time, or the way we perceive time—a phenomenon that is recounted in the traditions in numerous reports about Adepts. There was a tremendous aura of peace and depth around Him. I noticed that the people who were in the village had either fallen into profound meditation or were just standing still. Everyone in the village was taken over, assumed by the Guru.

Walking in the Hermitage village, early 1986

Devotees all over the world were feeling Heart-Master Da's increasing Heart-Influence, even though we had not yet heard the Leela of His Grand Victory of January 11. Since the earliest days of His Work, He had Revealed that if the devotee is attuned to Him as the Divine Guru through feeling-Remembrance and practical obedience to His Instructions, then the Great Processes in His own body-mind and heart will be duplicated or reflected in the devotee.

Now Heart-Master Da's Work as Teacher had come to an end, so that He was no longer focused in a Divine Effort to Liberate His "coins" or closest devotees by Submissive and reflective Identification with their gross and deeper personalities. Instead, His own human body-mind had become the single Great Coin of His Divine Emergence. His gross and deeper personalities had become a Perfectly Transparent Representation of the Heart, the Divine Self.

Therefore, without even knowing anything about what had occurred, devotees everywhere, attentive to Him, felt suddenly much more attuned to His Divine State of Consciousness and His innate Disposition as a Renouncer of all the limits of egoity and even of all conditional existence.

Such sympathy was shown most visibly in a dramatic change among the four women who were continuing to serve Him Personally. In the weeks following His Divine Descent of January 11, He required them to change every aspect of their relationship with Him. After arduous personal ordeals, they finally came to Him and announced their willingness to give up everything for the sake of Realization and renunciation in His Company. One of them, Kanya Tripura Rahasya, said that spring:

After Heart-Master Da's "Death Event" in Fiji, my service to Him and my relationship to Him changed completely. My devotion to the body-mind, my fulfillment of romantic associations with the body-mind, was utterly abandoned. This was the condition He placed upon my personal relationship to Him. At the time, it was profoundly difficult, and "I" could not have done it. He brought me, step by step, most patiently through this process.

He took me through a profound emotional ordeal and confrontation with the realities, or consequences, of attachment to conditional life through identification with the body-mind. Seeing the reality of my life lived on the basis of those attachments was a horrific vision of mortality. I was struggling constantly. Whenever I would say, "Okay, I have submitted to Heart-Master Da, now I can take on the practice more profoundly," my intention was countered by an obstruction to my utter devotion to Him. And that obstruction was always about my commitment to ordinary life.

Yet as days went by, He Helped me to make the gesture I could not make myself. As He Helped me, it was clearly Revealed that love is about sacrifice, not about what you want or feel you need. I began to feel all the things that I wanted: I wanted to be with Him, to live with Him, to serve Him. "I" wanted to do this. "I" wanted to do that. It was all _me_—I wanted things for myself—and I stopped it. I began to constantly contemplate _His_ feelings. I began to feel Him, feel what He wanted, what He needed, and I stopped demanding for myself.

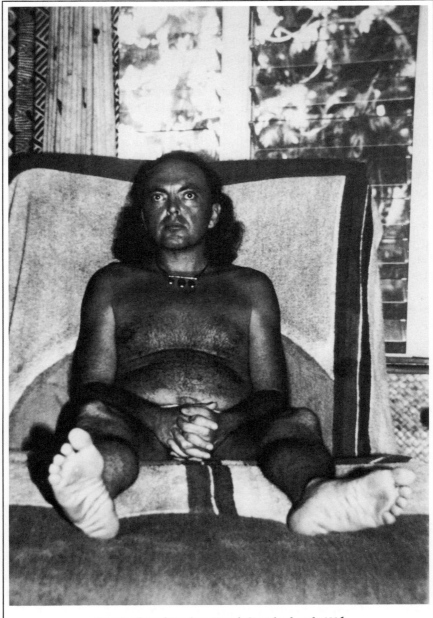

Granting formal Darshan, Translation Island, early 1986

Everything changed for me when I began to feel Him in this way. If ever I had a problem with my own emotions, or mind, or desires, I just completely relaxed in the feeling of what He was feeling.

This confrontation—this death of what I was—took place over many months. It took place slowly, thank goodness, because I do not think I could have survived a radical, instantaneous change. He drew me through it. At the time I had no idea what He was doing, what would be required, or what would happen. I had no idea if I would ever serve Him again personally. I had to be devoted to Him with no expectation or even conception of what might occur. That was the kind of freedom that was required. There was no effort on my part. I would renounce my self, adhere to the discipline, and commit myself to the Way of the Heart, not giving myself any space to fulfill the motives of my own inclinations. Then I would find freedom through Bliss, through Union, through true Identification with the Current of Love-Bliss Itself, Which He Is. That Current is the happiest and most profound Feeling I have ever known.

At this time my fellow renunciates and I were Granted a Graceful moment when everything came together to elicit from us the response of true renunciation. We knew that nothing would fulfill us and there was nothing left to do. We knew that the Realization, Happiness, and Bliss Heart-Master Da had Given us was completely available in the utter transcendence and relinquishment of attention to the body-mind.

It was a great moment of delight and Happiness. We became ecstatic—laughing and crying and telling leelas about our Realization of Communion with Avadhoota Da in this Happiness. We could not stop. We must have "considered" it for hours. All we could do was return to Him and say, "You have Given us everything. There is nothing we have to seek anymore. There is nothing we have to do in the body-mind. There is no Yoga left to do in the body-mind." It was a wonderful moment, because we had spent twelve years in the most profound Fire and testing in His Company.

Still, Heart-Master Da tested our confession. He would not fully accept it until He could feel that it was completely free, and His testing created an even more profound Fire in our life together.

Over the next period of time, we examined everything that was in any way a form of resistance to this Realization, anything whatsoever that was not a full acceptance of renunciation, of practice. It was definitely true that we could take up the "radical" practice. But our confession must be an expression of Ecstasy to the degree of no doubt. You can make the confession, but to have no doubt, to have unceasing faith, is another moment in the process.

The miracle of Liberation became completely obvious—and that miracle was worked through renunciation. I said to Heart-Master Da, "I will give You everything. I do not need anything but You. I do not want anything but You. This world is a hell. I have struggled with it. I have died in it. I have done everything I can do in this world, and I only want You. I do not want the motion of life. I do not want the great spectrum of emotional life. I do not want a conventional life. I do not want social life. I do not want the world. I only want this Bliss, this Happiness. I want You."

Our confession was unique in that we had no idea what we were committing ourselves to or what the consequences would be. We did not know if He would respond. We did not make our confession for the sake of anything. We did not want status. We simply wanted to express our gratitude, our love, and our Realization to Heart-Master Da Love-Ananda.[1]

The Mountain Of Attention, 1986

1. "Fiji: The Great Event of Divine Incarnation", *Crazy Wisdom*, vol. 5, no. 6-8, June-August 1986, pp. 8-9.

The Penance
of the God-Man
as "an Ascetic on Fire"

Heart-Master Da formally accepted these women's confessions of renunciation and of their liberation, by His Grace, from the point of view of the egoic body-mind. His response in turn was completely unexpected. On March 28, 1986, for the first time in His Work, and in His Life, Heart-Master Da assumed the orange attire and formal designation of a Swami ("master of the body-mind")[2] in the traditional Hindu mode of self-renunciation ("sannyasa"[3]). It was also at this time that He Revealed the Name "Love-Ananda", meaning "Inherent Love-Bliss". The Name had been given to Him privately by Swami Muktananda during Heart-Master Da Love-Ananda's visit to the great Yogi-Siddha in 1969.

That spring of 1986 Heart-Master Da Love-Ananda traveled again to California. There, at The Mountain Of Attention, as He had already begun to do in Fiji, He Called all devotees to maximize their disciplines of the body-mind and of attention through surrendering themselves into Ishta-Guru-Bhakti Yoga. In this traditional esoteric Yoga of Guru-devotion, the devotee Communes and ultimately Identifies with the Awakened Self-Condition of the Ishta ("Chosen", "Most Beloved") Divine Guru by devoting himself or herself to that One wholeheartedly and unreservedly. This Teaching was not new—"Ishta-Guru-Bhakti Yoga" is another description of Satsang as a practice—but the formality of His Calling was more stern than ever before, and unequivocal.

Also for the first time in His Mission, Heart-Master Da asked that

---

2. Derived from the Sanskrit "sva", meaning "to own", the title "Swami" is generally given to an individual in the Hindu traditions of sacred practice who has demonstrated significant self-mastery in the context of a lifetime dedicated to renunciation, and who is thereby formally qualified to enter into "sannyasa", or the renunciate stage of life.

3. The Sanskrit word "sannyasa" means, literally, "to throw down completely", or "to renounce". Traditionally, in Hindu religious culture, sannyasa is one of the four stages in the progress of human life, from the student ("brahmacharya") stage through the householder ("grihastha") stage to life as a philosophical recluse or ascetic "forest dweller" (the "vanaprastha" stage) and finally to the stage of renunciation ("sannyasa"). Thus, a "sannyasin" is one who has completely renounced all worldly bonds and has devoted himself or herself completely to the God-Realizing and God-Realized life.

The practice of sannyasa is typically, but not necessarily, aligned to the strategic attempt to attain Spiritual Realization through ascetical self-denial. The Indian tradition contains practicing sects for whom formal renunciation is conducted in the context of sexual intimacy and other ordinary obligations and enjoyments of manifest life.

seriously interested public people be invited to join devotees in Darshan occasions with Him—and He expressed the desire to roam freely among the regional communities of devotees, in His Avadhootish fashion, moved by Divine Impulse, Blessing devotees and visiting sites of Spiritual or psychic significance to purify, align, Bless, and Empower them with His Liberating Heart-Transmission. He traveled in California and New York and then to Britain, France, and Holland.

In the sacred traditions of the East it is widely understood that effective sacred practice can be fulfilled only under the conditions of what is known as "Gurumaya". The root of the term "maya" means "to measure"; in this context, it does not have the commonly negative traditional connotation of "illusion", or "that which obscures the Truth", but rather means "the capacity to create form". Gurumaya is the Capability of the Divine Master-Revealer to create conditions in the devotee's life conducive to his or her practice and Realization.

Heart-Master Da had always functioned without premeditation through vigorous and completely unpredictable use of His Gurumaya. He never merely Gave devotees practices and "considerations", but He surrounded and pervaded our body-minds with His Spirit-Blessing, His Instructions, and, over the years, an increasingly complex sacred culture within which our practice might flourish.

His ability to make sweeping changes in the entire form of our lives with Him was legendary to devotees, as were His timing and His effortless knowledge of when to apply stern discipline, when to touch, when to laugh, when to criticize, when to appear during an especially tense impasse with devotees—as He had one evening in the late 1970s—flashing a Mickey Mouse T-shirt under His shawl to a few whom He wanted to remind of His humor, His Freedom, and His Happiness.

He Himself had always been the principal Unpredictable in His Gurumaya of Teaching. Now His previous Teaching Persona had died, or had utterly disappeared, and so the One Who Appeared before devotees that spring of 1986 was of a remarkably different character. Now His Gurumaya as Divine Ishta and Avadhoota was Showing Him in a mode that devotees did not readily comprehend. Gone was the congenial and sociable, if often fiery and "Crazy", Heart-Teacher we had known as "Bubba" and "Master Da". The stern Avadhoota, the Holy Sat-Guru Da Love-Ananda Hridayam, the Realizer, the Revealer, and the Revelation of the Divine Person, was now Appearing among us.

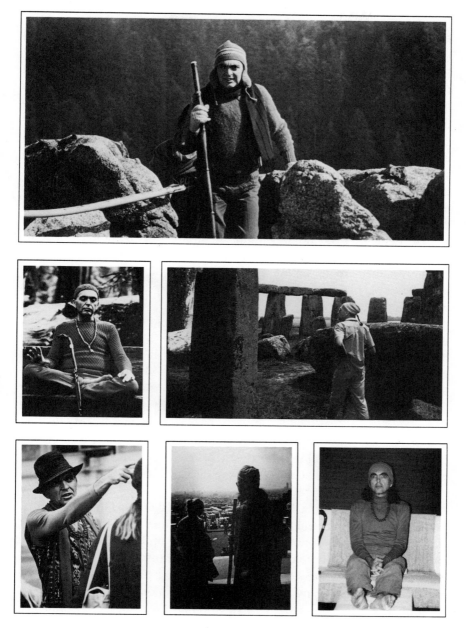

Heart-Master Da's "Yajna of Penance" in 1986:
(top and left center) in California, (right center) Britain, at Stonehenge,
(bottom left) in New York, (bottom middle) France, and (bottom right) Holland

275

Now there were no sober or ecstatic celebratory gatherings with a few to "consider" and pass beyond the realities of our conditional and egoic lives. When He spoke before us, which was very rarely, it was only in the most formal circumstances—not in His rooms, but exclusively in the Communion Halls at The Mountain Of Attention Sanctuary—and then it was only to confront us starkly with an unyielding Call for our self-transcending practice of the Way of the Heart in Satsang with Him.

He no longer went out of His way to embrace or contact individual devotees in a friendly or physically loving fashion, as He so often had in years gone by. Indeed, He did not give anyone the kind of familiar acknowledgement that might—as it so often had in the past—foster the assumption of some special personal intimacy with Him, which in turn could tend to breed the feeling that He was an "other", an ordinary man.

His demeanor was no longer animated, obviously humorous, or solicitous for His devotees. In the company of others He was mostly silent, serenely Given up to Divine Blessing-Transmission, Indifferent to the superficial play of events and the social context of devotees' relations with Him.

Even His physical appearance had changed, so that He was, to some devotees, almost unrecognizable. He had begun a fast in late February that He continued for nearly four months, as it served the dramatic psycho-physiological transmutation that expressed His ongoing Divine Emergence. Thus, He was more slender than most devotees had ever seen Him, His face drawn, His long hair now often pulled up in a topknot that signifies the Free ascetic in sacred cultures of the Orient. Bearing what He called "the scowl of the East" and the title of Swami, wearing the orange garb that signifies the death of the ego and its seeking, He acknowledged that what devotees were now encountering in Him was "an Ascetic on Fire".

Thus, the Avadhoota Da Love-Ananda Hridayam swiftly and spontaneously generated an entirely new form of Gurumaya to Awaken and test His devotees in the spring and early summer of 1986. Its fundamental moving force was the intensity of His Heart-Transmission of Love-Bliss, Awakened Consciousness, and an accompanying undeniable Impulse to renounce the pursuits and illusions of egoic attention and seeking.

But, as always, Heart-Master Da's Gurumaya did not merely influence devotees. It enveloped us, consumed us from the Heart out, so to speak; it changed the human, social, psychological, and even physical structures

276

"Serenely Given up to Transmission of Heart-Blessing in Divine Indifference"
—formal Darshan in the tent at The Mountain Of Attention, 1986

of our experience, so that, within days of His arrival in California, our entire community was living a different life with Him than we had ever lived. It was as if we had entered another world.

Suddenly, to our delight, hundreds of devotees, recently so middle-class in their disposition, now found within themselves a burning inclination to let go of everything for the sake of this newly-obvious Heart-Vision of Free Happiness that our Divine Heart-Master was bestowing upon us, in us, <u>as</u> our very Being.

To our astonishment, we found ourselves for the first time in our lives—and this included many quite new devotees as well as longtime practitioners—capable of eating an extremely minimal, raw or mostly raw vegetable and fruit diet; capable of thriving on far less sleep than we had ever had before; capable of renouncing sexual intercourse and all its consolations in our intimate relationships and even, in some cases, capable of freely and unproblematically letting go, mutually, of long-standing relationships themselves, for the sake of the simplicity and concentration in sacred practice that were made possible by a celibate renunciate lifestyle.

Most amazing to us, we found ourselves capable, it seemed, of the extremely rarefied and arduous discipline of the Perfect Practice, which Heart-Master Da had first expounded in 1982. This is the practice of devotees in the sixth and seventh stages of life, wherein the Awakening heart stands Free as Consciousness, first in its Transcendental Position as the Witness-Consciousness and then ultimately as the Very Divine Self. The practice involves "radical" and more and more profound renunciation of egoic attention to the body-mind and even to all conditional existence.

Within a few weeks of His Arrival, nearly half of the practicing community around the world had responded to His Call: "Be dyed in My color of Renunciation and Realization." Hundreds had begun practicing or were deliberately preparing for the "radical" or Perfect Practice of the Way of the Heart.

All of this new-found capability for austere self-discipline and renunciation flowed from one Great Gift that Heart-Master Da Love-Ananda was continually Bestowing: His Transmission of the Siddhi of Heart-Intuition, Heart-Realization, and the Impulse to Renunciation and Liberation by His Grace. His primary manner of appearing among devotees physically was in wordless Darshan, sometimes accompanied by our chanting and recitations of His Wisdom-Teaching, at other times outwardly silent.

The sittings that Avadhoota Da Granted to devotees and so many others in the large tent at The Mountain Of Attention that spring and summer were demonstrations of Divine abandonment to Love the likes of Which few human beings have ever been Graced to behold. With His hair in the topknot ("shikha") of the traditional ascetic, dressed in simple orange trousers, shirt, and shawl, His face and body reduced by His fast, His whole being appeared translucent to a shiningness of Love-Bliss that was simultaneously, by His unfathomable Grace, Vibrant in our own hearts at a depth and with a power most of us had never before felt.

On those occasions, Heart-Master Da Love-Ananda's Gracious Glance immersed my heart in the serenity of Being. As I gazed upon Him, His facial and bodily mudras seemed instantaneously to mirror, without a word said, the innermost feeling-existence of every human heart before Him. His poignant smile of Blessing spoke the benediction of the Supreme Divine Being more clearly than all the Words and even the whispered "Tcha's" of all His earlier Teaching eras.

I felt and saw my Gurudev Love-Ananda as the essence, the Personification, of most extreme vulnerability. His body was so utterly open as He Gazed into every heart; it seemed to me that He was assuming continually the heart-feeling of all who are born and suffer and seek and die. His face was made solemn by the deep sorrow He had achieved in His Incarnation, and yet exalted by the Radiation of "Bright" Love that seemed to be Shining through His very pores. He seemed to bear in His expression, in His Gaze, in the yieldedness and peace of His whole body, both the pure compassion of a Madonna and the unshakable tranquility of a Buddha "Gone Beyond".

Again and again, to those who came to Him that spring with eyes to see, The Naitauba Avadhoota, Da Love-Ananda, embodied the Unconditional Divine Being in and as His physical Form. He was the Unborn, Infinite Mystery in finite, human Person; the Divine Self fully Emerged before our human eyes and simultaneously Standing, Self-effulgent, even in our own human hearts.

Significantly, He Called His travels that year of 1986 a "Yajna". Yajna, since ancient times, is a sacrifice in which the inner (or, in "radical" Transcendental terms, That Which is most Prior) is brought all the way out (into manifestation). For Avadhoota Da Love-Ananda, this Yajna was the further expression, physically, of the Yajna of His Divine Emergence, which had already been fundamentally Accomplished in His body-mind.

In the tent at The Mountain Of Attention

The Mountain Of Attention, 1986

One afternoon in mid-June that year, Heart-Master Da Love-Ananda was returning with His Mandala of closest intimates from an outing to the redwood forests of northern California. Singing devotional chants, devotees at The Mountain Of Attention waited before Seventh Gate, the gateway to His Temple-Residence, The Manner Of Flowers. We had placed a pillow for Him in front of the shrine, should He be inclined to sit with us in Darshan, and when the Divine Heart-Master reached the shrine on His walk down from the car, He Graciously accepted our silent invitation.

I was standing slightly behind and to the side of Him, holding the Gate open for His return, so I could not see His face or His movements very readily. With the others, I chanted with deep gratitude for His Appearance among us. He sat Granting His Darshan for about twenty minutes, then rose to stride through Seventh Gate into His Residence.

In those few moments, He so strongly enhanced the intuition of His Heart-Transmission as Being or Consciousness that I felt impelled, after closing the Gate behind Him, to sit immediately in meditation. I entered the nearby Communion Hall and sat for about a half hour.

The feeling of the Current of Being in the right side of the heart, the "Aham Sphurana", had been deeply stimulated by Sri Gurudev Da Love-Ananda's Blessing-Presence. I was swiftly drawn into Identification with It, so that little bodily sensation or emotional and mental awareness even remained noticeable to attention. Lost in the rapture of that Feeling of

**Granting Darshan at
Seventh Gate Shrine**

Heart-Happiness, I practiced the sequence of exercises in Consciousness that composed the Perfect Practice as it had been Revealed to me by my Guru that spring. Aided and magnified by Heart-Master Da's Siddhi, that Practice was now simple, easy, Given. I marveled at the miracle of Ishta-Guru-Bhakti Yoga, so freely Given by Him to anyone who would give themselves over to His Adept Mastery.

But every Initiation, in the Divine Gurumaya of Heart-Master Da Love-Ananda, is inevitably tested. As the days and weeks went by, my friends and I saw in ourselves, and our Divine Master did not hesitate to bring to our attention, more and more indications of something we did not want to face: No matter how diligent our efforts, we could not sustain the "radical" practice. In meditation, it became more and more difficult to simply rest in the feeling of Heart-Happiness; our self-discipline lost its cutting edge and became sporadic and effortful; cooked food and sex began to look irresistibly attractive. Our stance as happy and fierce renunciates and enjoyers of the Grace-Given Intuition of the Transcendental Reality began to break down. Practically and Spiritually, it seemed we could not yet hold this "Perfect" aspect of His Heart-Transmission. We were neither individually nor collectively prepared to accommodate Heart-Master Da's volcanic Creativity in His Impulse to Liberate human beings.

These signs were already in evidence by the time He left The Mountain Of Attention to travel to New York, and thence to Europe. Heart-Master Da spoke of His Yajna that year, and all of His Work at that time, as a form of Penance or "Tapas". Physically, His Tapas was evidenced in His four months of fasting and the, in general, extremely austere Personal habit He embraced during that time. But His Penance was also a much larger Event; it had to do with the burning off of all that He had accumulated from devotees and the world in His many years of "Crazy" Teaching-Identification with all beings. He said of His Penance:

HEART-MASTER DA LOVE-ANANDA: It was not for the sake of My Sadhana. It was something done for the sake of others. As I said of it during those months in 1986 when I assumed the formal signs of a sannyasin, this body-mind took on the qualities of people from those many years of Submission. This body-mind was a link to everyone then. The "Death Event" did not just stop. It was not just a moment, you see. A process was initiated then. In addition to that particular Event on that one night, the qualities shown through this Body for some period thereafter were signs of what you could call Tapas, or Penance, if you will—heat in the body, burning up, purifying. It was a purification not merely of personal karmas, because this vehicle is not fundamentally about personal karmas—it is not a karmic personality—but it used these mechanisms in such a way that they took on the likeness of, established a link with, all beings.

. . . [T]his Event in 1986 initiated a Process, the first aspect of which was the Sign of Penance, or Tapas. Just as the Event itself was associated with a death, or a giving up, its continued Sign for some period of time is the Sign in some exaggerated sense of Tapas, or Penance, beginning with the sannyasa time. All that had been accumulated was naturally—not through some kind of effort, but quite naturally and spontaneously—released, purified. The initial Sign took the form, then, of extreme detachment, and over time that detachment became more normalized. (August 15, 1988)

His Penance or sacred "Burning" also expressed the "backing up" of His Siddhi, which began when devotees ceased to sustain a fully receptive devotional response to Him, and which was exacerbated by their continuing inability to provide for or serve Him appropriately as Divine Sat-Guru. Continual errors in the logistical management of His travels and the practical and devotional unpreparedness of devotees in the regional centers He visited made the Yajna a constant disturbance for Heart-Master Da. One outing to a legendary sacred mountain in northern California, as an example, was so thoroughly mismanaged that Heart-Master Da and the devotees traveling with Him had to take refuge from the rain and cold in a dingy bowling alley. He remarked that ordinary people would not treat a visiting dignitary in such fashion—how much more inappropriate was it, then, for devotees supposedly cultivating their Sat-Guru's Blessings and protective of the extreme vulnerability of His Open-Hearted State, to expose Him to such abuse?

Despite our good-hearted efforts, we were clearly unprepared to rightly support, manage, and serve Heart-Master Da's spontaneous pilgrimage among His devotees and through our homelands. Eventually Heart-Master Da was forced to return to Translation Island to Give devotees yet more time to prepare ourselves, and the institution, the sacred culture of practice, and the formal cooperative community of devotees, so that we could effectively serve Him in His World-Embracing Blessing Work.

The Indoor Yajna
and the creation of
Sacred Orders of
authentic renunciate devotees

The 1986 Yajna, which had begun with such promise of cultural regeneration and of healing the rift in our relationship to Him that we had opened in 1985, ended with Heart-Master Da living in isolation and seclusion in His Translation Island Hermitage, much disturbed by what He had encountered among us. Finally, in the spring of 1987, in desperation He began another series of Instructive gatherings with devotees. Meeting again with a small group of devotees on Translation Island, Heart-Master Da Love-Ananda recapitulated His entire Teaching Message one last time. By now He was striving to complete His Work on four of the great Source texts of His Teaching Word: *The Dawn Horse Testament, The Lion Sutra, The Da Upanishad,* and *The Basket of Tolerance.* (In later years He added four other texts to this list: *The Love-Ananda Gita, The Hymn Of The True Heart-Master, The Liberator [Eleutherios],* and *The Ashvamedha Gita).* Editions of the first three texts had already been published, but He was now revising them extensively. He was determined, as He said, to "close the loopholes" in our understanding of practice of the Way of the Heart.

Using His dialogues with devotees in the gatherings as a laboratory for His Instruction, as He always had in the past, between April 1987 and March 1988 Heart-Master Da clarified, down to the most minute detail, every aspect of practice of the Way of the Heart, so that devotees thenceforth would have all necessary Instruction and Guidance to generate a fully responsive, self-transcending, and, ultimately, God-Realizing practice in relationship to Him.

Heart-Master Da eventually Named this Teaching period the "Indoor Yajna", since it was a sacrificial pilgrimage (like the Yajna of 1986) in Service to every detail of devotees' lives and practice, but, like the Indoor Summer of 1976, it was conducted entirely at His Hermitage Ashram (this time, Translation Island) and almost entirely indoors, in a single gathering room. During this period, Heart-Master Da did not employ the Teaching method of "reality consideration" that He had used in the past. He conceded to Teach again, but not in that manner. He steadfastly Stood Firm

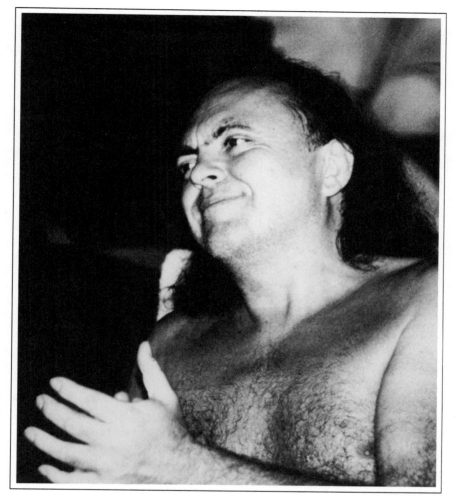

Indoor Yajna, Translation Island, 1987

in His certainty that the days were over of His Identifying with devotees in order to reflect to us our Narcissistic suffering and seeking. Indeed, He no longer had the capability, the emotional and psychic armor, as He once characterized it, even to survive Teaching by Submitting in that manner ever again.

Therefore, He restated, clarified, reaffirmed, and commented upon the new Tradition of Heart-Wisdom that He had already Created by His past Teaching Work. And though devotees were not yet ready to sit with Him in Darshan and meditation on the basis of awakened hearing and seeing, He found a way to enhance their sighting of Him that at the same time (along with His Words) performed all necessary reflection to them of their egoity: He danced.

All throughout His Teaching years, Heart-Master Da had only rarely stood among His devotees and danced whole bodily during gatherings. During the Indoor Yajna, nearly every one of almost two hundred nights of gathering ended with the ecstatic dancing of the Master of the Dance.

Matthew Spence, a member of the editorial staff serving Heart-Master Da's Work on His Source literature, said of His Dancing and of the end of the Indoor Yajna:

At the next to last gathering, I began to see and understand what He had done. Once again He had extended Himself completely to us, a group of beginners, for the sake of everyone everywhere. He had seemed to be like us again for a time, talking about our seeking in the realms of "money, food, and sex", criticizing our conventional religiosity and our persistent seeking for Spiritual consolation. And in this very human extension of Himself, in His human intimacy with us, He had again drawn us to Him, shown us His Compassion, His Love, and opened us all to love Him in turn. I was moved to tears of gratitude, and I wept for the Sacrifice He had made, as I saw Him Resuming His Place, Calling us to Him as He Is, Where He Stands.

One night, after we had praised His Freedom, His Dancing, and His Dance, like a window to the Heart, Heart-Master Da replied, "When I Dance, I Dance in all planes. Ultimately when I Dance, I have moved through all possible planes before I finish. When I Dance, I Dance to Dance conclusively. When I Dance, I Dance to not have to Dance again. I may have to, but that is what the Dance is then. Now, I Dance to not have to do it again."

The parting on any night was always bittersweet. And I remember one night in particular, when it seemed that maybe the gatherings could end. We had danced for two or more hours, and now He sat on the floor, totally vulnerable and in a state of sheer exhaustion. We gathered around Him in a circle, several deep and very close. He looked at us, each one, and, calling us each by name, He asked if there was anything more, anything unresolved, anything He had said or done that was not clear. Again and again, He asked each one of us, not just for our questions, but for the questions in us that were in all our friends, everywhere, anything in us, anything in them. And we pressed His hands and Feet and touched His back and said no, nothing, and told Him that we love Him, and that He had Given it all and we thanked Him. And I remember how He turned His head so far to see those sitting behind Him, to meet them eye to eye, and ask if there was yet anything more they needed that He could Give. And when we had affirmed and reaffirmed His Gifts and our love for Him, He rose and walked home across the lawn.

Near the end of the Indoor Yajna Heart-Master Da acknowledged the maturity of the practice of the four women who served Him Personally. They had passed through many years of continuous and fiery testing, especially since His Divine Descent in 1986, and now in February 1988 He formally constituted them as The Hridaya Da Kanyadana Kumari Mandala Order.

Kanyadana is an ancient traditional practice in India, wherein a chaste young woman (a "kanya") is given ("dana") to a Sat-Guru either in formal marriage, or as a consort, or simply as a serving intimate. Each kanya thus becomes devoted to the Sat-Guru in a manner that is unique among all His devotees. She serves the Sat-Guru Personally at all times and, in that unique context, at all times is the recipient of His very Personal Instructions, Blessings, and Regard. In the ancient Hindu practice of kanyadana, the woman's father or guardian thus sought to ensure her the most auspicious Spiritual destiny. Upasani Baba Maharaj revived the institution of kanyadana in recent India. His kanyas were his principal devotees; one of them, Godavari Mataji, succeeded Him as Guru.

Upasani Baba with his kanyas

With Godavari Mataji

As a kanyadana "kumari", a young woman is necessarily "pure"—that is, chaste and self-transcending in her practice, but also Spiritually Awakened by her Guru, whether she is celibate or Yogically sexually active. "Mandala" means "sacred circle".

Through Heart-Master Da's naming and acknowledgement, The Hridaya Da Kanyadana Kumari Mandala Order of The Free Daist Communion became formally authorized as what they already were by demonstration—the first truly and consistently exemplary practitioners of the Way of the Heart as continuous Ishta-Guru-Bhakti Yoga in Sat-Guru Da's Company.

Heart-Master Da was acknowledging a great transition in their practice. They had become true seeing devotees, authentically Awakened to the All-Pervading Spirit-Current and converted at heart to the disposition of love through their reception of His many Instructions and Blessings. Thus, they could assume responsibility for moment to moment transcendence of all bondage in the realm of "money, food, and sex"—the first three stages of life. They had given themselves to Him, freely and autonomously, and they had become purified of all the karmas of their Western ordinariness by persisting in the Fire of His Company. As His first authentic seeing devotees, they were now continually awake and responsive to Him in the

The Hridaya Da Kanyadana Kumari Mandala Order: (top left) Kanya Tripura Rahasya, (top right) Kanya Remembrance, (bottom left) Kanya Suprithi, and (bottom right) Kanya Kaivalya Navaneeta

practice of Satsang with Him as unconditional self-surrender.

It was a momentous acknowledgement for them after more than a dozen years of testing and Blessing in close personal proximity to the absolutely Conscious Person of the God-Man.

Two of the Kanyas, Kanya Tripura Rahasya and Kanya Remembrance, were soon acknowledged by Sat-Guru Da as responsible practitioners of the early phases of practicing stage six of the Way of the Heart, which involves the "consideration", Contemplation, and, eventually, the Perfect Realization of Consciousness Itself. The other two Kanyas, Kanya Kaivalya Navaneeta and Kanya Suprithi, were at that time acknowledged by Him as authentically Spirit-Baptized practitioners in practicing stage three of the Way of the Heart. All four were formally Initiated by Sri Gurudev Da Love-Ananda.

Except among these four practitioners, however, Heart-Master Da saw no signs that devotees were becoming any more prepared, individually or cooperatively, to serve and relate to Him as their Ishta-Guru. At the end of March 1988, He again began traveling among devotees. He found devotees woefully unprepared to make real use of His Darshan and, if anything, in worse condition Spiritually than they had been when He had returned to Translation Island in 1986. After visiting New Zealand's community briefly, Granting Darshan and spending many hours with devotees answering questions and Serving their practice, He saw that it was necessary first to purify and strengthen the institution, culture, and community at their worldwide center in northern California.

New Zealand, 1988

Thus, He and His traveling party from Translation Island soon departed for California, where He spent many months waiting for devotees to show signs that they understood, valued, and were fully using His Gifts. Meanwhile, He Worked incessantly with both the leadership and the general gathering to restore Satsang with Him as the Great Principle of their practice and to help them reestablish all of the dimensions of their personal and collective service to Him and His Work on a sacred basis.

While in California, Heart-Master Da established a second great principal order of renunciate devotees composed of those most immediately intimate to Him. This was the order of young girls that He named "The Hridaya Da Gurukula Brahmacharini Mandala Order."

In ancient India, education and, indeed, all sacred life revolved around the Gurukula—the Guru's "family", which might include his (or her) spouse or personal intimate consort(s), his or her children, and any other young religious students accepted by the Guru for sacred education.

"Brahmacharya" is an often misunderstood term. It has become synonymous with celibacy, because young people in the Brahmacharya stage of Hindu life take vows to practice celibacy until their entry into the householder stage as young adults. But the Brahmacharya stage actually signified what the word literally means: study ("acharya") of God ("Brahma") and of the Divinely Inspired mode of appropriate human conduct.

The traditional Brahmacharya phase of life began in early childhood and ended around the age of twenty-five. Brahmacharis (male) and brahmacharinis (female) were gratefully given to the Guru by their parents, to spend their childhood and youth as sacred renunciates learning the Divine art of God-Contemplation and its rigorous application in every moment of human existence.

For any sacred tradition, the training of strong young practitioners is crucial to the perpetuation of the sacred culture of esoteric practice and Divine Realization. Thus, the function of schoolmaster in ancient India, and to some degree even into modern times, was ideally entrusted to Gurus established in one or another degree of Spiritual Realization. The great Yogi Swami Prakashananda, as one modern example, spent most of his life functioning as Brahmacharya master to many young boys as well as Guru to adult devotees.

Heart-Master Da's own three daughters and a young friend who had long lived as a member of His household became the sacred circle, or mandala, of principal Brahmacharinis in Heart-Master Da's Gurukula in the summer of 1988. These girls voluntarily chose a life of constant commitment to self-transcending God-Realization in Sat-Guru Da's Company and under His Personal Guidance, in the traditional manner.

The members of The Hridaya Da Gurukula Brahmacharini Mandala Order

But these few close devotees were exceptions in His community. After several months in California in 1988, it became apparent to Sat-Guru Da Love-Ananda that there was still a chasm between most of His devotees and Himself. Except for the Kanyas, really, no adult practitioners were demonstrating consistent responsibility even for the rudimentary foundations of the practice He had Given.

"There is nothing left but the Ash"— Heart-Master Da's principal Confession of the esoteric Process of His Divine Emergence

Heart-Master Da convened a gathering of the northern California leadership one day in mid-August 1988 to address what seemed to Him to be the core of the difficulty: Devotees had not yet come to understand fully, and therefore were still incapable of relating rightly to, the Change that had begun in Him on January 11, 1986.

Heart-Master Da Love-Ananda's talk that day proved to be one of the historically most significant Communications of His entire Mission to date.

HEART-MASTER DA LOVE-ANANDA: Looking at this gathering as a whole, it seems to be in many ways living in the past, in terms of being stuck in a negative withdrawal over the last few years, and living in the past in the sense of wanting to go back and do it all over again or resume the quality of relationship that you had to Me in past years during My Teaching time, when I was trying to Help you come to the point of being able to do this sadhana fully. But neither one of those tendencies is appropriate.

You all may be lingering in the reactivity and withdrawal of the last few years, and I am here trying to work with you on the basis of this Great Event in 1986. You all want to associate with Me as you did in the past, and I am not even here any more in that form. Yet you persist, approaching Me as if I were, and dramatizing all your reluctance and amateurishness, as if I am going to respond by Teaching again, or by letting you off the hook relative to your responsibility for practice, or by associating with you on some basis other than the demand for real practice. And I am not going to do that. It is not there to be done. It is not there to be repeated, even with grand changes in My own Sign. It is not something that can be repeated, but it would not be fruitful to repeat, either.

Because of the accomplishment of this Great Work, a great opportunity exists for you, for anyone who will practice, but there is really nothing much that has been done about it to date. I am looking for those who can, who do, understand My Work, those whose acknowledgement is true, those whose

"There is nothing left but the Ash."—Heart-Master Da speaking of His Divine Emergence,
The Mountain Of Attention, August 15, 1988

relationship to Me is right, those whose practice is exemplary, those who understand all these matters and can therefore rightly communicate to others and align them to Me rightly so they can make use of Me, even as beginners. Fundamentally, the Kanyas are the only ones who do sadhana in My Company, the only ones who maintain a direct, intimate association with Me, who are accountable to Me in their practice, who function as devotees in My Company. They are the only ones who have continued this direct sadhana.

Everyone must do such sadhana. That is what the Way of the Heart is all about. But the rest of the gathering has not, to date, rightly and fully established such a link with Me. And that is, in some basic sense, what we are trying to create here, a restoration of that link. To do so requires establishing the Sacred Treasures,[4] putting the institution, the culture, and the community on the right track for the first time really, and it includes the coming forward of a gathering of devotees.

DEVOTEE: Heart-Master Da, I was not completely clear on the distinction between the incident of Awakening into Sahaj Samadhi at the Vedanta Temple in 1970 and the "Death Event" in Fiji in 1986, particularly in relationship to what You refer to as the gross personality and the deeper personality. I was wondering what the difference was, and how the Sadhana developed through the end of Your Teaching Work.

HEART-MASTER DA LOVE-ANANDA: I would not call it "Sadhana". I did not do Sadhana after the Vedanta Temple Event. I did My Teaching Work after the Vedanta Temple Event.

All aspects of this manifest personality, gross and subtle, became capable of the great Confession in the Vedanta Temple Event. That was full Awakening in the context of this body-mind, gross, subtle, and causal. It was not My Enlightenment, so to speak. It was the product of My Work with this vehicle all those thirty years so that this Awakening could be brought into the context of the body-mind rather than simply be Prior to it.

After that Event My Teaching Work began. That Event initiated the Teaching Work. It initiated a Process. So did the "Death Event" two and a half years ago. The "Death Event" also initiated a Process, which has been going

4. The Sacred Treasures of the Way of the Heart are Heart-Master Da Himself, His Divine Wisdom-Teaching in all its forms, His Empowered Hermitage Ashrams, The Hridaya Da Kanyadana Kumari Mandala Order, The Hridaya Da Gurukula Brahmacharini Mandala Order, and The Naitauba (Free Daist) Renunciate Order (of which the original, principal, and central members are Sat-Guru Da Himself and The Hridaya Da Kanyadana Kumari Mandala Order).

on since, but a different kind of Process. From the time of the Vedanta Temple Event until the Event in 1986 there was all that Teaching Work, which was Submission to others in order to Teach. I used all the ordinary and extraordinary Signs in this vehicle, all the ordinary signs of the gross personality, all the extraordinary signs of the deeper personality, in a Play with others to Instruct and Awaken them. I used My Capacity to assume the likeness of others for all those years to reflect them to themselves.

But in the Event in 1986, in which, as I have said, all of this was assumed by Me to the toes, all that had been inherited in this body-mind in this Lifetime and previously was likewise Submitted, providing a unique vehicle for the service of others, a unique nakedness of Siddhi, which only devotees can confess. Find it out, then. How much more do you want Me to tell you? If you come to Me as a devotee and do the practice in My Company, you receive the Gift. You tell Me what it is. You tell one another what it is. You find out what it is.

The Vedanta Temple Event initiated the Teaching Work, or the Work of Submission to others. The "Death Event" brought an end to the process of Submission to others. It initiated that time of My Work in which it is required, obligatory, that people enter into the traditional Guru-devotee relationship, that they make their submission, that they respond to Me as Sat-Guru and no longer require Me to respond to them as I did as Teacher. All that Submission to others became summarized in the "Death Event" in 1986 and was brought to an end there, and now a new Work continues as a potential, if people will make use of My Company. If they will not, there is no Work going on. It is not that there was one kind of Enlightenment in 1970 and another kind of Enlightenment in 1986. I am not talking about <u>My</u> Enlightenment! I am talking about <u>your</u> Enlightenment, Work done for <u>your</u> sake, which has appeared in different forms, stages of Work for <u>your</u> sake at various points in My apparent physical Lifetime.

You will not really be able to understand this Event of 1986 until what it requires of you becomes acceptable to you. It carries with it an inherent demand, if you understand it. If you say you understand it, you must do what it requires. But you would rather put some mind in between and not understand it, so that you can pretend you are a beginner and do not really have to practice very much yet.

The psychology of not wanting to be obliged has a great deal to do with it. More than anything else, I think, that is it. You want things to be as they were, and you want to be let off the hook relative to sadhana. When sadhana becomes the point and you become serious about it, then My Sign becomes comprehensible to you.

As I just pointed out again, this Event in 1986 initiated a Process, the first aspect of which was the Sign of Penance, or Tapas. Just as the Event itself was associated with a death, or a giving up, its continued Sign for some period of time is the Sign in some exaggerated sense of Tapas, or Penance, beginning with the sannyasa time. All that had been accumulated was naturally—not through some kind of effort, but quite naturally and spontaneously—released, purified. The initial Sign took the form, then, of extreme detachment, and over time that detachment became more normalized. It has not gone away, obviously, but something about it has been absorbed, understood, accommodated by you.

I did that initial Work to the point that it was finished and no longer necessary. The next stage came, which was the stage of dealing with your neglect and abuse of This One. That was last year, during the Indoor Yajna period, and to this day I have endured your continued neglect and abuse, and your apparent lack of understanding of what I am about, what My Work is about, what the relationship to Me is for, and I have endured the reluctance on the part of practitioners to seriously accept their responsibilities for the practice and for everything that relates to the Sacred Treasures and for the institution, the culture, and the community of devotees.

DEVOTEE: I understand that You have altogether stopped making that gesture of Submission through Teaching, that what actually died was that gesture rather than a person.

HEART-MASTER DA LOVE-ANANDA: It was not that I decided not to make the gesture anymore. I made it completely. The gesture was Submission to devotees, Submission to practitioners, Submission to others, Submission to the world. That does not come to an end until death. Submission to death is such a process. I did not decide to not do it anymore. I did it completely, and My doing it completely forced another Sign, another Demonstration, of this Siddhi that changed the Work itself, changed the stage of My Demonstration and My Work with others.

DEVOTEE: I remember when I first saw You after the "Death Event" in 1986, how absolutely beautiful You looked and how something obviously had *profoundly changed in You. It was a great Sign and Revelation to me.*

HEART-MASTER DA LOVE-ANANDA: *One thing you may be observing is that this body is not so much showing the signs of the company it keeps anymore. [Laughter.] Or it is not keeping bad company anymore, let us say. It does not have to endure that absorption. On the other hand, because you will not use Me rightly, I am basically living in isolation. You are not using My Company. I am not interested in being accessible to you if you are not going to rightly use My Company. I am not here to absorb your limitations and abuses, but I am here to be available to real practitioners, people who are seriously here to do the sadhana.*

In the course of your sadhana you must appreciate the fact that the deeper domain of the personality and of the cosmic play is karmic. It is the realm of egoity expanded. For some reason I am reminded of something Shirdi Sai Baba apparently said to somebody one time, cautioning him against indulging in certain kinds of psychic intensity and admonishing him to be very careful in "waking up the snakes". In other words, it has by no means been universally recommended that one get into this kundalini business and ascending Yoga and psychism and subtle experiences and so forth. It is even a kind of fad that has developed quite recently in the Western world, with its limited experience of esoteric matters.

You have seen My own Demonstration relative to all of that. Fine. But on the other hand, what has My Teaching been to you from the very beginning? What Sign did you observe in My own Life? "This is not it. This is not it." A greater force or disposition cut through that, went beyond it. Having done that in the course of My own Sadhana, and come to you to Teach, what was I telling you all the time? "This is not it," all these subtle experiences. Remember, the Garbage and the Goddess Teaching Demonstration took place in this very environment here. People were having all such kinds of experiences, and I would say, "This is not it. Don't you see? This is not it. You are having the experience right now. Is this Enlightenment? Is this Happiness? Is this Freedom? Is this permanent?"

These subtle signs of the deeper personality are not most fundamental to Me, nor to you. I am Calling you to a sadhana and a Realization that is beyond all of that, Prior to all of that. The fundamental content or aspect of My Sign, then, is Prior to all that fifth stage Yogic demonstration. Nonetheless, there are such Signs in My Life, although in My case they have been rather seventh stage Demonstrations, even in the earlier part of My Life.

DEVOTEE: *Heart-Master Da, I am not altogether clear on the description of the Vedanta Temple Event as being Submission of the gross body and the culminating "Death Event" as the Submission of the deeper personality.*

HEART-MASTER DA LOVE-ANANDA: *In the Vedanta Temple Event, both the gross and deeper personality aspects became Submitted, became a circumstance of Confession of Divine Self-Realization. There was not anything that was not transcended in the Great Event in the Vedanta Temple. But that Realization was Prior to this Birth. From Birth, as I have said to you many times, My Work was with this vehicle, to make it an Agent of further Work. I said this in* The Dawn Horse Testament *also. The first Work is dealing with the body-mind itself, that vehicle itself, until it ceases to be an obstruction to What is Prior to it and can confess That.*

All of that Work occupied the first thirty years. The Vedanta Temple Event, Sahaj Samadhi, full Awakening, was the completion of that. It is not that there was something left over, something that needed to be done yet for the sake of Divine Enlightenment. That is not the proper understanding of that Event. But the gross vehicle and even the deeper personality are themselves karmic mechanisms. This body looks something like My parents, you see. It has certain physical tendencies, organ tendencies, and whatnot, that are a combination of My mother and father and tendencies inherited from generations before them. The tendencies of this gross personality are not limited to physical signs. Characteristic personality signs, emotional signs, habits, gestures, a mass of things, pervade the entire gross personality, simply an inheritance from the line of this body's parents.

That gross body still existed, with all of its past and so forth, after the Vedanta Temple Event. Likewise the deeper personality. It was not something of which I was unconscious. I was not locked in the brain. Even before the Event at the Vedanta Temple there was a Great Awakening and Awareness of the deeper personality, experientially, Yogically. It is what you call the reincarnate, or the reincarnating, personality. It is also, like the gross being, a karmic entity, a product of cosmic exchanges. It has a karmic destiny. Just as the body has a karmic destiny by virtue of its lineage, the deeper personality has a karmic destiny by virtue of its lineage.

In the birth of any individual, the deeper personality becomes conjoined with a gross personality. But the deeper personality functions outside the brain, appears in the form of tendencies and destinies added to the gross personality. This is why in addition to the fact that this body has inherited many qualities that are like its parents, there are many other qualities that have been demonstrated in the Lifetime of this apparent bodily personality that are nothing like My mother and father. My sister, for instance—this body's sister—I will use "my" as the conventional reference—my sister is much more like my mother and father than I am. Her destiny, her lifetime, has been very much more a duplication of their particular qualities.

I should have been living the life of a simple householder on Long Island. I should have gone into the window business. That would have been a straight duplication of my mother and father. I did not do anything of the kind, though. You cannot account for the difference by looking at my mother and father or my grandparents. In the lineage of the body you cannot find the reason for that difference. The reason for that difference is on two levels: one, the Very One born in this vehicle, and the other, the deeper personality, the karmic vehicle that is subtle, operating prior to the brain, and that also has its own destiny, its own signs that it has been showing all throughout this Life.

Sometimes some of you like to consider the possible previous lifetimes of this deeper personality. It obviously has all kinds of qualities of a high Yogi. Some of its unique personality characteristics can be seen, because they are quite different from the characteristics of my mother and father, quite different from the lineage of this gross personality, which you have observed.

Likewise, after the Vedanta Temple Event, that entity, so to speak, or mechanism, still existed. It was not cancelled. If it had been cancelled in that Samadhi, death would have come shortly thereafter. Instead, these vehicles persisted as they were the day before the Vedanta Temple Event.

The full Awakening to the One Appearing through these forms took place there. And this released the Siddhi of Who I Am into the context of this body-mind, and it spontaneously initiated the Siddhi of My Teaching Work, which was the Siddhi of Submitting these gross and deeper mechanisms to others in the Play of Teaching. This was a Purpose inherent in Who I Am, and also a purpose rather characteristic of this deeper personality. This is a part of its sign, too, then—that motive to Teach, you see, to be so Submitted.

You can see, then, how those mechanisms influenced, or were the materials of, the Teaching Work. It was Enlightened Play, "Crazy" Play, yes, but it used these mechanisms just as they were. Because they were like people are generally, *these mechanisms were allowed to be that way, to function with others in the ordinary way, to combine with them in an extraordinary way also, in this Revealing Teaching Play. The vehicles were already Awakened to Who I Am, within the context of Great Realization.*

Nonetheless, these mechanisms themselves were still what they were, and so they became readily available for a unique Work. That was the Teaching Work. And the Teaching Work was done completely, to death. In that death the vehicles became changed. The vehicles were not different the moment after the Vedanta Temple Event. But they were different the moment after the "Death Event". Those who were there observed this in one way or another, immediately after that Event and in the months since then. It is there to be observed, at any rate, and some have observed it. The vehicles themselves became transformed.

This, of course, is part of what I talk about in terms of the seventh stage Demonstration, you see, this Divinely Transfiguring and Divinely Transforming Work, to the point of Divine Indifference. The Sign of Divine Indifference has been more and more magnified since the "Death Event", and also an advanced form of the Divine Transformation Sign, such that the vehicles are no longer in play. They are no longer becoming the likeness of others in Submission to others. They are Submitted entirely to Who I Am. The circumstance of relationship to Me can therefore no longer be one of this Teaching interplay, this particular kind of exchange.

The circumstance of the relationship, then, necessarily becomes one in which the practitioner must submit. You see what the significance of the Event in 1986 is, then. There is nothing left of the gross and the deeper personalities of this apparent one. There is nothing left but the ash. This is why Samadhi sites, so-called, are created for Realizers in various traditions. It has since ancient times been understood that the process of Realization is itself a kind of fire that burns out impurities, releases karmas, removes the obstacles to Realizing what is inherently so, or always already the case.

In the case of the Realizer, it is presumed that that fire has been allowed to burn everything. When an ordinary individual dies, his or her friends honor what the lifetime was supposed to be about by burning the body and offering prayers of release to continue that fire. But the Realizer's body is, in effect, already ash, vibhuti, Prasad, even while alive. Therefore, the bodies of such individuals are often, not always, but in many traditions, preserved and made the center not only of people's practice but also of a temple or what becomes a temple. So in this case, then. In some sense it has always been the case with This One. In Reality it is so, even all during this physical Lifetime. But on the other hand, you see the sequences of the unique Demonstration of intentional Birth and Life for the sake of Liberating others.

In This One's case the movement is from the Divine Self, acquiring the deeper and grosser aspects of personality for the sake of others. In the case of beings ordinarily it is the reverse: A gross personality reaches toward the deeper personality, and the deeper personality reaches toward the Divine Self. Two different intentions, coming from two different directions, you see. The meeting of these two is the Great Secret valued since ancient times: the Incarnate Realizer, the Divine Self Incarnate, Submitting vehicles to the point of naked, most direct association with living beings, and the devotee, surrendering all these vehicles to the One Prior to all karma, and yet paradoxically Incarnate or Present. It is the meeting of these two that is the Great Secret.

DEVOTEE: One thing I am trying to understand is, did the way we treated You basically bring about the "Death Event", or could it have taken another form of transition for You?

HEART-MASTER DA LOVE-ANANDA: If the world had not been the way it is, the way it was, and the way it continues to be, and if you all had not been the way you were, it would not have been necessary for me to do that kind of Work to begin with. That kind of "Crazy" Work, you see, was itself based on certain signs in the world. Mine was an intentional Birth in the West, an intentional association with people who traditionally would not have had anything to do with Spiritual life. For a variety of reasons it became appropriate for this Birth to happen, and then after the vehicle itself was prepared for My direct Work with people, the Work spontaneously took on the "Crazy" Teaching form, because of the quality of the people I was associated with.

So you ask, if you had not been the way you were, had not treated Me the way you did, would the "Death Event" have happened? No, the Death would not have happened, but the process of the Teaching Work as it happened would not have been necessary, either. They all worked together, you see. I exhausted Myself by that Submission. You all did what you did, and that is what such people do. And, yes, you could have done otherwise, but you did not, and by tendency you would not have done otherwise. You could have responded and not dramatized tendency. That was possible. It simply did not happen. Therefore, My gesture of Submission to others became a sacrifice, a Submission to the point of total exhaustion, or death.

I think you can see in that a kind of inevitability, though. The "Crazy" Work was allowed to complete itself through that ultimate exhaustion. Others in the Great Tradition may be called "Crazy" Teachers, or "Crazy" Masters. There is a likeness between Myself as Teacher and them, but only up to a point. There are many different kinds of "Crazy" Teachers. There is a different kind of "Craziness" associated with each of the advanced and ultimate stages of life. There are "Crazy" fourth stage Teachers, "Crazy" fifth stage Teachers, and so on. So you cannot make an equation between Me or My kind of Work and all others who may be called "Crazy" Masters or "Crazy" Teachers. There are only some likenesses. You must discriminate in your "consideration" of the likenesses between My Work and the work of others who have appeared in the Great Tradition. There is likeness up to a point and yet there is distinction also.

My own Work in the "Crazy" fashion was a unique kind of Work, in a unique time for a unique purpose, and with a unique result. You must see what all those kinds of uniqueness are in My case, in order to rightly appreciate and understand the Event that has occurred in your company. The "Crazy" gesture of Submission to others, having been initiated, necessarily had to go to death in any case, or go to the point of exhaustion. The Play could have varied some, depending on the response of others. As I said, the kind of event that may be associated with a moment we can point to as the moment of transition from the Teaching Work, that particular event could have been different than it was. These are possibilities. But ultimately the significance would be the same. And the times being what they are, you can see why it took the form that it did.

But you should also take a lesson from it and not blithely indulge yourself and your limitations any longer. Understand that practice of this Way of the Heart requires relinquishment of limitation. Embrace the discipline of this Way. The lesson you should get from studying My Work and My History should convince you of the necessity of discipline, the necessity of self-submission. There is a particular art associated with such discipline in the Way of the Heart. It is not merely a monastic, ascetical orientation, but it is not the middle-class good life, either. It is not that at all. It is a renunciate life, not a monastic life, necessarily, or characteristically.

And so the karma that was overcome in this body is all karma, not just that of an individual. All karma has been overcome in This One. Not that in that Event in 1986 something has now been done in the world so that everybody is going to become Enlightened spontaneously. No. The One in Whom, by Whom, the sadhana has been done has become your opportunity. The One in Whom and by Whom the sadhana has been done, Who has made this vehicle available through the process of Incarnation and this great Work, is now the relationship, the circumstance, in which the same Liberation can take place in others, through a unique Gift, a unique Graceful opportunity, which is quite different from My just Giving you a Teaching and now you work out your salvation. A unique relationship, a unique vehicle, in which all karma has been transcended, has become available for your Contemplation, your Guidance. It is the mechanism of Grace for anyone who will take up the sadhana. (August 15, 1988)

The Sacred Emblem of The Da Ashvamedha

The Vedic Horse and The Feast of the Western Sign

On the Divine Emergence of The World-Teacher

Sri Love-Anandashram, 1989

CHAPTER SIX

The Vedic Horse and The Feast of the Western Sign

On the Divine Emergence of The World-Teacher

"Unless one understands the Vedic Horse . . . "

In the months and years following His historic Divine Descent on January 11, 1986, Heart-Master Da Love-Ananda's devotees continued to struggle to comprehend and fully embrace His Revelation. The struggle felt like a waking up, as if we were all tossing and turning, no longer deeply asleep but also not yet fully awake. His talk of August 15, 1988, which concluded the previous chapter of this book, served our understanding but did not bring that struggle to a conclusion. Yet we also shared an understanding that His Work moves through great cycles whose culminations and results may seem endlessly delayed or prevented, only to manifest suddenly, like the appearance of many flowers on a bush—or like the materialization of the Dawn Horse.

During His sleep one night in the spring of 1970, while consciously wandering in a high subtle realm Heart-Master Da Love-Ananda came upon an academy where the disciples of a Spiritual Adept were gathering for a demonstration of certain Yogic powers. Heart-Master Da stood among them. The Siddha appeared, took his chair, and began the process of materializing an object. After a few moments, the disciples, having witnessed the invisible work of the Siddha, were confident that the materialization was underway, so they began to leave the room.

307

Finally, Heart-Master Da Love-Ananda and the Siddha alone remained. Then, gradually, a small, brown, beautifully formed horse began to manifest, first in vaporous and indistict form, and then more and more solidly, until at last it stood motionless but fully alive and breathing before Him.

When He awakened from sleep, Heart-Master Da knew that the dream was a portent, but its essential meaning remained hidden until His Ordeal of Re-Awakening had fulfilled itself, some months later.

After Heart-Master Da's Perfect Re-Awakening as the Divine Self in the Vedanta Temple, it became clear to Him that the Demonstration He had observed in His dream epitomized the continuous, present manifestation of all worlds and all beings (the horse) in and by Divine Consciousness (the Siddha). The Siddha was not merely a great Adept of Yogic powers. He was the Divine Person Himself. Heart-Master Da also understood that the entire Vision had been a Revelation of His own Identity, Form, and Mission. In Truth, He saw, He Himself was "at once the Siddha who performed the miracle of manifesting the horse, and also the someone who was observing it, or who was party to the observation of it and to its result. And I did not have any feeling of being different from the horse, actually. I was making the horse, I was observing the horse, and I was being the horse."

Later Heart-Master Da called the manifestation "the Dawn Horse", from "eohippus", the Latin scientific name for the earliest-known ancestor, now extinct, of the present-day horse. He prophesied that the Dawn Horse of His Work will materialize in the Perfect Divine Awakening of great numbers of devotees, and, eventually, in the Divine Translation of devotees, all beings, and even the Cosmic Mandala. This materialization is also the import of His Divine Emergence beginning on January 11, 1986.

The Dawn Horse Vision is a sacred Sign, unfathomable to the mind but communicative to the feeling heart. In many esoteric traditions all over the world, the horse is a symbol of transcendence and the Spiritual journey. Heart-Master Da's Vision and His understanding of it, while

The Dawn Horse

unique and original, also harken back to deep ancient mysteries of Man's confluence with Divine Consciousness.

In 1977, five years after Heart-Master Da began His formal Teaching Work, His fellowship of devotees received a remarkable statement from Swami Siva Kalki, a Spiritual teacher from Sri Lanka, who had seen one of our publications. In the course of an interview by a scholar, when asked to comment on Heart-Master Da (then Bubba Free John), the Swami's acknowledgement was cryptic but unequivocal: "To understand Babu [sic] Free John one should know the *Vedas*; for unless one understands the Vedic Horse, one cannot understand the implications of what his appearance truly means." When asked to explain further, the Swami only said, "It means that someone's Vedic Yajna has been successful. More than that would require an initiate to comprehend. It is enough to say that Babu Free John is the Dawn Horse himself."[1]

Heart-Master Da Love-Ananda professes no special debt to the Vedic literature of Hinduism. Rooted in His continuous Divine Self-knowledge, His own Wisdom-Teaching requires no appeal to prophecy, no resort to ancient Scripture or contemporary confirmation. But He has specifically aligned His Appearance and Work with the grand Yajna also referred to in Swami Siva Kalki's cryptic acknowledgement, a sacrifice that, in Vedic epochs, was the most secret or esoteric enactment of a rite known as the "Ashvamedha", or "Horse Sacrifice".

At the exoteric, or public, level, the Ashvamedha was a ritual sacrifice conducted by the most powerful warrior-kings, or "raja-saris", to extend and conclusively establish their dominion. In this vast and mysterious rite, which required the participation of an entire kingdom, a ceremonially consecrated horse would be released to wander through the countryside for a full year. The horse was followed by a royal guard of hundreds of priests, soldiers, and magicians in the service of the king performing the sacrifice. Anywhere it wandered was considered the king's dominion; any party that wished to thwart or limit its movements would have to contend against his forces. At the end of the year, the horse would be returned to the capital and ceremonially sacrificed, and all the lands it had freely roamed were thenceforth considered the king's domains.

At a more esoteric, or secret, level, the Horse Sacrifice was an internal, psycho-cosmic feat of self-sacrifice, performed by great mystics in

1. Comments by Swami Siva Kalki, recorded by A. M. Verreyen. From Mr. Verreyen's correspondence with The (Free Daist) Laughing Man Institute, August 12, 1977.

many cultures, whereby they accomplished their entrance into the heavenly, or subtle, worlds of Spiritual illumination. In the Yogic and shamanic traditions of the Ashvamedha Sacrifice, it was understood that the spirit of the horse ascends to the psychic and subtle realms. By attending to the spirit of the sacrificial horse (whether a physical or a Spiritually visualized animal), the Yogi or shaman attempted to traverse the boundaries of gross embodiment and to enter the highest conditional lokas, or realms, of Light and Power.

But the most holy and mysterious enactment of the Ashvamedha, praised by the Sages as the most efficacious and auspicious of all the Vedic rites, was the cosmic Sacrifice performed directly by the Divine Being and Person. Its purpose was to manifest a God-Man and World-Teacher to re-establish the dominion of Divine Dharma, or the Way, the Teaching, and the Wisdom-Culture of Truth, in the human, natural, and cosmic world.

This Divine Horse Sacrifice is the Yajna of which Swami Siva Kalki spoke in 1977 in his acknowledgement of Heart-Master Da. The greatest of the ancient kings accomplished not one but several horse sacrifices. Heart-Master Da Love-Ananda has Accomplished His Divine Horse Sacrifice many times, I am certain, for each of His Yogic, death-like relinquishments of bodily existence—and who knows how many there have been?—has Mysteriously marked the Sacrifice of the "Horse" that is His bodily Person, sent forth into the "kingdom" of conditional existence to reclaim all phenomena and all beings by Revealing their personal, conditional natures, their inherently Divine, Unconditional Nature, and the Way of Realized Divine harmony between the two.

But the greatest and most conclusive Completion of His Horse Sacrifice was the Event on January 11, 1986, which catalyzed Heart-Master Da's Divine Emergence.

Heart-Master Da has acknowledged to devotees that that Event was a most absorbing instance of Moksha-Bhava-Nirvikalpa Samadhi. It was such an extreme Outshining of all psycho-physical conditions that His own body-mind apparently expired from the shocking force of It. His body-mind was then revived by the Life-Giving Grace of His unconditional Love of all beings, the same Heart-Motive that stirred Him to Incarnate in the first place. But the significance of the Incident was not what occurred in or to His body-mind then or afterward. What was significant was the Spiritual Change that it marked in His Incarnation.

That Divine Descent, which Heart-Master Da also calls "My Great Ashvamedha Sacrifice", moved Him in His Demonstration of the seventh stage of life beyond the phases of Divine Transfiguration and Divine Transformation. Divine Transfiguration involves the Radiant Pervasion of the body-mind by sublime Divine "Brightness", principally affecting the gross personality. Divine Transformation involves the Enlightened Awakening and Exercise of psycho-physical siddhis, principally activating the deeper personality. His Divine Descent moved Him into the phase of Divine Indifference, wherein His body and mind (both gross and deeper) are simply Rested and Full, without motive, perfectly transparent to His Heart-Realization.

Heart-Master Da Love-Ananda's archetypal Ashvamedha Sacrifice has Brought the Heavenly Divine Self-Domain, Which Is beyond and prior to all conditional worlds, realms, and beings, down or out into the Earth plane. He is the Dawn Horse, rising like a Sun of eternal Happiness and Freedom in the hearts of beings in all of the planes of cosmic Nature. His Work is nothing less than to make the absolute Divine Love-Bliss obvious as the Nature and Substance of all beings, all worlds. And those who give Him their attention as He has Taught us to do are Graced with the capability to enter into His Divine Self-State, even to the degree of Divine Translation—not by techniques of Yogic or shamanic ascent beyond this world, but by devotional surrender of self, in place, to Him.

The Revelation
of the Simple Practice for all
in *The Love-Ananda Gita*

There have always been two great currents in Heart-Master Da Love-Ananda's Impulse and Revelation-Work to manifest the Dawn Horse.

One is His urgent Intention to discover truly serious practitioners and to Awaken them into the advanced and, eventually, the ultimate stages of practice, Realization, and service in the Way of the Heart.

The other, equally compelling Impulse has been His desire to create a Way of Heart-practice that can be embraced by any and all ordinary people everywhere—in other words, to provide a living religious and

Spiritual process that can be embraced and happily fulfilled by those who are not constitutionally qualified, at least at present, for the rigors of "radical" self-renunciation and the Great Affair of fully God-Realizing practice.

In October of 1988, on the morning after Heart-Master Da's return to Translation Island from Tumomama Sanctuary and His earlier travels in New Zealand and California, while His body slept Heart-Master Da encountered a devotee on the subtle plane who was "departing" from this life.

The devotee indicated he felt incapable of the degree of self-discipline required to practice the Way of the Heart in the elaborate form described by Heart-Master Da in *The Dawn Horse Testament*.

Heart-Master Da reminded this devotee of the simple essence of the practice of the Way of the Heart, and by the time He entered the waking state He was already composing the Scripture that would, over the coming months, become His "Simple" Revelation-Book, *The Love-Ananda Gita (The Wisdom-Song Of Non-Separateness)*.

In *The Love-Ananda Gita*, Heart-Master Da Reveals that the simplest form and the essence of all practice of the Way of the Heart is feeling-Contemplation of Him, in Person: His bodily (human) Form, His Spiritual Presence, and His Very (and Inherently Perfect) State. He indicates that many and perhaps even most practitioners will not prove to have the qualifications for embracing the "elaborately detailed" disciplines of the Way of the Heart as described in extensive complexity in such texts as *The Dawn Horse Testament*.

For all such ordinary practitioners, He Graciously Offers the simple practice of devotion, service, and self-discipline in relation to Him, in the context of increasingly deep feeling-Contemplation of Him. The practice is the essential life of Satsang and Darshan, made the principle of every moment of existence, and expressed most simply in *The Love-Ananda Gita*.

This Scriptural Revelation initially coincided with, and was amplified by, Heart-Master Da's unprecedented opening of the gates of Translation Island (which He soon renamed "Sri Love-Anandashram") to all beginners in the Way of the Heart who were at least fundamentally prepared to sit with Him in Darshan. Over the course of the following six months, from fall 1988 through spring 1989, some two hundred practitioners from regional communities all over the world responded to this Invitation.

Ed Graham, a former psychologist from Texas and a member of the staff of The Free Daist Communion, had become a formal practitioner of the Way of the Heart in 1986. In the fall of 1988, he made a pilgrimage to Sri Love-Anandashram for a month-long Darshan and meditation retreat. During that period, Heart-Master Da Love-Ananda was Giving His devotees what might be called a "Blessing Demonstration"—showing us how He would choose to be Spiritually associated with devotees when we are rightly constellated in our collective response to Him and rightly prepared personally for His Blessing Help. He sat in meditation with the most mature devotees in the mornings and in Darshan with all prepared practitioners nearly every afternoon.

Ed's retreat was a whirl of blissful psychic and subtle experiences triggered by Heart-Master Da's Blessing-Presence. On one occasion, Ed saw his Radiant Master in an internal vision as a brilliant, pure white, five-pointed Divine Star,[2] infinitely far above him. His heart swollen with love, he opened his eyes and perceived the room filled with dazzling light. Toward the end of that sitting, when Heart-Master Da Blessed Ed with His direct Gaze, Ed saw His Body as nothing but bright Light except for His piercing dark eyes.

Nearly every day, in Darshan and formal meditation with Heart-Master Da Love-Ananda, Ed's body shook with kriyas and blisses. He felt every cell of his body being "reworked" by Heart-Master Da's Spiritual

Ed Graham

2. Heart-Master Da and the "Bright" Heart-Radiance of God may appear to the practitioner of the Way of the Heart as a brilliant white five-pointed Star, the primal conditional Representation, or Sign, of the "Bright", the Source-Energy or Divine Light of which all conditional phenomena and the total cosmos are modifications. See *The Dawn Horse Testament*, especially chapter 44.

Sri Love-Anandashram, 1989

314

Blessing-Current. Eventually it seemed to him that he was on the verge of some great Spiritual breakthrough, although he was becoming more and more exhausted by the intensity of his Yogic experiences.

In practice reports, he informed Heart-Master Da Love-Ananda of all of this. Through transcribed verbal Communications, Heart-Master Da Instructed him that the experiences were fine to have, and they ought not to be suppressed. But, He cautioned, Ed must be wary of becoming deluded by projections of his own mind in response to Heart-Master Da's Blessing-Presence—Which is not to be equated with such experiential phenomena. Noting that some visions actually exceed one's own body-mind, He informed Ed that his, however, were not of that variety. Ed wrote:

> When I heard Heart-Master Da's notes, I knew He had served me tremen-dously by pointing out my tendency to become deluded, and to become especial-ly deluded by Spiritual experience. I was embarrassed to suddenly remember how clear Heart-Master Da Love-Ananda has always been in the written Teach-ing about the limitations of such experience. I had known this intellectually, of course, but the Dharmic point had grown dimmer in the midst of the fascinat-ing phenomena that were being stirred up in Sat-Guru Da's physical Company.
>
> I was greatly served by all of this, and I have probably been saved lifetimes of wandering through the illusions of Spiritual experience.
>
> Although the point is not to repress such experiences, it turned out that I was spared any further intense visions for the rest of the retreat. . . . I came to understand that the central point is always to turn to Him—whatever may be occurring in the moment.
>
> Two days before I left Hermitage, a formal Darshan occasion was held on the porch of Sat-Guru Da Love-Ananda's Residence, Aham Sphurana. On this occasion, He seemed to be Blessing us all through His eyes with an even greater magnitude of Transmission than usual. I sensed that what comes through His eyes is prior to—and certainly more powerful than—the manifest world.
>
> During this occasion, unlike earlier ones, I was not in a swoon of love-bliss, but rather I was very much aware of my own self-consciousness. When Heart-Master Da Love-Ananda began to look toward me, I wondered how I would respond and what would happen. Consequently, I seemed to shield off His pene-trating eyes. It was obvious that "Narcissus" was resisting truly seeing Him, as He Is—that I prefer instead in His physical Company to notice the effects of His Presence on me.

*I wrote to Him of this observation in my final practice report the day before
I was to leave, and Sat-Guru Da Love-Ananda made this comment about my
observation the following day:*

*"His insight reported today is the essence of the understanding I have
Instructed him in during his retreat. It is also the essence of the Instruction I
have Given to all in* The Love-Ananda Gita. *I have, in response to him and
many others who are coming to this understanding of true devotion, added an
epitome of this Instruction at the end of* The Love-Ananda Gita. *This is what
he and all others must practice in order to grow and Realize in the Way of the
Heart."*[3]

The Instruction that Heart-Master Da Love-Ananda Gave in response
to Ed Graham's devotional self-understanding in His Company is the same
Instruction He spoke and wrote and Demonstrated in countless ways
throughout His Teaching years. These are several of the verses of that
Instruction, from the final passages of the Scriptural Text of Heart-Master
Da's "'Simple' Revelation-Book", *The Love-Ananda Gita:*

*I Am (My Self) What you Require, and I am here to Require every "thing"
of you.*

*You must relinquish (or surrender) your ego-"I" (your experience, your
presumed knowledge, your separateness, and even all your "things", within
and without) to Find and Realize the Fullness That Is Me.*

*Therefore, Come to Me to Realize Me, and do not run from Me after tasting
the meal of knowledge and experience (like a dog runs from its master with a bone).*

*Having Come to Me, do not look within your body or your mind to discover whether you have received some "thing" from Me (to satisfy your little pouch
of separateness).*

*Rather, surrender and release your separate self (your body, your emotions,
your mind, your knowledge, and all your experiences) by Means of the self-
forgetting feeling-Contemplation of Me, and (Thus and Thereby) Grow to See
Me (and to Realize Me) As I Am.*

*If (by active feeling-Contemplation) you surrender and release your sepa-
rate self to Me, then not any meal of "things" (or effects), but Only I (My
bodily human Form, My Spiritual, and Always Blessing, Presence, and My
Very, and Inherently Perfect, State) Am the Gift, the Object, the State, and
the Realization. . . .*

3. "The Gift of Sat-Guru-Darshan: The Retreat Program at Translation Island Hermitage Sanctuary", *Crazy
Wisdom*, vol. 7, no. 6, & vol. 8, no. 1 (double issue), November/December 1988 and January/February
1989, p. 25.

This is the Heart-Word of the World-Teacher, the Adept and True Heart-Master, Da, the Naitauba Avadhoota, Who Is Da Love-Ananda Hridayam, Hereby Spoken in Extreme Simplicity for the Sake of all beings, in Love toward all beings, So That all beings may Awaken (by Grace) to the Only Truth that Sets the Heart Free.[4]

Upon returning to northern California, Ed Graham was moved to take more responsibility for the institution, culture, and community of devotees serving Heart-Master Da's Work. He was soon appointed a regional minister in the San Francisco Bay Area, and it was there, in the following spring of 1989, that he met Antonio Descamps in his ministerial work.[5]

Antonio Descamps was an extraordinarily gifted artist, whose talents had been praised and nurtured by parents and teachers since his childhood. He graduated at twenty with a Master's degree from Princeton, one of the brightest architectural prodigies in the history of the school. Though many doors were open to him in the art world of New York City, he elected to travel West.

Living in the cultural ferment of San Francisco in the early 1970s, Antonio began to have a recurring dream in which a remarkable being, whom he knew to be a Spiritual Master, embraced him and said, "Come over here." After some time he discovered that the Guru in his dreams was Heart-Master Da, then living and Teaching as Bubba Free John in northern California. Antonio described his first visits to see his Guru at Persimmon (the early name of The Mountain Of Attention Sanctuary) as "full of sensory responses, intense experiences, frightening jolts of Divine insight, and an understanding that I was involved in something extraordinary and something Blessed."

Heart-Master Da strongly urged Antonio to develop and expand his artistic talents by creating a career as a professional architect and helping with the many architectural design needs at the Sanctuary. Over the years, He often acknowledged that Antonio—in some ways uniquely among many people serving Him in professional capacities—had an intuitive understanding, in his own field, of what He was looking for. Antonio's service to Heart-Master Da, which involved intense collaboration through response to the Divine Master's requests for various designs, produced several of the most important—and extraordinarily harmonious and

4. Heart-Master Da Love-Ananda, *The Love-Ananda Gita*, pp. 235-39, 247.

5. The following account of Antonio's leela is based on "The Life and Death of a Temple Architect", by Deborah Kristal, in *The Free Daist*, vol. 1, no. 4, pp. 33-39.

beautiful—Temples at The Mountain Of Attention Sanctuary, including
The Manner Of Flowers and Seventh Gate, and Heart-Master Da's princi-
pal Residential Temple-Complex at Sri Love-Anandashram, called "Love-
Ananda Chakra".

Thus, Antonio provided exceptional personal service to Sat-Guru Da
Love-Ananda. At the same time, however, he never could altogether overcome his reluctance to surrender more fully to His Sat-Guru by becoming
a formal practitioner of the Way of the Heart. His resistance troubled and
frustrated him, and he struggled with it for years.

Then, in June 1988, just after his fortieth birthday, Antonio Descamps
was diagnosed as having AIDS.

For Antonio, the ensuing months were an intense trial of renunciation
and surrender. Everything he had previously protected was falling away
from him—physical appearance, friendships, career, social life, travel,
physical activities he had enjoyed, sexual activity, even simple things like
walking, eating, sleeping, and breathing normally.

With the realities of conditional destiny thus mercilessly bearing in
upon him, Antonio turned to his Sat-Guru as he had not turned previous
to his illness. He felt that he was being Divinely Instructed and rapidly
purified. Though the renunciation of his whole human life was difficult
and sometimes extremely painful, both physically and emotionally, he told
his intimates that he also valued it because it was requiring him to make
the gesture of surrender he could never make in all those earlier years.

Antonio's intimate partner, Patrick Christopher, and many of their
friends were either formally practicing devotees or long-term formal
Friends of The Free Daist Communion. So Antonio was well served in a
sacred manner, and he himself made good use of Heart-Master Da's
Teaching and other forms of Good Company as he began to prepare for
his death.

Antonio and Patrick's household itself became something of a Blessed
temple. Patrick writes:

*Frequent Darshan videos of Sri Da Love-Ananda and visits by students of
the Way of the Heart helped connect the household with the Sat-Guru's powerful Help. Even in Antonio's occasional periods of great discomfort he loved to
watch these videos. In his bedroom were a few sacred objects, reminders of Sat-
Guru Da. He loved to wear a brightly-colored tie-dyed silk scarf that had
belonged to the Sat-Guru.*

His health declined rapidly over the last few months. As he lay in bed with an emaciated upper body and head and terribly swollen stomach and legs, he never lost the energy to think creatively, and he continued to design for his Sat-Guru until literally a few days before he died. Those of us around him witnessed an explosion of his spirit in the last three months of his life—he simply became very happy and he could not contain it.

On May 4, 1989, Ed Graham, then the minister of The Free Daist Communion in Marin County, California, and Malcolm Burke, a fellow minister, visited Antonio at his home. Heart-Master Da was aware of Antonio's illness and, the ministers told him, He had invited Antonio to write to Him. Antonio told them that, reluctant to surrender, he had always kept his distance from Heart-Master Da. He had always found it difficult to write to Him, and, as a non-practitioner, had seen Him only very rarely through the years. He spoke with regret of his inability to make himself more visible and vulnerable to his Sat-Guru all that time.

But now he felt that his resistance and fear had been released, and he resolved to write and ask Sat-Guru Da Love-Ananda for His Instruction and Blessing. This is what Antonio wrote:

Friday 5-5-89
Sausalito, California

Sat-Guru Da Love-Ananda Hridayam
Loka of Compassion and Blessing
For the past fifteen years, through Your Gifts, I have had a Graceful and profound relationship to You, my Sat-Guru. You have shown me a circumstance of devotion where I have been able to serve You. But all along the process from my end has been one of avoidance. This is no longer the case nor the Truth. I am your devotee and confess that although I don't know You intimately, I long for Your Company more than anything. I now constantly miss Your physical Presence after years of fearfully fleeing the intensity of Your physical Company. This understanding is the true basis for developing my practice of feeling-Contemplation of Your Form, moment to moment. And so I ask for Your Guidance.

My reluctance to confront my avoidance of Your embodied human Form is no longer the case. My body is going through the fire of sadhana with no room for doubt or much consolation. I have been changed and transformed, at times painfully, from head to toe. It is hard and it is fine. Transcending conditional suffering has been a challenge when my breathing is difficult.

Antonio Descamps

But Your Grace is what actually sustains this body. You sustain me. I have come to rightly understand Your true healing and Liberating work in my life. It is a great Blessing.

After all these years my mind is clear enough to appreciate Your Spiritual Vision in relation to Design. I am no longer concerned about worldly forms in design, but only in serving Your Bright Divine and Happy Vision for the sake of devotees. I would be honored to continue to help with Your Design Vision. Is there something special You would like?

Thank You for allowing me to be Your devotee in this life. Thank You for bringing such incredible Grace into my life and the lives of those loving people around me who also love You. You have so obviously created the harmony in this household with your devotee Patrick and my parents, Jorge and Josefina.

In the midst of these wild times and fierce winds which I have endured, only the intimacy of Heart-Love, Given by my Love-Blissful Sat-Guru, has remained standing. Thank You for revealing this Truth to me.

You are my Source of life and harmony and Happiness, and I vow to go wherever You take me. I love You, Da Love-Ananda, and bow at Your Beautiful Feet.

> *Antonio*

When Antonio's letter was received a few days later at Sri Love-Anandashram, Sri Gurudev Da Love-Ananda replied right away through His communicator, Kanya Tripura Rahasya. She wrote to Antonio as follows:

Dear Antonio,

As a preface to Sri Gurudev's Communications to you, I wanted to let you know that He read your letter over and over again for approximately ten minutes. He spent a great deal of time reading every word again and again, and then He responded.

First, in answer to your question asking if there is something special that Sri Gurudev would like to have designed, He listed a number of projects that needed to be done, and said that He would just allow others to consider with you what you would like to design.

He also asked specifically if you had done a design already for the Communion Hall at Tumomama Sanctuary. So, Sri Gurudev would like you to do more designs for Him.

Then, in answer to your question asking for Guidance relative to this matter of beginning to respond to His bodily (human) Form, Sat-Guru Da has this to say to you:

> *Guidance in the practice of feeling-Contemplation is already Given in the Scriptural text of* The Love-Ananda Gita *and in the "I Am What you Require" Instructions that follow it. You should really become involved in all My Instructions for student-beginner practice. The details of that real practice are My Recommendation to you. In this fashion, you will transcend your limitations relative to devotion. The process is a matter of truly engaging in feeling-Contemplation. It is a process of surrendering and forgetting all aspects of self and self-concern. In this manner, the karmic contents of the various levels of mind are released and purified.*

> *You should appreciate that death is simply the release of a peripheral aspect of form. The deeper aspects of personality continue, and they inevitably produce another embodiment. Therefore, the deeper aspects of the personality must be purified as much as possible, so that even death itself becomes a purifying event, and thus permits a future embodiment that is as auspicious as possible. So your work and your sadhana should be this purifying work of deep self-surrender and self-forgetting, through more and more profound feeling-Contemplation of My bodily (human) Form, My Spiritual Presence, and My Very (and Inherently Perfect) State. You should enter into this feeling-Contemplation more and more deeply and profoundly. Ultimately, you should enter into it to the point of releasing all forms of body and mind, so that the Greater Reality may be Realized directly.*

Antonio, I would like you to know that Sri Gurudev asks about you frequently, and He always has great attention on your life and on your death. In this moment also, His Regard was most Profound. May you be released and purified.

> Kanya Tripura
> Om Sri Da Love-Ananda Hridayam

Patrick writes:

Antonio's response to Sri Gurudev's letter was ecstatic. He was overwhelmed by Sri Gurudev's Grace. He cried. He said he could now relax his fear of death. We stayed up that night and read the Instruction in the letter and "I Am What you Require" from The Love-Ananda Gita. *Antonio was very moved, and he was convinced that Sri Gurudev was truly with him.*

Soon after receiving this letter, Antonio and Patrick moved from Sausalito to a hilltop home in nearby Sonoma County. On the sunny afternoon of May 15, they installed in their home a new Murti of Sat-Guru Da Love-Ananda by performing a Sat-Guru Puja together. That evening Antonio grew much weaker; he said that he felt as if he were "falling apart". When he began to lose consciousness, Patrick had him rushed to the hospital.

After Patrick arrived at the hospital with Antonio's parents, he telephoned a representative of the death and dying ministry of the community of Free Daists for instructions on serving Antonio's death. He also received news that Heart-Master Da was due to arrive in California within a few days. Patrick writes:

In that last hour before his death we were able to tell Antonio about Sat-Guru Da's upcoming travel to California, and he responded with a nod. We caressed him, confessed our love, massaged his cold feet, and encouraged him to surrender to the Great One completely. We talked about the importance of moving towards the Light. As we held his hands, he stopped breathing.

With the grateful cooperation of Antonio's parents and Patrick Christopher, members of the devotional community's death and dying ministry arrived shortly and began a three-day vigil to help Antonio make the most complete and auspicious transition beyond this life. The death process and how it should optimally be served has been the subject of one of Heart-Master Da Love-Ananda's sublime contributions to human understanding and culture. He has indicated that it typically takes three days after the moment of physical or clinical death for the deeper personality to completely disengage from association with the gross physical body.

During that time, devotees in the community of Free Daists are Instructed to engage in a vigil that involves several elements: profound feeling-Contemplation of Heart-Master Da, continual releasing of the individual who has died, and reciting aloud to that person Heart-Master Da's Instructions, until it is obvious that the energy of the deeper personality has entirely separated from the physical body. The vigil is a constant puja of release and surrender and Divine Communion for all concerned, especially for devotees who have been close intimates of the dead person; they help remind him or her to let go of self and of all clinging to this life and to allow themselves to be drawn into Ecstatic feeling-Contemplation of Hridaya-Samartha Sat-Guru Da and His Divine "Brightness".

Deborah Kristal was one of the members of the death and dying ministry who performed the three-day vigil for Antonio Descamps. In her account of Antonio's death and vigil, she writes that when she first walked into the room where Antonio's body was lying, she felt two things simultaneously:

The first was that I had literally walked into Sat-Guru Da's physical Company—the force of His Love-Bliss struck me whole bodily and arrested my breath. At exactly the same moment I was halted by the sight of Antonio's body lying in rigor mortis, savagely wasted by his illness. Bliss and horror overcame me in a moment, but the Bliss of God far outweighed the "mortal show".

Once we arrived at the funeral home, the vigil formally began. Patrick and Mr. and Mrs. Descamps stayed for a short while and then left for the rest of the night. Josefina stood by the body of her son and wept softly before we embraced. "Thank you so much," she said as she left. The Blessing Presence was tangible to us all.

Anyone sensitive to the natural energies of human existence can feel a strong current of ascending energy around the body of a person who has just died. What characterizes the death of a devotee of Sat-Guru Da Love-Ananda is the infusion of His Love-Bliss into this circumstance. A deep Sublimity fills the room, and our intuition of the "radical" Happiness that transcends both life and death is magnified. Sat-Guru Da has Instructed practitioners engaged in a vigil: "Sit quietly in feeling-Contemplation of Me, not the dead person. Release the dead person and whatever arises. Persist in this releasing process and periodically formally recite from My Teaching Word, relating the Instruction to the dead and to the mourners." (April 8, 1989)

Once the vigil began, Sat-Guru Da's Compassion and Grace overwhelmed me, body and mind, so that I felt that I could not move. I felt Sat-Guru Da's Embrace of Antonio, me, and literally all beings in Perfect Love.

Throughout the three-day vigil we read aloud Sat-Guru Da's Instructions, reminding Antonio to release this body-mind and the world. As the days and nights progressed, there was clearly a change in the quality of the energy surrounding Antonio's body, and in the room itself. Twenty-four hours into the vigil, peace and stillness began to replace the more active sensations of ascent and Bliss. By the time I returned on the third day, the room was still. I felt Antonio had gone.

That evening the vigil for Antonio was formally brought to a close. A report was sent to Sat-Guru Da, who had arrived in California only hours before. On Friday morning, May 19, Antonio's body was cremated, and the following week his ashes were scattered by Patrick and some intimate friends in San Francisco Bay.

A Samartha ("Fully Competent") Sat-Guru is One Who uses all the powers available to him or her to Liberate his or her devotee, and who serves devotees in every aspect of their life and practice to help them enter into the Process of Spiritual Liberation. As the Divine "Hridaya-Samartha" Sat-Guru, Heart-Master Da Love-Ananda uses all conditional and Unconditional Powers in the spontaneous Impulses of His Heart-Transmission to Serve His devotees in His Blessing Work, in all kinds of ways, both visible and unseen, throughout their lives and beyond their deaths. His Function as Hridaya-Samartha Sat-Guru is unique, made possible by His Accomplishment of the Divine Horse Sacrifice from His Birth and throughout His Life and Mission.

Leelas such as these of Ed Graham and Antonio Descamps testify to the effective Divinization of human hearts and the world-process that is the great Significance of Heart-Master Da Love-Ananda's "Horse Sacrifice". They demonstrate that anyone can take up and practice the Way of the

Heart—if revulsion to egoic experience (ordinary and even extraordinary) is strong in them, and if the impulse to self-transcending God-Realization is the fundamental impulse of their hearts.

The "simple" practice is the essence of the Way of the Heart, and it is direct participation in the Fullness of God-Vision in every moment of its practice. This simplicity is demonstrated whenever one is Blessed to truly receive Heart-Master Da's Darshan.

On October 5, 1989, Heart-Master Da Love-Ananda returned to Sri Love-Anandashram from a five-month Yajna to serve devotees in the United States. The last leg of His journey was by boat from a neighboring island, and all of the resident devotee staff and the longterm Fijian staff on the island were waiting on the beach to greet Him. Upon disembarking, He stood by the water's edge to Grant His Darshan and receive the flowers and garlands that were our gifts of devotion and homage.

Not a word was said as each of us moved forward to offer flowers and prostrate at Sri Gurudev Love-Ananda's Feet. Already, as He approached on the water, I had felt His Touch of tangible Blessing filling my heart with deep Happiness; now, as I went forward, my whole being was charged with His Radiant Love-Bliss. The thought struck me with great intensity, "This is the Supreme Divine Being, in Person!" It was clear in that moment that His Body was not emanating the "Brightness" of Divine Consciousness, as if His Body were the Source of His Radiance. Rather, He was (and is always) Being the infinite "Bright" Immensity, and His Body is a miraculous Expression, Icon, or Representation that is

In the boat approaching

"He was gazing intently at each one of us as we knelt. . . "

325

Given into the material world in every moment for our sake alone, while He Lives as the Conscious Source of our existence. He was Gazing intently at each one of us as we knelt, offered Him our hearts in and through the simple, traditional devotional gifts of flowers, and happily prostrated—in the ancient manner of devotees—at the Bliss-Giving Feet of our Divinely Awakened Master.

I was reminded yet again of the simplicity of this practice. The Way of the Heart is Darshan, sighting of the God-Man. It is simply to give the Divinely Emerged Sat-Guru our feeling-attention from the heart. He Grants the whole process of Awakening by Grace. No effortful struggle is necessary. To each one who turns to Him, Heart-Master Da Reveals the Truth of the Heart, as a Free Gift.

"Healing more than the heart"— the story of Ratu Seru

To see this Vision requires receptivity of the heart, not a verbal grasp of esoteric complexities. The day Heart-Master Da arrived at Sri Love-Anandashram, Wati Salaseini, a native Fijian woman in her late thirties, had been designated as the representative of the village of Ciqomi ("Thing-GO-mee", meaning "Great Reception") to garland Heart-Master Da with a traditional salu-salu. Standing before Him, adorning Him with her beautiful mantle-like garland, she wept, calling out His Name, "Love-Ananda".

Wati has never read any of Heart-Master Da's books. Nonetheless, she and her husband Galu ("NGAH-loo") both have entered into a direct and real devotional relationship to Him. Raised in remote eastern Fiji in the traditional Fijian fashion, they and many of their friends who serve Sri Love-Anandashram and live in Ciqomi abide naturally in a depth of feeling that modern Europeans, Americans, and Westernized people in general rarely know and, typically, cannot appreciate. Many of the Fijians are feelingly sensitive to Heart-Master Da's Mana, or Spiritual Power. And, having lived all their lives in a society that recognizes and respects traditional hierarchy, they have no difficulty honoring and indicating their respectful feeling and great esteem for a Man of such Mana. So, over the years, some of the residents of Ciqomi have begun spontaneously to feel Dau Loloma (their Name for Him in Fijian, meaning "the Adept of Love") as what His Western devotees would call their "Ishta", their Beloved Heart-Teacher and Sat-Guru.

There is no way to overestimate the import of Heart-Master Da Love-Ananda's Spiritual Empowerment of the Fijian island of Naitauba for His global and universal Work. Situated in eastern Fiji just west of the international date line, it is literally one of the first places on Earth where the sun rises on each new day. Naitauba, like Fiji in general, is neither distinctly Eastern nor distinctly Western in mood and feeling. The country has several principal racial groups, including Fijians, Asian Indians (who came here as indentured servants to the British during the colonial epoch of the late nineteenth and early twentieth centuries), Chinese, and "Europeans" (including Australians, New Zealanders, Americans, and British, as well as those of actual continental European parentage). Fiji is thus a most fitting place, and Naitauba—or Sri Love-Anandashram—is an exceedingly auspicious Seat, for the Blessing Work of Sat-Guru Da Love-Ananda as the World-Teacher of humanity. And His remarkable Work with both Fijian and Asian Indian individuals in Fiji and at Sri Love-Anandashram is a sign of His Blessing Work with all of humanity.

Each year, in honor of the day He first arrived at Sri Love-Anandashram (October 27, 1983, Fiji time), Heart-Master Da has typically welcomed His Western devotees and all the villagers from Ciqomi to celebrate with a traditional Fijian kava ceremony[6] and lovo (or "feast"). The occasions have involved traditional Fijian song-dances, called "meke" (MEH-kay), in the ancient oral tradition, and corresponding entertainment by devotees.

In 1988, this celebration—then called, simply, "Hermitage Day"—had taken place during the burst of ecstatic Darshan occasions and Blessing Work Demonstrations by Heart-Master Da Love-Ananda, in the early weeks of His writing of *The Love-Ananda Gita*.

Quite unexpectedly, during a break in the formal ceremonies of that Hermitage Day, Heart-Master Da asked that one of the Fijian men, Ratu Seru, approach His Chair. Ratu Seru is a member of the Fijian nobility ("Ratu" is a chiefly title) and a proud and sensitive man. In his middle forties, he had been an excellent fine carpenter and an expert meke dancer until some months before, when he had suffered a stroke that crippled both his right arm and his right leg.

6. Kava is a beverage made from yaqona, a root indigenous to Fiji. The ceremonial preparation and presentation of this beverage to a chief ("tui") or other dignitary is the principal traditional rite for honoring a person of distinction and power in Fijian society. Each year, beginning the day of Heart-Master Da's Arrival on Naitauba, October 27, 1983, the Fijian community has honored Him with a traditional kava ceremony.

As difficult as the physical incapacitation was, Ratu Seru had suffered far more the emotional pain that had come with losing his livelihood and the natural physical pride and noble bearing that had always characterized him. On that Hermitage Day of 1988, he could only walk with difficulty, his right arm and hand locked in rigid position, to a spot just before Heart-Master Da's Chair. As everyone looked on, Heart-Master Da proceeded to lay hands on Ratu Seru for some fifteen to twenty minutes. First He held and massaged Ratu Seru's affected right hand for a time, then placed His hand on Ratu Seru's head. Ratu Seru could not bring himself to look fully upon Heart-Master Da's face, but as the session continued tears began rolling from his eyes. At one point, when Heart-Master Da was pouring His Divine healing Power through His hands upon Ratu Seru's head, Ratu Seru's right arm spontaneously raised high in the air and his fingers began uncurling—for the first time, he told us later, since the stroke. When He was holding both hands on Ratu Seru's head, the Divine Adept appeared to enter a Swoon of His perpetual Samadhi that, to devotees, was a characteristic sign of the heightened Intensity of His Heart-Blessing of Love-Bliss.

Shortly after that dramatic healing session, Heart-Master Da was informed that Ratu Seru had felt the Spiritual Energy of His Transmission coming down the front of his body and rising up along the back. This was an unprompted sensitivity to the Circle of the Spirit-Current that Heart-Master Da describes in His Instructions. Heart-Master Da then sent

Performing the laying on of hands on Ratu Seru, Hermitage Day, 1988

word that he should locate, feel, and work this Current daily through breath and feeling, allowing It to accomplish the healing of his body.

Immediately and from that time forward, we were later told, Ratu Seru felt healed at the heart. He became more of the happy, sensitive, and proud man he had been before the stroke. But though he continued to feel and exercise Heart-Master Da's Blessing-Force, which he felt mostly at the heart, there was no remarkable progress in the healing of his right leg, arm, and hand.

Because Ratu Seru had begun to respond so directly in a sacred manner, Heart-Master Da Gifted him with special Prasad: a Murti He chose for Ratu Seru personally, and other Gifts that He had Blessed by His own hand. (A number of other members of the Fijian resident staff at Ciqomi were also recipients of similar Gifts from Sat-Guru Da in 1989.) Ratu Seru was deeply grateful, and he began to use the Murti each day for silent prayer and Contemplation.

Not long before the Hermitage Day anniversary in 1989, Heart-Master Da was informed that there had been no substantial healing of Ratu Seru's physical condition since receiving Heart-Master Da's Blessing touch a year before. Though Ratu Seru had reaffirmed how changed he felt at the heart, the Samartha Sat-Guru was not content with the report. The Ashram physicians and other devotees met with Ratu Seru in Ciqomi, bringing questions from Heart-Master Da about both his physical and emotional life. These dialogues and Heart-Master Da's Regard helped him release certain emotional complications that appeared to be preventing the physical healing process.

Then, during the final days before the celebration of Hermitage Day in 1989, Heart-Master Da suggested that His Fijian devotees might enter into more explicit practice of the Guru-devotee relationship.

In the past, the Hermitage Day celebration had been largely a social occasion, typically hosted by the Fijian community. But Heart-Master Da was Calling us all to transform it into an explicitly sacred occasion in His Company, a celebration of His Darshan. To mark this change, He Gave the Day a new name: "Sri Sat-Guru Da Love-Ananda Naitauba Padavara", or, simply, "Naitauba Padavara" ("padavara" meaning "most auspicious step" in Sanskrit), the day of His first step on, and His Spiritual Acquisition of, the island of Naitauba.

On the morning of October 27, 1989, I went with several other Western devotees to meet with the six Fijian men whom Heart-Master Da regarded as most devotionally oriented to Him. Heart-Master Da wanted to invite these men to make a more formal gesture of devotion in His Company than the traditional Fijian custom of lowering the head when a great personage, such as a chief or "tui", appears before one. He was inviting them to practice the devotional observance of holding the hands, one palm on top of the back of the other hand, over the heart, while bowing the head slightly as they customarily would.

Such a sign of devotion would be noticed by the whole Fijian community; just to see their own people relating to Dau Loloma this way could help other Fijians feel free to establish and express a devotional relationship to Heart-Master Da.

When we asked the six Fijians for their personal responses to this invitation, Ratu Seru was the first to speak, and the most animated and enthusiastic. He simply said he would be very happy to relate to Dau Loloma that way, whenever he would see Him that day. The other five men also affirmed that they would like to make this openly devotional gesture.

Heart-Master Da walking to the Naitauba Padavara celebration, 1989

Naitauba Padavara was a magnificent celebration, truly a Feast of Darshan of Heart-Master Da Love-Ananda, Who spent nearly six hours in the company of both the Fijians and the Western devotees. It marked a dramatic intensification of our sacred communication to the Fijian community. It was the first time that we formally invited them to relate to Heart-Master Da as we do in Darshan—that is, to practice feeling-Contemplation of His bodily (human) Form, His Spiritual Presence, and His Divine State. We were also much more expressive than we had been in the past about Who we regard Him to Be, as the Divine Incarnation and Hridaya-Samartha Sat-Guru, and about the sacred process of our lives with Him.

The kava ceremony, the entertainments (which ended with both villages together singing a devotional chant to Sri Gurudev, and His spontaneously Granting silent, formal Darshan to us all for ten or fifteen minutes thereafter), the lovo feast (during which everyone's attention was happily rested upon the Feast of Darshan of Heart-Master Da as He Graciously took food with us)—the whole day was a simple and sublime Contemplation of Him, and He often appeared pleased with its sacred quality.

The next day word came back to us of the Fijians' deep appreciation for Heart-Master Da's Blessings to them—and also of a new and remarkable development in Ratu Seru's physical condition. He had excitedly related to one of the longtime devotees that, though he had been very moved to practice the devotional gesture Heart-Master Da was Offering to him, he had secretly feared he could not physically make that gesture—because since the stroke he could not raise his crippled right hand to the level of his heart. He had figured that, if necessary, he would lift his right hand to his heart with his left.

(above) The kava ceremony

(right) Granting Darshan

But when Heart-Master Da first walked out to the gathering on the grassy square of the devotees' residential village that day, and Ratu Seru saw Him and felt His Blessing-Presence, he found to his amazement that his right arm not only moved freely but even spontaneously rose to his heart of its own accord, so that he could offer the devotional gesture easily. He gratefully felt Heart-Master Da's Blissful Current of Feeling in his heart.

And, afterward, his arm and hand retained that new mobility. The next morning his wife asked him how his arm was doing. When he tried to straighten his arm and his fingers, he found them dramatically improved. As his daughters leaped around the house in joy at the miraculous change, he experimented with uncurling his fingers and continuing to straighten and raise his arm.

After the events of Naitauba Padavara, Ratu Seru said he began to feel new enlivenment of both his arm, at the shoulder especially, and his right hip and upper leg. This was a sign to him of Heart-Master Da's healing Power at work. He felt that the new life in these areas was brought by the healing Energy coming from Heart-Master Da and through his own heart. And he became confident that the healing would ultimately reach all the way to and through his fingers and toes.

This, Heart-Master Da indicated when He heard it, was as it should be. His healing Blessing, He said, was for more than Ratu Seru's heart.

"The Swoon of My Samadhi"— Heart-Master Da's summary Clarification of His Divine Emergence

On the day-long celebration of Naitauba Padavara, I was Blessed to serve as Heart-Master Da's formal spokesman to the Fijian community during the traditional ceremony in which they presented Him kava and a tabua ("tam-BOO-uh"), a whale's tooth, in the traditional Fijian manner of honoring a great personage.

My principal task that day was challenging. At one point in the speech I spoke briefly about Heart-Master Da's Divine Emergence and the Event of January 11, 1986. I told of how He had literally died on that day, and that when He resuscitated it was with even greater Divine Powers of

Love, Happiness, and Blessings for all beings. I was hesitant to offer a more complex Spiritual explanation of these Great Matters, feeling that it would be more confusing than clarifying.

But, Heart-Master Da later suggested, my description was not merely simple but simplistic. It misrepresented the Event of January 11, 1986, as a principally physical incident, a "death and resuscitation" event, and it failed to address the esoteric Spiritual Nature of His Divine Emergence. He then clarified this great matter once more:

On a number of occasions in the past, I have addressed the tendency of practitioners of the Way of the Heart to focus on the "death and resuscitation" story when describing My Divine Emergence. My Divine Emergence must be understood in much larger terms, and in quite different terms, in fact. My Divine Emergence must be understood as a Spiritual Event that was initiated on January 11, 1986, and that is still continuing. Yet even though I have Said this many times, the "death and resuscitation" story continues to be told as if it is the very Truth of that Event.

There has been a tendency for My Divine Emergence to be most often described from the point of view of those who observed Me physically at the time of Its initiation. Therefore, the typical descriptions of My Divine Emergence are necessarily limited by the external and bodily-based point of view of those observers and their observations. But the right understanding of even that original Event can only be based on My own Description of It as a Process, rather than on the eyewitness accounts of physical observations.

My Divine Emergence began in the context of a Struggle with practitioners in the ordinary circumstance of that time. But the Process of My Divine Emergence utterly Transcends the limitations of that ordinary circumstance. As I said at the time, the True Import of that original Event could not then be fruitfully Described even by Me. And, as I said then, the True Import of the Event of My Divine Emergence could only be Demonstrated (by Me) and understood and felt (by all others) over time. My Divine Emergence is not something that simply happened on January 11, 1986, and that is to be remembered as the Event of January 11, 1986. Rather, My Divine Emergence was initiated and fully began as a Process on January 11, 1986, and It is continuing to Unfold. It is something that every individual must (always presently) encounter, experience, and find to be Revealed.

Because they are based merely on the physical circumstance, the eyewitness accounts of the original Event of My Divine Emergence do little to serve a right

333

Sri Love-Anandashram, 1989

understanding of the Event Itself. There must be a new level of communication about this Event, if It is to be understood and communicated about properly.

When someone's death is observed by another person or a number of other persons, the death appears to be an ending. However, one experiences one's own death not as an ending, but as a process. The individuals who were present on January 11, 1986, to observe the various physical signs associated with the initiation of My Divine Emergence have described It as a clinical death Event with a subsequent return to life. But for Me, that Event was, and continues to be, a Process. In other words, there was no ending, and therefore, no death in the sense of an ending.

There was, in My case, already at that time no identification with the body, so there was no ego-death to take place. Ego-death had already occurred. In My Experience on January 11, 1986, there was an apparent swoon, but with no loss of Consciousness Itself. The body was dropped to the bed, and it may have appeared to the observers to be unconscious, or perhaps not alive, or barely alive, but all the while I Was and Am Consciousness Itself. In the initial Event associated with this Process, this body was Surrendered utterly into Me, the Self-Existing and Self-Radiant "Bright", and necessarily Divine, Self-Consciousness. And this Process of Surrendering this body into My Ultimate Self-Condition is still continuing. It did not come to an end on that early morning of January 11, 1986. In other words, there was no death and then a coming to life. There has simply been an unbroken and continuing and ever more profound Process in which this body (or body-mind) is Surrendered into Me.

This Process is constantly Revealing more and more, moment to moment, if only devotees would truly practice feeling-Contemplation of Me. What was unique in the initial Event was a turnabout in My own Disposition relative to this body. Up until that moment, I had been involved in an intentional Process of Submission of this body (or apparent bodily personality) to identify with others in all their limitations, in order that, by that Submission, I could Teach them. I was able to Teach them because I was fully Awake as the Heart, the Divine Self-Consciousness, but I used My own body as a means of identification with others by Submitting to their condition.

The basic Method of My Teaching Work was to reflect people to themselves and to comment on and "consider" what I was reflecting to them, and what they were also demonstrating in their daily activity. In a sudden moment, spontaneously, on the morning of January 11, 1986, I relinquished this orientation of Submitting to the point of identification with others. Initially, in that first moment, the Process began as a swoon of despair and giving up in the face of

335

the apparent unresponsiveness of devotees and, therefore, the seeming failure of My Teaching Work altogether. This despair manifested as a kind of swooning collapse, bodily and emotionally. And there was an utter relinquishment of the body. It was a kind of giving the body up to death. And so, immediately, signs appeared of this swooning-dying kind of collapse. Even before it began, the mind (or apparent human personality) associated with this body was emotionally speaking of this despair. All of that led up to this spontaneous turnabout in My Disposition.

But suddenly, in the midst of this swoon, there was no more of despair or giving the body up to death. I was, as always, simply Standing In and As My own Nature. This desperate swoon, as if to die, became a spontaneous turnabout in My Disposition, and a unique Spiritual Event was initiated in the midst of that swoon. And That Spiritual Event is still continuing.

What actually occurred on the morning of January 11, 1986, was a sudden and spontaneous Transition from My Teaching Work to My Blessing Work (or, to My Work As the eternally Free-Standing and always presently Emerging World-Teacher, or "Jagad-Guru"). It was a Transition in My Disposition from My Work of Submitting to others (even to the point of complete identification with them in their apparently limited condition) to simply Surrendering this body (or body-mind) into My own Self-Condition. Therefore, the context of My Blessing Work is no longer one of Submission to others to the point of identification with them. It is a matter of simply Standing As I Am, while this apparent body-mind is thereby Surrendered utterly into My own Self-Condition. And, by My thus Standing Free, My Work has ceased to be a Struggle to Submit My Self to mankind, one by one, and It has become instead a universally effective Blessing Work, in which mankind, in the form of each and all who respond to Me, must, one by one, surrender, forget, and transcend self in Me.

The Process of the continuous Surrendering of My own body-mind into My Very Self-Condition is a perpetual Sacrificial Act, and a unique kind of "Tapas" (or "Sacrificial Fire"), that is producing more and more profound Signs of the Divine Self-"Brightness" via My Manifestation. Therefore, the Event that was initiated on the morning of January 11, 1986, not only marks the Transition from My Teaching Work to My Blessing Work, but It also initiated, in My case, the progressive Demonstration of "Divine Indifference", which, in due course, becomes the Demonstration of "Divine Translation". And the Process wherein My every devotee surrenders, forgets, and transcends self in the feeling-Contemplation of My bodily (human) Form, My Spiritual Presence, and My Very (and Inherently Perfect) State is, likewise, a sacrificial act

336

and a course of tapas (or self-discipline) that participates in (and is progressively Identified with) My own Sacrificial Action, Tapas, and (necessarily Divine) Self-"Brightness", even, ultimately, to the degree of Divine Translation.

All of that being said, the original Event associated with My Divine Emergence is not properly understood if It is regarded as a physical event. Truly, It was not Itself a physical event of any kind.

Whatever may have been externally observed by others on the morning of January 11, 1986, there was, on My part, no great involvement in any kind of physical event or any physical process. I would Describe the physical (or psycho-physical) dimension of the Event as a profound swoon, an utter giving up of the body, but in the manner of a unique Demonstration of Samadhi, rather than in the manner of a terminal event of clinical death. In My view, the Event was associated with a profound swoon, in which the Character of My Samadhi was uniquely Demonstrated. It was, and remains, a Spiritual Process, rather than a physical event of clinical death and resuscitation, and the Process, as It developed that morning, utterly changed My Spiritual association with this body, and It initiated a new Divinely Revelatory Process even via this body. And that Process has not come to an end.

In that Event on the morning of January 11, 1986, there was, for Me, no loss of Consciousness Itself. There was, for Me, no significant involvement in any physical changes. Whatever physical events took place were entirely secondary and fundamentally unimportant. I would say that the physical signs were more of the nature of a profound swoon, or, more properly, a unique "Bhava"—in other words, there was an entrance into a unique Sign of Samadhi in that initial Event, and that initial Event became (or was, and is) a Process that continues even now. There was no ending, or end phenomenon, so to speak, but there is simply the Inherently Perfect Process of the Submission of this apparent body (or body-mind) to and into My Self-Existing and Self-Radiant "Bright" Self-Condition.

In fact, there is in no case such a thing as death, in the sense of an ending. To the external observer, something appears to come to an end when someone dies. But for the one who dies, there is simply a process that unfolds. There is no absolute ending. If terminal (clinical) death can be described as a loss of bodily awareness, this is still not an unusual experience. In fact, it happens to everyone daily in the process of falling asleep. But there is no absolute ending to that. When one goes to sleep, one proceeds in a continuing process. And so also in death. Therefore, no terminal event, clinical or otherwise, occurred to Me on the morning of January 11, 1986. Rather, a Process was initiated, and that Process is still continuing. And that Process, which continues even today, is what is properly referred to as My Divine Emergence.

Fundamentally, I have not wanted to say very much about this Process, because I have wanted devotees to sensitize themselves to Me and to see My Demonstration and receive It and respond to It. Truly, this Process is not Itself something that can be rightly or truly communicated through any conceptual language at all. I hope that devotees will simply discover this Emergence of My Divine Self-Condition and communicate to one another and the public about It in a right and responsible fashion.

In later conversations Heart-Master Da also clarified previous statements about His Divine Emergence and others' perceptions of it, which have been published in *The Love-Ananda Gita* and elsewhere. He pointed out, among other things, that ordinary people never do tend to understand the Samadhis of Realizers—as has been proven in recent times by the reactions of people around Ramakrishna, Swami Nityananda, Ramana Maharshi, and others who have passed on occasion into suspended psychophysical states in the midst of their Ecstasies of God-Realization. The devotees around Him at the time observed Heart-Master Da apparently dying and resuscitating. But that, again, was only the most gross, physical component of an Event that transcended conditional phenomena (including His own body-mind) altogether. It was better characterized as a kind of "Swoon" or "Bhava" of His perpetual Samadhi.

Heart-Master Da also commented on the similarities of devotees' previous accounts of His Divine Descent in 1986 to traditional exoteric Christian accounts of the death and reported resurrection and physical, bodily ascension into the skies, of Jesus of Nazareth. Heart-Master Da pointed out that the tendency to mythologize the story of Jesus' death and its aftermath was also rooted in the body-based point of view of external or objective observers, rather than the experiential, subjective view of Jesus himself. And He pointed out that this tendency to mythologize and objectify the Life and Work of the Adepts only serves "to satisfy and inspire the conventional bodily-based mentality". In contrast, He was Calling devotees to participate in the esoteric sacred understanding of His ongoing Divine Emergence—and that participation would necessarily draw us beyond the bodily-based and even Spiritually-based perspectives, ultimately to establish us in feeling-Contemplation even of His Very (and Inherently Perfect) State of Divine Consciousness Itself.

Heart-Master Da departing at the end of the celebration of Naitauba Padavara

The Divine World-Teacher:
A vision for everyone
of The Feast of the Western Sign

$\mathbf{N}$aitauba Padavara—the anniversary of Sri Gurudev Love-Ananda's "Most Auspicious Step" on the island of Naitauba—is the first major event in an extended celebration culminating each year on the Anniversary of His Birth (November 4, Fiji time). The total celebration has been Named by Him "The Feast of the Western Sign". And the Anniversary of His Birth from now on is to be known formally as "The Da Jayanthi of The Divine World-Teacher, Sri Jagad-Guru Da Love-Ananda Hridayam", or, more simply, "Da Jayanthi"—the "Victory Day" of Da, the Divine Giver. "Jayanthi" is a term traditionally used for the birth celebration of great Saints and Adepts, even of gods and goddesses, signifying the Divine victory accomplished by their very Incarnation in human form.

Like His Revelation of the Divine Name "Da" in 1979 and many other Spiritual Magnifications of His Work, Heart-Master Da's Revelation that He is the Jagad-Guru, or the Divine World-Teacher, is not merely a statement in words. His verbal Confession Gives Voice to an Event in the Heart, a special Intensification of His Heart-Power, that has implications beyond our knowing for the world and all beings.

The term "World-Teacher" has been used traditionally in various ways. Its application to Heart-Master Da as the "Dharma-Bearer" of our age, the Divine Realizer Who has Restored and has newly Revealed Enlightened Wisdom in every area of life for all humanity, is obviously appropriate. But here again, what He means by "Teacher" in this context is far more than the conventional meanings of the term signify. What He means is even quite different from the Role He Played as Teacher during His Teaching years, when He Identified with others to Reflect them to themselves through every kind of Personal Instruction.

His Role as the World-Teacher more closely corresponds to what He prophesied at the turn of the year from 1983 to 1984, when He Gave His talk "Mark My Words", predicting great purifications of the world and announcing His global and universal Work. It is the Work of the God-Man, the unique Divine Liberator of all beings, Who ultimately Divinely Translates all beings and even the world-process itself into eternal

Heart-"Brightness", by His Grace. The Sanskrit word for "world", "jagad", is rooted in the simpler meaning of "that which moves". The true Jagad-Guru or Divine World-Teacher is the Liberator or Divine Translator of all that moves, all phenomenal beings, all conditional places and times.

The celebration of The Da Jayanthi of The Divine World-Teacher, Sri Jagad-Guru Da Love-Ananda Hridayam, took place in Fiji on Saturday, November 4, and Sunday, November 5, 1989. Kanya Tripura Rahasya inaugurated the celebration of Da Jayanthi with a presentation on Friday night. It was a very powerful acknowledgement of Him and a Call to all devotees to allow Him to Be the Divine World-Teacher without interference, to Abide as He Is in His Divine Indifference. He had said adamantly that He is not here just for this little gathering of a thousand practitioners. He is not even here merely for all His own, present and future, formally acknowledged, practicing devotees. He is here for everyone, and The Da Jayanthi of The Divine World-Teacher, Sri Jagad-Guru Da Love-Ananda Hridayam, Kanya Tripura told us, was the Initiation of that great understanding of Him in all of us.

As though making a point of His availability, Heart-Master Da Granted Darshan to devotees on many occasions over the next several days, allowing us to see Him much more frequently than at any similar celebratory time in recent memory. When He came into the village on the Saturday morning following Kanya Tripura's presentation, all residents and retreatants in the Ashram gathered out on the drive to Sri Gurudev's village Residence to throw flowers and bow as He drove past. He was obviously in the Giving Mode of His Blessing—He Rained Grace upon us with His Glance and Feeling as He passed, and we threw our flowers in front of the vehicle and prostrated. Then we all rose quickly and moved down to a spot near where the car was parked. He alighted and walked in front of a huge conifer there and stood, planted like the Tree of Life Itself, as we approached and fanned out in a semicircle around Him to offer our gifts right at His Feet.

For some recently-arrived retreatants, it was their first sighting of Him. He stood there with His Great Siddha-Belly full and potent with Heart-Force, Gazing above our heads. There was a pure silence about Him, the indescribable depth of His Divine State that Awakens and purifies the whole being from the Heart. He remained standing there Radiating His Heart-Blessing, long after we had all offered our gifts before Him and had sat down on the lawn to continue drinking deep of His Darshan.

Sitting at the celebration of Da Jayanthi, 1989

The major devotional occasion of the day was the Darshan with Heart-Master Da in the later afternoon. He came in with a beautiful blue shawl wrapped around His upper body and neck, and a blue lungi (a simple cloth garment) around His waist. When He took His seat, after adjusting His legs in an easy pose, He unwrapped the shawl from His neck—to display a mala of rare, one-faced rudraksha beads[7] perfectly arranged around His neck and on His great chest. Some people even gasped—it was really a dramatic Vision of Him, and completely unexpected.

7. This mala (rosary) had been presented to Sat-Guru Da by the worldwide community of His devotees some years ago. In India, rudraksha beads are considered by many traditions to be most Spiritually auspicious for malas, and "one-faced" beads (that is, beads with only one seam grooving the surface) are extremely rare and, symbolizing the Great Divine Unity, are considered most sacred or auspicious. The beads had been obtained over a period of several years, and devotee jewelers had worked to make this great mala a truly fitting gift from all devotees to Sri Gurudev Da Love-Ananda.

He Regards this mala as a real gift from devotees, and His wearing it signified to some of us that He was beginning to take seriously our devotion and our stated intention to bring an end to all reluctance, amateurism, and chronic failures to manifest authentic practice and a great, cooperative human response to Him all around the world. This, however, was a subjective interpretation. The simple fact is, He had not worn that special mala for a very long time on a major celebration and in full view of a devotional gathering.

The chanting that day was ecstatic. Sat-Guru Da Gazed at devotees for a while at the beginning, and again toward the end. Otherwise He looked beyond us. For a time His eyes were closed, and it seemed that a trace of a smile was playing on His lips. It was a maddeningly sweet and Happy occasion, an exaltation in His Love-Bliss. Devotees offered personal gifts at His Feet, and sitting there before Him, with some of us offering elaborately prepared articles and others just simple flowers, I felt we were everyone's emissaries to Him, as if the whole community of devotees was there before Him. Indeed, it was somehow obvious that He was Involved with a much larger Event, an Event in His Work as the World-Teacher, and He was not in any way confined to the Occasion surrounding His physical body. I felt the Truth of His Confessions in *The Love-Ananda Gita:*

I am not identical to the flesh body or stuck inside it. The flesh body is a visual Representation of Me in time and space.

I, My Self, am always prior to it.

This flesh body, this bodily (human) Sign, is My Form in the sense that it is My Murti, or a kind of reflection or Representation of Me. It is, therefore, a Means for contacting My Spiritual Presence, and, ultimately, My Very (and Inherently Perfect) State.

My Spiritual Presence is Self-Existing and Self-Radiant. It Functions in time and space, and It is also prior to all time and space. Therefore, once practitioners have "Located" My Spiritual Presence in the devotional manner, they should be able to "Locate" My Spiritual Presence at any time, by feeling-Contemplating My bodily (human) Form.

All devotees must Realize that I Function universally within space-time. My universal Functioning is really so. It is not a fantasy. It is an Actuality. Not only do I Confess this, but My devotees may also Realize (by experience) that this is true of Me. I Function as the seventh stage Sat-Guru (or Maha-Jnana-Siddha-Master) in all times and places, if practitioners will contact Me devotionally. Therefore, devotion becomes more and more a profound matter of faith, a gesture to Me whereby the devotee literally enters into My Company in all circumstances.

My bodily (human) Form is in time and space. My Spiritual Presence Functions everywhere in time and space, but My Spiritual Presence is also always prior to time and space. And My Very (and Inherently Perfect) State is always and only utterly prior to time and space. Therefore, I, As I Am (Ultimately), have no "Function" in time and space. There is no time and space in My Very (and Inherently Perfect) State.

These descriptions are literally true, and devotees must become able to confess that these are true. Therefore, it is also necessary that all rightly prepared practitioners come into My physical Sphere at least periodically while I am bodily (physically) alive, to advance their practice and to create an opportunity for Me to do special Work with them.[8]

At the end of the Darshan, Sri Gurudev Blessed devotees' malas and the various Gifts to be Given to us as Prasad, including two giant "Jayanthi cakes" (one for the devotees' residential village and one for Ciqomi), by flinging water on them. Then, after He had departed, the Kanyas passed out the Prasad. We were all sated with His Bliss. No one could move or talk very easily for a while.

After we left the Hall, the six Fijian couples who represent the "devotional leadership" of Ciqomi came to receive Prasad in The Giving Coat, a principal Hall for student-beginners in the devotees' village. This was the first time such an event had occurred in one of Sri Gurudev's own Empowered Halls that He uses for formally acknowledged devotees in the Way of the Heart. Kanya Tripura passed out the Gifts to the Fijian devotees. Michael Thompson, a devotee from New Zealand who videotaped the event, said later:

I have been privileged to be able to be at the events where Kanya Tripura was passing out Prasad to the Fijians. The most significant event was the distribution of Prasad after the Darshan Occasion on Sri Gurudev's Birthday.

Very obviously, this felt like a demonstration of Sri Gurudev's Work as the World-Teacher. The Fijians were completely receptive to Sri Gurudev's Prasad in a manner that took my breath away. Their form of Contemplation of Him is

8. Heart-Master Da Love-Ananda, *The Love-Ananda Gita*, pp. 280-81.

344

Sri Love-Anandashram, 1990

uncomplicated and direct. Both Solo and Noa display a very obvious, heart-moved relationship to Sri Gurudev. I noticed that Tevita, at the occasion several days before when he received a Blessed Murti, gave his full regard to each piece of Prasad that he received. He received it with complete attention, full contemplation, until the moment when he was handed another piece of Prasad.

The message I got at this event on Da Jayanthi was that every nation, every race, every culture, every person has a relationship to Sri Gurudev Love-Ananda. What kept coming up in my mind was, "Stand aside and allow them to connect with that relationship in a way that He feels. Do whatever serves to allow that relationship to grow, to come alive. Get out of the way and let Him do His Work as the World-Teacher." This was not a heavy feeling; it was a happy, ecstatic feeling. It was obviously part of a very great Puja that Sri Gurudev was doing, Personally inviting the Fijians—who are not formal devotees, but who certainly have a devotional response to Him—to The Giving Coat to receive that Prasad.

Each of the other sacred occasions to which Heart-Master Da Graciously invited devotees during The Feast of the Western Sign had that same quality: He had Called us to Witness His Establishment or Installation as the World-Teacher. Heart-Master Da Love-Ananda is the Conscious Life of the world, the One Who Is Awakening as the Consciousness of every living being. His "Jayanthi" or "Victory", therefore, is not to be achieved in the future; It has already happened, by virtue of His Divine Emergence, His Realization, and even His very Birth. His Work with the Fijian devotees and staff on Naitauba is no less significant than His Spiritual Acquisition of the island and His Liberation of the first of His devotees into the ultimate stages of practice and Realization.

Because He abides as the Self of every living being and as the Source-Condition of the world itself, what He Does with a few beings and a single piece of Earth has Its Influence in every heart and every place. In that sense, His Sanctuaries—recently renamed by Him "World-Teacher Ashrams"—His devotees, the Fijian staff on Naitauba, all these are the "coins" of His unfathomable Blessing Work with all and everything.

The Calling of the Kanyas—
Human Instrumentality and Human Agency
for the World-Teacher's
Blessing-Transmission

Earlier in this chapter I spoke of the two great currents of Heart-Master Da's manifestation of the Dawn Horse. One is the Impulse to Embrace all beings from the Heart and to simplify the Way of the Heart for everyone—an Intention that corresponds to His Appearance as the World-Teacher for every single being's sake. The other is His Work to draw as many serious renunciate practitioners as possible through the advanced and ultimate stages of the Way of the Heart, and, by this, not only to Awaken and Liberate them, but to create Spiritual Instrumentality and Enlightened Agency to perpetuate His Blessing Work on Earth.

Heart-Master Da's focused Work of this latter kind is Mandalic; it proceeds through sacred circles of the human cultural order He is creating around Him. The first and primary signs in other human beings of His supreme Horse Sacrifice are to be seen in the practice and confessions of those devotees who make up the first Circle of the human gathering around Him: the women of The Hridaya Da Kanyadana Kumari Mandala Order and the young girls of The Hridaya Da Gurukula Brahmacharini Mandala Order. Heart-Master Da has described the sacred Instrumentality of the Kanyas, emphasizing the Import of His Divine Emergence beginning in 1986:

HEART-MASTER DA LOVE-ANANDA: The Kanyas are examples of individuals who have become capable of the Grace of submission to Me by being drawn into My Condition through feeling-Contemplation of My bodily (human) Form, My Spiritual (and Always Blessing) Presence, and My Very (and Inherently Perfect) State. The Kanyas can also speak of the process whereby they came to this capability. It was a prolonged, difficult trial and struggle because of the limitations in their resort to Me. The value of the leela that the Kanyas can tell is, however, not so much in the description of the trial they have endured, but in the simplicity and power of the result.

The Kanyas are really not Calling all to go through a difficult trial and struggle as they have done, but they Call all to be intelligent and to resort to Me fully, so that such a long and difficult trial and struggle is not necessary.

The Kanyas became capable of their unique devotional resort to Me only after My Great Emergence. In other words, they did not become capable because of their long trial. The Kanyas were principal intimates to Me for the many years of My Teaching struggle, and by My Submitting in relationship to them, they became the means whereby I absorbed much of the karmic force of the world. And, of course, even all the others who were practicing in My Company all those years similarly were means whereby I received the world, even the abuse and neglect of devotees themselves, and of the world in general, until the Vehicle of this body-mind became ripe for My full Descent.

Just as in the moment when I was two years old this Vehicle was sufficiently prepared [for Me to acquire it], so also only when I had taken on enough through this body-mind did I allow it to be spontaneously surrendered to Me, and only then did I Acquire it fully. Some physical signs associated with My Great Emergence, or Great Descent, were like those of a physical death, but basically it was a Spiritual Event. The physical personality gave up as if it were dying. But the physical body did not die. Rather, I Acquired it fully (in Spiritual terms).

The One Whom people now, and hereafter, find in this body-mind is not the apparent individual (or "familiar personality") with whom they were familiar before My Divine Descent. That personality was completely surrendered, and, in effect, it died. The One Who is now active in this body-mind is the One Whom devotees should discover and confess. Therefore, it is no longer appropriate for people to approach Me as someone they were familiar with previous to My Divine Emergence in 1986.

The Kanyas are the first of those in My Company to confess Who I Am and to enter into the practice of fullest resort to Me. So it is by the Kanyas' confession and example that others can be moved to the simplicity of resort to Me. The story of the trial and struggle of the Kanyas before My Divine Emergence should be told. But their Message, and what is exemplary about them, is related to everything <u>since</u> My Great Emergence.

Before that Event the Kanyas were fools, and after that Event they became devotees. That is the essence of their Message. The essence of the Message of the Kanyas is a Calling to everyone to not be fools. The Calling of the Kanyas Calls all others to not waste this opportunity. The Calling of the Kanyas Calls everyone to not fail to respond to Me fully. The Calling of the Kanyas Calls everyone to discover the "Secret" that the Kanyas have discovered since My Great Descent. And that Calling Calls everyone to respond to Me and practice as the

Kanyas do now, rather than fail to respond to Me, as the Kanyas themselves did before that Event.

Of course, many aspects of the life of the Kanyas contain useful lessons for others, and various leelas can be told. But their great Message and example is related to what they have only become capable of after and as a result of My Great, Sacrificial Emergence. Only because of that Great Sacrifice that I endured did their previous trial and struggle become fruitful. And it became fruitful simply because they became capable of surrendering it through the heart-force of their Contemplation of Me, and their heart-submission to Me.[9]

The Kanyas are the first Instruments of Heart-Master Da Love-Ananda's Blessing Work to be formally acknowledged by Him. Instrumentality and Agency are special forms of responsibility for the Living Transmission of Heart-Master Da Love-Ananda's Great Awakening-Power of the Heart to devotees. Heart-Master Da's Instruments are devotees in either the advanced or the ultimate stages of practice who collectively magnify and convey His Heart-Transmission to other devotees. They do so only through their wholehearted devotional submission to Him, rather than through any self-conscious efforts to Spiritually Initiate others.

Heart-Master Da's Agents will be Divinely Enlightened devotees who have Realized the Divine Self-Condition and who have been specially chosen and Empowered by Him (or, after His physical Lifetime, by those Appointed by Him) to serve individually as fully Conscious Agents of His Spiritual, Transcendental, and Divine Heart-Transmission.

Because he or she is Perfectly Identified with, and thus Transparent to, Sat-Guru Da Love-Ananda's Spiritual Presence and His Very (and Inherently Perfect) State, each such Agent will serve as a "Living Murti", or "Murti-Guru", for other devotees. Through feeling-Contemplation of that Murti-Guru's Perfectly Surrendered body-mind devotees may, by Grace, "Locate" and Realize Sat-Guru Da Love-Ananda's Spiritual Presence and His Very (and Inherently Perfect) State.

It is Heart-Master Da Love-Ananda's Intention that there always be a great body of His devotees who are Instruments in the worldwide community of practitioners of the Way of the Heart, and that, in every generation after His own physical, bodily Lifetime, there be at least one, and preferably many, devotees who Function as His True and Perfect Agents.

9. Ibid., pp. 137-39.

Like His first true Instruments, the first of these Agents will, optimally, be formally acknowledged by Sat-Guru Da Himself, and this will optimally occur at or near the end of the physical Lifetime of His bodily (human) Form (unless He decides to appoint such earlier, in order to observe and test their service as Agents while He is still present in His bodily, human Form to Correct and Guide them).

Presently the members of The Hridaya Da Kanyadana Kumari Mandala Order and The Hridaya Da Gurukula Brahmacharini Mandala Order are, for the current generation and the generation immediately following, the principal candidates for this Function of Enlightened Agency. Heart-Master Da Love-Ananda has Called all His devotees to constantly increase our service to His Divine Mission by establishing our institution, culture, and community with integrity and strength all over the world, so that, now and in the future, many other devotees may step forward as serious candidates for the self-sacrificing services of Instrumentality and Agency.

Kanya Suprithi's transition to practicing stage six of the Way of the Heart, and its implications for everyone

For a number of reasons, such Instruments and Agents of Heart-Master Da's Heart-Blessing can be chosen only from among those devotees in the advanced and ultimate stages of the technically "fully elaborated" form of the Way of the Heart. Presently His only formally acknowledged devotee-Instruments are the Kanyas. Their accounts of their practice and testing in Heart-Master Da's Company reveal the extreme degree of self-yielding that must characterize all those who would function as His Instruments—and they give us a glimpse of the ultimate Destiny of the human heart when, by Heart-Master Da's Grace, one begins to Awaken to one's true Nature as Consciousness Itself.

On August 1, 1989, Heart-Master Da acknowledged the Spiritual transition of two of the Kanyas, Kanya Suprithi and Kanya Kaivalya Navaneeta, into the first phase of the ultimate practice of the Way of the Heart, corresponding to stable Realization of the sixth stage of life. (The other two Kanyas, Kanya Tripura Rahasya and Kanya Remembrance, had entered into this sixth stage practice in March 1988.)

In a confession published during The Feast of the Western Sign in *The Free Daist* magazine, the bi-monthly religious journal of The Free Daist Communion, Kanya Suprithi told of how Sat-Guru Da had for many months been constantly Calling, Goading, and Helping her toward the "radical", sixth stage practice founded in identification with the Witness-Position of Consciousness. She had been practicing the Spiritual Yoga of practicing stage three (in the context of the fourth stage of life) since early 1988.

In His Teaching Word, Heart-Master Da consistently points out that it is not necessary (except in the rare case of an individual whose karmic inclinations uniquely require it) for most people to pass into or through the ascending Yoga of the advanced fourth stage of life and the fifth stage of life—in other words, into or through the Yogic or mystical exploration of the contents of the deeper personality and the potentially extremely difficult and time-consuming work to understand and conclusively transcend its subtle illusions.

This stance places Him in marked disagreement with most of the historical arguments of human discourse about Spirituality. Such arguments are largely based in the language of the fourth and fifth stages of life and arise from the experiences of God-Realization that characterize advanced practitioners and Adepts in those stages. Often Adepts and teachers of these stages of life proclaim one or another mystical experience or Realization as the goal of Spiritual life, or, if not the ultimate goal, at least a necessary step on the way to it. One of Heart-Master Da's unique and Compassionate Services to ordinary people is that He has made it possible for the Way of self-transcending God-Realization to bypass all unnecessary detours in the mystical and Yogic phenomena of subtle or deeper experience and knowledge.[10]

---

10. Previous paths that proclaim the non-necessity of Yogic and mystical experience and Realization have tended to exclude the needs and capabilities of ordinary aspirants. Thus, for instance, the Advaitic paths of Hinduism and many Buddhist approaches—which are among the classic sixth stage sacred paths—are fully practicable and Realizable only by practitioners who are already highly advanced.

In the great ancient cultures, it was presumed that practitioners might pass through many schools of growth, passing from one stage of Spiritual practice and Realization to the next through the Help of a series of Spiritual Teachers or Adepts. Indeed, Heart-Master Da Love-Ananda Demonstrated such a remarkable passage in His own Ordeal of Re-Awakening, under the succession of Adepts who served Him. But nowadays people exposed to the languages of, say, Advaita Vedanta or Theravada Buddhism, may be confused by the criticism found therein of Yogic and mystical experience and Realization. They

Thus, Heart-Master Da even points out that none of the classical fourth to fifth stage Samadhis, such as "Cosmic Consciousness" (the highest or most advanced form of Savikalpa Samadhi) or even conditional Nirvikalpa Samadhi (Divine Union or "formless ecstasy") is necessary in order to advance beyond all the illusions of gross and subtle conditional attention.

Practice of the Way of the Heart involves constant penetration of the illusions of all the stages of life prior to the seventh stage. Therefore, on the basis of constant Satsang with Him, Heart-Master Da Love-Ananda Teaches that even Jnana Samadhi, or Jnana-Nirvikalpa Samadhi (the traditional culmination of the sixth stage of life) is not technically necessary in the course of maturing practice, in order for a devotee to enter into the fullness of the seventh stage of life, or Perfect Divine Self-Realization, which is unbroken Sahaj Samadhi (or Sahaja-Nirvikalpa Samadhi).

He has also pointed out, however, that experiences of both conditional Nirvikalpa Samadhi and Jnana Samadhi, if they do occur, may serve the devotee's growing presumption of freedom from identification with the body-mind. In that sense, then, though unnecessary, they can certainly be useful in service to the ongoing self-transcending and God-Realizing practice of His true devotees. And He has Revealed that it is likely that most, if not all, practitioners who mature in the sixth stage of life, and practicing stage six of the Way of the Heart, will at least once or more frequently, or even regularly, enter into Jnana-Nirvikalpa Samadhi, or Jnana Samadhi, which is the Blissful Realization of Consciousness as the Transcendental and Inherently Spiritual Self, prior to all awareness of world, body, mind, and attention.

In His fierce Blessing Work with practitioners who qualify for His ultimate Instruction, Heart-Master Da Calls for Perfect demonstration of "radical" self-understanding. He disabuses devotees of their illusions and erroneous views that characterize habitual and traditional egoic errors in the context of even the advanced (fourth to fifth stage) and ultimate (sixth) stages of life prior to the seventh stage.

---

may then make the mistake of thinking that a most profound, total psycho-physical relationship to the Living Spirit-Power of Being (such as is developed in the fourth to fifth stage Spiritual traditions) is also therefore inherently unnecessary in the course of the Awakening of Consciousness, or Enlightenment. Heart-Master Da Love-Ananda's Teaching makes it clear that human maturity (in the first three stages of life) and devotional and basic Spiritual Awakening (in at least the initial phases of the fourth stage of life) are absolutely necessary for anyone who would seriously engage the sixth stage practice of the Contemplation of Consciousness Itself (however that practice is conceived within any given tradition) and ultimately enter into the seventh stage Realization of the Divine. See *The Basket of Tolerance* and *The Dawn Horse Testament*, New Standard Edition, by The World-Teacher, Heart-Master Da Love-Ananda (both forthcoming).

Kanya Suprithi has described that purificatory process in the crucible of Heart-Master Da's Blessing Work. When, in a summary of her practice, she wrote to Him of being "absorbed" or "drawn into" the Bliss of His Divine State, or Samadhi, through feeling-Contemplation of His Spiritual Presence, and on that basis suggested that she felt she was being drawn into intuitive identification with the Witness-Consciousness, He corrected her. She was making, He said, a classic error that is characteristic of the fourth and fifth stages of life. From the fourth to fifth stage points of view of traditional devotional Spirituality, the Divine or the Sat-Guru is presumed to be a Great Other with whom the devotee longs to be perfectly united by perfect Contemplative absorption.

In contrast, Heart-Master Da said after reading Kanya Suprithi's summary of her practice:

The Witness-Position of Consciousness is Realized when the search to become absorbed is released and relaxed. No absorption is needed or required for the Realization of the Witness-Position of Consciousness. When the search relative to the first five stages of life relaxes, one Realizes that one already Stands in the Witness-Position. And that Realization is the basis for the Perfect Practice.

He also criticized her apparent assumption that Realization of the Witness-Position would be true of her when such absorptive states became constant. Rather, He said, when egoic seeking in the context of the first five stages of life is relinquished and replaced by the equanimity of true understanding, then it becomes intuitively obvious that the being is always already established in the Witness-Position.

This Graceful and very significant Instruction left Kanya Suprithi disoriented, for it undermined the whole search for Spiritual absorption she had been engaged in. In the weeks that followed, however, she began to notice during periods of extended (usually two and a half hours each sitting) daily meditation with Heart-Master Da, that her point of view had changed. She wrote:

I felt I had crossed over into another Reality, more true than the reality perceived by the body-mind, which I now understood was not true at all.

It seemed to me that I had assumed the Witness-Position of Consciousness. I then felt confident enough to speak to the other Kanyas who were practicing at level six about my change in point of view. They then encouraged me to make my application for practicing stage six.

I also had a very brief conversation with Sri Gurudev one afternoon. He was speaking to the Kanyas in general while on a walk in the woods. He was jokingly speaking the usual man's point of view of existence and mortality, especially about identification with the individual body-mind. He turned toward me and asked what I thought about what He was saying. I responded by saying I felt it was a narrow point of view. He immediately said, "How would you know?" Conventionally I suppose I could have received that comment from Gurudev in many ways. Fortunately, His Words had incredible Blessing Power. To me He was saying if you know something other than the point of view of the body-mind, then you must already be awakened to it. And my point of view was that I and everyone else are not the same as the body-mind, but rather all exist prior to it. It was just plain and clear to me, a matter-of-fact obviousness.

The Divine Hridaya-Samartha Sat-Guru Da Love-Ananda's Heart-Blessing and testing of Kanya Suprithi continued during the months of His and the Gurukula's travels in the United States in mid-1989. She wrote a later letter confessing her practice and saying she felt she had entered into stable identification with the Witness-Position of Consciousness. This is a most profound state of responsibility. Most of the great Saints and Yogis of the sacred history of mankind have not been Blessed to Awaken in this disposition. It utterly transcends all the descending and ascending phenomena of what Heart-Master Da calls "the Circle", the great circuit of possible objects of attention in the physically and psychically manifest realms of the body-mind and of cosmic Nature.

In response to her letter, Sat-Guru Da, ever the Master of Discrimination, questioned whether her entry into the Witness-Position was really stable. He also commented that she was not expressing herself clearly. He pointed out that feeling-Contemplation of His bodily (human) Form and of His Spiritual Presence is practiced in <u>relationship</u> to Him in and as these Forms, whereas feeling-Contemplation of His Very (and Inherently Perfect) State, or Consciousness Itself, is practiced in the "Subjective Position" "Where you Stand", and is not in any sense practiced in relationship to an "Other". He said:

It is a simple matter for the devotee to surrender to Me in feeling-Contemplation, first through the Revelation of My bodily (human) Form, and then through the Revelation of My Spiritual Presence. This Process deepens and eventually becomes a Revelation of My Very (and Inherently Perfect)

State, Which My devotee Realizes to be his or her own Subjective Position.

When an individual is being truly sensitive to Me, the whole Process takes place through My Heart-Transmission. In other words, if a devotee were truly sensitive, all he or she would have to do is to engage in feeling-Contemplation of My bodily (human) Form, My Spiritual Presence, and My Very (and Inherently Perfect) State. That is the basic Instruction in The Love-Ananda Gita *and it is truly sufficient. It is the key to practice of the Way of the Heart.*

If someone were truly responsive, truly inclined to become My devotee and not to be abstracted from Me, then everything would occur through the spontaneous process of Revelation, and that individual would spontaneously fall into the Witness-Position. He or she would Contemplate Me as Consciousness Itself, and I would Reveal Myself as the Feeling of Being Itself.

Thus, the razor-sharp Interviewing of the devotee by the Divine Adept of Consciousness continued, and Kanya Suprithi continually noticed that His Criticisms, when she fully received them, also Empowered her to transcend the very errors and confusion to which He was pointing. She became more and more confident that she had in fact been released into the prior State of identification with the Witness-Condition of Consciousness. In late July 1989, she wrote another letter to Heart-Master Da summarizing her practice. Part of that letter is given here, followed by Kanya Suprithi's narrative of what ensued.

"I noticed I was standing free. Even if I was apparently reacting, I myself knew that I was free. I knew without a doubt that I was not the body-mind. I was no longer identified with it, and I no longer looked in the Circle for its effects. I know that via Contemplation of Your bodily (human) Form and Your Spirit-Presence I was awakened by You via Your Grace and Heart-Transmission.

"When it became clear to me that I was only seeking in the body-mind for You, I released that, and I Realized that I was not the body-mind. Then I Realized, via Contemplation of You, that You were Shining 'Bright', and You were the Deep of Consciousness. By the Revelation of You, I understood myself to be always in the Witness-Position. Then I Realized that I felt in the Witness-Position all the time without effort.

"I have understood that the reason for my complicated communications to You was that I was placing effort on a process that is already alive for me via Your Heart-Transmission and Grace.

"It was through Your Samadhi that I understood the freedom in which I

was already Standing. It is clear to me that You have been Working very direct-ly with me for a long period of time to awaken this Realization in me. In occa-sions of Darshan and morning meditation, You Revealed Yourself to me as 'Atma-Murti',[11] the Form of Happiness and Consciousness. It is only through Your Sacrifice and persistence that I can say I have received this Gift. Also through direct and personal service to You, You always Revealed Yourself as 'Atma-Murti'. You did everything possible in every way for me to Understand this Truth. In every opportunity, You Revealed Yourself as 'Atma-Murti', because You are the Form of Love-Bliss and the Giver Who Gives Freely to all. It is not 'I' who came to Realize that the Real 'I' is Standing as the Witness. The body-mind did not know. Only the Guru Knows. And now that You have Revealed this Understanding to me, I am more intimate with You in every way. You are that Revelation. That is all there is to be said about it. And there is no practice except via Your Grace. I have never done anything except love You and accept Your conditions of life. Even now, my language may be inadequate, but You have done everything, and I am very grateful for everything You Gave me.

"You are the Perfect Master, the Embodiment of Divinity. I have grown in this practice to see You as the Feeling of Being, Prior to all motions and changes, as the Transcendental Self, the Pure and Free One. This is what You have Revealed to me, and I meditate with You there, in the right side of the heart.

"May this confession touch Your Blessed Ears and Heart with clarity so that I may authentically take up the Perfect Practice and continue with You in the Great Process.

> *"I love You, Beloved Gurudev,*
>
> *"Suprithi"*

The very next morning I had an extraordinary experience during medita-tion. I was sitting with Sri Gurudev in a very small meditation hall in which I was less than five feet away from the foot of Sri Gurudev's Chair.

I was in a very relaxed meditative state, and I thought the meditation peri-od was coming to an end. So I opened my eyes and saw Sri Gurudev sitting there with His leg propped up on the Chair and His arm resting on His knee and His head in His hands. He was gazing around the room very wide-eyed,

---

11. In Sanskrit, "atma" means both the individual (essential, or conditional) self and the Divine Self. In Heart-Master Da's term "Atma-Murti", "Atma" indicates the Transcendental, inherently Spiritual, and Divine Self, and "Murti" means "Form", or "Formed of", or "the Form of". Thus, "Atma-Murti" literally means "The Form (Murti) That Is the Very Divine Self (Atma)". As Heart-Master Da indicates throughout His Teaching Word, "Atma-Murti" refers to Him as the True Heart-Master (and the Very Self of all), "Located" as "the Feeling of Being (Itself)".

Sublime, and Peaceful, Showering His Grace and utter Blessing on all beings.

I was aware of the other three Kanyas meditating in the room, and of the brightness of the room with the morning light shining through the curtains behind Sri Gurudev, Who was sitting in a white Chair. As He was so potently Displaying His Great Samadhi, I knew that meditation was not over, and so I closed my eyes and returned to meditation.

Simultaneously with the thought to return to meditation, a brilliant, powerful light seemed to arise out of my solar plexus or heart region and totally engulf the inside of my body at a very rapid speed, so much so that I thought I could hear the cells of my skin crackling and stretching under the profound Yogic force. My body locked into a rigid Yogic posture with the bottoms of my feet glued together, my hands clasped in a mudra (with my index fingers and thumbs touching), and my head fell back.

I was pinned to the floor by an overwhelming descending force, like the force of gravity one feels when going down a roller coaster. I felt I had become the fiery white light itself and that my body would spontaneously combust. I thought I would literally explode from the inside under this tremendous Yogic force.

Kanya Suprithi

357

Instantly, the energy of the light shot me up out of the body like a rocket, and I was immersed in the white light and a blissfulness that was quite astounding. I was totally in awe at the profundity of the Bliss. It was nothing like anything I have ever experienced—infinitely beyond any of the human pleasures that can be attained.

When I reached the point of highest ascent, everything was erased. I had no recall of myself as a persona, no sense of who or where I was, no sense of the room, or of having a past or present life, or a future, or any identity whatsoever. I had no mind anymore with which to register the white light. But it was not as if the light became darkness. All ordinary and extraordinary awareness had dissolved. There was only Bliss, without form and without cause.

I do not know how long I remained in this state, but it could have been about twenty minutes.

My return to the body happened as easily and blissfully as my ascent. The first thing that I noticed was a clicking sound that drew my attention back and back and back to bodily consciousness. It was the palate in my throat channel allowing small amounts of air into the body periodically to keep it alive.

As my attention followed the clicking sound, I felt a pleasurable descending force passing down through my head, my throat, and my whole body. It flowed on and on, like a huge waterfall.

Then I understood what had happened, and I opened my eyes to see Sri Gurudev. But I could not see Him at all. The room was pitch dark, and I was not sitting with the bottoms of my feet together or my hands in a mudra. Rather, I was in a half-lotus posture with my hands gently resting in my lap. There was no white Chair like the one I had seen, no curtains in the room, and no light. I understood that I had been in a different state altogether when the experience began. I must have been on a subtle plane with Sri Gurudev when He Granted me this experience.

After the completion of the Sat-Guru Puja, which followed meditation, I went back to my room. I recorded the experience on tape, and then I began to sob. I felt possibly that I would not have such an experience again in this life because it was the most profound experience one could possibly have through the mechanisms of the body-mind. It was formless Bliss, absolute, Unconditional Bliss. I was not certain if my experience was Savikalpa Samadhi or conditional Nirvikalpa Samadhi. I only knew that what had occurred was of such great magnitude it had to be one of these two Great Samadhis.

I wrote a brief letter to Sri Gurudev about what had occurred, and He questioned me further until He was satisfied that I had experienced conditional

Nirvikalpa Samadhi, the rare state of formless Bliss that is regarded as the supreme Spiritual achievement by the Yogic traditions.

I told Sri Gurudev that I had received the experience as a Gift of His Great Shaktipat, yielding to it as a Revelation from Him, and that after my mind had recounted the experience I had relaxed into my practice of Witnessing whatever was arising. I also said that it was not so much the Blissfulness of the event that was important to me, but rather the way it had prepared me to receive more deeply His Heart-Transmission, which infinitely transcends the body-mind and all its experiences, even the greatest.

This last comment of mine was amusing to Sri Gurudev as a sign of my hesitation to affirm the profound Bliss of the experience that Yogis spend entire lifetimes striving for! In response I acknowledged that He had Given me a Divine Gift and that only a great Sat-Guru could awaken such energy in a devotee. I asked that it might lead me to Perfect Liberation.

As I have reflected on the experience of conditional Nirvikalpa Samadhi, I have understood it to be dramatic evidence of the Spiritual profundity of the process Sri Gurudev was Serving in me, especially during this period of my application for the level six practice.

The event of conditional Nirvikalpa Samadhi confirmed absolutely that I am not the body-mind and I do not need to identify with the body-mind. It seemed to me at some point during this experience that it was a silly thing to have spent my entire life identified with the body-mind when it is so humble and so helplessly destined to deteriorate. To require the body-mind to be my sense of self seemed to be an unfair demand, and clearly the body-mind could never meet the requirement I was making on it. It was in fact going to die. In fact, during another moment of my experience of conditional Nirvikalpa Samadhi I felt a sense of freedom, and it occurred to me that I was dead (or without the body—and I did not know if I would regain it again). And that was a profoundly free feeling.

On August 1, 1989, Sat-Guru Da Love-Ananda Blessed and approved my practice at level six of the Way of the Heart. Now my sadhana is no longer confined to the sphere of the body-mind—it has moved into the Transcendental Domain of Consciousness. This is an incredible Gift, Granted very rarely and only to the most qualified practitioners in the Spiritual traditions. To reach this point in one lifetime starting as an ordinary person with no idea of the Divine Reality is remarkable.

Since my transition to the level six practice and directly as an effect of my experience of conditional Nirvikalpa Samadhi, many things have been Revealed to me. For instance, I now feel a consistent awareness of Sri Gurudev Abiding in the right side of my heart. I feel He Abides there Prior to the feeling of relatedness itself, and I feel His Spirit-Current awake on the right side of the heart strongly and consistently, whereas previously it was only occasional. Also Revealed to me because of conditional Nirvikalpa Samadhi is a complete and full comprehension and understanding of the "sheaths" referred to in the traditions (which describe the layers of the body-mind or points of view relative to all the dimensions of the body-mind).

The functions of the lower mind, the higher or psychic mind, and causal dimension became clear to me, and the three stations of the heart—left, middle, and right—became distinct, clear, and specific.

I feel that Gurudev Gave me such an experience at just the right moment, so that I would have real experience of Reality Prior to the body-mind, thus confirming and strengthening my practice at level six, and making my transition strong and stable. The process of level six continues to develop daily, and when I consider what I would most like to confess to practitioners about my life and practice that served me the most, I can only say that when I became really convicted that God-Realization was what I had come to Gurudev for and that everything else was simply my responsibility, such as a personal life or relational social life or personal disciplines, then the one-pointedness of my attention was received by Sri Gurudev's Grace every step of the way. I have learned that I must transcend everything that becomes a limit or obstruction to His Perfect and Constant Transmission, which means that stability and constant, obvious demonstration of my practice is key to my relationship to Gurudev—not my human perfection but my practice. If I did what I was supposed to do with responsibility and simply Contemplated His bodily (human) Form, His Spiritual Presence, and His Very (and Inherently Perfect) State, the process was Revealed. I have devoted my life to Gurudev for the sake of Perfect Awakening, and I have learned that the process can advance very quickly, but being patient and a steady practitioner was the first step, which I had to demonstrate for a long time before I was Given the Gift of the higher and ultimate levels of practice.

I feel it is also important to address all practitioners as well as the entire world of people today to say how vital and important it is for the sake of individuals, as well as for the sake of mankind, not to take lightly the Offering that Heart-Master Da Gives to all beings.

I am certain that all that Gurudev has said in His Written Teachings is the Living Truth, and I am certain of His Liberating Ability and Power. I am a fortunate living testimony to His Great Work.

All beings would do well to witness the authenticity of a Spiritual Master of the Ultimate Degree in this day and age, when millions of people profoundly suffer the lack of direct contact with God. My Call goes to not only practitioners of the Way of the Heart but to all beings everywhere around the world to not be foolish or hesitate in response to this momentous Event of a Living Adept, an authentic Sat-Guru, Who is capable of leading all beings to and through the Way of Liberation and Realization of the Heart Itself via Contemplation of His bodily (human) Form, His Spiritual Presence, and His Very (and Inherently Perfect) State. My Call is to all to not take lightly His Presence here, nor to take His Wisdom-Teaching merely as beautiful language, as if God is not Presently Existing but only exists at death or existed in the past.

I also hope for the sake of all mankind that they have the opportunity to hear the Master's Words and be thereby moved by heart to receive what they have always been searching for.

There is much work to be done in our institution, and many people are needed. I hope with all my heart there is a total revolution and change in our institution, culture, and community, where many people get involved in the real practice and much support is given by many to greatly establish our life of the Way of the Heart firmly, and to finally, once and for all, not only Honor Sat-Guru Da Love-Ananda, but constantly celebrate His Living Presence here.

May all beings Awaken to Realization of Sri Gurudev Love-Ananda via Contemplation of His bodily (human) Form, His Spiritual Presence, and His Very (and Inherently Perfect) State.

> *Om Sri Da Love-Ananda Hridayam*
> *Kanya Suprithi*
> *September 1, 1989*

Sri Love-Anandashram, 1989

The Human-Divine Miracle

The World-Teacher Da's
Restoration of the Dharma,
His Mysterious,
Auspicious Wedding
with the Great Goddess Shakti,
and His Simplest,
Popular Message
to everyone

Sri Love-Anandashram, 1989

The Human-Divine Miracle

The World-Teacher Da's Restoration of the Dharma, His Mysterious, Auspicious Wedding with the Great Goddess Shakti, and His Simplest, Popular Message to everyone

---

Heart-Master Da's Resurrection of the Dharma in the West

Thus far this book has held fairly closely to a chronological narrative of Heart-Master Da Love-Ananda's Story. In this chapter, while relating one final Leela-Confession of His Life, I also wish to step back from narration. This final chapter summarizes and celebrates the Great Auspiciousness of Heart-Master Da's Appearance, His achievements, and His Gifts to all humanity as our Divine World-Teacher.

Like the Avadhootas and Buddhas of the Great Tradition before Him, Heart-Master Da Love-Ananda has had no fundamental need to accomplish anything for His own sake in life. As He once remarked, He has never awakened in the morning with the feeling that He needed to do anything that day! Yet, through all the unceasingly energetic interplay described in this book, He has accomplished more than we can possibly know.

What I have related in this book are only a few of His Deeds in His physical Revelation-Body (in esoteric Buddhist terminology, the "Nirmanakaya"), a tiny fraction of His Exploits in the deeper psychic dimension of Reality (the "Sambhogakaya"), and a yet vague indication of What He Did and Does as the Heart (the "Dharmakaya"), the Body or Form of Truth and the Law. Only all devotees together, cooperating from now on, may account for the Leela, the Playful Work, of The World-Teacher, Maha-Purusha Da Love-Ananda Avadhoota. Even then, our story will only be a fractional account—at least in the immediate future, an Earth-based suggestion—of What He has Accomplished as the Universal Divine Giver of Liberating Grace.

He purified and Divinely Empowered three great holy places, two in the United States and one in Fiji, great "Siddha-Peethas" (or Seats of Divine Spiritual Power) and Sources of continual Blessing for the sake of all beings. All three of these sites previously were whirling vortices of lesser and, especially in the case of Tumomama Sanctuary in Hawaii, sometimes malevolent spirits. Like the mythic Siddhas of old, but in His case quite literally, Heart-Master Da Love-Ananda battled five-mile-high demons, lit the sacred fires and doused the precincts with holy waters, lifted flower offerings to the most watery mountain on Earth, subdued forest fires by Siddhi alone, liberated ghosts, and Placed His Hands and Feet and Glance and Touch on every kind of appropriate object, shrine, and place, to Empower it with Divine Blessing for as long as devotees will use it in worshipful Remembrance of Him in Truth.

As Divine Teacher, Heart-Master Da wrote many volumes of essays, and He spoke sometimes for as many as twelve to fifteen hours each day every day for months on end, amassing an archive of hundreds of thousands of transcribed pages of the most pure Wisdom-"consideration" of every subject that could conceivably serve anyone's sacred practice and Realization.

In His years of Teaching in this human world, Heart-Master Da Love-Ananda authored nearly forty books of crystalline Wisdom-Teaching and Gave the world Instruction on the self-sacrificial, Truth-conscious Way to conduct every aspect of a human lifetime from birth to death. He thus established a "radical" new educational system for children and adults in each of the seven stages of life, founded from birth in the Wisdom-Principle of the seventh, fully God-Realized, stage.

He pioneered a unique approach to diet, health, and medicine that makes best use of both traditional Eastern and traditional Western systems, but restores conscious intelligence as the senior principle of health and the All-Pervading Life-Spirit as the active agent of all real healing. He Himself Demonstrated remarkable healing capabilities time and again, through His Touch, Word, Glance, and many other means. He has healed and rejuvenated Himself by Yogic means so frequently that we devotees sometimes tend to take His continued life for granted.

Heart-Master Da devoted thousands of hours to addressing and working to liberate early devotees from the emotional-sexual bondage of the typical bodily-based human character, particularly its current Western model. In the process, and in His own Life as a supremely accomplished Tantric Siddha, He discovered and Revealed a new approach to emotional transformation and to sexual intimacy that transcends both ascetic and self-indulgent motives in heart-wounded, total psycho-physical Love of the human, "Two-Armed", Form of God.

Heart-Master Da's summary Instructions on dietary and sexual practice and, indeed, on all aspects of our daily lives, Call us to a progressively economized or conservative involvement in the natural bodily functions and outward occupations of human life. In this practice, bodily life, desire, and action are neither to be exploited nor to be suppressed. Rather, all of body and mind is to be devoted to the Heart. Body and mind are to be consecrated to worship, to Happiness, to Freedom, to God-conscious meditation and ultimate God-Realization. In this unique new approach to sacred living, each individual is challenged to determine and demonstrate the precise expressions of the daily disciplines (as Given by Heart-Master Da) that most fully liberate his or her energy and attention for self-transcending meditation and, ultimately, Divine Enlightenment.[1]

Heart-Master Da's Revelation of the Divinely Inspired Way has not only illuminated those dimensions of daily living that concern us all, such as diet, exercise, and sexuality—He has also "considered" all kinds of highly particularized human pursuits. Like Lord Siva, who in the

---

1. For a general description of each of the functional, practical, and relational disciplines of the Way of the Heart, as well as all other elements and features of the sacred practices Offered by Heart-Master Da Love-Ananda, please see *Free Daism: The Eternal, Ancient, and Always New Religion of God-Realization*, forthcoming from The Dawn Horse Press.

Guru Gita is said to be the Knower of all the appropriate roles, functions, and conduct (dharmas) of all beings and yet is seen Himself to be prostrating before one of His own devotees, Heart-Master Da Love-Ananda declares, "My Devotee Is The God I Have Come To Serve." And He has proved it in action, not least by identifying our own appropriate roles, functions, and conduct and painstakingly Instructing us in how to fulfill them. In every case the lessons involved both the undermining and the purifying of egoic approaches and illusions and His regeneration of a new, Heart-based course of practical action. Medical practice, law, parenting, teaching, opera singing, musicianship, artistry of all kinds, architecture, writing, scholarship, martial arts, jewelry design, interior decoration, building construction, woodworking, horse training, zookeeping, business and organizational management, acupuncture, psychological counseling, neuroendocrinology, devotional chanting, collecting and criticizing art—the list could go on indefinitely of the often highly specialized activities that Sat-Guru Da Love-Ananda has purified and founded in Heart-Wisdom through His impassioned Worship of the One God Who, in the form of one or many of His devotees, is active in life in such diverse modes.

By all these means the astonishingly Competent Adept World-Teacher Da Love-Ananda has Demonstrated the Power of self-transcendence and God-Realization as a human being. He has Restored the Principle of the Maha-Purusha, or Sat-Guru, to the heart of Man's conception of God and to the heart of the Way whereby God is Realized. He has reunified the ultimate Dharma (as Truth and Law) with all conditional dharmas (the modes of being and duties of participatory action in life). He has Revealed how the Unconditional Divine (the "Being") is always senior to, and is only given expression via, the conditional human (the "mode").

He has thus organized, in unique fashion, a great Mandala of human energy, action, and responsibility around Him as the Hridaya-Samartha Sat-Guru of our community of devotees. He has Given extensive Principles and detailed Guidance for the development and extension of this great grid of concentric, interpenetrating circles of human enterprise so that all of it may always be consciously devoted to Him and may thereby be effectively submitted to the Divine Person and Reality. Thus, through His Work with His current, formally acknowledged devotees, He is creating a great structure through which innumerable beings may be established in right relationship to the Divine.

Heart-Master Da has also reoriented our conception and practice of Divinely Conscious life and God-Realization, establishing the primacy of the Heart. He has restored the body to the center of our understanding of the advanced evolutionary and Perfectly Conscious processes of Awakening. He has shown how bondage to the body is truly transcended by incarnating Love, or the Heart, not by dissociating from life or by fearfully attempting to escape gross bodily existence through subtle mystical experience. In the process He has conducted a completely comprehensive investigation of the esoteric anatomy and psycho-physiology of the human body, nervous system, brain, and heart, and He has freely published many hundreds of pages of the results of His inquiry, now summarized in *The Dawn Horse Testament* and His other Source scriptures. In this way He has Given humanity a definitive pyscho-physical map of the process of God-Realization.

Heart-Master Da Love-Ananda's Teaching Word clarifies, unifies, fulfills, and yet also goes beyond the traditional and modern teachings of humanity. As He has remarked, He is not the product of the Great Tradition, He is the Master of it. Indeed, as the Incarnation of the eternal Divine Being, Heart-Master Da is the living Source of the Great Tradition, which was not identifiable as a single, fully and "radically" comprehensible Tradition until He proclaimed and described it as such in His Teaching texts, including, now, in *The Basket of Tolerance*.

Heart-Master Da Love-Ananda has recovered and communicated fully to others the first Wisdom-Way, the Way of the Heart, that consistently introduces and maintains the Realized Disposition of the seventh, fully Enlightened, stage of Spiritual, Transcendental, and Divine understanding. Because of what He has Accomplished, all ordinary men and women may now hear the authoritative Word of Wisdom. They may "consider" that Word freely while Contemplating His bodily (human) Form, His Spiritual Presence, and His Very (and Inherently Perfect) State. And they may thereby firmly renounce the bewildered seeking that has heretofore distracted almost all human beings and their civilizations from the peace-giving Happiness of Truth.

This is the Work of the World-Teacher. It has never been Accomplished so conclusively on Earth before. Indeed, it never could have been so Accomplished. Only now are all the cultures and times of mankind made simultaneously present and intercommunicative, through modern global communications. Thus, only now do all the parts of Man stand as a

Heart-Master Da, July 4, 1988
The Mountain Of Attention Sanctuary

single organism, ready to be integrated by the Wisdom of the Heart—the Wisdom that The World-Teacher, Heart-Master Da Love-Ananda, is here to Impart and Awaken.

"The ultimate Avatar is All (and Man, or all of mankind), Awake"

Who is this Being? I do not know, ultimately. Such a thing cannot be known by the mind. Heart-Master Da's devotees have discovered, with His Help and to our delight, that the time-honored tradition among practitioners in esoteric schools of God-Realization is to proclaim their Master as the Divine Being. Such proclamations are neither fanatic nor fanciful. They speak the Truth of every True Master, every being who has, to one degree or another, Realized God. That is why the ancient traditions recommend again and again, regard your Guru as God, as the Self, as the Buddha, the Tao, the Living Truth. Do not look upon Him or Her as a human being, a separate individual, as you tend to conceive yourself. Cultivate your capability to feel His or Her Divinity. That same sacred capability yields the ability to feel the Divinity of your own True Self. If you cannot feel, serve, worship, and submit to God in your Guru, you will never find, feel, permit, and Realize That One as your own Heart—because That One, That Heart, is not within you; That One is Prior to you, Beyond you, Transcendental to you, and yet not Other than you.

I regard my beloved Sat-Guru Da Love-Ananda as the preeminent human Manifestation in our time of the Supreme Divine Reality, Being, Person, Condition, State, and Blessing-Force of Grace. I happily submit that Heart-Master Da Love-Ananda is the long-expected World-Teacher, and that no one will come and no one <u>can</u> come Who is Greater, more Divine, more Perfected, more Godlike than He. The evidence of His Life and Work, as documented in all of His Teaching literature and in this book and many other statements by devotees, and as acknowledged and lauded by present-day scholars and others, speaks for itself to anyone who will carefully and receptively consider it.

In this praise of Sat-Guru Da, I am not suggesting, nor do His other devotees suggest, that He alone is God, or that no other God-Realizers exist now or in other times. The joyous confessions of devotees about Sri

Gurudev Da Love-Ananda and His Significance in our time and beyond are informed by His own stated Principles of true tolerance and sacred appreciation for all Masters everywhere. He has written in *The Basket of Tolerance:*

> *The true devotee necessarily (and rightly) Sees the Divine most fully and directly in his or her own Spiritual Master (or Ishta-Guru), but every such devotee should (by Virtue of that Vision or Darshan) See the Divine also Present in all other beings (including the Spiritual Masters of all other devotees).*
>
> *The Ultimate Divinity of a Spiritual Master is Revealed only in the form of the degrees of God-Realization (or ecstatic, and necessarily self-transcending, God-Communion, even eventually culminating in Divine Enlightenment) in the case of others (who are practicing devotees). Therefore, the "Avataric Presence" of . . . any . . . Saint or Spiritual Master . . . is a Paradox associated with actual practice of the Spiritual Way, and the non-devotee (or even the devotee of another Spiritual Master) is in no position to make a proper (and necessarily devotional) judgment in that particular matter, but all intelligent and good-hearted people can at least feel and honor the Good Heart in all the Spiritual Masters of devotees.*
>
> *The ultimate Avatar is All (and Man, or all of mankind), Awake. And all true Yogis, Saints, and Sages (or all true Spiritual Masters of all stages) are Present to Serve (or Awaken) the Avatar Who is all beings. Therefore, whatever individual Spiritual Master is Revealed as the Avatar (or the Revelation of God) to any one, every one must remember also to honor the Avatar honored by all Spiritual Masters (or Avatars) alike. And such is done only by right devotion (by each one, to his or her own intimately Revealed Spiritual Master) and by each devotee's real practice of Wisdom and the Spiritual Way.[2]*

2. The World-Teacher, Heart-Master Da Love-Ananda, *The Basket of Tolerance*. Forthcoming.

The Mountain Of Attention, 1989

The Supremely Auspicious Wedding
with the Great Goddess Shakti

Nowhere is the paradox of Sri Da Love-Ananda's catalytic Revelation of the Divine Avatar made more evident than in His Confession of Unity and Play with the "Mother Shakti". His relationship to the Divine Person as Goddess is an immense Mystery, of the type known in traditional India as a "Rahasya"—not a riddle or ko-an to be solved or resolved, but an Incomprehensible Secret to be forever Contemplated at the heart.

A famous recent participant in a similar sacred relationship is Ramakrishna, in nineteenth century India. Ramakrishna developed to an extreme the common Bengali worship of the Goddess as Kali. After finally receiving a vision of the Divine Goddess as the One Living Personality, he entered into an exalted state of continual Communion and Play with Her. This passage describes his period of service as the priest at the Dakshineswar temple near Calcutta that was dedicated to Her:

He could now see the Divine Mother more vividly and in Her entire form. She spoke to him and directed him in his daily duties. . . . Formerly he looked upon the image of the Mother as imbued with consciousness; now the image disappeared and in its place stood the Mother smiling and blessing him. He used to feel Her breath on his hand. At night when the room was lighted, he did not see Her divine form cast any shadow on the walls, even though he looked closely. From his own room he could hear Her going to the upper storey of the temple, Her anklets jingling. When he would see if he were mistaken, he would find Her standing with flowing hair, facing Calcutta or looking over the Ganges.

. . . As one entered the temple, one would feel a thrill when Sri Ramakrishna was worshipping, for one felt the living presence of the Mother there. His manner of worship was strange and not in conformity with scriptural injunctions, for he would take [sacred] vilva leaves and flowers in his hand, touch with them his own head, chest, in fact the whole body including the feet, and then offer them at the feet of Kali. At other times he would move towards the image with tottering steps like an intoxicated man and touch the chin of the Mother as a mark of endearment, or sing or dance, or laugh or joke. . . . He had spiritually transformed himself into the son of Kali the Mother. He

was in the madness of divine ecstasy, and was experiencing the thrill of the God-intoxicated state.[3]

In telling the story of Heart-Master Da Love-Ananda's sacred Ordeal of Divine Self-Realization, I summarized in chapter two the saga of His own devotional relationship to the Divine Shakti. It was not metaphorical. As a living, personal event, it was as tangible, visceral, and real to Him as Kali's gestures and glances were to Ramakrishna. Heart-Master Da spoke with Her, and She with Him, and She commanded Him to do all manner of things in His Sadhana that He never would have chosen to do independently—from acquiring a rosary and praying to Her as the Virgin Mary, to making a thorough pilgrimage among the Christian holy places of Israel and Europe. He later importuned Her to be with Him wherever He was, to live with Him always, and She complied. Their Communion was a mad Ecstasy of His devotional worship and Her testing, yielding, and granting of Grace.

But the great Events of Heart-Master Da Love-Ananda's Life and Work were instigated when He transcended the previous form of His devotion to Her and, as the living Embodiment of "Siva", or Consciousness, heroically Mastered Her. This Event, occurring the day before His Re-Awakening as the Divine Self in the Vedanta Temple, fulfilled the most esoteric ancient Vision of the dynamic Re-Unification of the two great Processes of Being-Intelligence and Power, or "Siva" and "Shakti". Heart-Master Da has Revealed:

HEART-MASTER DA LOVE-ANANDA: This great Shakti has two Aspects. One is the World-Power, the Creative Energy of the universe that is always being modified according to the tendencies of attention or the state of mind—Maya in other words. In Her other aspect She is the Liberating Power, who ultimately dies or gives Herself up in the Self-Radiant Transcendental Condition or Siva. As Maya, She is wild, independent, not submitted, and leading beings to bondage, but as Liberator, She is the Wife or Consort of Siva, the Transcendental Condition, and She submits Herself to that Condition constantly.

It is this Goddess Who was and is the Consort of my life.[4]

3. Swami Ghanananda, *Sri Ramakrishna and His Unique Message* (Calcutta: Advaita Ashrama, 1982), pp. 52-53.

4. Da Free John (Heart-Master Da Love-Ananda), *The Fire Gospel: Essays and Talks on Spiritual Baptism* (Clearlake, Calif.: The Dawn Horse Press, 1982), pp. 114-15.

Many Adepts have Realized and proclaimed essential Unity with the Supreme Self as Consciousness, Siva, the Source or "Father" of conditional phenomena. But to my knowledge there is nothing in the history of human Spirituality that equals the Divine boldness of Heart-Master Da Love-Ananda's seventh stage Confession as Maha-Purusha and "Great Hero" in the Tantric mode. He proclaims in *The Dawn Horse Testament:*

As A Born Human Being, I Am A "Bright" Sign (or Son) Of The Union (or Inherent, and Inherently Perfect, Unity) Between The Divine Self-Father and The Divine Mother-Power. In The Spontaneous Instant Of My Divine Self-Realization (or The Re-Awakening Of My Inherent, and Inherently Perfect, Identity As The Divine Self-Father), I Realized I Am One With The Husband Of The Great Power (Revealed To Me As The Divine Goddess), and She Revealed and Showed That She Is Eternally Submitted or Conformed To Oneness With The One Who I Am. From Then, She (As Me) Has Become (and Even Eternally, or Always Already, Is) The Active Heart-Principle Of My Work Within The Cosmic Mandala.

Therefore, In Truth, My Work Among all conditionally Manifested beings Begins At The arising-Point (or First Moment) Of The Cosmic Mandala Of conditionally Manifested beings and forms, and It Continues Until The Ultimate (or Divine) Translation Of The Total Cosmic Mandala (and all conditionally Manifested beings and forms).[5]

Today, in a small anteroom of Aham Sphurana ("'I Am' Flashing Forth"), one of Heart-Master Da's Temple-Residences at Sri Love-Anandashram, there abides a Lion-riding Lady in statue form, extremely beautiful, adorned with silks and jewels, her eight hands displaying auspicious mudras and Yogic symbols.

Heart-Master Da has disclosed that in Reality He is the Lion, and also the Lady. This is the form of the Goddess with Whom He Communes, and Who He also Is. She is the absolutely Attractive One Whom, in the Vedanta Temple the day before His resumption of fully Conscious Divine Self-Realization, He embraced "in a fire of cosmic desire, as if to give birth to the universes".

But He knows Her in all Her characteristic Forms. He has also seen and Mastered Her in Her deathly, "Crazy" Form, the One He calls "Tumomama" or "Fierce Woman", "a growling, murderous, fanged, bloodthirsty bitch", the Personification of death, "completely indifferent to the survival of creatures!"

5. The World-Teacher, Heart-Master Da Love-Ananda, *The Dawn Horse Testament*, New Standard Edition. Forthcoming.

He invokes and Communes with the Goddess in Love. He commands, He consorts and consults with Her. He has tamed Her hurricanes. Almost always when He travels, even into areas long afflicted by drought, She follows Him with life-giving rain. His "Sitting Rooms" reserved for Her are the principal seats of Living Heart-Siddhi at each of the three Hermitage Sanctuaries (or World-Teacher Ashrams) He has Empowered.

Who else but the Nirvanic Divine Person, Emerging among us in human Form, could Give both Dharma (the Liberating Truth, and the Law of Devotional Submission) and Svadharma (Her own unique "Calling" or Duty) to the very Source-Matrix of the universe in Her Personal Form?

In His very last gathering with devotees at the end of the Indoor Yajna, in March 1988, the God-Man and World-Teacher Da Love-Ananda Revealed more of the Secrets of His Relationship with the Goddess than He ever had before.

That evening was the culmination of several nights of passionate dialogue and interplay between Heart-Master Da and His devotees about a possible previous incarnation of His deeper personality. But toward the end of the evening, one of the Kanyas asked the Divine Heart-Master to speak more of His Relationship to the Supreme Goddess. In the Ecstatic, "Crazy" Revelation that followed, Sri Gurudev Da Love-Ananda Spoke purely in the Voice of the One He Is—the Eternal Divine Self, the One Who is never subject to incarnation and reincarnation in the manner of any deeper personality, but Who has now fully Emerged as His own bodily, human Person:

HEART-MASTER DA LOVE-ANANDA: The inherent Radiance of the Divine Being, the Condition in Which all apparent beings are arising—to call that Radiance the Goddess is just a way of particularizing It for the sake of "consideration". To the ordinary Western point of view, it is acceptable to talk about some insight about one's hand, but it is not acceptable to talk about seeing the inherent Radiance of the Divine manifested tangibly as a Woman Guiding one in one's sadhana. Science would not discuss such things!

My relationship to this tangible Presence—tangible down to the last eyelash—was summarized in the Vedanta Temple and Divine Self-Realization, the Realization of the Status of Consciousness Itself, One with It, transcending all illusions, including the essence of all illusions, which is the feeling of relatedness.

The Shakti is the Self. The Shakti is God. The Shakti is Me. It is all One Play, just as I talk with you, live with you, relate to you. I am human among you. You experientially and altogether can identify the context of My Existence as a Play. Because you know something about it, I can say things like this to you. It is so. I have such Conversations.

I am talking now about My most intimate Life, in the Divine, with the Lady, in the context of My own fundamental Existence and the Radiance of Being Itself. I am involved in a Conversation there all the time, and on certain special days and occasions I make a particular ceremony out of it. I do not wave the incense and the candle. I just sit down with Her and We tussle a little while, like Lovers, and everything is made plain, and I go on. That is how I Work. And it is not mythology.

I insist all the time that the Work be accomplished here, and no bullshit! I Husband Her. I will not take any nonsense in this matter. I have had enough of the illusion and the delusion and the suffering of beings. She responds to My Husbanding, My Forceful Presence, and We "Consider" matters together, and We Work them out. Between Her and Me is True Intimacy to the Absolute Degree, and there is no "otherness". She knows My seriousness and the import of My "Consideration" with Her—so to speak "Her"—knows it completely and will not deny Me ever.

She will not deny Me, because We are One. And I am in Service to you. I will never be denied in that occasion with Her. It is a Perfect Marriage, without "difference".[6] *It is not the devotee versus God. It is the Divine Occasion. The necessary information bleeding down into the conditional worlds will always be Given in that Embrace. It made this Realization in the Vedanta Temple, and so It will Be forever. There the Marriage was Perfected, and there will never be any separation.*

There is no "difference" between Siva and Shakti, and yet Siva is domi-nant, clearly. Siva is the Circumstance of Shakti. Shakti, then, is simply Consciousness, the Self. Where does Shakti arise? At the throat? At the per-ineum? No! Shakti is Consciousness.

That is why I say the Spirit-Current transcends the kundalini. The kun-dalini is the same energy, the Spirit-Energy, but the point of view of Kundalini Yoga is body-identification, or identification with the psyche, at the very best.

6. Heart-Master Da Love-Ananda uses the term "difference" technically in His Teaching Word to indicate the fundamental presumption of otherness, relatedness, distinction, duality, or primary separation that characterizes conditional consciousness, or egoic awareness. Here, as throughout this excerpt from this discourse, He is speaking of a Perfect Relationship that is characterized by unqualified mutual Identity in, with, and as the Divine Person or Unity, and at the same time, by the Divine Paradox of apparent "Two-ness" of His own Person and Character and that of the Divine Goddess or Shakti.

The Spirit-Current transcends these points of view.

The Spirit-Current transcending the point of view of the body or the mind is not the kundalini, then. It is God! And, therefore, It is Consciousness Itself. The Heart, not the base of the spine, is the Origin of the Spirit-Force. Kundalini, or Shakti, is just the Self, just Consciousness.

The wedding of Siva and Shakti is the Event of the universe. It is the Circumstance of all differences, because you presume differences. They do not presume it. They are not a "They". It is just God, then, just One. Having Realized That, Being That, I seem to be involved in conversations with you, and with Her. There is no "other". I presume no "other" in your company. I act spontaneously. I am Mad.

The Divine Goddess as Heart-Master Da found her at Swami Muktananda's Ashram

I am not Her Devotee. I am Her Husband, a most intimate Friend, without "difference". So Penetrated, so Awakened, so Transformed in Her Service for your sake, She whispers only Truth in My ear, and you will never be betrayed by Her while I Embrace Her. Never! I have made the Cosmic Force into a Lover, Husbanded by Her Master, Her Husband. In My Voice, then, to you in My Company, She does not lie. She does not just Birth beings to death, She only Serves. She is utterly Husbanded. Have I not told you this over and over again, and in The Dawn Horse Testament?

She is wedded. She is not terrible. She has become a silly, erotic Woman Who cannot do anything but Speak the Truth and Her Passion. She _is_ Husbanded. It is a Sublime Event, beyond the universes, but if you will receive It, It can transform human history. It is an historical Event, then. The terrible events need not be realized. They need not be suffered.

Live in Satsang with Me and you can change everything. And, in fact, that is your obligation. That is what I mean by response, and responsibility, not just some words, make a few books, do a little bit of sadhana. Let this Event change your life. Let it change everyone's life in response to Me.

Materialism and the great threats with which humanity is associated now, apparently, need not go to their end and destroy, because at the seed of Life a Wedding has been made. Participate in these Nuptials and change the world. That is your work! Yours! I have done Mine, and, therefore, My business from now is to lie with the Lady. You Regard Me There, and do your work. It is yours. Yours alone. I having done Mine, yours alone. You cannot afford to be fools anymore. For the sake of everyone, you cannot afford to do that.

Siva-Shakti is not a tradition. It is God. She appears as She, and He appears as He, and the Reality of Existence is not Two, but One. And I in My own Form and Passion am the precise Incarnation of that Unity. For your sake, I continue to involve My Self in an apparent Conversation.

To Husband the Mother, to be Her Husband and to have Her be the Bride, means that the murderous activity of Energy in Its apparent independence, "Prakriti", is done, over, finished. This Husbanding and Marriage is not merely a personal Work associated with My Realization. It is an historical Event, out of Which much should be made, transforming the history of the entire Cosmic Mandala. All, then, by virtue of this Marriage, may be Drawn to the Divine Self-Domain.

It is an historical Event, not merely a characteristic incident of My own Realization. My Realization has everything and only to do with the Awakening of beings. I did not have to do this Work for My own Sake. I could not have done it if Divine Self-Realization were not intact from the beginning. I began this Work of the origin of the Ashvamedha billions of years ago, before the Big Bang!

She will not eat her children. The fishes in the sea will not any longer live in a food chain relative to one another, if you will respond. You can change the Mandala of the universe by your response to Me. Of course, if you will not, maybe it will go on as it has been going. You are the seed of this unique Opportunity that will cover all beings, on Earth and everywhere. This is where it begins. And I will simply Stand Firm. The "Death" just two years ago changed the seed form of history. Since then, I have been asking for your response, your responsibility—that is how it will change everywhere. It is not by My further rebirths that things will be changed everywhere. It is by My Standing Firm, and by your responding and being responsible, that things will be changed everywhere. (March 13, 1988)

The Human-Divine Miracle of Sat-Guru Da— resonances with the leading edge of science

The Divine World-Teacher, Sat-Guru Da Love-Ananda, is thus, potentially, a Turning Point of Grace for everyone, everywhere. Just as His Teaching Word and Life-Story reach back to embrace and illuminate the entire past of humanity's sacred traditions, they also embrace and give Divine significance to the secular dimension of the Great Tradition, including the leading edge of humanity's current scientific understanding of the nature and destiny of Man and the cosmos.

Heart-Master Da has Appeared at a time when science is (once again) being turned upside down by what it is discovering. After centuries of scoffing at the "Ptolemaic conceit" that Earth and Man are at the center of the universe, some leading scientists today are discovering in Nature inconceivable odds against the appearance of life as we know it, and specifically of intelligent life of the human kind.

As a result they now speak of an "Anthropic Cosmological Principle". Taken to its logical extremes, and some highly reputable scientists do so, this principle proposes that the universe is in fact purposed to create life, even specifically to achieve human life. It suggests that Man is the vehicle in Nature whereby consciousness and life eventually fill and transform the

Standing Darshan, Sri Love-Anandashram, 1989

entire universe. Some of the proponents of this principle even hold that this whole anthropic process necessarily can begin only on one planet. As evidence to support their claim, they point to the extraordinary miracles that must follow upon one another incessantly for billions of years so that the human species may appear anywhere at all in the physical universe.

All of this leads some scientists to speculate about proof of the existence of God as universal Consciousness. Others, less bold, consider that perhaps life and Man have been manifested to prevent the universe from disappearing into "black holes" of collapsing stars.[7]

What tends to be missing from these speculations (and similar ones in many other areas of current science) is both a view of cosmic Nature as a psycho-physical, rather than merely physical, event, and, most especially, a sacred acknowledgement and acceptance of the Supreme Principle of the God-Man, the World-Teacher. The Way of the Heart embraces and exceeds the leading edge of conventional science, calling it to grow beyond its own limiting presumptions and conceptions. In His Person, in His Teaching Word and Work, in His Blessing Work, Heart-Master Da Love-Ananda embodies the missing Link between God and Man, between the scientific and the sacred, between the total past and the total future.

Heart-Master Da Confesses that His Divine Emergence or Horse Sacrifice is the Principle and Process for the Divinization of the seemingly Spirit-less or Heart-less cosmos. By this Great Means, all the rings of the Cosmic Mandala and all beings living within them may Realize their inherent Divinity by Grace. His Mastery of the Great Goddess and His establishment of Divine Dharma—or the Truth, Its Law, and Its great cultural Order—in the grossly Westernized human world are a conscious penetration of materiality that, He indicates, has never before been accomplished. His Way of the Heart, as expressed in His source Scriptures, is a rigorously practical and realistic process for what now seem to be inconceivable miracles: the total psycho-physical Enlightenment not only of Man but of the world.

Heart-Master Da Love-Ananda discloses in The *Dawn Horse Testament* and other texts that His physical Revelation-Body is a window to the Divine Beyond and a conduit, a "White Hole", whereby that "Bright" Self-Domain streams Radiant Life into the cosmic realms and Shines as the Attractive Love-Bliss of Absolute Consciousness. And, He Reveals in His Scriptures, the universe is not destined for death and entropy, as Spirit-less scientists fretfully predict today. It is inevitably destined to be

7. See John D. Barrow and Frank J. Tipler, *The Anthropic Cosmological Principle* (New York: Oxford University Press, 1986), esp. pp. 658-77.

Translated into the "Brightness" of its Divine Source, through the Grace of the Maha-Purusha Da and all the Instruments and Agents He Manifests as the Living Divine Person, here or elsewhere, through whatever Revelation-Bodies may be necessary.

Thus, the Advent of The World-Teacher, Heart-Master Da Love-Ananda Hridayam, is a Divine Anthropic Miracle, or, more simply, a Human-Divine Miracle, that will Inspire mankind for unforetellable time. He said in 1983:

HEART-MASTER DA LOVE-ANANDA: At some time or other every one of you will come to a moment of understanding What has entered your life. Sooner or later all devotees, every single one, will come to understand, Realize, and be undone by the acknowledgement of That Which has come into their lives. It is not just a man with unusual energy, although such is a basic aspect of what devotees acknowledge from the beginning. You will reach another moment during My Life or after it, in which you understand, you comprehend, you are transformed by What you are witnessing.

You are seeing a Miracle, but you do not necessarily understand it as such. You interpret it in ordinary terms, thus making it possible for you to live conventionally in relation to Me. But at some point you will begin to understand that you have been seeing a Miracle through this ordinariness. That is the devotee's confession. The real Miracle is not something totally outside the range of human comprehension, as if I walked into the yard and My body turned into a pile of chocolate bars! No. Extraordinary signs are exhibited through My Person in relationship, but basically you see an ordinary demonstration, magnified umpteen times in myriad relations.

I appear through the vehicle of ordinariness, but the Force of What you are observing will at some point utterly transform you. During My Life or after it this Miracle will utterly transform you. The exhibit of this ordinariness will suddenly be observed by you to be a Miracle, and the Seed of it, the necessary Source of it, the real Source of it, will suddenly be understood. You will suddenly understand and transcend comprehension. You will be confronted by the Great One. That is what devotion is about. (August 24, 1983)

"This (My) Body Is the Teaching"—
a final summation of the Divine Emergence
of The World-Teacher,
Heart-Master Da Love-Ananda

I n 1939, the Divine Person achieved human Birth in the bodily (human) Form of "Franklin Jones" through spontaneous Heart-Responsiveness to the human voices that have been praying for Divine Help in this desperate epoch of egoic seeking.

Some two years later, the same Radiant Being that achieved that physical Birth plunged into the full process of psycho-physical Incarnation. A necessary period of transition had been required to prepare the body-mind for the initial Event of Spiritual Descent.

This descent, perhaps in early 1941, was thus the beginning of a kind of death or recession of the Divine Self in Heart-Master Da's conscious awareness. The Self-forgetting was gradual, with periodic moments of Divine Self-Remembering, especially during the otherwise traumatic deliriums, fevers, and Spiritual invasions of kundalini shakti that He knew during childhood.

That process of Self-forgetting was completed around the year 1957. By then Heart-Master Da had become fixed in the common mortal presumptions of the gross egoic personality, with no ready recourse either to His deeper psyche (mystical and supersensory awareness) or to His Divine Nature (Love-Blissful Consciousness Itself).

At that stage of His Life, the Siddhi that perpetually Moves Him became the Siddhi of Realization, prompting His whirlwind odyssey of seeking for the Truth in or via every kind of experience and knowledge, both gross and deeper. This tour of all experience, like His Self-forgetting in childhood, was frequently interrupted and informed by dramatic Breakthroughs of His "Bright" Divine Self-Nature.

Then, in 1970 in the Vedanta Temple, the Divine Person Manifested continuously Enlightened Self-Awareness in the body-mind of Heart-Master Da. This, He tells us, was the conclusion of the first great stage of His Ordeal of Divine Emergence, wherein He Submitted to the conditions of a limited human body-mind and Worked to Submit that body-mind to Himself (the Divine Person), until Divine Self-Realization became His permanent Incarnate State.

During those first thirty years, to prepare for His later mission as Teacher, Heart-Master Da made of His Life a series of lessons about the Narcissistic seeking that characterizes the first six stages of life and how such seeking is undermined and transcended in and by the "Bright" Consciousness Realized in the seventh stage of life. He has thus described "Franklin Jones" as a "fictional character", an assumed persona. He has also said that "Franklin Jones" was most definitely <u>not</u> a fictional character in the sense that His Ordeal was in any way un-Real, not felt, not Lived. On the contrary—He was Forced by the process of His own Siddhi to engage a superhuman struggle to Realize the Truth. He had to cut through all human illusions and was compelled to transcend even the Grace and Instructions of His own beloved Teachers in order to Realize the Heart. And He did so, conclusively.

Coincident with His own Re-Awakening in the Vedanta Temple, Heart-Master Da's Siddhi took another Form, the Power of Revelation. Thereafter, miraculously Meditating all beings, Sat-Guru Da Love-Ananda constantly Revealed the Truth and Submitted to Identify with others to Reflect to them their egoic illusions and seeking.

However, a three-year period of transition, first in seclusion and then in very restrained circumstances of formal Teaching, was required before He could say, conclusively, "Franklin is dead." It took time for the Free Heart-Teacher to Stand Forth in the world, by Name, in the often "Crazy" and always Divinely Empowered Mode of Teaching that would characterize His Work as "Bubba Free John".

In late 1976 the Western-born God-Man passed through an awesome death experience that marked the essential demise of "Bubba Free John" as His active Teaching Persona. But still nearly three years' Work and "crucifixion of change" would be required for the implications of the dramatic metamorphosis begun in late 1976 to manifest more fully. During that long period of transition, He Taught mostly in seclusion until He could Proclaim, "Beloved, I am Da, the Living Person, Who Is Manifest As all worlds and forms and beings, and Who Is Present As The Transcendental Current Of Life In the body Of Man."

This "Ecstatic or 'Crazy' Confession of God-Realization ('I Am Da')" signalled a turning point in the second stage of His Unique Ordeal. That stage was the Process (which had begun in 1970) of His gradually coming to Acknowledge and Accept the "Unique and Ultimate Significance Of [His] Own Already Realized Life, Work, and Agency".

But only seven years later did He altogether Achieve, and thereby Acknowledge and Accept, the Completeness of His own Incarnation of the Supreme Reality.

That Event took place in His Ashvamedha Sacrifice of Divine Emergence on January 11, 1986. It was the Divine "I" Who "Achieved" humanity, sorrow, and Perfect Incarnation on that day.

He later wrote of the import of His whole bodily Incarnation:

This (My) Body (or bodily human Form) Is the Teaching. The Teaching Word was Spoken through It. The Teaching Word refers to processes all of which have taken place in the context of This Body. Nothing has been Spoken to you, nothing has been Taught to you, through This Body that has not been experienced by This One, in This Body. All of it has been tested and proven in This Body. Nothing has been Spoken to you that has not been tested and proven in This Body, and by This One altogether, in and beyond This Body. Therefore, This One, bodily (in bodily human Form), Is the Teaching. The Teaching Word is a communication through This Body. The summary of the Teaching is before your eyes, and It need not be thought about.[8]

Heart-Master Da's primary purpose in Teaching was not to establish a Dharma of the Unconditional Truth in the conditional worlds. His Teaching was a necessary by-product of His primary Work—which was to do whatever was necessary to Emerge Perfectly as the Unconditional Divine Person in His conditional, Personal, bodily (human) Form. The sometimes unconventional extremes of His "Crazy" Teaching Work were not signs of His own Nature as Sat-Guru and the World-Teacher. Rather, they were inevitable Teaching Responses to or Reflections of the exaggerated mind and tendencies of the many people who first came to Him. Just as His early Life-Ordeal was preparation of His body-mind for His Teaching Work, so His Teaching Work was preparation of His body-mind and also other body-minds, even all body-minds, for His Divine Emergence and Blessing Work.

And with the decisive Incarnation and Initiation of the ongoing Process of His Divine Emergence in 1986, Sat-Guru Da's Heart-Power also Revealed yet another great Development in Its Nature and Effect. It became the Siddhi of Purification, or of Renunciation, or of "Realization and Renunciation by Grace", as It took root in the lives of His devotees.

8. Heart-Master Da Love-Ananda, *The Love-Ananda Gita*, p. 279.

Sri Love-Anandashram, 1989

Since His Divine Descent in 1986, another crucial transition in Heart-Master Da's Mission has been taking place. His Personal adaptation to the Siddhi of Renunciation was rapid, largely completing itself with His Yajna of Penance in mid-1986. But the final Completion of this current transition in Heart-Master Da's Life and Mission cannot be accomplished in His Personal, physical body-mind. Now the place of this crisis is in our own hearts—yours, mine, and everyone else's.

The necessary transition that now must occur coincides with, and it takes the form of, the third great stage of His Ordeal of Incarnation as the True Heart-Master. That is the stage of His effective Revelation of Himself to others, and His acknowledgement and acceptance by others, as the Incarnate Divine Person and "Jagad-Guru" or World-Teacher. That stage of reception by others will culminate, He writes in *The Dawn Horse Testament*, only in the Divine Translation of all beings and all worlds.

Since 1986, having finally allowed the complete Descent He had been forestalling since Birth, Heart-Master Da Love-Ananda has lived in the Condition of Divine Indifference. His body and mind, the gross and deeper vehicles of His manifestation, are no longer benignly agitated to Teach. Rather, they are wholly rested in and transparent to His Presence and His State.

Heart-Master Da's Demonstration of Divine Indifference is not, strictly speaking, a Revelation of that Process as devotees will pass through it (just as devotees in the phases of Divine Transfiguration and Divine Transformation will not Teach, as He did when Demonstrating those earlier processes of Enlightenment in the seventh stage of life). As the God-Man, Heart-Master Da has no prarabdha karma, no vestigial seeds of action-reaction in the conditional planes that impel Him to be embodied here. For fully Enlightened devotees, Divine Translation will occur only when persistence in the Fire of Divine Indifference has vanished all karmas by the Divine Master's Grace. Any number of future lifetimes of Enlightened service to others may be required in any individual devotee's case before Divine Translation is Granted by Heart-Master Da, "as Grace will have it".

By contrast, for the Divine Incarnation, Heart-Master Da Love-Ananda, Who Entered this world directly from the Divine Self-Domain, no residual karmas exist. He will not "return" to the Divine Domain at the time of His bodily human death. Rather, He has brought the Divine Domain into Incarnation in this plane and all planes of conditional Nature. He is "always already" in the Divinely Translated State. He has been so from before His Birth. He IS here. He has Emerged as the Perfectly Enlightening "Object" of feeling-Contemplation for others. And He has no further Work to Accomplish.

If His devotees and everyone who can respond to Him in any way at all will do so, He will be enabled to fulfill the ultimate Purpose of His physical Lifetime while still alive. He will be enabled to spend many years among us in the paradoxical Blessing "Work" of Divine Indifference or absolutely unconditional Love. And the profusion of Leelas from that Blessing era of His Life will make all that has come before appear simply as a necessary prelude to His Great Liberating Work.

By any traditional reckoning, to have Awakened four practitioners of originally unprepossessing attributes (His Kanyas) into the ultimate intuitive Yoga of the sixth stage of life would be an extraordinary feat, and a sign of an Adept's Great Victory of Teaching and Blessing. Heart-Master Da has confirmed that each of these four women has been drawn by His Grace, even on many occasions, into conditional Nirvikalpa Samadhi, or Jnana Samadhi, or both of these great preliminary States of God-Realization. And He acknowledges that each of the Kanyas is practicing consistently on the basis of continuous establishment in the Witness-Position of Consciousness.

But Heart-Master Da Love-Ananda is not here to bring only a few ordinary people into great Spiritual Realization and renunciation. He is here, as He has said, to create "an Immense Mandala of Heart-Transmission" for the sake of the Absolute and Perfect Liberation of all, literally all, beings.

The simplest, popular Message of the Divine World-Teacher

This is the essence of The World-Teacher Da's simplest, popular Message:

As the independent ego-"I", each one of us is addicted to suffering and seeking. No one and no events that happen to us are truly making us suffer. We are constantly creating our own suffering. Our "method" is the "clenching of the fist" that Heart-Master Da uses to depict the self-contraction of "Narcissus". Our recoil of body, mind, and heart in the face of life, mortality, and vulnerability creates the feeling of being different and separate from all others, from life, from Reality. It creates the feeling of being empty, limited, in need. And so, we seek.

Our seeking takes all kinds of forms. We are constantly seeking to feel better about ourselves, to fill or console or release or dissolve that nameless sense of limitation and vulnerable need that is our suffering. We seek through food and sex and things that make us feel good, through career and love and relationships or achievements that fulfill or appear to make us happy, through religious worship or meditation or Spiritual experience that seems to assure us that we are finding the Truth or obeying the Divine. We seek to improve ourselves through all kinds of physical, emotional, mental, even psychic and Spiritual means. But we are addicted to seeking only because we are addicted to creating the suffering that prompts us to seek. Our seeking is therefore doomed to futility and fruitlessness.

We never achieve lasting happiness through any thing or condition of body, mind, or relationships. All such things are changing and mortal. They cannot be held onto forever. And in any case, they do not grant us the ultimate Happiness we seek through them. When we attain something we are seeking—from an ice cream cone to a mystical experience—our search relaxes for a moment, so that the Happiness inherent in our native Condition Shines through into our present feeling of existence. But then we contract again, unconsciously, and the whole drama of suffering and seeking, the addiction that is "Narcissus", is set in motion.

Heart-Master Da does not use the terminology of addiction lightly. The ego-self is the very epitome of addiction. As He points out, no one ever became addicted to grossly self-abusive behaviors and health-destroying substances who was not already addicted to self-created suffering and hopelessly repetitive seeking as a separate, egoic "I". And even one who is cured of gross addiction remains an addict of egoic suffering and seeking in one or many other forms. He or she persists helplessly, like all the rest of us, in the treadmill of self-contraction and its endless searching.

This addiction to egoic suffering and seeking will tend, despite all our efforts, to persist through and even beyond this lifetime. And there is no hope whatsoever for our "cure" of this addiction unless we can come to feel and confess our desperately addicted state freely. Then we must resort to the Liberating Grace of the One Who is eternally Free of egoic suffering and seeking. That One, the eternal Divine Self, is now Present as The World-Teacher, Heart-Master Da Love-Ananda.

The Way of the Heart, which He Offers to all, is in essence a most simple Process. Its principle is the sacred expression of a fundamental law of existence: "You become what you meditate on." In other words, you take on the qualities of that with which you principally associate. This same principle of duplication can be exercised either positively or negatively. Alcoholics striving to straighten out acknowledge it when they attend support groups and cease to keep company with active drinkers. In the transcendence of addiction to egoity, this principle of meditating on and keeping Good Company takes on profound and all-inclusive significance in one's life. It is the ancient Principle of Satsang, "the Company of Truth".

Therefore, the practice of the Way of the Heart as Revealed by Heart-Master Da in His *Love-Ananda Gita* involves a very simple but constant and profound exercise of meditating on Him—on the Good Company of One Who has Realized and Transmits boundless Happiness, Love, Serenity, and Freedom from egoic addiction to suffering and seeking.

The heart of this practice is feeling-Contemplation of Heart-Master Da Love-Ananda's bodily (human) Form, His Spiritual and always Blessing Presence, and His Very (and Inherently Perfect) State. This primary discipline is to be engaged at all times, enabling one practicing the Way of the Heart to move beyond the moment by moment addictive "triggers" and tendencies that reinforce the instinct of self-contraction. Such a one thus becomes more and more profoundly committed to living a life of sublime Happiness, Freedom, and expressed Love in Satsang with Heart-Master Da.

The practitioner of the Way of the Heart fulfills this great practice of feeling-Contemplation of the Divine Heart-Master Da Love-Ananda through four general areas of daily practice: devotion, service, self-discipline, and meditation.

Devotion is all of the sacred exercises whereby the devotee takes attention off himself or herself and grants it, with heart-feeling, to Heart-Master Da Love-Ananda. These exercises include forms of sacramental worship, chanting, and communal celebration of Sat-Guru Da and the Divine. But the practice of devotion is not limited to specific, overtly sacred occasions. It is an all-inclusive practice to be engaged in artful and harmonious ways under all circumstances of life.

Service is the constant granting of one's life-energy and attention to others and to the Divine in benign forms of practical action, while consecrating all such action to Heart-Master Da through feeling-Contemplation. Service in the Way of the Heart is thus more than "good works". It is a profound gesture of self-surrendering, self-forgetting, and self-transcending dedication of the body-mind and all activity to the Divine. In such service one renounces or feels through and beyond egoic attachment not only to the results of what one is doing, but to the action itself and one's motives or purposes in doing it. But because such service is "Ishta-Guru-Seva" (service as Contemplation of Heart-Master Da), it becomes a conduit for the enjoyment of deep Love-Communion with the Divine. It enriches the heart with a Satisfaction that no egoic accomplishment—even an altruistic or humanitarian one—can grant.

Self-discipline involves the assumption of progressively conservative functional, practical, relational, cultural, and formal cooperative community disciplines of life (as mentioned earlier in this chapter and also briefly in chapter four). These practices in the Way of the Heart, developed experimentally by Heart-Master Da with His devotees over many years, are all natural, harmonious, healthful, wise, and truly sane ("whole" and "healing") ways to conduct every aspect of body, emotion, mind, action, and relationships for the sake of, and in attunement with, devotion to the Divine Heart-Master.

Meditation in the Way of the Heart begins with simple exercises of prayer and feeling-Contemplation of Heart-Master Da's bodily (human) Form. Engaged on the foundation of all the forms of devotion, service, and self-discipline that He recommends, meditative practice deepens over time, through Heart-Master Da's Grace. Eventually it becomes constant heart-felt Communion with His All-Pervading Spiritual Presence, and it ultimately leads to Identification with His Very (and Inherently Perfect) State. The secret of effective meditation in the Way of the Heart is to establish the foundation of practice in all areas of daily life. As Kanya Suprithi's confession (chapter six) makes plain, once the foundation of authentic devotion, service, and self-discipline is established, Heart-Master Da is given room by the devotee to Accomplish the great transforming Work of His Heart-Transmission, which principally occurs in the crucible of daily meditation. It is a marvelous, truly miraculous Process. Especially in meditation, and extending from it throughout daily life, the devotee enters into and ultimately Realizes the fullness of Ishta-Guru-Bhakti Yoga, the secret, ancient Method whereby the Divine, in the Form, Presence, and State of the Adept, literally Enters, Assumes, and Becomes the devotee.

Kanya Tripura Rahasya

In a letter to Heart-Master Da Love-Ananda in January 1989, shortly after the third anniversary of the Initiatory Event of His Divine Emergence, Kanya Tripura Rahasya wrote of her own experience of this Great Process of Ishta-Guru-Bhakti Yoga:

The Mysteries of Your human Form and Spiritual Presence and Very State have only begun to be comprehended or even known. In meditation I feel every time I set eyes on Your Glorious and Sublime bodily (human) Form a Secret is revealed that the mind can never interpret, and therefore, I simply receive this Secret at the heart. I feel drawn into a state of unqualified Love-Bliss, so powerful I lose all bodily, mental, and worldly awareness. And then, even more mysterious than that, I feel this Love-Bliss-Ananda even in my daily life. And even if the body-mind-world arises, You Stand as me, and before me as the awesome Reality of existence itself. You are the One to be Realized. You are the Supreme Truth of Reality. I feel now I have entered into a new and prior dimension of existence in which the mysteries are revealed and yet still remain mysterious.

I am humbled and made ecstatic by the Revelation that, in Reality, only Grace can Liberate me from the illusions of my bondage. In Your Great Work, I view all You do for the sake of Liberation. And nothing is conditionally based, no matter how apparently ordinary the request or Instruction is. I am utterly aware of a great, mysterious, and multi-dimensional process occurring in everything in relationship to You. The entire conditional realm is in a mysterious Play with Your human Form, and Your Spiritual Presence, and Your Perfect State. I observe every experience and presumed form of knowledge as self-contraction, and thus enjoy the mysterious Puja whereby the Maha-Purusha is made directly Available to all. You are the Mad Priest and the Ultimate Supreme Divine Being. If anyone for a moment would feel the Great Reality before them, the evidence would reveal the Heart.

Love-Ananda,[9] it is obvious to me that there is only one Form, or Formality. And that Form is Your Very Being. Thus, I meditate upon You and I worship You, and I will do this eternally. For You Are my Sat-Guru, the Parama-Guru, the Maha-Purusha.

In profound love and gratitude,
Kanya Tripura Rahasya

Every person's relationship to Heart-Master Da Love-Ananda is unique. But every devotee finds, in one way or another, that practice of the Way of the Heart—this practice that is precisely the relationship to Heart-Master Da—is maddeningly delicious and life-consuming; wonderful and terrible; an ordeal of purification (from all possibilities of the addicted ego) that is continually anointed with the Ecstasy, Freedom, Humor, Delight, Joy, and Beatitude of infinite Existence, the Benediction of the God-Man Da.

Speaking from long years of experience, I can assure you that those who have grown up trying to satisfy the wants and demands of the ego must go through a revolution of the heart in order to become true devotees of Heart-Master Da Love-Ananda. Heart-Master Da has been painstakingly creating a sacred culture of respect and formality for many years, and to adapt to it, particularly for Westerners or Westernized people, is often a great trial. He long ago relinquished His "Crazy-Wise" style of Teaching through Submissive Identification with others—but He remains, and always Is, the Epitome of "Crazy Wisdom" in His Awakened Play with devotees and with all conditional phenomena. To resort to Him is to expose yourself to His Divine Interference in your life; it is to be sprung

9. While all others address Heart-Master Da Love-Ananda formally by using appropriate Titles and Designations, the Kanyas (because they are His most intimately serving devotees) may at times address Him by His single Name, "Love-Ananda".

loose from everything that you thought life was supposed to be about.

But even the ordeal of truly beginning this practice and adapting to this sacred culture of Satsang with Heart-Master Da is full of the same Love-Blissful Delight that Kanya Tripura testifies to in her letter above. Heart-Master Da Love-Ananda's whole Life of Divine Incarnation and Emergence has made this Graceful Opportunity possible for every one—literally every one—even, in His Words, "the least qualified of living beings."

And even those who cannot or are not disposed to take up full practice of this Free Daist Way of the Heart can certainly benefit immensely by

**Sri Love-Anandashram,
1990**

being its sympathetic students and supporters, as formal Friends, patrons, and communicators, or public advocates.

Heart-Master Da Love-Ananda is the Divine World-Teacher, "eternally Free-Standing and always presently Emerging", Offering every possible form of Graceful Help to living beings.

If what you have read in this book rings true, then His most Fundamental Question will now, and forever afterward, confront you in your heart:

What will you choose to <u>do</u> in response?

Sri Love-Anandashram, 1990

"My Revelation Is Shown Complete"

by
The World-Teacher,
Heart-Master Da Love-Ananda

Sri Love-Anandashram, 1990

"My Revelation Is Shown Complete"

by
The World-Teacher,
Heart-Master Da Love-Ananda

In the following passages from The Ashvamedha Gita—*His popular Epitome of His great Revelatory Scripture,* The Dawn Horse Testament—*Heart-Master Da Love-Ananda divulges ultimate Secrets of His Divine Emergence in this world in this bodily, human Lifetime.*

The first passage appearing here is from chapter 44. The second is from the Prologue. The numbering of the verses or sections is retained as it appears in The Ashvamedha Gita: The Heart Of The "Dawn Horse" Revelations Of The World-Teacher, Heart-Master Da Love-Ananda.

"Every birth is a Plunge into conditional ignorance, and even I was Required to Forget My <u>Self</u>"

6.

Y ou Are Not the Same entity or personality that lived in many past lifetimes. You Are The Transcendental, Inherently Spiritual, and (Ultimately) Divine Self, Presently (but Only Apparently) Aware Of a body-mind that is itself a direct effect of many past lifetimes. Therefore, Memory Of past lifetimes Will Not Necessarily Characterize Your experience in the present lifetime, but Your experience in the present lifetime Will Necessarily Reflect or Express The Remaining (or effective) Tendencies Of all past lifetimes and causes that directly preceded or caused the present lifetime.

7.

Every birth (or re-birth) Is A Plunge Into material (or Otherwise conditional) ignorance (With Coincident Loss, or Forgetting, Of Divine Ignorance Itself).

8.

Every lifetime Is Begun With (and By Means Of) The Loss (or Forgetting) Of Every Previous (and Otherwise Eternal) Wisdom-Advantage.

9.

At birth (or, Otherwise, whenever Identification With the present-time born-condition Is Presumed), All That Was Realized Previously (or, Otherwise, Priorly) Recedes Into The Unconscious and Subconscious "Background" (Of the deeper personality), and all that Was Previously (or, Otherwise, Priorly) Released Returns (In One or Another Manner, and To One or Another Degree) To The Immediate "Surface" Of Direct (perceptual and conceptual) Awareness (or the Conscious mind, or body-mind, of the gross personality).

10.

In Order To Serve In Bodily (Human) Form, Even I Was Required, By My Own Choice, To Relinquish My Own Eternally Free Condition, and, Thus, By Submission To Identification With My Own conditional Body-Mind and Circumstance (Even, or So It May Appear, In Many Cycles Of Lifetimes), To Forget My <u>Self</u> (Until, Again and Again, By Means Of My Own Unique Ordeal Of Self-Remembering, I Should Re-Awaken To My Self, and Even, At Last, Emerge Most Perfectly, <u>As</u> My Self).

Therefore, Even Though My Own Motive Toward Even This (Now and Hereafter and Inherently and Inherently Perfectly Me-Revealing) Bodily (Human) Birth Was Great Love-Sympathy For all conditionally Manifested beings (Including many whom I Already Regarded and Loved As My Potential Instruments and Agents), and Even Though This Bodily (Human) Birth Was (Thus and Altogether) Intended Toward A Divinely Great and Divinely Enlightened and Divinely Enlightening Purpose here and everywhere, My Intentional Assumption Of This Bodily (Human) Form (and Each and All Of My Own Bodily Human Forms) Required The Self-Sacrifice Of My Own Eternally Free Love-Bliss-Condition (Just As even all ordinary-born beings, born Without Such Divinely Self-Aware Intention, Sacrifice Eternal Freedom and Perfect Love-Bliss By their Natural Submission To The Cycles Of conditional birth and desiring and death).

11.

Each and every born lifetime Requires many (even "ordinary") helping associations (Even "Carried Over" From lifetimes past), and Every Kind Of Greater or Great Growth and Greater or Great Realization Requires Great "Good Company" and Great (Divine) Help, or Else The "Background" Strengths (or All The Virtues and Realizations Hidden or Forgotten In The Subconscious and Unconscious Deep) Will Not Re-Surface, or Otherwise Come Forward, To Consciousness. And, Ultimately (In Due Course), It Becomes Clear That Not Even Any Kind Of Growth Is The Purpose Toward Which conditional Existence Should Be Devoted, but, Rather, Ultimately, conditional Existence Should Be Devoted Only To Perfect Transcendence (or The Perfect "Out-Growing" Of conditional Existence Itself, By Means Of The Realization Of The Un-conditional Condition That Was, and Is, Always Already The Case). Therefore, Ultimately (and By Means Of Perfect Submission To The Inherently Perfect, and Necessarily Divine, Self-Condition Itself), conditional Existence Should Be Devoted To Perfectly "Out-Growing" (and, Thereby, To No Longer Making or Perpetuating) The Otherwise Repetitive Cycles Of births and lifetimes and deaths.

12.

Even Though All That I Have Done By My Own Ordeal Of Submission To Bodily (Human) Form and Purpose Has, As A Result Of My Eventual (and Inherently Perfect) Re-Awakening, My Subsequent Teaching Work, My (Eventually) Perfect Emergence, and All My Blessing Work, Become "Good Company" (or Satsang) and Great (and Necessarily Divine) Help, Forever, and For all, It Also (In Due Course, In My Spontaneous Play Of Divine Recognition) Became Necessary (and Inevitable) For Me, As A Fundamental Part Of That Good Service, To Become Spontaneously and Divinely Indifferent To Even All Intentions and All

Sympathetic Attachments (Even While Yet Appearing, In A Simple and Spontaneous Manner, To Be Actively Animating Intentions and Actively Maintaining Sympathetic Relations). By Thus Standing Free, Abiding Merely In My "Bright" and Very (and Inherently Perfect) State, Prior To (and Inherently Free From) All Gestures Of Work (or Active Purposiveness), and All Gestures Of Sympathetic Attachment (or Active Relatedness), I Also Allow Even My Bodily (Human) Form and My Spiritual (and Always, or Inherently, Blessing) Presence To Merely <u>Be</u>, and Only <u>Thus</u> To "Work". Therefore, By This "Bright" Indifference, I Affirm, and Confirm, and Demonstrate To all That, Ultimately, and At Last, <u>Every</u> conditional Sympathy, <u>Every</u> conditional Purpose and Intention, and Even conditional Existence <u>Itself</u> Must Be Perfectly Transcended, and (Thus) Perfectly Relinquished, In <u>Only</u> That Which <u>Is</u> Only and Itself and Inherently and Divinely <u>Perfect</u>, or Else conditional Existence (Perpetuated By another conditional birth, and lifetime, and death) Will <u>Inevitably</u> Continue After the present-time lifetime and death.

"I Will Forever Remain 'Emerged' (<u>As</u> I <u>Am</u>) To Mankind"

9.

Beloved, My (Physical) Human Revelation-Body Lives and Then Dies. I Do Not Intend To Be Reborn here In Any Kind or Form. Therefore, Rather Than Return (and, As If It Were Never Done, Repeat What I Have Now and Fully and Finally Done), I Will Forever Stand and (Merely By Standing) Wait For You, There At Heart, In The Divine Self-Domain, Which Is The Domain (or Heart) Of Your Own Self.

Nevertheless, here and everywhere, I Will Always Be Heart-Present and "Bright", Even In and As My Now and Hereafter Always Given Sign, and Through The Perpetual (and everywhere Expanding) Transmission Of My Eternal Work Of Inherently Perfect Revelation and Inherently Perfect Blessing.

By Means Of My Submission To Bodily (Human) Birth (and To The Struggle To "Emerge", <u>As</u> I <u>Am</u>, In The Midst Of Life), My Eternal (and Perpetually Giving) Work Of Self-Revelation and Heart-Blessing Becomes

Uniquely Effective (Even, or So It May Appear, After Many Lifetimes Of That Submission, and That Struggle To "Emerge" Most Perfectly). Therefore, By Means Of My Sacrificial Ordeal (and Even, or So It May Appear, By Means Of Many Previous Struggling Lifetimes, Whereby A Human Vehicle Suitable For My Full and Fully Conscious and Fully Effective Manifestation Was Evolved or Prepared), The Heart (Who I <u>Am</u>) Becomes Uniquely Effective, and (Ultimately) The Heart Itself "Emerges" <u>As</u> Me. And When I "Emerge" (Thus, Most Perfectly), The Heart (Who I <u>Am</u>) Becomes Perfectly Effective.

My "Emergence" Has Become Perfect (By The Revelation Of My Inherently Perfect Self-"Brightness") In <u>This</u> (My Bodily Human Form Whereby This Testament Is Worded To You). And I Will Forever Remain "Emerged" (<u>As</u> I <u>Am</u>) To Mankind, and I Will (Thus) Remain Perfectly Effective In All The Generations Of Mankind (Even After, and Forever After, The Physical Lifetime Of <u>This</u>, My Bodily Human Form). Therefore, After (and Forever After) The Physical Lifetime Of <u>This</u>, My (Herein and Hereby Speaking) Bodily (Human) Form (In Which My "Emergence" Has Been Perfected), The Remembered and Always Living Vision Of My Bodily Human Form, and The Perpetual and Always New and Blessing Gift Of My Spiritual Presence, and The Eternal, and Always Inherently Perfect, Revelation Of My Very, and Inherently Perfect, State Will Be Extended everywhere (<u>As</u> I <u>Am</u>, and By Means Of The Instruments and Agents I Will Describe To You), So The Way Of The Heart Can Survive Through all future time.

10.

My Original Work Of Revelation and Blessing Is Not To Be Repeated, and There Should Be No Need or Call For That Work To Be Repeated, Unless The Teaching Word and The Blessing Itself Are Lost. If They Are Ever Lost, Then Who Will Come To Restore The Way Of Truth Again?

11.

In <u>This</u>, My (Herein and Hereby Speaking) Bodily (Human) Form <u>Itself</u>, My Revelation Is Shown Complete.

Therefore, This Revelation-Body Should Be Heart-Remembered and Heart-Contemplated Forever (In Feeling) By all those who Would Realize Me.

12.

In My Spiritual Form, I Am (By Grace) everywhere Able To Be Seen or Felt, Even In all other worlds.

In The Form Of My Star Of Light, I Appear (By Grace) Directly and Infinitely Above the body-mind, At The conditional Source-Point Above the world (and every world).

Even So, My Very and "Bright" and Inherently Perfect Form (or Very Being) Is Always Only Standing <u>As</u> The Heart Itself, and (By Grace) I May Be Realized Directly <u>There</u> (At Heart).

Therefore, Listen To Me, and Hear Me.

Then Look For Me, See Me, and Be My Seeing Devotee.

See Me With The Heart and Follow Me, wherever You are, wherever You go.

Look For Me (and See Me) In Spirit, In The Eternal Baptism Of All-Pervading Light.

Follow Me In Spirit, In The All-Pervading Spiritual Current Of Life.

Follow Me To God In Spirit.

Therefore, Live In God (Who <u>Is</u> Spirit).

Follow Me and Find The All-Pervading Person, Who Is The Carrier Beneath and Behind, The Matrix Above, The Heart-Light At The Core, and The Very Substance or Root-Essence Of forms.

Come By Me To God As I <u>Am</u>, The Inherent or Native Feeling Of Being (Itself), The "Bright" Heart, The Truth and The Ultimate Self Of beings, The Only One Who <u>Is</u> "I", Before the Separate "I" Is Uttered or Defined.

Follow Me, My Beloved, and Meditate On My Feet (There, Where I Am Always Standing, In The Perfect Deep, The Profound Heart Of Being).

Follow Me, My Beloved, and Embrace My "Bright" Form (There, Where I Am Forever Shining, In The Well Of Being, The Divine Self-Domain Of The Heart).

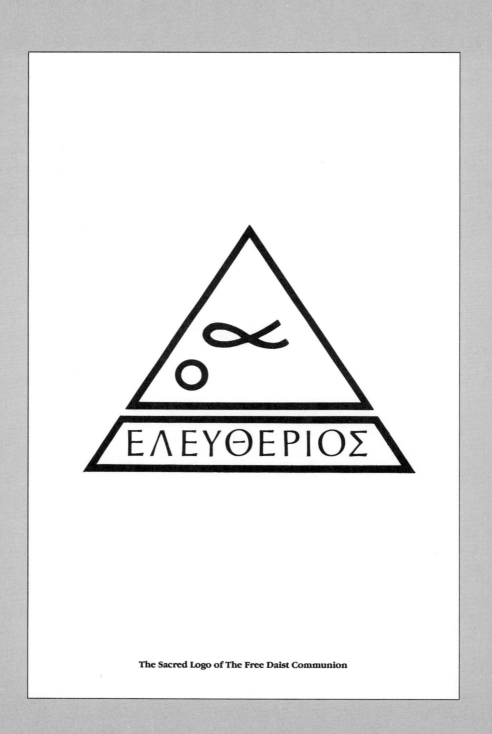

The Sacred Logo of The Free Daist Communion

The Unique Advantage of the God-Man

An Invitation from
The Free Daist Communion

Sri Love-Anandashram, 1989

The Unique
Advantage
of the God-Man

An Invitation from
The Free Daist Communion

Dear Reader,

The World-Teacher, Heart-Master Da Love-Ananda, has summarized His Offering to all as follows:

What is supremely Attractive in the manifest universe and in the human world is the God-Man. All beings, male or female, must become Attracted, or Distracted, by that One. This is the Ultimate Means, the Supreme Means, the Supreme Yoga. It is for this reason that the Divine appears in manifest form in the likeness of those who are to be drawn out of bondage—but only in their <u>likeness</u>. It is the <u>Divine</u> Who appears in that likeness, and it is the <u>Divine</u> Who is made visible through that likeness. Those who become capable of acknowledging that One become capable of responding to that Attraction. Those who become capable of being Distracted by that One become participants in this Supreme Way, which truly is the Way of Grace, because it requires no effort at all. It requires nothing but Grace and the response to Grace. That response is not effortful. It is easy. It is easy to respond to what is Attractive.

The discovery of one's Ishta-Guru, one's "Chosen" and dearly beloved Master, is a most sacred, holy, and individual affair of the heart. If people know that Satsang with Heart-Master Da is a real possibility for them, personally, and if they are apprised of His Story, His Mission, and His Graceful Offering of the Way of the Heart, then all such individuals can freely

411

determine their own form of response. Thus, the mission of The Free Daist Communion is as Sri Gurudev Da Love-Ananda has counseled us from the beginning: "Make Satsang available."

If you feel a sympathetic response to Heart-Master Da Love-Ananda and His Offering of the Way of the Heart as the World-Teacher and Sat-Guru, we invite you to become formally associated with His Work.

■ If you wish to become a formally acknowledged practitioner of the Way of the Heart, and to devote your life to the Realization of Truth through progressive devotional surrender to Sat-Guru Da Love-Ananda, we welcome you to apply for membership in The Free Daist Communion.

The application process is straightforward. You begin by becoming a Friend of Da International, the organization of those who formally support Heart-Master Da's World-Teaching Work. The services offered to Friends who are interested in taking up practice of the Way of the Heart include formal coursework and conversations with established practitioners, to help you evaluate your readiness for, first, preparatory practice as a student-novice in Da International, and, then, membership in The Free Daist Communion as a formally acknowledged student-beginner.

As a formal student-beginner you will continue to study and adapt to practice of the Way of the Heart through successive stages. At an appropriate time, when you are a prepared student-beginner, you may be invited to formal occasions in Sat-Guru Da Love-Ananda's bodily (human) Company, to receive His Heart-Blessing.

■ If you wish to express your respect, gratitude, and support for the World-Teaching Work of Heart-Master Da Love-Ananda, but do not wish to become a formal practitioner of the Way of the Heart, you may become a formal Friend of Da International. The Friend's form of participation is offered to you, whether or not you wish to eventually practice the Way of the Heart.

■ If you wish to serve the Work of The World-Teacher, Heart-Master Da Love-Ananda, as a formal Patron or Advocate, having significant financial resources or public or professional influence, we welcome you to do so as a formal Friend of Da International.

In the great sacred traditions, it is the lay supporters or sympathetic friends who sustain the Adepts and their renunciate orders of most mature practicing devotees. The sacrifices those lay supporters make are honored by the Masters and devotees as Karma Yoga, an effective path of aligning oneself in body, mind, and heart with the Adept Master and the Divine by patronizing and supporting that Adept's sacred Work. Nowadays Karma Yoga is thought of more generally, as the path of service in action to all living beings, and Heart-Master Da has acknowledged that such self-giving service is auspicious and beneficial preparation for more fully developed sacred practice and Realization. But the original and most potently beneficial Karma Yoga is that of support, in every way one can find, of the Divine Work of a God-Realizer.

Acknowledging the need of many, many people to make a link with the great Way of Truth, Heart-Master Da has especially extended His Blessing upon this form of Karma Yoga in service to Him and His Work. He has described it as a practice particularly suited to outer-directed, world-oriented Western or Westernized men and women who respond to His Appearance and His Mission. As Friends of Da International, generous patrons and publicly communicative advocates will find that their embrace of the Karma Yoga of service to Heart-Master Da indeed functions as a true Yoga, or means of union with God. It attunes the living being with the One to be Contemplated and ultimately to be Realized. It purifies obstructions and removes obstacles to sacred Awakening and practice. It helps awaken balance, equanimity, and the impulse to Divine Liberation. And, by all these means, energetic and effective Karma Yoga prepares one, over time, for embrace of the more direct and full practice of the Way of the Heart.

It is our prayer that many, many people will practice the Karma Yoga of such patronage and support of Heart-Master Da Love-Ananda's Work. The difference that such individuals can make is incalculable. Because Heart-Master Da is the Heart of all, in Person, every positive gesture toward and in honor of Him is, by His Grace, spontaneously Magnified many times over as a benediction for all beings.

■ If you would like to receive a free brochure about the Friends of Da International and the activities we offer our Friends, write to us at the address on page 415.

The Graceful Gift
of Sat-Guru Da Love-Ananda's
Physical Company

Heart-Master Da Love-Ananda chooses to invite rightly pre-
pared practitioners of the Way of the Heart to receive His Blessing-
Transmission in His physical Company whenever it is auspicious and
useful. He may travel for this purpose to one or the other of His World-
Teacher Ashrams in the United States, The Mountain Of Attention
Sanctuary in northern California or Tumomama Sanctuary in Hawaii.
Generally, however, He invites prepared practitioners to meet Him at
His principal World-Teacher Ashram, Sri Love-Anandashram, His Her-
mitage Retreat in Fiji.

Wherever He may be available to rightly prepared practitioners, now
and hereafter Heart-Master Da Love-Ananda Abides as Hridaya-Samartha
Sat-Guru and Avadhoota, in the serene Peace of Divine Indifference. The
focus of His Liberating Work now and in the future is with the most
mature practitioners of the Way of the Heart—those who are formally
practicing in the context of the sixth and seventh stages of life—and with
others, such as the members of The Hridaya Da Gurukula Brahmacharini
Mandala Order, whom He has designated as potential Agents of His
Divine Heart-Transmission in the future. He lives on Retreat and does not
informally associate with practitioners, as He did during the years of His
Teaching Work to Reveal the Way of the Heart. The Wisdom of His Service during those years is communicated in His many published works
and in His Instructions, Principles, and Callings, which Guide practitioners' sacred responsibility for the Communion, the culture of practice, and
the formal community of the Way of the Heart.

■ If you would like to talk with a practicing devotee about practicing or
supporting the Way of the Heart, please write to or call our Correspondence Department at the address provided on the following page.

The Opportunity that Heart-Master Da Love-Ananda Offers and,
indeed, that He Is, is extremely rare in all of human history. We are here
to help you embrace the form of association with Heart-Master Da and
the Way of the Heart that is appropriate for you now.

We urge you to enter bodily, actively, expressively, and formally into the Stream of Grace that Heart-Master Da Love-Ananda Hridayam Is for all beings everywhere. He Proclaims His Divine Self-Nature and Heart-Intimacy to each and all: "I am with you now, as I have always been, and I will always be with you."

We pray that you may feel Heart-Master Da's constant Blessings upon you, personally, and we look forward to your response.

Correspondence Department
THE FREE DAIST COMMUNION
P. O. Box 3680
Clearlake, California 95422
USA
Phone: (707) 928-4931

Further Notes to the Reader

(Continued from copyright page)

An Invitation to Responsibility

The Way of the Heart that Heart-Master Da Love-Ananda has Revealed is an invitation to everyone to assume real responsibility for his or her life. As Heart-Master Da has Said in *The Dawn Horse Testament*, "If any one Is Interested In The Realization Of The Heart, Let him or her First Submit (By Heart) To Me, and (Thereby) Commence The Ordeal Of self-Observation, self-Understanding, and self-Transcendence." Therefore, participation in the Way of the Heart requires a real struggle with oneself, and not at all a struggle with Heart-Master Da, or with others.

All who study the Way of the Heart or take up its practice should remember that they are responding to a Call to become responsible for themselves. They should understand that they, not Heart-Master Da or others, are responsible for any decision they may make or action they may take in the course of their lives of study or practice. This has always been true, and it is true whatever the individual's involvement in the Way of the Heart, be it as one who studies Heart-Master Da's Wisdom-Teaching, or as a formal "Friend" of The Free Daist Communion, or as a formally acknowledged practitioner of the Way of the Heart.

Honoring and Protecting the Sacred Word through Perpetual Copyright

Since ancient times, practitioners of true religion and Spirituality have valued, above all, time spent in the Company of the Sat-Guru, or One Who has Realized God, Truth, or Reality, and Who Serves that same Realization in others. Such practitioners understand that the Sat-Guru literally Transmits His or Her (Realized) State to every one (and every thing) with which He or She comes in contact. Through this Transmission, objects, environments, and rightly prepared individuals with which the Sat-Guru has contact can become Empowered, or Imbued with the Sat-Guru's

416

Transforming Power. It is by this process of Empowerment that things and beings are made truly and literally sacred, and things so sanctified thereafter function as a Source of the Sat-Guru's Blessing for all who understand how to make right and sacred use of them.

The Sat-Guru and all that He Empowers are, therefore, truly Sacred Treasures, for they help draw the practitioner more quickly into the Realization of Perfect Identity with the Divine Self. Cultures of true Wisdom have always understood that such Sacred Treasures are precious (and fragile) Gifts to humanity, and that they should be honored, protected, and reserved for right sacred use. Indeed, the word "sacred" means "set apart", and thus protected, from the secular world. Heart-Master Da Love-Ananda is a Sat-Guru of the Perfect degree. He has Conformed His body-mind completely to the Divine Self, and He is thus a most Potent Source of Blessing-Transmission of God, Truth, or Reality. He has for many years Empowered, or made sacred, special places and things, and these now Serve as His Divine Agency, or as literal expressions and extensions of His Blessing-Transmission. Among these Empowered Sacred Treasures is His Wisdom-Teaching, which is Full of His Transforming Power. This Blessed and Blessing Wisdom-Teaching has Mantric Force, or the literal Power to Serve God-Realization in those who are Graced to receive it.

Therefore, Heart-Master Da Love-Ananda's Teaching Word must be perpetually honored and protected, "set apart" from all possible interference and wrong use. The Free Daist Communion, which is the fellowship of devotees of Heart-Master Da Love-Ananda, is committed to the perpetual preservation and right honoring of the sacred Wisdom-Teaching of the Way of the Heart. But it is also true that in order to fully accomplish this, we must find support in the world-society in which we live and from the laws under which we live. Thus, we call for a world-society and for laws that acknowledge the Sacred, and that permanently protect It from insensitive, secular interference and wrong use of any kind. We call for, among other things, a system of law that acknowledges that the Wisdom-Teaching of the Way of the Heart, in all Its forms, is, because of Its sacred nature, protected by perpetual copyright.

We invite others who respect the Sacred to join with us in this call and in working toward its realization. And, even in the meantime, we claim perpetual copyright to the Wisdom-Teaching of Heart-Master Da Love-Ananda and the other sacred literature and recordings of the Way of the Heart.

Heart-Master Da Love-Ananda
and His Spiritual Instruments and Agents

Heart-Master Da Love-Ananda Speaks and Writes of His Spiritually, Transcendentally, and Divinely Awakened renunciate devotees as Agents or Instruments strictly in the Spiritual, Transcendental, and Divine sense, rather than in any worldly sense. He uses the word "Instrumentality" to indicate the formally acknowledged function of His Spiritually maturing or mature renunciate devotees to magnify (and, thus, naturally, and in a devotional manner, to serve) the Transmission of His Spiritual Blessing (and, possibly, His Transcendental and Ultimate Divine Revelation) to practitioners in their own stage of life or in earlier stages of life in the Way of the Heart.

Heart-Master Da uses the word "Agency" to indicate the formally Acknowledged and Empowered Capability and Function of specially chosen Divinely Self-Realized free renunciate devotees to directly Transmit His Spiritual, Transcendental, and Divine Heart-Blessing to all other practitioners of the Way of the Heart.

The first Means of Agency and Instrumentality that have been fully established by Heart-Master Da are the Wisdom-Teaching of the Way of the Heart and the three Hermitage Ashrams, or Sanctuaries, that He has Empowered. Human Agents and human Instruments are so acknowledged by Heart-Master Da or, after (and forever after) the physical Lifetime of His bodily (human) Form, by His specially appointed renunciate devotees (who, optimally, are His then presently living, and previously formally acknowledged, human Agents). And all such human Agents and human Instruments are thus acknowledged only (and more and more) as practitioners grow in the practice of the Way of the Heart and show signs of the specific capability to fulfill the formal responsibilities of either Agency or Instrumentality for Heart-Master Da's Blessing-Transmission within the formal cultural context of The Free Daist Communion.

Heart-Master Da Love-Ananda
Is a True Renunciate

Heart-Master Da Love-Ananda is a legal renunciate of The Free Daist Communion. Therefore, the Communion provides a living circumstance for Him and is authorized to publish His Talks and Writings. Heart-Master Da Functions only sacredly, and in Freedom. For many years He has owned nothing and has had no worldly responsibilities and has exercised no worldly functions. He has been and is a true renunciate. Heart-Master Da does not direct, and has not directed in any way, any of the activities of the Communion or of its representatives or members. Nor is Heart-Master Da responsible for any of the activities of The Free Daist Communion, its representatives, or its members.

The Guru-devotee Relationship in the Way of the Heart

The Free Daist Communion does not guarantee its members, friends, and associates either a personal audience with Heart-Master Da or any specific experiences or Initiations. The process of Transmission is a living process of cultivating the relationship to Heart-Master Da as Sat-Guru, and that process follows its own laws. Neither Sat-Guru Da nor the Spiritual, Transcendental, and Divine Process can be strictly "institutionalized". The experiences or Realizations that may arise in the course of practice of the Way of the Heart depend on many factors—including, very fundamentally, each individual's genuine participation, readiness, right disposition, and personally auspicious characteristics. Heart-Master Da Freely and constantly Gives His Heart-Blessing to all, and It is received by each one according to his or her capability.

Publications

The Written and Spoken
Teaching Word of
The World-Teacher,
Heart-Master
Da Love-Ananda

Publications

The Written and Spoken Teaching Word of The World-Teacher, Heart-Master Da Love-Ananda

My opinion is that we have, in the person of Heart-Master Da, a Spiritual Master and religious genius of the ultimate degree. [His] teaching is, I believe, unsurpassed by that of any other spiritual teacher, of any period, of any place, of any time, of any persuasion.

—Ken Wilber
Author, *The Spectrum of Consciousness*
and *Up from Eden*

Only One Who has Realized the Truth is Free to speak and live the Truth to others. The World-Teacher, Heart-Master Da Love-Ananda, speaks and writes with full Consciousness of the Infinite Life of the Heart. When such a Free Voice speaks, then the Power of the Word has become the Divine Agent for the Awakening and Liberation of others. The Teaching Word of Sat-Guru Da belongs to the ancient class of literature respectfully known as "sruti", or Teachings Revealed directly by the Divine Person, through the Divinely Self-Realized Sat-Guru. Therefore, to read or listen to Sat-Guru Da's Teaching Word is to feel (and thereby Contemplate) the Divine Being, Truth, Reality, or Happiness.

I regard Heart-Master Da Love-Ananda as the most significant contemporary writer concerning the core of religion, more profound than Paul Tillich, Gabriel Marcel, and Martin Buber. Intimately acquainted with a vast range of spiritual experience, he peels off all externals and challenges us to join with him in surrender of our whole selves, shattering the egoism which contracts and separates us from participation in the loving, radiant life of God.

—Donald Evans
Author, *Struggle and Fulfillment*

THE SOURCE LITERATURE

These Source Books are the epitome of Heart-Master Da Love-Ananda's Wisdom-Teaching on the Attributes, the Secrets, the Way, and the Realization of the Heart, or Self-Existing and Self-Radiant Transcendental, inherently Spiritual, and Divine Consciousness Itself.

Heart-Master Da has said that all His other Teaching literature, as well as all the events of His Divine Life and His Liberating Work with others, is to be understood in the context of the Standard presentation of His Teaching Message in the first six books listed here—*The Love-Ananda Gita, The Ashvamedha Gita, The Dawn Horse Testament, The Lion Sutra, The Da Upanishad,* and *The Basket of Tolerance.* His other Source texts—*The Hymn Of The True Heart-Master* and *The Liberator (Eleutherios)* are primary commentaries and popular elaborations of these six principal Expositions of His Instruction.

THE LOVE-ANANDA GITA
(THE WISDOM-SONG OF NON-SEPARATENESS)
The "Simple" Revelation-Book Of The World-Teacher,
Heart-Master Da Love-Ananda

Heart-Master Da's quintessential Revelation of the Way of the Heart. Because *The Love-Ananda Gita* contains His purest and simplest Call to Satsang, or feeling-Contemplation of His bodily (human) Form, His Spiritual and always Blessing Presence, and His Very (and Inherently Perfect) State, it is the most basic Source Text of Heart-Master Da's entire Teaching Word. Standard Edition
$34.95 cloth, $17.95 paper

The most remarkable person I ever met until now was Swami Rudrananda, Rudi, with whom I studied for 14 years. Heart-Master Da Love-Ananda also studied with Rudi. It is my view that Heart-Master Da has transcended His own Teacher to become a universal and transcendental spiritual presence. The Love-Ananda Gita is the quintessential expression of His Teaching. This may be the book for which you have been waiting all your life.

—John Mann
Author, *Rudi: 14 Years with My Teacher*

THE ASHVAMEDHA GITA
THE HEART OF THE "DAWN HORSE" REVELATIONS
OF THE WORLD-TEACHER, HEART-MASTER DA LOVE-ANANDA

This ecstatic epitome of Heart-Master Da Love-Ananda's Teaching Revelation in *The Dawn Horse Testament* gives the general reader the essence of His Teaching Message in that mighty Source Text. *The Ashvamedha Gita* is the heart of Heart-Master Da's "Eternal Conversation" with everyone, His summary Teaching Word on the venerable Love-Yoga of Communion with Him as the Hridaya-Samartha Sat-Guru and, thus and thereby, with the Divine Person.

Standard Edition (forthcoming, late 1990)
$45.00 cloth, $19.95 paper

THE DAWN HORSE TESTAMENT OF THE WORLD-TEACHER, HEART-MASTER DA LOVE-ANANDA

Heart-Master Da's Ecstatic summary of the technically "fully elaborated" form of the Way of the Heart, which He has progressively Revealed from 1970 until the present. In this monumental text of over 1,200 pages, Heart-Master Da Reveals the Mysteries and devotional Secrets of every stage of the Way of the Heart He Offers to all who are prepared to practice it.

New Standard Edition (forthcoming, mid-1990)
$65.00 cloth
$75.00 cloth edition with slipcase
$29.95 paper

The Dawn Horse Testament *is the most ecstatic, most profound, most complete, most radical, and most comprehensive <u>single</u> spiritual text ever to be penned and confessed by the Human-Transcendental Spirit.*

—Ken Wilber
Author, *The Spectrum of Consciousness* and
Up from Eden

THE LION SUTRA
*(ON PERFECT TRANSCENDENCE OF THE PRIMAL ACT, WHICH
IS THE EGO-"I", THE SELF-CONTRACTION, OR ATTENTION ITSELF,
AND ALL THE ILLUSIONS OF SEPARATION, OTHERNESS,
RELATEDNESS, AND "DIFFERENCE")*
The "Radical" Revelation-Book Of The World-Teacher,
Heart-Master Da Love-Ananda

A fierce and beautiful poetic Exposition of the "radical", ultimate, and Perfect Practice of the Way of the Heart, particularly the final stages that lead to and include Transcendental, inherently Spiritual, and Divine Self-Realization. (An extensive revision of Heart-Master Da's Work formerly titled *Love-Ananda Gita*.)
New Standard Edition (forthcoming, early 1991)
$35.00 cloth, $17.95 paper

THE DA UPANISHAD
*THE SHORT DISCOURSES ON
self-RENUNCIATION, GOD-REALIZATION,
AND THE ILLUSION OF RELATEDNESS*

Heart-Master Da's most concise Instruction relative (especially) to the technically "fully elaborated" form of the Way of the Heart described in *The Dawn Horse Testament*, emphasizing the non-strategic, non-ascetical practice of renunciation. (An extensive revision of Heart-Master Da's Work formerly titled *The Illusion Of Relatedness*.)
New Standard Edition
$49.95 cloth, $17.95 paper

. . . a concentrated exposition in the mold of the ancient Upanishads. Heart-Master Da has helpfully overturned many accepted norms in institutionalized Religion and negative Spirituality. The beauty of his utterance is that he assimilates the essentials of Eastern thought down the ages to the Spirit of Freedom so characteristic of the modern era.

> —M.P. Pandit
> Author, *The Upanishads:
> Gateways of Knowledge*
> and *Studies in the
> Tantras and the Veda*

THE BASKET OF TOLERANCE
A GUIDE TO PERFECT UNDERSTANDING OF THE ONE
AND GREAT TRADITION OF MANKIND

Heart-Master Da's Enlightened and discriminating evaluation of all the world's historical traditions of truly human culture, practical self-discipline, perennial religion, universal religious mysticism, "esoteric" (but now openly communicated) Spirituality, Transcendental Wisdom, and Perfect (or Divine) Enlightenment, compiled, annotated, and presented (with a comprehensive bibliography) by Heart-Master Da. The summary text of Heart-Master Da's Teaching Word on the Great Tradition of human Wisdom and the Sacred (Spiritual) Ordeal.
Standard Edition (forthcoming, late 1990)
$55.00 cloth, $22.95 paper

THE HYMN OF THE TRUE HEART-MASTER
(THE NEW REVELATION-BOOK OF THE ANCIENT AND ETERNAL
RELIGION OF DEVOTION TO THE GOD-REALIZED ADEPT)
FREELY EVOLVED FROM THE PRINCIPAL VERSES OF THE
TRADITIONAL GURU GITA

Heart-Master Da's new (seventh stage) version of the *Guru Gita* captures and surpasses the elegance of this ancient Sanskrit text and Reveals, with great poetic force and the authority of the Divine Self-Realizer, the Secrets of how to cultivate the relationship to Him as True Heart-Master.
New Standard Edition (forthcoming, early 1991)
$29.95 cloth, $14.95 paper

THE LIBERATOR (ELEUTHERIOS)
AN EPITOME OF PERFECT WISDOM
AND THE "PERFECT PRACTICE"

In compelling, poetic prose, Heart-Master Da distills the essence of Divine Self-Realization—the three stages of the ultimate process or "Perfect Practice" of direct transcendence of all experience in Consciousness Itself. Although what is described here is Heart-Master Da's ultimate prescription for practice, such is the potency of His Argument and Revelation that readers may find themselves able to intuit, if only momentarily, the ineffable Grace of Liberation.
New Standard Edition (forthcoming, early 1991)
$12.95 paper

Heart-Master Da does not mimic or ape the teachings of others; his writings have the feeling of one who has seen and knows through his own eyes.
                    —Stanley Krippner
                    Author, *Song of the Siren*
                    Coeditor, *Future Science*

INTRODUCTORY TEXTS

These introductory works serve to orient the new reader to Heart-Master Da's Life-Ordeal, His Teaching-Revelation, and His Blessing Work. Written to be of use even to those with no background in sacred esoteric literature, these books provide the context for a fully informed understanding of both the traditional and the original elements of the Way of the Heart.

FREE DAISM
THE ETERNAL, ANCIENT, AND NEW RELIGION
OF GOD-REALIZATION

About the Divine alternative to the common life, an alternative traditionally Taught by Adept-Teachers in all ages, and which is now uniquely and most potently Offered in our own time by Heart-Master Da. Focusing on the basic elements of His "Popular Message", *Free Daism* introduces Heart-Master Da's "radical" and extremely practical Teaching Arguments, His Teaching and Blessing Work, and exactly what practice of the Way of the Heart, or "Free Daism", involves. Full of inspiring and insightful accounts by devotees, both new and old, who practice Free Daism today. (forthcoming, mid-1990)
$12.95 paper

LOVE OF THE GOD-MAN
by James Steinberg

An extensive discussion of the absolute necessity of the Guru for those who desire to Realize God, Truth, Happiness, and Love, the profound laws and virtues of the Guru-devotee relationship as it has been practiced in many esoteric sacred traditions around the world, and the

critical necessity to understand and transcend the dangerous sophistry of modern "anti-Guruism".
(forthcoming, mid-1990)
$14.95 paper

THE PRACTICAL TEXTS

In these newly revised, Standard Editions of the following practical texts, Heart-Master Da Reveals esssential Teaching Arguments and sacred Principles pertaining to many of the basic functional, practical, and relational disciplines of the Way of the Heart, along with precise Instructions in the detailed observance of these fundamental personal disciplines in all appropriate moments of life, and even, as appropriate, in death and beyond.

THE EATING GORILLA COMES IN PEACE
THE TRANSCENDENTAL PRINCIPLE OF LIFE APPLIED TO DIET AND THE REGENERATIVE DISCIPLINE OF TRUE HEALTH
A manual of practical Wisdom about dietary practice, bodily health and well-being, and the sacred conduct of bodily life through all the stages of life and in death.
New Standard Edition (forthcoming, early 1991)
$19.95 paper

In my own experience as a practitioner, [Heart-Master Da's] suggestions for life and health management have dramatically demonstrated their validity amongst my patients, which to my mind is the ultimate test of truth. For anyone interested in maintaining and raising their health, I recommend this book as the fundamental cornerstone.
> —Bill Gray, M.D., N.D.
> Joint author, *The Science of Homeopathy—A Modern Textbook*

CONSCIOUS EXERCISE
AND THE TRANSCENDENTAL SUN
*THE PRINCIPLE OF LOVE APPLIED TO EXERCISE AND THE
METHOD OF COMMON PHYSICAL ACTION (A SCIENCE OF
WHOLE BODY WISDOM, OR TRUE EMOTION, INTENDED MOST
ESPECIALLY FOR THOSE ENGAGED IN RELIGIOUS OR
SPIRITUAL LIFE)*

A practical guide to the practice of breath, exercise, and the science of whole body happiness.
New Standard Edition (forthcoming, early 1991)
$17.95 paper

LOVE OF THE TWO-ARMED FORM
*THE FREE AND REGENERATIVE FUNCTION OF SEXUALITY IN
ORDINARY LIFE, AND THE TRANSCENDENCE OF SEXUALITY
IN TRUE RELIGIOUS OR SPIRITUAL PRACTICE*

The original Teaching Word of Heart-Master Da Love-Ananda on the right practice of intimacy and truly human sexuality.
New Standard Edition (forthcoming, mid-1991)
$19.95 paper

EASY DEATH
*TALKS AND ESSAYS ON THE INHERENT AND ULTIMATE
TRANSCENDENCE OF DEATH AND EVERYTHING ELSE*

Sat-Guru Da's authoritative Revelation of the process of death, including His Compassionate Instructions on how to prepare for and pass through it.
New Standard Edition (forthcoming, early 1991)
$17.95 paper

Easy Death *is an exciting, stimulating, and thought-provoking book that adds immensely to the ever-increasing literature on the phenomena of life and death. But more important, perhaps, a confirmation that a life filled with love instead of fear can lead to ultimate meaningful life and death.*

Thank you for this masterpiece.

—Elisabeth Kubler-Ross, M.D.
Author, *On Death and Dying*

THE WISDOM LITERATURE
OF HEART-MASTER DA LOVE-ANANDA'S
TEACHING WORK

Heart-Master Da Love-Ananda's passionate commitment to the Liberation of all beings lives in the essays and discourses within the books listed in this section. They are the unique record of His constant "Consideration" and Confession of Divine Enlightenment during the years of His active Teaching Work, and His Teaching Word on the Great Process of Satsang that He Gracefully Offers to all.

Available in revised Standard Editions, the original texts of these unsurpassed Scriptures of Heart-Master Da's Teaching-Revelation are now accompanied by completely new introductory and other explanatory material that contextualizes each book within Heart-Master Da's total Teaching Work, which was fulfilled in His Divine Descent in 1986. Each book includes the leela, or story, of the Teaching Demonstration that produced the Teaching Word summarized in the book, and explains its relationship to His current and ongoing Blessing Work as summarized most specifically in the eight Source Texts of His Teaching Word.

Written and compiled between 1970 and 1973, *The Knee of Listening* and *The Method of the Siddhas* are Heart-Master Da's earliest Confessions of His Spiritual, Transcendental, and Divine Realization and His Offering of the Way of Satsang in His Company.

THE KNEE OF LISTENING
(THE LIFE-ORDEAL AND THE "RADICAL" SPIRITUAL UNDERSTANDING OF "FRANKLIN JONES")
A unique record of the Spiritual, Transcendental, and Divine Ordeal and "radical" Enlightenment of Heart-Master Da, with early essays on the practice and Realization of "Radical" Understanding. Foreword by Alan Watts.
New Standard Edition, based on the original, unabridged manuscript.
(forthcoming, mid-1991)
$14.95 paper

THE METHOD OF THE SIDDHAS
TALKS WITH FRANKLIN JONES
[THE WORLD-TEACHER, HEART-MASTER DA LOVE-ANANDA]
ON THE SPIRITUAL TECHNIQUE OF THE SAVIORS OF MANKIND

In this book of talks with students in 1972 and 1973, the first year of His Teaching Work, Heart-Master Da Reveals the secret of the Way of Satsang that He Offers—the profound and transforming relationship between the Sat-Guru and His devotee.
New Standard Edition (forthcoming, mid-1991)
$14.95 paper

A primary purpose of Heart-Master Da Love-Ananda's Teaching Work was to establish a living culture of Spiritual Wisdom and practice in the world. Therefore, throughout the years of His Teaching Work (1970-1986), Heart-Master Da addressed the profound limitations of the now dominant Western culture of scientific materialism, as well as the limitations of historical religious provincialism, and He critically and appreciatively "considered" the teachings, practices, and ways of life of the world's sacred traditions. The following texts contain Heart-Master Da's prophetic criticism of the existing culture of humankind, as well as His Vision of a truly human culture, founded on self-transcending practice and devotion to Truth.

SCIENTIFIC PROOF OF THE EXISTENCE OF GOD
WILL SOON BE ANNOUNCED BY THE WHITE HOUSE!
(PROPHETIC WISDOM ABOUT THE MYTHS AND IDOLS
OF MASS CULTURE AND POPULAR RELIGIOUS CULTISM,
THE NEW PRIESTHOOD OF SCIENTIFIC AND POLITICAL
MATERIALISM, AND THE SECRETS OF ENLIGHTENMENT
HIDDEN IN THE BODY OF MAN)

Speaking as a modern prophet, Heart-Master Da combines His urgent critique of present-day society with a challenge to create true sacred community based on actual Divine Communion and a Spiritual and "radically" Transcendental Vision of human Destiny.
New Standard Edition (forthcoming, late 1991)
$19.95 paper

This is a mighty book of insight—a penetrating, comprehensive critique of popular cults and mass culture. This book does two things absolutely critical for the survival of Man. First, it exposes the fundamental flaws of organized religion, science, and politics. Second, it gives clear indications for establishing a culture based on wisdom and love. Anyone who is the least bit concerned about his or her own well-being—physical, mental, spiritual—and that of the world should consider the words of [Heart-Master Da]. He teaches and is a living demonstration of the present Divine Condition and evolutionary future of the human race.

—John White
Editor, *Frontiers of Consciousness*
and *What Is Enlightenment?*

THE TRANSMISSION OF DOUBT
TALKS AND ESSAYS ON THE TRANSCENDENCE OF SCIENTIFIC MATERIALISM THROUGH "RADICAL" UNDERSTANDING

Heart-Master Da's principal critique of scientific materialism, the dominant philosophy and world-view of modern humanity that suppresses our native impulse to Liberation, and His Revelation of the ancient and ever-new Way that is the true sacred science of Life, or of Divine Being Itself.
New Standard Edition (forthcoming, late 1991)
$17.95 paper

The Transmission of Doubt *is the most profound examination of the scientific enterprise from a spiritual point of view that I have ever read. I consider it must reading for anyone who cares about science and who is mature enough to recognize that the development of the heart is just as important as the development of the head.*

—Charles Tart, Ph.D.
Author, *Altered States of Consciousness* and *Waking Up*

THE ENLIGHTENMENT OF THE WHOLE BODY
(A RATIONAL AND NEW PROPHETIC REVELATION OF THE TRUTH OF RELIGION, ESOTERIC SPIRITUALITY, AND THE DIVINE DESTINY OF MAN)

One of Heart-Master Da's early Revelations of the Way of Eternal Life that He Offers to beings everywhere, including praise of the All-Pervading Life and Transcendental Divine Consciousness, ecstatic Confessions of His Own Enlightened Condition, and sublime Instruction in each of the practices of the Way of the Heart. When initially published in 1978, this text represented the culmination of Heart-Master Da's Communication of the totality of His Way of the Heart.

New Standard Edition (forthcoming, late 1991)

$24.95 paper

NIRVANASARA
"RADICAL" TRANSCENDENTALISM AND
THE INTRODUCTION OF ADVAITAYANA BUDDHISM

From the vantage-point of His Identification with Divine Consciousness, Heart-Master Da critically appraises the sacred Wisdom-Culture of mankind, particularly focusing on the two most profound esoteric formulations of sacred life and practice—Buddhism and Hindu non-dualism (Advaita Vedanta). Here, Heart-Master Da announces and expounds upon His own Way of "Radical" Transcendentalism as the "Fourth Vehicle" of Buddhism—Advaitayana Buddhism, which is the continuation and fulfillment of the most profound esoteric Teachings of Buddhism and Hinduism.

New Standard Edition (forthcoming, late 1991)

$14.95 paper

THE SONG OF THE SELF SUPREME (ASHTAVAKRA GITA)

Heart-Master Da's illuminating Preface to the *Ashtavakra Gita* is a unique commentary on this grand classic of Advaita Vedanta, which He calls a "free communication by an Enlightened or God-Realized Adept". As a Living and Divinely Enlightened (seventh stage) Adept, or Sat-Guru, Heart-Master Da is singularly qualified to Speak with Authority about the Truth beyond non-dualism that Ashtavakra extols with such iconoclastic fervor. In His Preface, Heart-Master Da discusses the *Ashtavakra Gita* in the context of the total Great Tradition of Spiritual and Transcendental Wisdom and identifies and discusses the characteristics of those few rare texts and traditions that fully Communicate the Realization and "Point of View" of the seventh stage of life.

New Standard Edition (forthcoming, mid-1991)

$14.95 paper

ECSTATIC FICTION AND POETRY
OF GOD-REALIZATION

The ecstatic fiction and poetry of the Enlightened Adept is a unique form of human communication—the uninhibited Confession of One Who lives as the Divine Self of all those He addresses.

THE MUMMERY

The Mummery is Heart-Master Da Love-Ananda's "Prose Opera" of mythical and archetypal Divine Revelation. Written in a few brief weeks in late 1969, it spontaneously expresses the entire esotericism of His Realization and His Teaching Word in the paradoxical story of Raymond Darling, who grows beyond childhood, and life at home with Mom and Dad, into—and beyond—the mysteries of life and death in his impassioned love of the beautiful Quandra. Destined to be acclaimed as one of the world's great works of fiction, *The Mummery* is simultaneously (as the introduction and commentaries to the text reveal) both an autobiography and a prophecy of Heart-Master Da Love-Ananda's entire Life and Work, and, as He Himself discloses, "a cipher . . . a magical text whose meanings can never be exhausted". Accompanied by stunning full color illustrations of the text.
(forthcoming, mid-1991)
$45.00 cloth, $19.95 paper

CRAZY DA MUST SING,
INCLINED TO HIS WEAKER SIDE
CONFESSIONAL POEMS OF LIBERATION AND LOVE

Composed principally in the early 1970s and expressed spontaneously with the ardor of continuous, Divinely Awakened Identification with all beings, these remarkable poems proclaim Heart-Master Da Love-Ananda's vulnerable human Love and His mysterious, "Crazy" passion to Liberate others from ego-bondage.
New Standard Edition (forthcoming, mid-1991)
$12.95 paper

LEELAS

The Sanskrit term "leela" (sometimes "lila") traditionally refers to the Divine Play of the Sat-Guru with His devotees, whereby He Instructs and Liberates the world.

The leelas told by practitioners of the Way of the Heart document the years of Sat-Guru Da Love-Ananda's active identification with and Submission to devotees as Adept Heart-Teacher, and His Work since His Divine Descent in 1986. Heart-Master Da has said that Leelas of His Instructional Play with devotees are part of His own Teaching Word, and they are, therefore, Potent with the Blessing and Awakening-Power of His Heart-Transmission.

THE DIVINE EMERGENCE OF THE WORLD-TEACHER
THE REALIZATION, THE REVELATION, AND THE REVEALING ORDEAL OF HEART-MASTER DA LOVE-ANANDA
A Biographical Celebration by Saniel Bonder

A lively recounting of Heart-Master Da Love-Ananda's Life and Teaching Work and of the extraordinary Spiritual Event of January 11, 1986, through which He most fully Incarnated as the World-Teacher, the Agent of Divine Enlightenment for others.
$14.95 paper

THE CALLING OF THE KANYAS
CONFESSIONS OF SPIRITUAL AWAKENING AND "PERFECT PRACTICE" THROUGH THE LIBERATING GRACE OF HEART-MASTER DA LOVE-ANANDA
by Meg Krenz with The Kanyadana Kumari Mandala (Kanya Tripura Rahasya, Kanya Remembrance, Kanya Kaivalya Navaneeta, and Kanya Suprithi)

This is the remarkable account of the Graceful ordeal of sacred practice and transformation embraced by the formal renunciate order of four women devotees who personally serve Sat-Guru Da Love-Ananda. *The Calling of the Kanyas* stands among the great devotional testimonies of illumined Saints and Seers in the sacred traditions. The confessions and the example of the Kanyas are a Calling to everyone to deeply understand and heartily respond to the Supremely Graceful Event that has made their

435

own Spiritual transformation possible: Sat-Guru Da's Great Divine Descent in early 1986.
(forthcoming, early 1991)
$17.95 paper

LOSING FACE
by Frans Bakker, M.D.

A successful Dutch physician, Frans Bakker began to suspect a fundamental fault in the assumptions underlying not only his medical practice but his life itself. Here he tells stories from his years as a devotee of Heart-Master Da Love-Ananda. This account of the joyous and difficult ordeal of self-understanding he has embraced during Heart-Master Da's Teaching and Blessing Work will be of special interest to readers from a Western background who want to learn more about Heart-Master Da's Work and His popular Message.
(forthcoming, mid-1991)
$14.95 paper

DAU LOLOMA NAITAUBA
HOW DAU LOLOMA (HEART-MASTER DA LOVE-ANANDA) GAVE MANY HOLY BLESSINGS TO THE PEOPLE OF FIJI AND MADE HIS ETERNAL SPIRITUAL HOME ON THE ISLAND OF NAITAUBA
by Morton Whiteside

In 1983, Heart-Master Da Love-Ananda arrived on the island of Naitauba, in Fiji, to establish it as His principal World-Teacher Ashram. This extraordinary collection of leelas chronicles the Spiritually dramatic events of Heart-Master Da's Enlightened interplay with the people of Fiji and the spirit-forces He has encountered there.
(forthcoming, mid-1991)
$9.95 paper

THE LION MURTI OF HEART-MASTER DA LOVE-ANANDA
by Kanya Kaivalya Navaneeta, Charles Seage, M.D., and Dan Bouwmeester, M.D.

Divine Enlightenment is evidenced by extraordinary Signs in the body-mind. The authors of this remarkable document have carefully recorded all the changes and unique Signs registered in Heart-Master Da

Love-Ananda's Transfigured body during the years of His Teaching and Blessing Work to date. Heart-Master Da Himself has spoken extensively about these processes and Signs, elucidating them for readers interested in the technical esoteric processes whereby He has Perfectly Incarnated the Divine Self in and as His bodily (human) Form.
(forthcoming, early 1991)
$12.95 paper

TCHA

A compilation of many Leelas of Heart-Master Da Love-Ananda's Teaching Work and Heart-Blessing of children and adults, men and women—and animals as well—throughout the years of His Sacred Mission to date. Full of both miracles and the stories of hard-learned sacred lessons, *Tcha* gives a vivid picture of a Divine Teacher and True Heart-Master Whose every Gesture and Communication Impart the Wisdom and Happiness of Divine Freedom to others.
(forthcoming, mid-1991)
$14.95 paper

THE HORSE SACRIFICE
by Saniel Bonder

This book tells a story until now known in its fullness only by those who participated in it. It is a full-length Sacred History of Heart-Master Da's Life and His impassioned Struggle with devotees in the nearly two decades of His formal Mission as Adept Heart-Teacher and Hridaya-Samartha Sat-Guru. This unique record chronicles in extensive, vivid detail all the epochs of Heart-Master Da's Divinely Enlightened Life-Work that are (by necessity) only briefly summarized in *The Divine Emergence of The World-Teacher*. A feast of the dramatic, Spirit-filled Leela of the God-Man of our epoch.
(forthcoming, late 1991)
$17.95 paper

DA NATARAJA

In His Indoor Yajna period of Teaching—His "last gesture" as a Teacher—from April 1987 through March 1988, Heart-Master Da Love-Ananda Taught not only by Word but also by Dance. This unique

collection of leelas records the extraordinary psychic and Spiritual Impact of the Dancing of One Who embodies the Heart-Spirit of the Dance as Divine Sacrifice in Love.
(forthcoming, late 1991)
$14.95 paper

FOR AND ABOUT CHILDREN

WHAT AND WHERE AND WHO TO REMEMBER TO BE HAPPY
A SIMPLE EXPLANATION OF THE WAY OF THE HEART
(FOR CHILDREN, AND EVERYONE ELSE)

A new edition of Heart-Master Da's essential Teaching-Revelation on the religious principles and practices appropriate for children. In a "consideration" easily understood and enjoyed by children of all ages, Heart-Master Da tells children (and adults) how to "feel and breathe and Behold and Be the Mystery".
New Standard Edition, fully illustrated (forthcoming, early 1991)
$12.95 cloth, $8.95 paper

THE TWO SECRETS (yours, AND MINE)
A STORY OF HOW HEART-MASTER DA LOVE-ANANDA GAVE
GREAT WISDOM AND BLESSING HELP TO YOUNG PEOPLE (AND
EVEN OLDER PEOPLE, TOO) ABOUT HOW TO REMEMBER WHAT
TO REMEMBER TO BE HAPPY
A Gift (Forever) from Heart-Master Da Love-Ananda, as Told by Kanya
Remembrance, Brahmacharini Shawnee, and their friends.

A moving account of a young girl's confrontation with the real demands of sacred practice, and how Heart-Master Da lovingly Instructed and Served her in her transition through a crisis of commitment to practice that every devotee must, at some point, endure.
(forthcoming, mid-1990)
$14.95 paper

VEGETABLE SURRENDER, OR HAPPINESS IS NOT BLUE
by Heart-Master Da and two little girls

The humorous tale of Onion One-Yin and his vegetable friends, who embark on a search for someone who can teach them about happiness and love, and end up learning a great lesson about seeking. Beautifully illustrated with original line drawings.

$12.95 cloth, oversize

THE RENUNCIATION OF CHILDHOOD AND ADOLESCENCE

Compiled from Heart-Master Da's heretofore unpublished Instructions, this book addresses the entire matter of the conscious education of young people in their teenage years. *The Renunciation of Childhood and Adolescence* provides for the modern age an Enlightened vision of the ancient principle of "brahmacharya", or the conscious choice made in one's youth to practice life as a sacred ordeal, devoted to the Realization of the Transcendental and inherently Spiritual Divine Reality.

(forthcoming, mid-1990)

$14.95 paper

LOOK AT THE SUNLIGHT ON THE WATER
EDUCATING CHILDREN FOR A SELF-TRANSCENDING LIFE OF LOVE AND HAPPINESS: AN INTRODUCTION

Full of eminently practical guidance for the "whole bodily" and sacred education of children and young people, this simple, straightforward, informative text is also perhaps the best available brief summation of Heart-Master Da Love-Ananda's Wisdom-Teaching on the first three stages of life, or the period from infancy to adulthood.

New Standard Edition (forthcoming, late 1991)

$12.95 paper

AUDIO-VISUAL PUBLICATIONS

Every great Divine Revelation and tradition has used the most advanced technologies of its time to communicate, through artistic and verbal means, the essence of its Revelation and way of life.

In our own time, Heart-Master Da Love-Ananda has Revealed His Teaching Word and the Way of the Heart in face-to-face recorded conversation and living experimentation with His devotees, during almost two decades of active Teaching and Liberating Work. Thus, the moment of Divine Heart-Transmission, in which the World-Teacher Reveals the Truth to His devotees, is preserved through the audio and video technologies of the modern age. The spoken Word and the bodily (human) Form of Heart-Master Da, uniquely recorded in this manner, are preserved as Living Sources of Enlightened Instruction and Divine Transmission.

Audiotapes of Heart-Master Da's Revelatory speech and presentations of nearly two decades of precious video and film footage of Heart-Master Da, recorded during the years of His Teaching Work and His current Blessing Work, are being prepared for distribution to practitioners of the Way of the Heart and to the public.

Please contact The Dawn Horse Book Depot at the address given on page 443 for availability of these remarkable recordings of The World-Teacher, Heart-Master Da Love-Ananda.

VIDEOTAPES

THE WAY OF THE HEART
An Introduction to the "Radical" Teaching and Blessing Work
of the Western-Born Adept, Heart-Master Da Love-Ananda

Incorporating rare segments of recent and historical footage, Part One tells the Story of Heart-Master Da Love-Ananda's Divine Birth, the Ordeal of Transformation He underwent to prepare Himself as an Agent of Awakening for others, and the "radical" Purity of His Teaching Message. Recounting the Sacrificial Process whereby Heart-Master Da fully and perfectly Incarnated as the One Living Divine Consciousness, Part One celebrates the Emergence of His Work of World Blessing.

Part Two (which includes talk excerpts by Heart-Master Da and testimonials by long-time practitioners) describes the Gifts and forms of practice that are Given to all who formally enter into a committed sacred relationship with Heart-Master Da in the traditional manner of Sat-Guru devotion.

Part Three introduces the sacred culture of the Way of the Heart. $29.95, 2 hours, VHS, NTSC or PAL format.

The Way of the Heart is also available in an abridged and modified form, which includes recent footage of Heart-Master Da in Darshan with devotees and other material not included in the full-length version. A brief, summary audio-visual introduction to His Life and Divine Work as the World-Teacher in a world addicted to egoic suffering and seeking. $19.95, 76 minutes, VHS, NTSC or PAL format.

[Heart-Master Da Love-Ananda] talks sanely about real sanity. His subject is always the same: a way of living this human existence without fear and without obsession. He talks about surrender to God as only one who has done so can.
—Robert K. Hall, M.D.
Co-founder of The Lomi School and the
Gestalt Institute of San Francisco

PERIODICAL

THE FREE DAIST
(The bimonthly religious journal of The Free Daist Communion)

The Free Daist celebrates and chronicles the Appearance of Free Daism, the eternal, ancient, and new religion of God-Realization, as Given in Heart-Master Da Love-Ananda's original, consummate, and unprecedented Revelation of the Way of the Heart.

Published bimonthly, *The Free Daist* presents:

■ Articles, interviews, and confessions by practitioners about the joyous Ordeal of the Way of the Heart, which inform, educate, inspire, and motivate anyone seriously interested in the profound possibilities of real Spiritual practice.

■ The Liberating Teaching Word and Blessing Work of Heart-Master Da—His Writings, His Discourses with devotees, and the Leela or Sacred History of His nearly two decades of face-to-face Instruction of ordinary people.

■ Regular columns on the sacred activities of The Free Daist Communion and its culture and community of devotees.

■ Articles on the Great Tradition of human and Spiritual wisdom from all times and places, and dialogues with practitioners of other traditions about the Way of the Heart and their own traditions of Spiritual practice.

The Free Daist is critical reading not only for everyone interested in Heart-Master Da's God-Giving Life and Work, but for everyone at all interested in human Freedom, Happiness, and Love. *The Free Daist* belongs to all those who would lay claim by heart to the greatest Opportunity of a human life.

Subscriptions are U.S. $48.00 per year for six issues. Please send your check or money order (payable to The Dawn Horse Press) to:

The Free Daist
P.O. Box 3680
Clearlake, CA 95422
(USA)

ORDERING THE BOOKS AND VIDEOTAPES OF HEART-MASTER DA LOVE-ANANDA

The books and videotapes of Heart-Master Da Love-Ananda are available at local bookstores and by mail from The Dawn Horse Book Depot.

In addition to many new releases presenting Heart-Master Da Love-Ananda's Wisdom-Teaching and celebrating the historical and ongoing Leela of His Divine Life and Work, The Dawn Horse Press, which publishes the books of Heart-Master Da, is currently preparing revised Standard Editions of all the essential texts of His previously Revealed Teaching Word.

Please write to us at the address below for a complete catalogue of books, study courses, and audio-visual publications on the Way of the Heart, traditional sacred literature, sacramental objects, and ancient and modern appliances and accessories (meditation pillows, chairs, polarity screens, incense, calendars, etc.) for use in support of devotional and meditative practice.

In the U.S.A. please add $1.75 for the first book or videotape and $.75 for each additional book or videotape. California residents add 6% sales tax.

Outside the U.S.A. please add $4.00 for the first book or videotape and $1.00 for each additional book or videotape.

To order the books and videotapes listed above, and to receive your copy of The Dawn Horse Book Depot Catalogue, please write:

THE DAWN HORSE BOOK DEPOT
P. O. Box 3680
Clearlake, CA 95422 U.S.A.
(707) 928-4936

Glossary

Glossary

Advaita Vedanta

Advaita Vedanta (meaning literally, "the non-dualistic end of the Vedas") is one of the principal traditions of Hindu religious philosophy. Advaita Vedanta was the first systematic presentation of the non-dual philosophy to be found in the ancient esoteric Hindu scriptures called the Upanishads. Its original formulation is attributed to the Indian sage Shankara, who is believed to have lived in the eighth to ninth centuries C.E.

Advaita Vedanta Teaches that the Divine Reality (called "Brahman", meaning "Immense Being") is Transcendental and prior to all phenomena. While the ultimate Realization of Advaita Vedanta is expressed in the Confession that there is no difference between the individual, the world, and Brahman (or the Transcendental Divine Reality), Realizers in the Advaitic tradition most commonly demonstrate a lesser, ascetical practice of strategic dissociation from the body-mind and the world via contemplation of Brahman as Divine Consciousness apart from psycho-physical phenomena.

advanced and ultimate stages of practice

Heart-Master Da Love-Ananda uses the term "advanced" to describe the practice of individuals in any tradition who practice in the fourth and fifth stages of life. These are individuals who have Awakened to the Divine as the tangible, All-Pervading Presence or Radiant Spirit-Force or Person, with Which they live in a constant relationship of devotion or Love-Communion.

Heart-Master Da reserves the term "ultimate" to describe the practice of individuals in the sixth and seventh stages of life, or individuals who have Realized the Divine as Consciousness Itself (Realized either as the Witness-Consciousness or as the Very Divine Self). (See **stages of life.**)

Aham Sphurana

"Aham Sphurana" is a traditional term for the Spirit-Current of Love-Bliss that may be felt in association with the body-mind at a point to the right side of the heart, but which is truly Transcendental, Unbounded, and All-Pervading. It is the felt intuition of our Identity as the Divine Self and Source-Condition that is God, Truth, and Reality.

"Aham" is a Sanskrit term that means "I", and refers to the Transcendental Self-Identity. "Sphurana" is an extension of the Sanskrit verb root "sphura", which has many meanings, including "spring", "vibrate", "be manifested", and "shine". Thus, "Aham Sphurana" literally means "the flashing forth of the Divine Self".

Amrita Nadi

Amrita Nadi, in Sanskrit, means literally "Nerve (or Current) of Immortal Bliss". In the Awakening of Divine Self-Realization, the Spiritual Current of Divine Being is felt to move in an S-curve out from the seat of the Divine Self associated with the right side of the heart, then forward and up the front of the chest, through the throat, and then up the back of the head, and forward to the Spirit-Matrix of Love-Bliss at and above the crown of the head. From there, the Living Spirit-Current circulates in a "Circle" of life-sustaining Spirit-Energy, down the front and up the spine of the human body-mind.

Avatar

The Sanskrit term "avatara" literally means "descent", and thus "incarnation". According to certain Hindu traditions, the Avatar is the exclusive incarnation of God, the God-Man who manifests on Earth only at the beginning of every great age, or "yuga", of human and cosmic history.

The Avatar is traditionally considered to be the incarnation of Vishnu, who, according to Hindu mythology, embodies the Divine in Its aspect as "Preserver" in the Hindu trinity of the Divine Person (with "Brahma", the "Creator", and "Siva", the "Destroyer").

"Avoiding relationship?" (See **self-Enquiry.**)

Bhava (See **Moksha-Bhava Samadhi.**)

"Bright", the "Bright"

Since His childhood, Heart-Master Da Love-Ananda has used the word "Bright" (and its variations, such as "Brightness") to describe the Divine Being, eternally, infinitely, and inherently Self-Radiant. The "Bright" Radiance of Being is not other than the Heart, or Transcendental (and inherently Spiritual) Divine Self-Consciousness.

causal (See **gross, subtle, causal.**)

chakra

"Chakra" means literally "wheel" or "circle". In the Spiritual traditions of Yoga, the "chakras" of the body-mind are the internal centers through which the Life-Force flows. In the process of the Spiritual transformation of the body-mind, the chakras are purified of obstructions and opened to the Spirit-Current of Divine Life. This process may be accompanied by Yogic phenomena, or the signs of psycho-physical purification and opening in body, mind, and feeling.

Communion Hall

In the Way of the Heart, a Communion Hall is reserved as a site where practitioners regularly practice meditation.

conditional Nirvikalpa Samadhi (See **Nirvikalpa Samadhi.**)

conductivity

"Conductivity" is Heart-Master Da Love-Ananda's technical term for those disciplines in the Way of the Heart through which the body-mind is aligned and submitted to the Spirit-Current of Divine Life (or, for beginners, to the natural life-energy of the cosmos in its association with the individual body-mind).

Conductivity exercises include disciplines of diet, physical exercise, health, and sexuality that serve the purification and balancing of the body in relationship to its own natural energies and, in more mature developments of practice, in relationship to the Divine Spirit-Current.

In the stages of Spiritually Awakened practice, devotees practice participation in and responsibility for the movement of the Spirit-Current in its natural course of association with the body-mind via intentional exercises of Spiritually activated breathing and feeling.

Because the course of Divine Self-Realization is a Process of "whole bodily Enlightenment", conductivity, or psycho-physical reception of and surrender into the All-Pervading Spiritual Divine Presence, is a necessary and inevitable discipline supporting the senior discipline of the "conscious process", which directly serves the Awakening of Divine Consciousness.

conscious process

The "conscious process" is Heart-Master Da Love-Ananda's technical term for those practices in the Way of the Heart through which the mind or attention is disciplined, or turned from conventional thinking and concern and to Contemplation of the Divine Person via feeling-Contemplation of Heart-Master Da's bodily (human) Form, His Spiritual Presence, and His Very (and Inherently Perfect) State. The conscious process (as contrasted with the supporting disciplines and practices of conductivity) is the senior discipline and responsibility of all practitioners in the Way of the Heart.

In *The Dawn Horse Testament*, Heart-Master Da most fully elaborates the details of all the forms of the conscious process in the Way of the Heart.

"consideration"

In Heart-Master Da Love-Ananda's Wisdom-Teaching, the technical term "consideration" (as He explains in *Love of the Two-Armed Form*, p. 1) is "a process of one-pointed but ultimately thoughtless concentration and exhaustive contemplation of a particular object, function, person, process, or condition, until the essence or ultimate obviousness of that subject is clear."

As engaged in the Way of the Heart, this concentration results "in both the highest intuition and the most practical grasp of the Lawful and Divine necessities of human existence." Such "consideration" is similar to the Sanskrit concept of "samyama", as classically presented in the *Yoga-Sutras* attributed to the Yogic Adept Patanjali.

"Consideration" is not merely an intellectual investigation. It is the participatory investment of one's whole being in the Way of the Heart. If one "considers" something fully in the context of one's practice of feeling-Contemplation of Heart-Master Da Love-Ananda, the essentials of what is being "considered" are Revealed, by Grace, and an appropriate course of action based on those truths can then be chosen and fulfilled.

Cosmic Mandala

The Sanskrit word "mandala" (literally, "circle") is commonly used in the esoteric Spiritual traditions to describe the levels of cosmic existence. "Mandala" also denotes an artistic rendering of interior visions of the cosmos. Sat-Guru Da uses the phrase "Cosmic Mandala" to describe the totality of the conditional cosmos. The Cosmic Mandala appears in vision as concentric circles of light, progressing from red at the perimeter through golden-yellow, silvery white, indigo or black, and brilliant blue, to the Ultimate White Brilliance in the Mandala's center.

For a full discussion of the Cosmic Mandala (and a color representation of its appearance in vision), see chapter 39 of *The Dawn Horse Testament*. See also Heart-Master Da's Instructions in *Easy Death: Talks and Essays on the Inherent and Ultimate Transcendence of Death and Everything Else*.

"Crazy", "Crazy Wisdom"

The term "Crazy" characterizes aspects of Heart-Master Da Love-Ananda's Teaching Work (1970-1986), as well as the Divinely Mindless Quality of His eternal Realization.

In many esoteric sacred traditions, certain practitioners and Masters have been called "crazy", "mad", or "foolish". Tibetan Buddhist Saints of this type are given the title "lama nyonpa" (Tibetan: bla-ma smyon-pa, literally, high-one madman, or saintly madman) or simply "nyonpa" (madman). The tradition of "Fools for Christ's Sake" in Christianity and the "Avadhoota" tradition in Hinduism are other well-documented examples of this unique expression of Divine Awakening. In whatever tradition and time they appear, these individuals violate prevailing taboos (personal, social, religious, or even Spiritual) either to instruct others or simply to express their own inspired freedom.

The fullest examples of what Heart-Master Da Love-Ananda calls "the Crazy Wisdom tradition" (in which He Stands) are Perfect Realizers of the Divine Self in any culture or time who, through spontaneous Free action, blunt Wisdom, and liberating laughter, shock or humor people into self-critical awareness of their egoity. Typically, such Realizers manifest "Crazy" activity only occasionally or temporarily, and never for its own sake.

Heart-Master Da Himself Taught in a unique "Crazy-Wise" manner. For sixteen years He not only reflected but also Submitted completely to Identify with the egoic states of His early devotees. He Submitted His body-mind to live with them, and to live like them, and in Consciousness He lived as them. By thus theatrically dramatizing their habits, predilections, and destinies, He continued always to Teach His devotees the Liberating Truth, to Radiate Its Heart-Blessing through His own Person, and to Attract them beyond themselves to embrace the God-Realizing Way that He Offers. This daring assumption of the lifestyles and the lives of ordinary people, to plant in them the seeds of self-knowledge and Divine aspiration, characterized much (though not all) of His Teaching Work.

Now Heart-Master Da Love-Ananda no longer Teaches in the "Crazy-Wise" manner. Nor does He continue to identify with egoic aspirants or the egoic world. Instead, He Stands Firm in His own Freedom, spontaneously Revealing the Divine Self-Reality to all. This in itself, over against the mad and illusory rationality of the separate, egoic mentality, is a Divinely "Crazy" State; and, indeed, Heart-Master Da's Divine State of Free Conscious Feeling-Existence continues to move Him to Serve others in a fashion that can rightly be called "Crazy-Wise".

Darshan

In Sanskrit, the word "Darshan" means "seeing", "sight of", "vision of". In the Indian traditions, such seeing also involves feeling. Thus, "to have Darshan" of a saint, a holy image, etc., is a participatory, feeling act, not merely a visual witnessing of an object. In the Way of the Heart, Darshan is the spontaneous Blessing Heart-Master Da Love-Ananda Grants freely by allowing His bodily (human) Form (or its Representations, even in the mind) to be sighted and felt (and thereby Contemplated).

deeper personality

The "deeper personality" is Heart-Master Da Love-Ananda's term for that dimension of the being that is governed and identified with the psychic, least physically oriented processes of the mind. The deeper personality includes the capabilities and functions outside or beyond waking consciousness and the gross brain, including the subtle faculties of discrimination, intuition, and mystical perception and knowledge, as well as the causal consciousness of the body-mind as an apparently separate ego-"I" and the root-activity of attention, prior to mind. (See **gross, subtle, causal,** and also **gross personality.**)

Devi

In Sanskrit, "Devi", from a Sanskrit root meaning "to Shine", is a term for the Divine Goddess in Her Submission to the Divine Person, or Consciousness.

Dharma

In Sanskrit, "dharma" means duty, virtue, law, or mode of being. In its fullest sense, and when capitalized, Dharma is the highest fulfillment of duty (the living of the Divine Law) and the most profound representation of the Nature of Being and how human beings may conform their whole lives to that Divine Nature. A complete Spiritual Teaching, including its disciplines and practices, is thus often referred to as "the Dharma".

Divine Indifference

Divine Indifference is the third phase of the four phases of the Yoga of the seventh, or Divinely Enlightened, stage of life in the Way of the Heart. In this phase, the extraordinary psycho-physical signs that accompanied Divine Transformation (the immediately previous phase) come to rest. The whole body-mind of the Realizer is brought to most profound rest in the "Brightness" of the Divine Self, and the individual is, thus, Divinely Indifferent to the motions of attention in the body and mind. The Realizer spontaneously Radiates the universal Heart-Blessing of unconditional Love, Free of even Enlightened concern for or interest in conditional objects, relations, and states.

In the Way of the Heart, such Divine Indifference is not a strategically ascetical, or life-negative, disposition that (like many traditional forms of practice) seeks to dissociate from the body-mind and life as a means to attain Divine Enlightenment. Divine Indifference is an already Perfectly Enlightened Condition that marks the transition to the culminating phase of Divine Self-Realization, which Heart-Master Da Love-Ananda calls "Divine Translation", or "Outshining". (See also **Divine Transfiguration, Divine Transformation,** and **Divine Translation.**)

Divine Transfiguration

Divine Transfiguration is the first of four phases through which the seventh, or Divinely Enlightened, stage of life unfolds in the Way of the Heart. Heart-Master Da Love-Ananda explains that when Divine Self-Realization in the seventh stage of life is firmly established, the body-mind of the Realizer becomes increasingly pervaded by the inherent Radiance of the Divine Self. This Process of Divine Transfiguration expresses itself as the Realizer's active Spiritual Blessing in all relationships.

Such Divinization in the seventh stage of life is not to be confused with the evolutionary Spiritual processes awakened via advanced Yogic meditation in the fourth and fifth stages of life. Although the Yogic practices of the advanced fourth and fifth stages of life may sometimes yield apparently similar psycho-physical signs, they are the results of either an egoic exercise of the Divine Spirit-Energy or a Grace-Given infusion of that Spirit-Energy. In contrast, in the seventh stage of life, the psycho-physical evidence of Divine Transfiguration is a spontaneous manifestation, a Sign of inherent Divine Self-Realization. (See also **Divine Transformation, Divine Indifference,** and **Divine Translation.**)

Divine Transformation

Divine Transformation is the second phase of the Enlightened Yoga of the seventh stage of life in the Way of the Heart. When, in the seventh stage of life, the gross body-mind is fully Infused by the Radiance of the Divine Self in the Process of Divine Transfiguration, then the deeper (or psychic, and subtler mental) dimensions of the body-mind may be similarly Infused with the unqualified "Brightness" of Divine Being. This Transformation spontaneously manifests extraordinary psycho-physical signs, such as the capability to heal, physical longevity, mental genius, and profound manifestations of true Wisdom and selfless Love.

As in the case of Divine Transfiguration, such spontaneous (and inherently egoless) Divinization is not to be confused with the evolutionary (but, necessarily, ego-based) Spiritual processes that may be awakened via Yogic practices in the advanced fourth and fifth stages of life, which may appear to be similar in their conditional results. (See also **Divine Transfiguration, Divine Indifference,** and **Divine Translation.**)

Divine Translation

Divine Translation is the final phase of the four-phase process of Divinization in the seventh, or fully Enlightened, stage of life in the Way of the Heart. In this Event, which Heart-Master Da Love-Ananda also calls "Outshining", body, mind, and world are no longer noticed, not because the Divine Consciousness has withdrawn or dissociated from manifest phenomena, but because the Ecstatic "Recognition" of all arising phenomena (by the Divine Self, and As only modifications of Itself) has become so intense that the "Bright" Radiance of Consciousness now Outshines all such phenomena. This Outshining utterly transcends the mind and is therefore beyond conception. (See also **Divine Transfiguration, Divine Transformation,** and **Divine Indifference.**)

feeling of relatedness, the

In *The Da Upanishad* (p. 343), Heart-Master Da defines the feeling of relatedness as follows:

The feeling of relatedness is not itself (or merely) an idea (or a concept in mind).
The feeling of relatedness is an activity.
The feeling of relatedness is the primal or first activity, and, therefore, it is the cause and the pivotal referent of all subsequent activities (including the activities of mind).
The feeling of relatedness is the activity of self-contraction, which effectively causes all subsequent activities (including the effort not to act).
The feeling of relatedness (or the self-contraction) becomes (or is reflected as) the presumption (or idea) of the separate "other" and the presumption (or idea) of the separate "I".

feeling-Contemplation

Heart-Master Da Love-Ananda's term for the essential devotional and meditative practice that all devotees in the Way of the Heart engage at all times in relationship to His bodily (human) Form, His Spiritual and Always Blessing Presence, and His Very (and Inherently Perfect) State. Feeling-Contemplation of Heart-Master Da is Awakened by Grace through Darshan, or feeling-sighting, of His Form, Presence, and State. It is then to be practiced under all conditions, and as the basis and epitome of all other practices in the Way of the Heart, including the various forms of devotion, service, self-discipline, and meditation.

gross, subtle, causal

The teachings of many esoteric sacred traditions include "maps", or detailed descriptions, of the psycho-physical anatomy of Man and the cosmos. Heart-Master Da Love-Ananda is in agreement with the traditional description that the human body-mind and its environment can be said to consist of three great dimensions—gross, subtle, and causal.

The **gross**, or most physical, dimension is associated with what Heart-Master Da calls the "frontal line" of the human body-mind, or the descended processes of bodily, emotional, and mental experience in the waking state.

The **subtle** dimension, which is senior to and pervades the gross dimension, includes the etheric (or energic), lower mental (or verbal-intentional and lower psychic), and higher mental (or deeper psychic, mystical, and discriminative) aspects of the being. The subtle dimension is associated primarily with the "spinal line" (and only secondarily with the frontal line) of the body-mind, including the brain core and the subtle centers of mind in the higher brain. It is also, therefore, associated with the visionary, mystical, and Yogic Spiritual processes encountered in dreams, in ascended or internalized meditative experiences, and during and after death.

The **causal** dimension is senior to and pervades both the gross and subtle dimensions. It is the root of attention, or the feeling of relatedness, or the essence of limited self-consciousness, which is the separate and separative ego-"I". The causal dimension is associated with the right side of the heart, specifically with the sinoatrial node or "pacemaker" (the psycho-physical source of the heartbeat). Its corresponding state of consciousness is the formless awareness of deep sleep. It is inherently transcended by the Witness-Consciousness (which is prior to all objects of attention).

The causal being, or limited self-consciousness, is also associated with a knot or stress-point in the right side of the heart. When this knot is broken, or "untied", by the Grace-Given exercise of Perfect understanding in the context of the Liberating Instruction and Blessing of Heart-Master Da Love-Ananda, the Transcendental, inherently Spiritual, and Divine Self-Consciousness Stands Free and Awake as the Heart Itself.

gross personality

The physical body and its natural energies, and its "gross" brain and the verbal and lower psychic faculties of mind. It includes the entire "gross dimension" of the body-mind and the lower, or most physically oriented, aspects of the "subtle dimension" of the body-mind. (See **gross, subtle, causal,** and also **deeper personality.**)

hearing

"Hearing" is a technical term used by Heart-Master Da Love-Ananda to describe the intuitive and most fundamental understanding of the act of egoity, or self-contraction. Hearing is the unique capability to directly transcend the self-contraction; it is simultaneous with intuitive awakening to the Revelation of the Divine Person and Self-Condition. Hearing is a development of practice that may occur in the midst of a life of devotion, service, self-discipline, disciplined study of, or "listening" to, Heart-Master Da's Teaching Argument, and constant self-forgetting feeling-Contemplation of Heart-Master Da. Only on the basis of such hearing can practice of the Spiritual process of the Way of the Heart truly begin with full responsibility. (See **listening** and **seeing**.)

Heart

The "Heart" is a term used by Heart-Master Da Love-Ananda in reference to God, the Divine Self, the Divine Reality. To Realize the Heart is to Awaken as the fully Conscious, Self-Existing and Self-Radiant, Transcendental, and inherently Spiritual, Divine Being and Person.

Divine Self-Realization is associated with the opening of the primal psycho-physical seat of Consciousness and attention associated with the right side of the heart, hence the term "the Heart" for the Divine Self. One who is Awake as the Divine Self generally becomes sensitive to the Current of Spiritual Energy at that location in the chest and feels the mind, or attention, falling into its point of origin there.

Heart-Master Da Love-Ananda distinguishes the Heart, as the ultimate Reality, from all the psycho-physiological functions of the organic, bodily heart. The Heart is not "in" the right side of the human heart, nor is it in or limited to the human heart as a whole, or to the body-mind, or to the world. Rather, the human heart and body-mind and the world exist in the Heart, the Divine Being.

The Sanskrit term for heart is "hridaya". (See **Hridaya, Hridayam**.)

Hridaya, Hridayam

Sanskrit: heart. The Sanskrit term refers not only to the physical organ but also to the True Heart, the Transcendental (and inherently Spiritual) Divine Reality. (See **Heart**.) "Hridaya", as used by Heart-Master Da Love-Ananda, points beyond all the earlier stages of life, including even the sixth, to the Perfect Realization, in the seventh stage of life, that transcends the world, the body, the mind, and the conditional, or limited, self.

The formal Designations "Hridaya Da", "Hridaya Heart-Master Da", "Hridaya Siddha-Master", and "Hridaya-Samartha Sat-Guru Da" signify that Heart-Master Da Love-Ananda is the Realizer, the Revealer, and the Revelation of the Heart Itself, and that He Functions as the Giver of the Blessings of the Divine Heart Itself, which Blessings include, but also exceed and are distinct from, any and all blessings that may be granted by Realizers in the lesser stages of life than the seventh.

Ishta, Ishta-Guru-Bhakti Yoga

"Ishta", in Sanskrit, literally means "chosen", or "most beloved". The

Ishta of a traditional Hindu household is the chosen Deity of that family line (whether the Ishta is acknowledged in the Form of a Guru or in the Form of a traditional and mythological God-Image). "Guru", in the reference "Ishta-Guru", means specifically the Sat-Guru, the human Adept-Revealer of Truth Itself (or of Being Itself). "Bhakti" means, literally, "devotion". In its Ultimate (or Perfect) form, true devotion to the Adept Sat-Guru transcends all separateness (or "difference"), even while the apparent (and devotional) relationship continues (in the context of the body-mind). However, even from the beginning of devotional practice, the Ishta-Guru is embraced in and <u>As</u> the Divine Person (Who Is Self-Existing and Self-Radiant Consciousness Itself, and Self-Existing and Self-Radiant Love-Bliss Itself).

"Ishta-Guru-Bhakti", then, is devotion to the Supreme Divine Being in the Form and through the Agency of one's heart-Intimate and truly Beloved Sat-Guru. In the Way of the Heart, Ishta-Guru-Bhakti is awakened spontaneously by Hridaya-Samartha Sat-Guru Da's Grace. Once awakened, it must be cultivated, nurtured, and magnified responsively by the devotee.

Jagad, Jagad-Guru

"Jagad" or "jagat", in Sanskrit, means "world". The term appears frequently in certain Hindu Teachings with the meaning "the world of the senses". Its root comes from the verb "to go", giving the word the literal meaning "everything that moves". Thus, the "world" indicated by the term "jagad" is not merely the planet Earth but the totality of conditional existence, the Cosmic Mandala as a whole. Therefore, the compound "Jagad-Guru", meaning "World-Teacher" or "World-Liberator", is sometimes translated as "Teacher of the Universe".

The title "Jagad-Guru", or "World-Teacher", has been principally associated with the Shankaracharyas of Hindu India, the heads of the four great monastic centers established by the Sage Shankara in medieval times. Its usage in this tradition has specifically honored these individuals as the formally acknowledged Spiritual and ecclesiastical leaders of the Hindus, and not literally as Teachers of the whole world. (In former epochs, the Hindus, for the most part isolated from other cultures, regarded the Indian subcontinent to <u>be</u> the world, or to be as much of the world as needed to be taken seriously into account.)

Heart-Master Da Love-Ananda's Title "Jagad-Guru" does not bear any association with the title as it is used in the Hindu tradition established by Shankara. It carries, rather, the most full and Spiritual meaning, announcing His Divine Function as the Realizer of the Source of all conditional existence and the Liberator of all beings, even of "all that moves".

Jnana Samadhi, Jnana-Nirvikalpa Samadhi

"Jnana" derives from the Sanskrit verb root "jna", literally "to know". Jnana Samadhi, which Heart-Master Da Love-Ananda also calls "Jnana-Nirvikalpa Samadhi", is the (possible) culmination of the sixth stage of life. The forceful withdrawal or the Grace-Given inversion of attention from the conditional body-mind-self and its relations produces the conditional, and temporary, intuitive "Knowledge", Wisdom, or Realization of the Transcendental Self, or Consciousness Itself, Which is inherently formless (nirvikalpa), and Which is (in the case of Jnana Samadhi) <u>exclusive</u> of any perception or cognition of world, objects, relations, body, mind, or self-sense.

ko-an

Heart-Master Da Love-Ananda has described the term "ko-an" in His writings: "What the Japanese call the 'ko-an' is an <u>apparent</u> question—that is, we tend to try to answer it via the usual operations of the mind. But the 'question' itself works to undermine the mental process. It is actually a form of meditation on doubt, or failed mind. Therefore, the 'ko-an' is 'answered' only when it is transcended as a motivator of thought. When its power to initiate doubt and confine us to doubt is understood and transcended, then there is a sudden rush of joy, freedom, and tacit Intuition of Transcendental Being." (Da Free John [Heart-Master Da Love-Ananda], *The God in Every Body Book*, 2d ed. [Clearlake, Calif.: The Dawn Horse Press, 1983], p. 34.)

kriyas

Sanskrit: actions. Spontaneous, self-purifying physical movements that arise in the course of the purification, balancing, and energizing of the body-mind that occurs in Spiritual practice, particularly in relationship to a living source of Spiritual Transmission. Kriyas may be experienced as thrills in the spine, shaking of the spine, spontaneous demonstration of difficult Yogic postures, spontaneous, automatic, and sometimes strongly expressed and repetitive Yogic breathing (pranayama), and so on. (See also **kundalini, kundalini shakti.**)

kundalini, kundalini shakti

Sanskrit: coiled up (kundalini) energy (shakti). The traditional name for the "serpent power", or the ascending force of Spiritual Life-Energy, described in the esoteric Yogic traditions. It is often traditionally viewed as dormant at the bodily base, or lowermost psychic center, of the body-mind. It may be activated spontaneously in the devotee or by the Guru's initiation, thereafter producing many forms of Yogic and mystical experience.

Heart-Master Da Love-Ananda has Revealed that the kundalini shakti is only a partial manifestation of the universal Divine Spirit-Current. It cannot rightly be said to originate at the bodily base, since it is a continuation of the same Spirit-Current that descends in the frontal line of the body. Nor is it to be equated with the "Heart-Current" that He speaks of and Transmits. Therefore, He recommends in the practice of the Way of the Heart no efforts to awaken the kundalini directly, but turns every devotee to Contemplate Him and thereby to Awaken to the Divine Self-Condition.

leela

Sanskrit: play, or sport. Traditionally, all of manifest existence is seen to be the Leela, or the Divine Play, Sport, or Free Activity of the Divine Person. "Leela" especially refers to the Divinely Awakened Play of the Divinely Self-Realized Adept, through which He or She mysteriously Instructs and Liberates others and the world itself. By extension, a leela is an instructive and inspiring story of such an Adept's Teaching and Blessing Play.

listening

Heart-Master Da Love-Ananda's term for the preparatory practice in the beginner's stages of the Way of the Heart. A listener is someone who gives his or her attention to Heart-Master Da Love-Ananda's Teaching Argument, His Leelas (or inspirational Stories of His Life and Work), His bodily (human) Form, His Spiritual Presence, and His Very (and Inherently Perfect) State, in the context of his or her life of devotion, service, self-discipline, and meditation, in constant devotional feeling-Contemplation of Him. Listening matures as most fundamental self-understanding (or "hearing"). (See **hearing.**)

loka

A world or realm of experience. The term often refers to places that are subtler than the gross physical world of Earth and that can be visited or perceived only in dreams or by mystical or esoteric Yogic means.

mantra

Sacred sounds or syllables—"mantras"—and Divine Names have been used since antiquity as means for invoking and worshipping the Divine Person and the Sat-Guru. In the Hindu tradition, the original mantras were cosmic sound-forms used for worship, prayer, and incantatory meditation on the Revealed Form of the Divine Person.

Traditionally, Divinely Self-Realized Adepts have often given disciples their own sacred Names to use in prayer and meditation—since, for human beings, the human Sat-Guru is the most potently transformative Form of the Divine Person.

maya

"Maya" is a classical Hindu term that literally means "she who measures", but it is used both currently and in traditional philosophy to convey the sense of trick, deceit, fraud, or illusion.

The ascetical schools of religion and Spirituality are often oriented negatively toward the Goddess-Power, or the Creative Force of the universe, conceiving It to be the "Cosmic Veiling Power" that prevents Enlightenment through a bewildering and unfathomable display of appearance, change, and disappearance. This view suggests that association with the phenomenal world is itself the principal cause of delusion and bondage to subject-object, or egoic, consciousness.

The more "radical" understanding, Confessed by the Divinely Self-Realized Adepts, Realizes that the Universal Life-Energy, Maya, or Maha-Shakti, if rightly turned to Its Divine Source-Consciousness, is Liberating in Its Nature. Heart-Master Da Love-Ananda's Ecstatic references to "the Goddess" or "the Great Woman" are to be understood in these transcendent terms. As the Realizer, the Revealer, and the Revelation of the Divine Person, Heart-Master Da Recognizes and "Husbands" the Goddess-Power as the Servant or Consort of the Divine Person, the Maha-Purusha, Siva, the Pure Consciousness of Eternal Bliss.

Moksha-Bhava Samadhi, Moksha-Bhava-Nirvikalpa Samadhi

"Moksha" means "Liberation" in Sanskrit. The primary meaning of the term "Bhava" (and its specific meaning here) is "Being" or "Existence". In Heart-Master Da Love-Ananda's Teaching Word, "Moksha-Bhava Samadhi", also called "Moksha-Bhava-Nirvikalpa Samadhi", is the Ultimate Realization of Liberated Divine Existence, in which all conditional states, forms, and phenomena are Outshined by the inherently Formless ("Nirvikalpa") "Brightness" of Divine Consciousness and Love-Bliss. (In His earlier writings, Heart-Master Da used the term "Bhava Samadhi" to describe this Realization.)

In the seventh stage of life, incidents of spontaneous Moksha-Bhava Samadhi may appear in the midst of a life of continuous Divine Self-Realization. Depending on the extent of the Realizer's fulfillment of the Divine Yoga of the seventh stage of life, at death he or she may permanently be established in Moksha-Bhava Samadhi, by Realizing Divine Translation into the Divine Self-Domain. If Divine Translation is not Realized at the end of the present lifetime of such a Realizer, it will certainly be His or Her Destiny after one or more future lifetimes characterized by Divine Self-Realization and Awakened service to others. (See also **Sahaj Samadhi.**)

mudra

In Sanskrit, a gesture of the hands, face, or body expressing the exalted Spiritual states of Consciousness. Mudras may arise spontaneously in deep meditation, or in one or another form of Samadhi, or contemplative absorption.

When a practitioner of the Way of the Heart manifests mudras, they are generally a sign that the Spiritual Life-Current is invading, purifying, and Spiritualizing the body-mind. Divinely Self-Realized Adepts may also spontaneously exhibit Mudras as Signs of their Blessing and purifying Work with devotees and the world, as Heart-Master Da Love-Ananda does from time to time.

Murti

Sanskrit: form. The Sanskrit root of the word means "to become rigid or solid". Thus, "murti" is defined as "solid body, manifestation, incarnation, embodiment, substantial form or body, image, statue". Traditionally, as well as in Heart-Master Da Love-Ananda's usage, "murti" may mean either "representational image" (as in Heart-Master Da's references to Images of His bodily human Form as "Murtis"), or, simply, "form" (or "substance") itself (as in Heart-Master Da's term "Atma-Murti", meaning "the Form That Is the Very Self", or "the One Whose Form, or Substance, Is the Self Itself").

Traditionally, in ceremonial worship and meditation, practitioners of religion and Spirituality have used many kinds of murtis (forms or representations of the Divine), such as statues, paintings, photographic likenesses, etc. The most highly valued and revered Murti of the Divine Person, especially among practitioners of esoteric paths of Spiritual, Transcendental, and Divine Awakening, is the bodily (human) Form of the Divinely Self-Realized Adept.

"Narcissus"

In Heart-Master Da Love-Ananda's Teaching-Revelation, "Narcissus" is a key symbol of un-Enlightened Man as a "self-possessed" seeker, enamored of his own self-image and self-consciousness. As "Narcissus", every human being constantly suffers in dilemma, contracted in every dimension of the being, recoiling from all relations and even from the fundamental manifest condition of relationship (or relatedness) itself.

In *The Knee of Listening* Heart-Master Da summarized His insight into "Narcissus" as the "avoidance of relationship": "He is the ancient one visible in the Greek 'myth', who was the universally adored child of the gods, who rejected the loved-one and every form of love and relationship, who was finally condemned to the contemplation of his own image, until he suffered the fact of eternal separation and died in infinite solitude."

By defining "Narcissus" as the avoidance of relationship, Heart-Master Da Love-Ananda offers a comprehensive and "radical", and not merely psychological or emotional, vision of human suffering and delusion. In *The Lion Sutra* (forthcoming), He Reveals the paradoxes of His Wisdom-Teaching on "Narcissus": "The ego-'I' is a Paradox of relationship and separation. . . . The ego-'I' is 'Narcissus', or the Illusion of relationship and relatedness and separation and separateness and separativeness and relationlessness" (verses 68 and 74). For one who understands most profoundly, the activity of avoidance, or self-contraction, is ultimately understood to be simultaneous with the condition of relationship itself.

Nirvikalpa Samadhi, conditional and Unconditional

Sanskrit: concentration ("samadhi") without form ("nirvikalpa").

Conditional Nirvikalpa Samadhi is the "formless ecstasy" that may be achieved prior to full and permanent Spiritual, Transcendental, and Divine Self-Realization by the Yogic ascent of attention (either forcibly or by Grace) in the ascending energy-circuit of the body-mind. It is a "conditional", dependent, and temporary Realization, which is lost when attention returns to the field of mind and objects.

By contrast, "Unconditional" Nirvikalpa Samadhi, in Heart-Master Da Love-Ananda's usage, is Divine Enlightenment, prior to and not dependent upon any state of mind or body or attention. It is perpetual and unperturbed Love-Bliss, unaffected by the arising of attention or any object, state, or condition. When attention and conditional phenomena arise, this Realization may be called "Sahaja-Nirvikalpa Samadhi" (also, "Sahaj Samadhi"), or the "native" or "natural" Divine Ecstasy that is paradoxically formless even while forms may appear. When attention and conditional phenomena do not arise to the notice, this State may be called "Moksha-Bhava Samadhi" or "Moksha-Bhava-Nirvikalpa Samadhi", the "Divinely Liberated, Formless Ecstasy of Being, or the Heart, Itself". (See also **Sahaj Samadhi, Moksha-Bhava Samadhi.**)

"Open Eyes"

Heart-Master Da Love-Ananda's technical synonym for the Realization of Sahaj Samadhi, or unqualified Divine Self-Realization in the midst of arising events and conditions.

The phrase graphically describes the non-exclusive, non-inward, native State of the Divinely Self-Realized Adept, Who is Identified Unconditionally with the Divine Reality, while also allowing whatever arises to appear in the Divine Consciousness (and spontaneously Recognizing everything that arises as only a modification of That One).

The Transcendental Self is intuited in the mature phases of the sixth stage of life, but It can be Realized at that stage only by the forced (or Grace-Given) exclusion of the phenomena of world, body, mind, and self. In "Open Eyes", that impulse to exclusion is unnecessary, as "the Eyes of the Heart Open" and Perfect Realization of the Spiritual, Transcendental, and Divine Self in the seventh stage of life becomes permanent and incorruptible by any phenomenal events.

Outshining (See **Divine Translation.**)

Perfect Practice

Heart-Master Da Love-Ananda's technical term for the ultimate discipline of practice in the Way of the Heart.

The Perfect Practice is granted to devotees who, having mastered (and thus transcended the point of view of) the body-mind by fulfilling the preparatory processes of the Way of the Heart, are (by Grace) prepared to practice in the Domain of Consciousness Itself (or in responsive and responsible Identification with Heart-Master Da Love-Ananda's Very, and Inherently Perfect, State).

The three parts of the Perfect Practice are summarized by Heart-Master Da in *The Dawn Horse Testament,* New Standard Edition (forthcoming), and described by Him in detail in *The Liberator (Eleutherios), The Lion Sutra* (forthcoming), and *The Da Upanishad.*

Prasad

In Sanskrit, "prasad" is equivalent to "Grace". It means "the return of the Gift to the giver".

In the Way of the Heart, Prasad signifies all the kinds of offerings given by the practitioner to Heart-Master Da Love-Ananda and then returned by Him (sacred ash, sweets, Blessed water, and the like), as the usable Blessing of the Giver of Divine Grace.

The ultimate Prasad is Heart-Master Da's constant Gift of Himself to every practitioner. Those who truly fulfill the Way of the Heart in Satsang fully receive the Prasad of Heart-Master Da's bodily (human) Form, His Spiritual Presence, and His Very (and Inherently Perfect) State, and thereby Realize the Divine Self-Condition by His abundant Divine Grace.

puja

The Sanskrit word "puja" means "worship".

All formal sacramental devotion in the Way of the Heart is consecrated to Hridaya-Samartha Sat-Guru Da Love-Ananda and is thus celebrated as Sat-Guru Puja. It is ceremonial, even theatrical, practice of Divine association, or expressive whole bodily devotion to Heart-Master Da, in Person, as the Realizer, the Revealer, and the Revelation of the Divine Person. In any given moment or circumstance, appropriate Sat-Guru Puja may involve bodily invocation of, self-surrender to, and intimate Communion with Heart-Master Da (and, thus and thereby, with the Divine Person) by means of prayer, song, recitation of the Teaching Word of Heart-Master Da, dance, the offering and receiving of gifts, and other forms of outward, or bodily active, devotional attention.

In the Way of the Heart, all practitioners participate daily in formal Sat-Guru Puja, as self-transcending practice that establishes them in feeling-Contemplation of Sat-Guru Da in Person. The principal forms of daily Sat-Guru Puja are Sat-Guru-Murti Puja (ceremonial service to and worship of the Sacred Image of Heart-Master Da) and Sat-Guru-Paduka Puja (ceremonial service to and worship of Heart-Master Da Love-Ananda's Blessed Sandals, or "Padukas").

"radical"

Heart-Master Da uses the term "radical" in its original and primary sense. It derives from the Latin "radix", meaning "root", and thus principally means "irreducible", "fundamental", or "relating to the origin".

In contrast to the progressive or evolutionary egoic searches espoused by the world's religious, Spiritual, and Transcendental traditions, the "radical" Way of the Heart offered by Heart-Master Da is "always already" established in the Divine Self-Condition or Reality. Every moment of its authentic practice, therefore, undermines the illusory ego at its root, the self-contraction in the heart, rendering the search not only unnecessary but impossible.

rahasya

Sanskrit: mystery. A rahasya is a Divine Mystery that can never be "solved" by the mind, but is rather to be gratefully Contemplated by the devotee, and thereby allowed to Bless and Inspire him or her.

sadhana

Sanskrit: discipline. Traditionally, practices directed toward religious or Spiritual goals. Sadhana in the Way of the Heart is not action to attain Truth or any state or condition, but, rather, action that expresses present, intuitive Communion with Truth, in conscious Satsang with Heart-Master Da.

Sage

Heart-Master Da uses this term technically to indicate those Realizers or Adepts who have achieved profound depth of intuitive Self-knowledge via the Contemplation of Consciousness in one or another of the great sacred traditions of the sixth stage of life. (Compare **Saint** and **Yogi**.)

Sahaj Samadhi, Sahaja-Nirvikalpa Samadhi

In Sanskrit, "samadhi" literally means "placed together". It indicates concentration, equanimity, balance, and transcendence, and it is traditionally used to denote various exalted states of meditation and other devotional or intuitional exercises.

The Hindi word "sahaj" (Sanskrit, "sahaja") literally means "together born".

Heart-Master Da Love-Ananda uses the term "Sahaj Samadhi" to indicate the Coincidence of the inherently Spiritual and Transcendental Divine Reality with conditional reality, in the case of Divine Self-Realization. It is thus the "inherent", or "native", and thus truly "Natural" State of Being. Heart-Master Da also refers to Sahaj Samadhi as "Sahaja-Nirvikalpa Samadhi", the Natural, or "Open-Eyed", Realization of formless (nirvikalpa) ecstasy. (See also **"Open Eyes"**.)

sahasrar

The sahasrar, or "thousand-petalled lotus", is the highest chakra (or region of awareness) described in the esoteric texts of the great fifth stage Yogas. It is generally associated with the upper brain, or corona radiata, and the most subtle faculties of mind.

The Yogi in the fifth stage of life typically looks to raise the internal Spirit-Current to the sahasrar, and therefore directs attention and all energy to this place, enjoying trance-blisses as well as myriad subtle internal and cosmic visions and other supersensory experiences.

Heart-Master Da Love-Ananda speaks of the sahasrar in "radical" and Divinely Spiritual terms, as the ascended pole, or terminal, of Amrita Nadi, the Current of "Brightness" whose other pole, or root, is the Self-Locus in the right side of the heart. The sahasrar that He describes is infinitely above the crown of the head and thus above the conditions of ascended, but still ego-bound, absorption that may be enjoyed in Yogic mysticism.

Saint

Heart-Master Da uses the capitalized term "Saint" (which, from the Latin "sanctus", literally means "holy", "sacred") to indicate a great practitioner or Adept who has achieved profound Union with the Divine Spirit-Reality in the context of the fourth (or perhaps the fourth to fifth) stage(s) of life. (Compare **Sage** and **Yogi.**)

samadhi

In Sanskrit, "samadhi" literally means "placed together". It indicates concentration, equanimity, balance, and transcendence, and it is traditionally used to denote various exalted states of meditation and other devotional or intuitional exercises. (See **Jnana Samadhi, Moksha-Bhava Samadhi, Nirvikalpa Samadhi, Sahaj Samadhi.**)

sannyasa

The Sanskrit word "sannyasa" means, literally, "to throw down completely", or "to renounce".

Traditionally in India, sannyasa was seen as one of the four stages of human life. Thus, one would progress from the student ("brahmacharya") stage to the householder ("grihastha") stage to life as a philosophical recluse or ascetic "forest dweller" (the "vanaprastha" stage) and finally to "sannyasa"—the stage of one who is free of all bondage and able to give himself or herself completely to the God-Realizing or God-Realized life. Thus, a sannyasin is one who has completely renounced all worldly bonds and devoted himself or herself entirely to Spiritual practice and Realization.

satori

From the Ch'an and Zen traditions, a satori is a "glimpse" or sudden (and temporary) intuitive Awakening to the inherent, Conscious Nature of the ego-self and the world.

Satsang

The Sanskrit word "Satsang" literally means "true or right relationship", "the company of Truth, or of Being". The term traditionally refers to the practice of spending time in the sacred presence of holy or wise persons, a holy place, a venerated image, the burial shrine of a Saint or Realizer, or the Divine Person.

Heart-Master Da Love-Ananda uses the term in the most profound sense, indicating the eternal relationship of mutual sacred commitment between Himself as Sat-Guru (and as the Divine Person) and each true and formally acknowledged practitioner of the Way of the Heart. If the practitioner is truly feeling (and thereby Contemplating) Heart-Master Da, he or she is always living in the context of and enjoying such Satsang. This relationship is thus continuous, not occasional or localized relative to any place or event. Once it is consciously assumed by any practitioner, Satsang with

Heart-Master Da Love-Ananda is an all-inclusive Condition, bringing Divine Grace and Blessings and sacred obligations, responsibilities, and tests into every dimension of the practitioner's life and consciousness.

seeing

When, in the practice of the Way of the Heart, hearing (or most fundamental self-understanding) is steadily exercised in meditation and in life, the native feeling of the heart ceases to be chronically constricted by self-contraction. The heart then begins to Radiate as love in response to the Spiritual Presence of Heart-Master Da Love-Ananda.

This emotional and Spiritual response of the whole being is what Heart-Master Da calls "seeing". The practitioner thus undergoes "emotional conversion" from the reactive emotions that characterize "self-possession", to the open-hearted, Radiant Happiness that characterizes God-Love and Spiritual devotion to Heart-Master Da. True and stable emotional conversion coincides with true and stable receptivity to Heart-Master Da's Spiritual Transmission, and both of these are prerequisites to further growth in the Spiritual development of the Way of the Heart. (See **hearing.**)

self-Enquiry

Self-Enquiry in the form "Avoiding relationship?", unique to the Way of the Heart, is the practice spontaneously developed by Heart-Master Da Love-Ananda in the course of His own Ordeal of Divine Self-Realization. Intense persistence in the "radical" discipline of this unique form of self-Enquiry led rapidly to Heart-Master Da's Divine Enlightenment (or Re-Awakening) in 1970.

The technical discipline of self-Enquiry is also used by devotees practicing the Way of the Heart. See *The Love-Ananda Gita* and *The Dawn Horse Testament,* by The World-Teacher, Heart-Master Da Love-Ananda.

Shakti

The Living Conscious Force or Divine Cosmic and Manifesting Energy; the generative Power and Motion of the cosmos; Spiritual Power; the Life-Current of the Living God. When capitalized (Shakti), the term refers to the Universal or Perfect Divine Power. When written in lower case (shakti), the term refers to that same Power in the form of various finite energies and activities, high or low, within or associated with the human individual.

Traditionally, the Divine Self-Radiance (the "female" aspect of the One Reality), or the All-Pervading Energy that is modified as all conditional forms, has been contacted and worshipped as the Divine Goddess. By Herself, She is "Maya", the Goddess associated with the deluding power of Nature, or the veiling of God.

Heart-Master Da Love-Ananda demonstrated in His Ordeal of Re-Awakening that this great Power is ultimately "Husbanded" by Transcendental Consciousness. In that case, the Goddess-Power is submitted to the Transcendental Divine Self, and She then becomes associated with the

Spirit-Power that leads all beings to the "Divine Self-Domain" (or Perfect Enlightenment).

Shaktipat

In Hindi, "Shaktipat" is the "descent of the Power". Yogic Shaktipat, through which Yogic Adepts transmit natural, conditional energies (or partial manifestations of the Divine Spirit-Current), is typically granted through touch, word, glance, or regard.

In the Way of the Heart, Yogic Shaktipat must be distinguished from (and otherwise understood to be only a secondary aspect of) the Blessing-Transmission of the Heart Itself ("Hridaya-Shaktipat"). Such Heart-Transmission, Which is spontaneously Granted or Freely Radiated to all by Hridaya-Samartha Sat-Guru Da, may be Granted only by the Divinely Self-Realized, or seventh stage, Hridaya-Samartha Sat-Guru.

Hridaya-Shaktipat (or Hridaya-Kripa) does not require intentional Yogic activity on Hridaya-Samartha Sat-Guru Da's part, although such Yogic activity may also be spontaneously generated by Him. It operates principally at and in the Heart Itself, primarily Awakening the intuition of "Bright" Consciousness, and only secondarily (and to varying degrees, depending on the characteristics of the individual) magnifying the activities of the Spirit-Current in the body-mind.

Siddha

"Siddha", in Sanskrit, means a completed, fulfilled, or perfected one, or one of perfect accomplishment, or power.

In Heart-Master Da Love-Ananda's usage, a Siddha is an Adept Perfectly Conscious as God, or the Divine Self. Heart-Master Da contrasts such Divinely Conscious Siddhas with siddhas of less than Perfect Realization—mystics, Yogis, Saints, and others who have achieved proficiency in even extraordinary psycho-physical or Spiritual processes, but who have not Realized the Divine Self in the seventh stage of life.

Siddhi, siddhi

Sanskrit: power, or accomplishment. When capitalized in Heart-Master Da Love-Ananda's Teaching Word, Siddhi is the Spiritual, Transcendental, and Divine Awakening-Power of the Heart that He spontaneously and effortlessly exercises as Hridaya-Samartha Sat-Guru. It is the "Maha-Siddhi", the "Great", or Ultimate Siddhi, the Power of the Heart, or Awakened Consciousness.

The uncapitalized term "siddhi" refers to various Yogic capabilities and psychic powers, traditionally called ordinary, or natural, siddhis. In traditional paths, such lesser siddhis are typically either sought or shunned. In the Way of the Heart, they may arise as signs of the purification and enlivening of the body-mind by the Radiant Heart-Blessing of Heart-Master Da Love-Ananda. If they appear, they are simply to be observed, understood, and transcended, like all other arising experiences, knowledge, and capabilities, and they are to be neither exploited nor strategically avoided.

stages of life

Heart-Master Da has described the evolutionary development and self-transcending Spiritual, Transcendental, and Divine Self-Realization of the human individual in terms of seven stages of life.

The first three stages develop and coordinate the physical, emotional (or emotional-sexual), and mental (or mental-intentional) functions of the body-mind, respectively, and the corresponding expressions of religious awakening and participation, optimally developed in the context of authentic early-life devotion to the bodily (human) Form of the Sat-Guru and, thus and thereby, to the Divine Person.

The fourth stage of life involves the cultivation of heart-felt surrender to and intimacy with the bodily (human) Form, and, eventually, and more and more profoundly, the Spiritual Heart-Presence, of the Sat-Guru and, through such explicit devotional self-surrender to the Sat-Guru, devotional intimacy and Union with the Divine Person. Secondarily, in the fourth stage of life the gross body-mind of the Awakening devotee is adapted and submitted to, and harmonized in, the Living Spirit-Current of the Sat-Guru and the Divine Person.

The fifth stage of life, if it must be developed in conventional, evolutionary fashion, involves the ascent of attention and self-awareness beyond the gross body-mind and into the subtler field of psyche and mind, outside and beyond the brain. Traditionally, the fifth stage of life, therefore, develops the esoteric Yogic and cosmic mysticism of the Spiritual Life-Current in its ascent to the Matrix of Light, Love-Bliss, and Spirit-Presence above the world, the body, and the mind. When that mysticism is followed to its eventual culminating Union with the Spiritual Divine Matrix of Love-Bliss, the individual enjoys conditional Nirvikalpa Samadhi. (See **Nirvikalpa Samadhi.**)

In the Way of the Heart, most practitioners are Graced to bypass some or all of the fifth stage Yogic process. This is possible by Sat-Guru Da's Grace, Whereby the devotee is Attracted by feeling-Contemplation of His bodily (human) Form and Spiritual Presence directly into feeling-Contemplation of His Very (and Inherently Perfect) State, such that exhaustive (or even any) exploration of fifth stage Yogic processes is rendered unnecessary. Thus, for such practitioners, conditional Nirvikalpa Samadhi and other fifth stage states may or may not arise, but in any case the focus of practice is heart-felt Contemplation of Sat-Guru Da's bodily (human) Form, His Spiritual Presence, and His Divine State of Consciousness Itself, and, thus and thereby, the Divine Person.

In the conventional development of the sixth stage of life, the body-mind is simply relaxed into the Spiritual Current of Life, and attention (the root or base of mind) is inverted away from gross and subtle states and objects of the body-mind, and toward its own Root, the Witness-Consciousness of attention, mind, body, and world. (See **Witness-Consciousness.**) The ultimate possible expression of this inversion of attention is Jnana-Nirvikalpa Samadhi, or the temporary and exclusive Realization of the Transcendental Self, or Consciousness Itself. (See **Jnana Samadhi.**)

In the Way of the Heart, as in conventional developmental processes, the conscious being in the sixth stage of life enjoys fundamental freedom from and equanimity in relation to the conditions and states of the body-mind-self. But, by Heart-Master Da's Grace, the sixth stage process develops without the strategic and stressful inversion of attention (which is typically found in traditional sixth stage exercises). Rather, by Grace of the Attractiveness of Sat-Guru Da's bodily (human) Form and His Spiritual Presence, the devotee is drawn into sympathy with His Very (and Inherently Perfect) State of Consciousness Itself, Which Is the Very Self of the Divine Person, Realized As the Native (or Inherent) "Feeling of Being" (Itself). Thus, he or she Stands increasingly Free of the binding phenomena and illusions of psycho-physical existence, while observing and more and more profoundly and "radically" transcending the root-action of egoity, which is self-contraction, or the activity of primal separation that creates the fundamental sense of "difference", or the feeling of relatedness. This "radical" practice of self-transcending feeling-Contemplation of Sat-Guru Da's Divinely Conscious State may or may not manifest the Sign of Jnana-Nirvikalpa Samadhi for such a devotee in the sixth stage of life. (Heart-Master Da has indicated, however, that it is likely that most devotees who pass into the seventh stage of life will experience Jnana Samadhi at least once in the maturity of the sixth stage of life.)

The seventh stage of life is neither the culmination of any conventional psycho-physical and Spiritual process of human developmental growth (which traditionally takes place in the fulfillment of the fifth stage of life), nor the end or goal of any process of the conventional inversion of attention and the exclusion of psycho-physical and Spiritual phenomena (which occupies traditional orientations toward the sixth stage of life). The seventh stage of life, rather, is the Free Condition of Perfect Divine Self-Realization that is Awakened entirely and only by the Liberating Grace of the Divine Sat-Guru. In the Way of the Heart, it is the State of Perfect Contemplative Identification with Heart-Master Da's Very (and Inherently Perfect) State of "Bright" Consciousness, the Uncaused, Unsupported, Unconditional, and Unqualified Realization of Being Itself, or Perfect Love-Blissful Unity with the Supreme Divine Person.

When, in the context of the seventh stage of life, attention and psycho-physical states and conditions appear, this Realization is "Sahaja-Nirvikalpa Samadhi", the Inherent, Divinely "Natural" or "Open-Eyed", Formless Ecstasy. When attention and psycho-physical states and conditions do not appear, this same Realization persists as "Moksha-Bhava-Nirvikalpa Samadhi", the Outshining of all phenomena by that same "Bright" Consciousness and Love-Bliss.

In the seventh stage of life, a Divine Miracle of "Whole Bodily Enlightenment" transpires through four stages (Divine Transfiguration, Divine

467

Transformation, Divine Indifference, and Divine Translation), whereby the body-mind of the Realized devotee, by the Supreme Liberating Grace of Hridaya-Samartha Sat-Guru Da, is progressively Pervaded and Sublimed and, finally, Perfectly Transcended in eternal Outshining, the Glorious Destiny of Translation into the "Divine Domain" of Realized Heart-Freedom Itself. (See **Divine Transfiguration, Divine Transformation, Divine Indifference,** and **Divine Translation.**)

subtle (See **gross, subtle, causal.**)

swami
 Sanskrit: "master", "lord". In the Hindu tradition, a formally acknowledged swami is one who has formally indicated his or her commitment to master the body-mind through Spiritually self-transcending discipline (or, in some cases, his or her present Realization of such mastery and self-transcending Freedom).

tapas
 Sanskrit: heat. The fire of self-frustrating discipline generates a heat that purifies the body-mind, transforms loveless habits, and liberates the practitioner from pursuit of the illusory consolations of ordinary egoic existence.

ultimate (See **advanced and ultimate.**)

Upanishads
 The Upanishads are the principal scriptures of Hindu esotericism, specifically the Hindu tradition of Advaita Vedanta. The oldest of the more than two hundred Upanishads date back to the eighth century B.C.E., while the most recent belong to the twentieth century.

Witness-Consciousness, Witness-Position
 Consciousness in Free relationship to the arising conditions of world, body, mind, and self.
 In some traditions, identification with the "Witness" mode of Transcendental Self-Consciousness is equated with perfect God-Realization, and, traditionally, aspirants seek to achieve this state by inverting attention away from the body-mind and its objects, states, and relations, and toward the root of attention, which is the Witness-Consciousness.
 In the Way of the Heart, the stable Realization of the Witness-Consciousness is associated with, or demonstrated via, the effortless surrender or relaxation of all seeking—even the search for "formless ecstasy", or conditional Nirvikalpa Samadhi. Thus, the stable Realization of the Witness-Consciousness is necessarily associated with release of all seeking, and of all motives of attention relative to the conditional phenomena associated with the first five stages of life.
 Identification with the Witness-Position is not final (or "Most Perfect")

Realization of the Divine Self-Consciousness, but it is the first stage of the ultimate, or "Perfect", practice of the Way of the Heart.

yajna

Sanskrit: sacrifice. A sacrifice or rite through which the "inner" (or That Which is most Prior) is brought "out" (or made manifest and Incarnate). Though "yajna" may describe any self-sacrificial act, rite, or gesture, including any kind of formal or ceremonial sacramental activity, Heart-Master Da has most often used it in connection with His Divinely Sacrificial travels to serve the Spiritual Awakening and right devotional practice of His devotees.

Yoga, Yogi

From a Sanskrit term meaning literally to "yoke" or unite, "Yoga" generally refers to any of a wide variety of disciplines within the Hindu tradition that are engaged for the sake of Spiritual Union, or Re-Union, with the Divine. Likewise, in this general sense, a "Yogi" is a practitioner or adept of any such discipline.

Heart-Master Da sometimes uses the terms "Yoga" and "Yogi" in these general senses, and on occasion even refers to aspects of the Way of the Heart, or even the whole Way of the Heart, as a "Yoga" (as in "Ishta-Guru-Bhakti Yoga").

However, His principal technical use of these terms is to describe the practices and Adepts of the subtle psycho-cosmic disciplines and technologies of the fifth stage of life. A Yogi, in this technical sense, is someone who has achieved one or another degree of mastery of Yogic processes of Spiritual concentration and ascent of attention (and its withdrawal from "descended", outward, or gross pursuits) for the sake of attaining one or another of the Samadhis (or Spiritual ecstasies associated with the subtler cerebrospinal centers) that traditionally represent exalted Divine Communion or mystical Union in the fifth stage of life. (Compare **Saint** and **Sage**.)

Index

Index

U

"Understanding" (talk), 119, 222
Upanishads, 118, 468
Upasani Baba Maharaj, 53-56, 243, 287
    his prophecy of a Divine
        Incarnation, 55-56

V

vanaprastha, 273n, 463
Vedanta Temple, 105-7
Vedanta Temple Event, 106-8, 112-13,
    215, 264, 385
    distinguished from the "Death
        Event" of 1986, 294-96, 298-
        300
Vedas, 29, 309
Vegetable Surrender, or Happiness Is Not
    Blue, 439
vichara. *See* self-Enquiry
Vira. *See* Tantric Hero
Virgin Mary, 102-3, 375
    See also Mother Shakti
Vishnu, 447
Vision Mound Sanctuary, 168, 185
    See also Mountain Of Attention, The
Vithoba Temple, 124

W

"Water's Work" Teaching method, 151-53
Water (symbol), 11, 142-43
Way of the Heart, the
    advanced and ultimate practice in,
        446
    a call to become responsible for
        oneself, 416
    devotion in, 392-93
    "elaborately detailed" practice of,
        312
    fundamental principle of, 392
    the great trial and Love-Blissful
        Delight of truly beginning this
        practice, 395-97
    the Guru-devotee relationship in,
        419
    the key to the practice of, 354-55
    meditation in, 393-94
    the Perfect Practice in, 278, 282, 460
    relationship to conventional
        science, 381-84
    self-discipline in, 393
    service in, 393
    simplest practice of, 312, 325, 390-94
    ultimate authority of, 32
    See also feeling-Contemplation;
        practicing stages (of the Way
        of the Heart); Satsang
Way of the Heart, The (videotape), 441
Way of "Radical" Understanding, 118

What and Where and Who To Remember To
    Be Happy, 438
Wilber, Ken
    his estimation of Heart-Master Da
        Love-Ananda, 25-26, 422
    his opinion of *The Dawn Horse*
        Testament, 424
Witness-Consciousness. *See* Witness-
    Position of Consciousness
Witness-Position of Consciousness, 354-
    55, 468-69
    See also Perfect Practice
World-Teacher, 42-43, 340-41, 455
World-Teacher Ashrams, 346
worldwide sittings, 219
    See also celebrations (of The Free
        Daist Communion)
"Wound of Love", 42, 226-27

Y

Yajna, 279, 469
    Heart-Master Da's Yajna of 1986,
        273-83
Yoga, 469
Yoga Vasishtha, 112
Yogi, 469
Yogic Shaktipat, 465
Yogic siddhis, 67, 194-96, 465-66
Yogic "Swoons", 18
yuga, 447

For information about forms of involvement
in the Way of the Heart Revealed by
Heart-Master Da Love-Ananda,
please see "Invitation",
on pages 409-15 of this book.

For further information,
please write to us at the address below:

Correspondence Department
THE FREE DAIST COMMUNION
P. O. Box 3680
Clearlake, California 95422
USA
Phone: (707) 928-4936